American Immigration and Ethnicity

American Immigration and Ethnicity

A Reader

David A. Gerber, Alan M. Kraut

AMERICAN IMMIGRATION AND ETHNICITY
© David A. Gerber and Alan M. Kraut, 2005.

First published in 2005 by
PALGRAVE MACMILLAN™
175 Fifth Avenue, New York, N.Y. 10010 and
Houndmills, Basingstoke, Hampshire, England RG21 6XS
Companies and representatives throughout the world.

PALGRAVE MACMILLAN is the global academic imprint of the Palgrave Macmillan division of St. Martin's Press, LLC and of Palgrave Macmillan Ltd. Macmillan® is a registered trademark in the United States, United Kingdom and other countries. Palgrave is a registered trademark in the European Union and other countries.

ISBN 0–312–29349–6

Library of Congress Cataloging-in-Publication Data is available from the Library of Congress.

A catalogue record for this book is available from the British Library.

Design by Newgen Imaging Systems (P) Ltd., Chennai, India.

First edition: November 2005

10 9 8 7 6 5 4 3 2 1

Printed in the United States of America.

For the teachers who have inspired us, and the students
who have challenged us to inspire them

• • • • •

The editors gratefully acknowledge the
assistance of Jane C. Morris and the support of the
University at Buffalo (SUNY), the Baldy Center for Law and Social
Policy, and the College of Arts and Science of American University.

CONTENTS

LIST OF ILLUSTRATIONS

Preface and Introduction

There are so many textbooks for undergraduate history courses currently on the market that authors and editors offering yet another for the consideration of instructors and students are under an obligation to explain what they have in mind. In the case of the present volume, the editors feel confident that we are able to make a strong case for the usefulness of this volume, especially at this moment in both national history and in the development of the writing of American immigration history. Our justification will bring together immigration history and the ways in which it has been conceived, exploring the interface of historiography and the past as people in history have lived it, and demonstrating the consequences for our national self-understanding of how we think along that interface. In this way, we are going to merge a "Preface," in which we explain our editorial choices, with an "Introduction," in which we review the development and significance of immigration in the American past and present.

International migrations have been central to defining the character of American society, culture, and politics from the beginning of European settlement in North America. Without them, of course, the evolution of North American civilization from Native American to neo-European over the course of the last five centuries could not have taken place. Other present-day societies—for example, Canada, Australia, Argentina, and New Zealand—have been formed largely on the basis of voluntary international migrations, but none of them has experienced such immigrations as continuously, in as large numbers, with such large samplings from among as broad an array of the world's peoples.

For the first two centuries of European settlement, those migrations took place in the context of British imperial policy and served the needs and goals of the British crown. After the American Revolution and over the course of the next two centuries and into the present third century of American national life, however, international migration worked to add definition and character to the singular society and polity that Americans themselves have created. We are concerned in this volume with migrations that took place after 1789, in the context of American national life. Colonial migrations offered precedents for the future in the diversity of the peoples who voluntarily came to British North America—or, in the case of millions of Africans, were forced there by the slave trade, or of Europeans who were to varying degrees forced there as indentured servants or transported criminals. But in terms of numbers, consequences, and the scope of diversity itself, the voluntary international migrations of the nineteenth and twentieth centuries offered an entirely different situation that served repeatedly to make and remake the character of an independent nation. They contributed toward the shaping of its democratic political practices and institutions, the diversity and cosmopolitanism of its popular culture, and, through the immigrants' labors, the dynamism of its capitalist economy.

The Old Immigration and the New Immigration: Europeans Come to the United States

International migrations to the United States occurred without interruption, if unevenly, after 1789, but most Americans are probably familiar with the fact that American immigration history has witnessed several periods of especially voluminous mass migration. These periods of mass migration have become personally familiar, because they serve as convenient places from which to chart the American genesis of millions of families in their evolutions from foreign to American. The 1840s and 1850s saw the first of these human tides, as immigrants from northern and western Europe, principally Germany and Great Britain (then including Ireland), streamed into the United States. The second took place from the late 1890s to the inception of World War I, years which saw an even larger flow of immigrants, now from southern and eastern Europe. The spreading eastward and southward of the origins of European immigration reflected the movement in those directions of the capitalist modernizing processes that had begun in the north and west in the late eighteenth century, and that continued to remake the rest of Europe well into the twentieth century. Industrialization and the commercialization of agriculture rendered insecure the traditional ways of life and of earning a living that had sustained peasants, farmers, artisans, and petty traders, but now exposed enough of them to the possibilities that modernization held out for the improvement of individual and family circumstances. They were open to radical changes in their circumstances in pursuit of the conservative goal of security and, they had begun to dream, even prosperity. Often that dream of prosperity had less to do with permanent residence in the United States than with returning with one's earnings to buy land or establish a small business in the homeland. Return migration became increasingly feasible throughout the nineteenth century with the improvements in the speed, safety, and scheduling of trans-Atlantic shipping, as sailing ships came to be replaced by steam-powered ones.

On the other side of the ocean lay the United States, rich in resources and increasingly in investment capital, but lacking in labor equal to its economic potential. As far as Europeans were concerned, American immigration policy reflected this insatiable need for labor for well over a century.

For all practical purposes, American borders were open to European immigrants, excluding only limited categories of individuals—those with physical or mental illnesses or impairments, paupers, and those on the extreme left of the political spectrum. The immigration laws were much less generous to Asians, Africans, and other peoples from outside the European continent. Subject to exclusions or restrictions, their numbers grew slowly, constrained by both law and popular hostility. Race was always a potent factor in American immigration policy, though, as we see in this volume, it did not work as simply, along the stark lines of simple distinctions between white and non-white, as we might be tempted to guess.

As a consequence largely of these two waves of international migrants, and by no means insignificant numbers of migrants accreting annually between them, perhaps as many as 50,000,000 people came to the United States in the century between 1820 and 1920. The mid-nineteenth-century European immigrants came to be known as *the Old Immigration* to distinguish them from subsequent European arrivals, *the New Immigration*, of the late nineteenth and early twentieth century. Both migrations took place amidst plateaus in the development of the American capitalist economy. The mid-nineteenth century saw a vast expansion of the scope and scale of markets, as new lands opened for cultivation, cities developed to process agricultural goods, and the beginnings of factory production took root in the North. The late nineteenth and early twentieth centuries witnessed the transition to an industrial economy, characterized by mass production, large factories, and vast workforces of wage-earning machine tenders.

For contemporaries, the distinction between the Old Immigration and the New Immigration covered more ground than simply the chronology of arrival, for the seemingly exotic Catholic, Orthodox, and Jewish migrants of southern and eastern Europe in their massive numbers seemed profoundly different from the often Protestant and English-speaking immigrants of the earlier period. In fact, they were often considered indigestible by those native-born Americans worried about the loss of cultural coherence and political unity their presence seemed to threaten. The Old Immigration had prompted some of the same fears, which crystallized among the antiforeign groups of American nativists into political programs to limit immigration and the political rights of immigrants, in the nineteenth century. But by the twentieth century, the Germans, British, Irish, and Scandinavians had taken great strides toward making themselves at home in America and becoming in many ways like their American-stock neighbors. The fears they had once inspired were largely forgotten, while those inspired by the New Immigration continued to grow in proportion to the unprecedented number and the cultural diversity of new peoples streaming into the nation's cities and factories, where they provided much of the raw material that facilitated the American Industrial Revolution. Immigrants were again, as in the mid-nineteenth century, associated with disease, subversive political ideologies, vicious and antisocial habits, and inferior cultures. After a century of relatively open borders, legislation to sharply restrict immigration from anywhere outside northern and western Europe was passed between

1917 and 1929. Immigrants over sixteen were required to be literate. Asian immigration was completely banned. A quota system, which was based on percentages of the foreign-born by national origin reflected in the 1890 census, sharply limited the New Immigrants.

For the next four decades, until the next major revision of the immigration laws in 1965, the numbers of immigrants were small, and the attention of the nation focused more on the question of creating policy to accommodate the growing number of refugees created by war, political instability, and repressive political regimes. One consequence was to speed the assimilation of the New Immigrants, who many pessimists had thought would never assimilate into American society, for without the need to continually assimilate newly arrived family, kin, friends, and fellow villagers from the Old World, and without the newly arrived setting the cultural tone of ethnic group life, these peoples and their children and grandchildren were exposed to the daily processes of work and of social life, in such forms as public schooling, mass media, and shopping, that made them more similar than different from their neighbors. They were subject as well to the various homogenizing influences exerted by the national crises of the Great Depression, World War II, and the Cold War—the rise of labor unions in the mass production industries, the rise of the national Democratic Party as a social democratic coalition of peoples, classes, and races, and the vast mobilizations of men into the American military. The prosperity of the first decades after World War II propelled large numbers of people into middle-class lifestyles, which were characterized by common consumer aspirations centered around family and home ownership. By the mid-twentieth century, it was easy to forget the anxieties that European immigration had once prompted.

Interpreting European Immigration

The optimism about the destiny of European immigrants was reflected in the historical and social science research and writing on immigration during the mid-century. Interpretations of immigration, however, were never a simple reflection of cultural moods and social trends. They also reflected trends in the academic disciplines and related understandings of the dynamics of modern urban, industrial society. The dominant interpretation of the American lives of European immigrants, which centered around the concept of assimilation, dated back to the years before World War I and to developments in the infant discipline of sociology. The founding generation of academic sociologists, particularly those at the University of Chicago, were creating both a language of concepts and new research methods for understanding the modern American industrial city, one of the most striking aspects of which was the massive presence of foreign-born residents. While many Americans were pessimistic about the nation's ability to absorb the New Immigration, the Chicago sociologists argued that the principal social processes of modernization—urbanization, industrialization, bureaucratization, and centralization—worked over time to lessen social differences. While at first, the Chicago sociologists said, immigrant life was certainly characterized by such symptoms of social disorganization as family breakup, juvenile delinquency, and alcoholism, the immigrants and especially their children would slowly build the foundations of economic security, social order, and cultural coherence for themselves. Mid-twentieth century analysts such as Milton Gordon, whose *Assimilation in American Life* (1964) is considered the most important review of these trends then under-way in the decades just after World War II, seemed to validate the projections of the Chicago sociologists of the previous generation. For Gordon and others of his generation, however, assimilation was not understood as the disappearance of differences, eventuating in the complete homogenization of all of America's ethnic peoples. While a common American way of life was in the process of creation, the descendants of the immigrants of the nineteenth and early twentieth centuries nonetheless continued to have an ethnic group life and ethnic identities, which were based on common memories and shared patterns of socializing, sometimes reinforced by common religious affiliations and often by common voting preferences. While the desire of immigrants to create a common group life in the United States had once been looked at suspiciously, as divisive and hence dangerous, the ethnic group had come by mid-century to seem exactly the opposite. It was a common pattern of life shared by Americans, uniting them in their declining differences.

Late-Twentieth-Century Immigration: A Contemporary "New Immigration"

It was in this frame of mind that Americans in the mid-1960s confronted the revision of the 1920s immigration quota laws, which were seen as a remnant of a less tolerant, racist, and anti-Semitic America that had allowed irrational prejudice to guide public policy. A certain degree of cultural diversity now seemed, in fact, a significant asset in American life, and it had to be acknowledged that immigrants had helped to build up the country economically and thus create the material and political foundations for its remarkable rise from isolation to world power. The necessity of rethinking parochial prejudices in light of contemporary history also led Americans to introspection. The horrors created by Nazi racism were fresh in people's consciousness and experience, as were the profound inequalities created by American racism as they came to be understood in the context of both the Civil Rights Revolution and the Black Power movement. The Cold War made the United States vulnerable to criticism by Communist regimes, which mocked American claims to leadership of a democratic "Free World." The Immigration Law of 1965 ended the system of national quotas, and set the number of immigrants allowed at 170,000 per year. But numerous groups—principally, political refugees, those with family in the United States, and those with skills deemed necessary to sustain economic development—were exempted.

Within a decade, immigrants were again streaming into the United States, and soon their numbers, further enhanced by incalculable masses of largely Mexican illegal immigrants, were equaling and perhaps even surpassing the yearly totals of the first decade of the twentieth century. But numbers were not the only aspect of late-twentieth-century immigration that drew attention as well as a resurgence of the conventional fears that we have seen characterized responses in the past to periods of mass migration. In the midst of a rapid recovery from the destruction of World War II, Europe no longer sent forth millions of desperate but hopeful migrants. The conditions of urban, industrial development that had once created the forces pushing Europeans out of their homelands now had reached the developing countries of Asia, Africa, the Middle East, and South and Central America, and were stimulating emigration from places that relatively few, if any, migrants had ever reached, or been allowed to reach, American shores. The United States beckoned these people, as it had previous waves of immigrants. The American economy was transformed in the last quarter of the twentieth century from an industrial economy to a more mixed economy, with an increasingly robust service sector that required masses of low-wage janitors, cooks, maids, groundskeepers, security guards, sales staff, waiters, and others for its hotels, restaurants, malls and plazas, airports, convention centers, and office complexes. This was work that Americans rejected, because it was servile as well as poorly paid, even as the industrial economy deteriorated, and large numbers of them were thrown out of previously well-paying factory jobs. Immigrants often filled the vacuum in the service sector, but they also became increasingly the main labor force in old industries, such as meat-packing, where low-wage labor was sought to do work that had long reputed to be as noxious a way to make a living as any in existence.

If the emerging economy opened itself up to these newer immigrants, Americans, including the aging European immigrants of the early twentieth century, their children and grandchildren, were much more ambivalent about their presence. The comfortable homogeneity amidst unthreatening diversity that had become the model, if not exactly—amidst racial strife— the reality, for American culture and society in the mid-twentieth century seemed menaced by peoples who were mostly non-European in culture, non-Christian in religion, and non-white in race. Now asked once more was the old question: would these people ever succeed in assimilating, let alone desire to; or would their unassimilated presence lead to changes in American society that established Americans did not want? Contentious old issues that had not been debated in decades, such as whether English should be the official language of government services and public education or whether immigrant languages should be accommodated in such official and public contexts, were again being debated. Often they were debated without knowledge that they had ever been debated before, thus closing off to the present the wisdom and experience of those who had debated them in the distant past. To the extent also that large numbers, estimated in the millions, of these migrants were illegal, the situation raised anger and fear about the porousness of the nation's borders, the wholesale contempt for its laws, the decline of wage scales, and the extent to which employers of illegal immigrants' labor were willing to subvert the nation for their own economic gain. When illegal immigrants with American-born children, who automatically became citizens under the constitution, claimed their children's right to social services, such anger spread rapidly. Economic contraction in the 1970s, 1980s, and the early 1990s exacerbated the tensions. Unemployment levels were high across the country and, as tax revenues declined, social services deteriorated. Some angry Americans targeted the legal immigrant population, streaming into the United States, to escape even worse conditions in their homelands. Soon there would be calls for the reimposition of strict immigration ceilings and quotas.

Interpreting Recent Immigration

Although there is not one dominant interpretive tradition for analyzing the lives and projecting the future of America's third wave of mass immigration, there are some notable departures from the assimilation model that had dominated the study of the European immigrants. These departures have been forcefully advanced by those who argue from a variety of perspectives that past immigration history and the ways of interpreting it are not necessarily relevant to understanding contemporary immigration.

What are the principal arguments for the contention that contemporary immigration is more different than similar from past immigrations, and thus requires different interpretive frameworks? There are three central points repeatedly raised to advance this viewpoint:

(1) Contemporary immigrants are non-whites entering an intensely race conscious society, in which power, privilege, and resources continue to be closely structured according to skin color. The European immigrants of the past were white people, and to that extent, while their lives were in many ways touched by adversity, they were accorded the benefits that came with being white people. Contemporary immigrants may define their identities by their national origins and homeland cultures, but their Americanized children will probably do so considerably less. Yet the children will find it difficult to identify with and be part of the American mainstream to the extent they will be defined in ways that place them at and cause them to identify with the bottom of an emerging new racial hierarchy, alongside the African American inner city poor. In comparison with the European immigrants, therefore, their assimilation will be blocked or stunted.

(2) Intensifying this trend is the nature of the contemporary service economy, with its shortage, relative to the industrial employment of late-nineteenth and early-twentieth-century European immigrants, of steady and high-paying jobs. Service jobs offer the prospect of low wages, periodic unemployment and routine underemployment, and poor employee health and pension benefits, and hence are unlikely to provide a sound foundation for upward socioeconomic mobility.

These two arguments together are thought to suggest the *segmented assimilation* of contemporary immigrants: the idea that in contrast to the Europeans of the past, who are said to have been able to sort themselves out throughout the existing social structure at all class levels, today's immigrants will be concentrated toward the bottom of American society.

(3) Contemporary communication and transportation make it possible for today's immigrants to keep in constant touch with their respective homelands and to return to those homelands as frequently as they are able to afford to do so. The racial and economic difficulties that today's immigrants will face that will block their ability to fit themselves easily into American society will be an additional factor in leading them to remain interested in their homelands, complementing the desire to keep in touch with loved ones and friends and to return for visits to familiar landscapes and people. For all of the problems in doing so, it might be easier to make a living in the United States than in one's homeland, but rejections and discrimination and the attraction of the familiar make the long-term prospect of permanent return attractive. Meanwhile, immigrants may live from at least a psychological perspective in neither their homelands nor in the United States, but in a sense simultaneously in both of them. From a practical standpoint, they may save money and send it back to their homelands, for example to invest in property, in anticipation of the day when they might resettle permanently. At the same time, in the United States, certain sociological factors, such as high degrees of residential concentration in neighborhoods of cities and very large numbers of particular groups sharing a common language, combined with federal government policies that encourage cultural diversity, will reinforce the tendency to retain a sense of being foreign and provide a further impediment to assimilation.

This argument is usually referred to as the *transnational* interpretation of contemporary immigration. The word "transnational" is intended to imply that today's immigrants cannot be understood solely within the bounded or narrow confines of one nation, but must be understood as creating social and cultural spaces, networks, and institutions that span national borders, and in fact act, to the extent laws make it possible to do so, as if borders were irrelevant. In light of these trends, the assimilation model, which worked so well in thinking about the American lives of European immigrants, appears especially irrelevant, for the logic of transnational analysis is not simply that today's immigrants will find it difficult to assimilate, but rather that they may not want to assimilate.

To the extent that the validity of these new views of immigration are projections of future developments, their accuracy can only be proven in the distant future, when we have the opportunity to observe the lives of the children and grandchildren of today's immigrants. Meanwhile, of course, because immigration is such an important feature of contemporary

American culture, society, and politics, we cannot stop trying to understand it. We need to continue to understand immigration and its consequences, even if we cannot resolve all of the many issues that obstruct our understanding.

One place to begin to resolve this dilemma is to ask ourselves whether the history of European immigration is helpful to understanding the present and thinking about the shape of the future. The editors of this volume, both historians, answer, "Yes, it is." Our contention is that the past is indeed relevant to thinking about where we are and where we might be going. But we go further in our understanding of American immigration history itself to advance the argument that we may think of studying immigration, in both the distant and the recent past, as a conceptual unity. By this we mean that, whether we are discussing Irish immigrants in the 1840s or Korean immigrants in the 1990s, we may profitably employ the same analytical categories and ask the same questions about the immigrants' aspirations, experiences, identities, and groups. We cannot realistically expect the same answers, of course. Indeed we should anticipate that the questions themselves will have to be modified. After all, in the case of the Irish and the Koreans, they are peoples who differ not simply in the national histories that have produced them, but also in culture. They have not entered similar economies in the United States, so the opportunity structures they have confronted have been different. But, it is our view, the larger outlines of their American lives are similar enough for comparison. Immigration confronts each group with similar practical problems of resettlement, making a living, and creating the foundations of a secure family life, all within the framework of abiding American institutions. Thus, there is more that makes their histories similar than makes them different. At the very least, we can say with confidence that these histories are enough alike that there are reasons to compare them profitably. Interestingly, in making such comparisons, we will find that the newer analytical frameworks, such as transnationalization, that have been advanced to understand contemporary immigration, are useful for understanding the past as well as the present.

This book, therefore, is an exercise in comparison. It juxtaposes the distant and recent pasts for the sake of understanding the similarities and differences between them. In doing so, the editors hope that it will not only help us to understand the relevance of the past to making sense of the present, but also help us to feel more comfortable in the present. Understanding that previous generations have passed through periods of unsettling change, and not simply survived, but frequently confronted challenges humanely, creatively, and intelligently is one of the best antidotes we know to the pessimism that makes us incapable of acting in the present and leads us to dread the future. Understanding the similarities between the European immigrants of the past, who now seem retrospectively so familiar to many Americans but were deemed exotic and dangerous by many when they arrived in the United States, and today's immigrants, who seem similarly strange and threatening to many Americans today, is equally important for helping us to feel comfortable in the present. So, too, is understanding the formidable absorptive capacities of American society, which has continuously throughout our national history met the challenge of accommodating immigration, and doing so on a larger scope and scale than perhaps any other immigrant-receiving nation in the world.

At this time, in the third century of its existence, the United States can lay claim to being a truly international society, in which peoples from every region of Planet Earth now reside. Whether we allow the view to prevail that this is a desperate problem that needs correcting, or the view that our's is the opportunity to forge a unique and vital American unity amidst this global diversity, will depend on our ability to understand our past and see its links to the present and the future.

Using This Volume

Comparisons

How is this volume to be used? From what has just been said, it should be no surprise that we hope that the volume inspires students to exercise comparisons between past and present immigrations in the search for differences and similarities. Some of the readings specifically engage in comparative analysis and systematically guide students through comparisons among these immigration waves. In light of the persistence of immigration throughout American national history, under a variety of different social, economic, cultural, and political circumstances, one would think that the challenge of analyzing issues of change and continuity over significant historical time would yield a great deal of comparative analytical work. This is not the case, however, for most analysts of today's immigration, when they recognize history at all, are content to allude briefly to the past as precedent or as a totally *other* situation, and devote their time exclusively to the present. For their part, historians shy away from the study of the recent past, believing that it is too contemporary, and that they are too immersed in it, for it to yield to their skills and imagination. The comparative work put together here has been largely, though not exclusively, restricted to analysis of contemporary immigration and the more widely studied New Immigration of the late nineteenth and early twentieth centuries. Much work remains for historians seeking a comparative approach. Comparative analysis between present and an even more distant past, the Old Immigration of the mid-nineteenth century, is virtually uncharted scholarly territory.

In light of the dearth of explicitly comparative work that juxtaposes all three waves of mass migration, most of the readings in this volume invite students to do their own comparisons in chapters in which the readings suggest comparison but do not themselves directly engage in it. The introductions to each chapter point students in the direction of thinking comparatively. Students need also to be encouraged by instructors to use their own experience and their perceptions of the world around them to inform their comparative imagination. Evidence of immigration and the cultural diversity it prompts are everywhere around us—on campus, and at the mall, the airport, the thruway rest-stop, and all the other locations of ordinary daily life. Minds can be cultivated by observation as well as by reading, but better yet, by both working in tandem.

Chapters and Selections

The chapters of this book have been organized according to commonsense categories that largely reflect an interest in the consciousness and daily experiences of ordinary people. The readings are of many kinds: analytical interpretations, autobiographical narratives, excerpts of public speeches, and newspaper articles. Wherever possible, first-person documents and other types of popular literature have been juxtaposed with analytical treatments to cast familiar and informal light on problems professional researchers confront through the interpretation of data and documentary evidence. The relationship within each chapter between the analytical work and the more popular selections are not always self-evident. The selections do not necessarily validate each other's viewpoints, and may lie in a state of tension to each other. We ask students to attempt to work out these contrasting or conflicting viewpoints where they occur, or simply to see the ways in which one reading within a chapter qualifies or contextualizes the others. The readings have been chosen with the goal of putting students in charge of making these connections. They are guided in doing so by the chapter introductions, which contain general comments as well as comments that are intended to assist students in interpreting individual selections.

CHAPTER ONE

A Comparison of Contemporary Immigration and the New Immigration of the Late Nineteenth and Early Twentieth Centuries

Introduction

The first selection, appropriately, is an essay that lays out a comparison between turn-of-the-century European immigrants and contemporary immigrants. Pyong Gap Min, a sociologist, outlines a very comprehensive argument for the contention that today's immigrants will follow a different trajectory in making lives for themselves within American society than did European immigrants a century ago. Min's argument is based on a number of economic, cultural, political, and social factors that are said to separate the experience of the two groups. The familiar arguments, based on segmented assimilation theory and transnationalization, are complemented here by discussions of both governmental policies and the internal social character- istics and settlement patterns of the contemporary immigration that serve to reinforce the view that the assimilation model is not a useful way to understand immigration today. Thus, past experience, which helped to cre- ate the theory that analysts took to understanding European immigration, is presumed not to be an adequate guide to present immigration experience.

As Min notes, however, we must keep in mind that the European immi- grants of the turn of the century were also deemed unlikely to assimilate into American society, which, in fact, was one of the most important reasons that the nativist movement to restrict their numbers grew and was ulti- mately successful in gaining federal legislation to impose strict quotas on all immigrants from outside northern and western Europe. The quota system

Pyong Gap Min, "A Comparison of Post-1965 and Turn-of-the-Century Immigrants in Intergenerational Mobility and Cultural Transmission" in *Journal of American Ethnic History*, v.18 (Spring, 1999): 65–94. Copyright ©1999 by Transaction Publishers. Reprinted by permission of Transaction Publishers.

did provide a context for the more rapid integration of European newcomers, because it cut off the immigration of people from their homelands who continuously revitalized homeland languages, cultures, identities, and ethnic groups in the United States. While some nativists did indeed favor just such efforts to speed the process of Americanization, many others were concerned simply with protecting American society against foreigners who seemed to threaten American democracy and social order, and who seemed inherently to be poor material for American citizenship. In retrospect, these fears of peoples like Italians, Eastern European Jews, Poles, Greeks, and others, who over the course of several generations found their way into the American mainstream and are now firmly lodged there, seem irrational, exaggerated, and deeply bigoted.

One question that is immediately called to mind in light of the pessimism and the hostility that turn-of-the-century European immigration inspired at the time is whether the pessimism about, and in some quarters, too, the hostility directed at contemporary immigrants is similarly exaggerated. Just as it was difficult amidst the confusing welter of daily events to project a more positive outcome for the European immigrants and for American society a century ago, so, too, might it be the case today that pessimism seems more realistic than putting one's hopes on the formidable absorptive powers of American society. Nonetheless, American society has proven itself able to integrate large numbers of immigrants, both by changing the immigrants and by changing such institutions as schools and political parties to accommodate their presence. Moreover, as some selections in this book will demonstrate, the lives and the aspirations of contemporary immigrants often do not really seem much different from the European immigrants of the past. Ask yourself, then, whether there are alternative futures to the one projected in the essay you are about to read.

Suggestions for Further Reading

Alejandro Portes and Robert Bach, *Latin Journey: Cuban and Mexican Immigration in the United States* (Berkeley: University of California Press, 1985).

John Bodnar, *The Transplanted: A History of Immigrants in Urban America* (Bloomington: Indiana University Press, 1985).

Nancy Foner, *From Ellis Island to JFK: New York's Two Great Waves of Immigration* (New Haven and New York: Yale University Press and the Russell Sage Foundation, 2000).

Oscar Handlin, *The Uprooted: The Epic Story of the Great Migrations That Made the American People* (Boston: Little Brown, 1951).

Rudolfo Acuña, *Occupied America: A History of Chicanos* (New York: Pearson, Longman, 1988, third edition).

Sucheng Chan, *Asian Americans: An Interpretive History* (Boston: Gale Group, 1991).

Thomas Archdeacon, *Becoming American: An Ethnic History* (New York: Free Press, 1983).

Pyong Gap Min, "A Comparison of Post–1965 and Turn-of-the-Century Immigrants in Intergenerational Mobility and Cultural Transmission"

BETWEEN 1880 AND 1930, approximately 28 million people immigrated to the United States. About half of the immigrants during this mass migration period originated from southern and eastern European countries. While the vast majority of the earlier northwestern European immigrant groups were Protestant, these later immigrants were mostly Catholic or Jewish. Initially, these *non*-Protestant, "new immigrant" groups were considered different races and encountered prejudice, discrimination, and racial violence by native-born Americans of northwestern ancestry. However, as classical assimilation theory predicted, these non-Protestant, white ethnic groups quickly acculturated to the American mainstream and achieved gradual social assimilation and socioeconomic mobility over generations. Although their ancestors were labelled as "inassimilable races," they have been incorporated into the white American mainstream culturally and structurally.

National origin discriminatory immigration laws in the early 1920s, the Great Depression, and World War II caused the immigration flow to drop to its nadir in the next four decades beginning in 1930. Yet, the liberalization of immigration laws, the United States government's political and military involvement in many Third World countries, and other factors have accelerated the flow of immigration since 1965, ushering in the second mass migration period in American history. While the majority of immigrants during the first mass migration period were whites who originated in European countries, the vast majority of post–1965 immigrants were drawn from non-European, Third World countries.

An important issue regarding the adaptation of the descendants of these new immigrant groups is whether they will follow the descendants of the earlier white immigrant groups at the turn of the twentieth century. To put the question differently, what will the major differences be between the descendants of earlier white ethnic groups and those of contemporary immigrant groups in patterns of adaptation?

This article intends to compare the descendants of contemporary, Third World immigrants and those of the turn-of-the-century white immigrants in their adaptation patterns. To compare the adaptation patterns systematically, we need to examine the differences in (1) patterns of ethnicity and acculturation and (2) patterns of social mobility separately.

"Inassimilable Races" Have Become White Americans

Table 1.1 provides an overview of historical trends between 1841 and 1996 in immigration size and regions of immigrants' origin, with a focus on the

Table 1.1 Immigration to the U.S. by decade, region, and race, 1841–1996

| | | Region (%) | | | | | | U.S. totals | | |
Decade	Total N (in 1000s)	N.&W. Europe	S.&E. Europe[2]	Canada & N.F.[3]	Total White	L.A.[1] &C.I.[4]	Asia & M.E[5]	Year	% of Foreign Born	% of White
1841–50	1,713	93.0	0.3	2.4	95.7	1.2	0.0	1850	9.7	84.3
1851–60	2,598	93.6	0.8	2.3	96.7	0.6	1.6	1860	13.1	85.6
1861–70	2,315	87.8	1.5	6.7	96.0	0.6	2.8	1870	14.0	87.1
1871–80	2,812	73.6	7.7	13.6	94.9	0.7	4.4	1880	13.3	86.5
1881–90	5,247	72.0	18.2	7.5	97.7	0.7	1.3	1890	14.7	87.5
1891–1900	3,688	44.6	51.9	0.1	96.6	1.0	2.0	1900	13.6	87.9
1901–10	8,795	21.7	69.9	2.0	93.6	2.1	3.7	1910	14.6	88.9
1911–20	5,763	25.3	50.0	12.9	88.2	6.0	4.3	1920	13.1	89.7
1921–30	4,107	32.5	27.5	22.2	82.2	14.4	2.7	1930	11.5	89.8
1931–40	528	38.7	27.2	20.5	86.4	9.7	3.0	1940	8.6	89.8
1941–50	1,035	49.9	10.1	16.6	76.6	17.7	3.1	1950	6.9	89.3
1951–60	2,516	38.2	14.5	15.0	67.7	24.6	6.1	1960	5.4	88.6
1961–70	3,322	18.3	15.5	12.4	46.2	39.3	12.9	1970	4.7	87.6
1971–80	4,493	11.6	10.0	23.8	45.4	40.3	35.3	1980	6.2	79.6
1981–90	7,338	4.6	5.2	1.8	11.6	46.8	38.0	1990	8.0	75.6
1991–96	6,146	3.3	10.2	1.5	15.0	48.7	31.6	1997	9.7	72.0

Notes

1. Latin America.
2. Up to 1910, data for Austria and Hungary were tabulated together by the Immigration and Naturalization Service. In this table, the data for these two countries up to 1910 were included in the category of southeastern Europe, although only Hungary actually belongs to southeastern Europe.
3. Newfoundland.
4. Caribbean Islands.
5. Middle East.

Sources: U.S. Bureau of the Census, *Historical Statistics of the United States, Colonial Times to 1957*, Series A 9–22, A 34–50, C 23–38 & C 228–295 (Washington, D.C., 1960); U.S. Bureau Of the Census, *Historical Statistics of the United States, Colonial Times to 1970*, Series A 9–22, A 44–50, C 23–28 & C 228–295 (Washington, D.C., 1975); U.S. Bureau of the Census, *1980 Census of Population*, PC-80-1-B1, U.S. Summary, Table 39 and PC-80–D I-A, *United States Summary*, Table 253 (Washington, D.C., 1983); U.S. Bureau of the Census, *1990 Census of Population, Social and Economic Characteristics, United States*, Table 24 (Washington, D.C., 1993); U.S. Bureau of the Census, 1997 Demographic File, March Current Population Survey; Immigration and Naturalization Service, *Statistical Yearbook, 1985*, Tables 1.1, 1.2 & 1.3 and 1996, Table 3 (Washington, D.C., 1986 and 1997).

two mass migration periods. The period of 1881–1930, the first mass migration period, differs from the previous migration period both in the size of annual immigration and in the region of origin of immigrants. While an over-whelming majority of immigrants admitted before 1881 were drawn from northwestern European, Protestant countries—the United Kingdom, Germany, and Ireland in particular—the proportion of southeastern, non-Protestant immigrants began to increase in the 1880s, reaching the majority of immigrants in the next three decades. The phenomenal increase in the number of immigrants from these less-developed European countries con-tributed to the sharp rise in the overall immigration scale during the period. In the peak decade of the 1900s, Italy, Russia, Hungary, and Poland were among the top source countries of immigrants, with the first two replacing the United Kingdom and Germany as the top two source countries.

The immigrants from these economically less-developed European countries were mostly Catholic, Jewish, or Eastern Orthodox Christian. Their language, religious, "racial," and other differences, along with nativism, led native-born Protestants to consider their mass migration as a threat to the very foundation of American cultural and political systems. The negative atti-tudes toward Italians resulted in racial violence against and killings of Italian immigrants in the early twentieth century. Jews, who left Russia and other Eastern European countries to escape pogroms, encountered new forms of anti-Semitic prejudice and discrimination. The nativist reactions to the "new immigrants" developed into scientific racism in the 1910s, according to which "scientific evidence" was alleged to support the biological superiority of the "old stock," or the "Teutonic race," to southern and eastern Europeans.

Immigrants' class background is one of the key variables that determine their and their children's socioeconomic adjustments. A large proportion of the southern and eastern European immigrants of the first mass migration period were farmers and unskilled workers who were illiterate, although there were significant national origin differences in the immigrants' class back-ground. Among the European immigrants of 1889–1910 who reported their occupations, 94 percent of Rumanians, 83 percent of Russians, 78 percent of southern Italians, and 76 percent of Poles were unskilled workers or farmers, compared to only 12 percent of Scotch and 14 percent of Jews and English. The illiteracy rates of major southern and eastern European immigrant groups admitted in 1920 were 60 percent for the Portuguese, 47 percent for Italians, 32 percent for Poles, and 23 percent for Jews. As a result, most of the Southern and Eastern European immigrants, with the exception of Jews who had largely urban and higher educational backgrounds, occupied the bottom of the occupational hierarchy in American society. In 1910, only 6 percent of foreign-born white workers engaged in professional and other white-collar occupations (public service and clerical) in comparison to 17 percent of native white workers with native parentage, while they were overrepresented in manufacturing with the ratio of 43 percent to 26 percent. Partly because of their class disadvantages and partly because of the industrial structure of the time, even many of their second-generation descendants remained in blue-collar occupations.

Earlier southern and eastern European immigrants of a heavy rural background kept their "old world traits" in urban America. Many working-class immigrants who settled in ethnic enclaves were able to transmit their ethnic language and customs to their children. However, these "inassimilable" white ethnic groups also experienced an inexorable march toward acculturation. Beyond the second generation, they lost their ethnic language and much of their ethnic customs. Already in the 1970s, their third and fourth generations achieved cultural and social assimilation to the extent that they maintained their ethnicity loosely, using only ethnic symbols such as ethnic food and ethnic festivals. In the 1950s and 1960s, descendants of southern and eastern European immigrants were slightly behind those of Protestant ethnic groups in their socioeconomic statistics. However, by the 1970s most of the non-Protestant ethnic groups caught up with or outperformed Protestant ethnic groups socioeconomically. In the process of racial formation in the United States, these "inassimilable races" have become white Americans.

Contemporary Immigrants' Contribution to Racial and Ethnic Diversity and Disadvantages for Intergenerational Mobility

The contemporary migration period is similar to the first mass migration period in that an exceptionally large number of immigrants were admitted annually to the United States. Yet the differences in the region of origin and physical characteristics of immigrants sharply separate the two waves. While nearly 90 percent of immigrants admitted between 1881 and 1930 were drawn from Europe and Canada, only about 15 percent of post–1965 immigrants have originated from these regions. Mexico, the Dominican Republic, El Salvador, Guatemala, Cuba, the Philippines, Vietnam, China, and South Korea are among the major sending countries of contemporary immigration to the United States, with Jews from the former Soviet Union and the Middle East being the only major contemporary white immigrant group.

Contribution to Racial and Ethnic Diversity

As shown in table 1.1, the mass migration of immigrants beginning in 1880 did not change the racial composition of American society at all. Until the 1960s the white population had maintained its numerical supremacy with almost 90 percent. The only significant racial minority group before the 1960s was African American; thus race relations in the United States was synonymous with black–white relations. However, the influx of immigrants from Latin American, Asian, and Caribbean countries since the late 1960s has led to a phenomenal increase in Latino and Asian populations, while it has gradually reduced the proportion of the non-Hispanic white population.

In 1997, the non-Hispanic white population dropped to 72 percent, while the Latino and Asian/Pacific Islander populations rose to 11 and 4 percent, respectively. In the population estimate made in March 1997, there was no statistically significant differential between non-Hispanic black (12.6 percent) and Latino (11.1 percent) populations. Considering that the majority of the approximately four million illegals are Latinos, Latinos may have already outnumbered non-Hispanic blacks in 1997.

The liberalization of immigration law in 1965 is partly responsible for the mass migration of immigrants from Third World countries in the post–1965 era. But the United States government's military and political linkages with many Latin American, Asian, and Caribbean countries, along with other structural factors, are mainly responsible for the current flow of migration. There is little chance that the immigration laws will be drastically revised in the foreseeable future to substantially reduce the current level of immigration. Further, many researchers have warned that the government cannot stem the tide of the current immigration flow through its policies. If that is the case, Latino and Asian populations will continue to increase, with a concomitant decline in the proportion of the white population. According to population projections, the non-Hispanic white population will be reduced to 53 percent in 2050 while the Latino, black, and Asian American populations will grow to 25 percent, 14 percent, and 8 percent, respectively.

As will be shown in the next section, the contemporary Third World immigrants are concentrated in several states and metropolitan areas, and much more highly concentrated than turn-of-the-century white immigrants. As a result, non-Hispanic whites have already become a numerical minority in several metropolitan cities, including New York, Los Angeles, San Francisco, and Miami. American cities have grown far more multiracial and multiethnic than they were thirty years ago; they will grow racially and ethnically more diverse in the future. Thus the influx of immigrants in the post–1965 era has made American racial and ethnic relations far more complex than before. Many scholars have pointed out that racial and ethnic theories based on the black–white dichotomy cannot explain complex racial and ethnic relations in contemporary America.

Disadvantages for Intergenerational Mobility

Although the contemporary mass migration of Third World people has made American society far more diverse than before, it has not changed the racial stratification system in which white Americans dominate other racial minorities. While descendants of the earlier European immigrants have melted into white society structurally as well as culturally, African Americans and some Latino groups (like Puerto Ricans and Mexicans) have not been incorporated into American society structurally. Civil rights laws enacted in the 1960s have eliminated legal barriers encountered by minority groups; affirmative action programs have given minority members and women some advantages for finding jobs and gaining admission to colleges and universities. However, blacks and other racial minorities are still subject to prejudice and subtle forms of discrimination. A gradual increase in minority populations and a concomitant decline in the white population in the future may further moderate racial prejudice and discrimination. Yet white racism and racial inequality are unlikely to disappear in the foreseeable future.

Thus, the descendants of post–1965 immigrants, with the exception of the descendants of white immigrants, will encounter barriers to social mobility and structural assimilation that the descendants of turn-of-the-century white immigrants did not experience. The children of black immigrants from the Caribbean Basin, and those of lower-class black immigrants in particular, are more likely to assimilate to black Americans than to white Americans, although, as will be discussed below, the social class variable will have effects on the children's socioeconomic adjustments in interaction with race. Overall, the descendants of contemporary Latino immigrants will be better accepted than those of black immigrants. But the children of darker-skinned Latino immigrants, like Dominicans, are likely to encounter more social barriers than light-skinned Latinos and Asian Americans. The 1990 census shows that United States-born Dominican households have a higher poverty rate than their foreign-born counterparts.

As far as socioeconomic adjustments are concerned, Asian Americans seem to do very well. The 1990 census reveals that for all Asian groups, with the exception of Filipinos, the native-born populations fare better than both the foreign-born and white Americans in their socioeconomic status in general and in educational level in particular. However, even second-generation Asian Americans, regardless of their socioeconomic status, are subjected to a moderate level of prejudice by white Americans because of their color. Personal interviews with 1.5[1]—and second-generation Asian American adults and their narratives reveal that even native-born Asian American children suffer from prejudice and harassment by white children because of their physical differences. The later-generation descendants of the earlier white immigrants are now accepted as one-hundred-percent Americans. Thus for them ethnic identity is a matter of a personal choice mainly to meet their psychological need to belong to a community. However, even later-generation Asian Americans cannot but accept their ethnic identity because they are not accepted by "real Americans."

The class background of immigrants, along with their race, is an important determinant of their own and their descendants' socioeconomic adjustment. While immigrants' skin color is likely to have long-term effects on the socioeconomic adjustment of not only the second but also later generations, their class background will have positive effects particularly on their children's socioeconomic adaptations. As noted above, the 1884–1930 white immigrants, with the exception of Jews, had heavily rural and lower class backgrounds, lower than the native population in the United States, which partly contributed to their initial adjustment difficulties and their slower intergenerational mobility. By contrast, the vast majority of contemporary immigrants originated from urban areas, with a significant proportion having professional and middle-class backgrounds. Asian immigrants, with the exception of Indochinese refugees and Chinese immigrants from mainland China, were predominantly from metropolitan cities and were drawn heavily from professional and middle-class segments of the populations. The 1990 census shows that 36 percent of Asian immigrants had completed at least four years of college, compared to only 22 percent of the white population. Latino and Caribbean immigrants on average represent a lower premigrant class background than both Asian immigrants and white Americans. In the 1990 census, only 9 percent of Latino and Caribbean immigrants reported that they completed a four-year college. Yet, Latino and Caribbean migrants in the United States, even illegals, lived in cities prior to migration and they represent a higher class background than the general populations in their home countries.

Segmented assimilation theory proposes that immigrants' race and social class have combined effects on their locale of residence, which, in turn, determine their children's acculturation patterns. New Asian immigrants and many oldtimers with lower-class backgrounds tend to reside in immigrant enclaves, while professional and middle-class Asian immigrants generally live in white middle-class neighborhoods either through the initial settlement upon immigration or through re-migration from immigrant enclaves. Asian American and other children who live in immigrant enclaves can maintain their language and ethnic culture successfully, although they may not be fluent in English. These children will find an opportunity for socioeconomic mobility in an ethnic community. The children who grow up in white middle-class neighborhoods are likely to acculturate to the white middle class. Proponents of segmented assimilation assume that the acculturation to the white middle class has positive effects on children's school performance. Thus, the children of Asian and other immigrants settled in white middle-class neighborhoods have a greater chance to achieve high social mobility in the mainstream economy through a high level of education. This mode of adaptation that requires acculturation and education as prerequisites for social mobility is a replication of a path suggested by classical assimilationist theorists.

Lower-class immigrants in general and poor Latino and Caribbean immigrants in particular often settle in inner-city, low-income minority neighborhoods. [Sociologist Alejandro] Portes and his associates argue that their settlement in low-income, minority neighborhoods is likely to lead their children to have contact with native-born minority children and thereby to assimilate to the "adversarial subculture developed by marginalized native youth." The idea that native-born minority youth create their own subculture "adversarial" to academic performance was originally developed in the late 1980s to explain the poor academic performance of blacks. Drawing from these anthropological studies, proponents of segmented assimilation theory propose that the acculturation of the children of immigrants to the minority youth culture will block their academic achievements and thereby their social mobility. However, not all immigrant groups settled in low-income, minority neighborhoods are vulnerable to their children's acculturation to the adversarial subculture. Vietnamese refugees settled in a black neighborhood in New Orleans were able to teach their children immigrant values through strong family and community ties and thereby helped them to resist the adversarial minority youth culture.

Because of the differences in the structure of economic opportunities, education is far more important for social mobility for the children of contemporary immigrants than for those of turn-of-the-century white immigrants. At the beginning of the twentieth century, when the United States economy was in its industrial stage, a large number of well-paying blue-collar jobs were available to the children of immigrants. Thus many second-generation white ethnics were able to achieve intergenerational mobility without getting a higher education. However, the deindustrialization process during recent decades has drastically reduced the proportion of manufacturing and particularly unskilled jobs, while creating a large number of high-paying high-tech and professional occupations. Moreover, the earnings gap between the high earners and the low earners has significantly increased recently. This means that the highly educated children of contemporary immigrants can achieve a high level of intergenerational mobility within one generation—probably from their parents' small business to a computer programmer or a medical doctor—while those with no high school degree do not have an opportunity to find stable jobs.

Social scientists consider a combination of the residents' low education and the disappearance and exodus of low-level blue-collar jobs as major factors for an exceptionally high unemployment rate and poverty in inner-city, low-income black neighborhoods. As noted above, as a result of their acculturation to a local youth culture, the children of Caribbean and Latino immigrants who live in inner-city, minority neighborhoods may not have the motivation to excel in school. These children, like the children of native-born minority members, are likely to be trapped in permanent poverty. Many of their immigrant parents can escape from poverty because they are ready to undertake low-level blue-collar and service-related jobs and work long hours. The second-generation children who do not hold their immigrant parents' values of work and mobility will not accept these unattractive jobs that demand long hours of work. This is why some sociologists predict that a large segment of the new second generation will experience downward mobility.

The New Second Generation's Advantages for Retaining their Ethnic Culture and Remaining Bicultural

Almost all contemporary immigrant parents would want their children to achieve high social mobility while maintaining their ethnic cultural traditions. The above observations indicate that the descendants of post–1965 immigrants are disadvantaged for social assimilation (being accepted as full American citizens) and social mobility compared to those of the earlier white immigrants because of their skin color and a changed economic structure. While the new second generation have disadvantages for their social assimilation and social mobility, they have advantages for retaining their ethnic language and culture. This does not mean that the descendants of contemporary immigrants will be slower in adopting American culture than those of turn-of-the-century white immigrants. There are also strong forces that push the children of contemporary immigrants toward acculturation. As a result of their retention of ethnic culture and a high level of acculturation, a large proportion of the second- and even third-generation descendants of post–1965 immigrants are likely to remain bicultural.

Contemporary Immigrants' Higher Level of Concentration

There are four major reasons that contemporary immigrants have advantages for transmitting their cultural traditions to their descendants over the 1880–1930 waves of immigrants. First, contemporary immigrants have a higher level of population concentration. Table 1.2 shows the differences in settlement patterns between the earlier and contemporary immigrants based on 1910 and 1990 census reports. While New York State and the New York metropolitan area were the premier immigrant state and city in the 1880–1930 era, California and Los Angeles have replaced New York as the major immigrant state and city in the post–1965 era. This is not surprising, considering the fact that Los Angeles and other California cities are major destinations of many Latino and Asian immigrants. In 1990, 34 percent of Latinos were concentrated in California and 21 percent in the Los Angeles

Table 1.2   Major foreign-born states and metropolitan cities in 1910 and 1990

Year	Major States	Number (in 1,000s)	% of Total Foreign Born	Major Cities	Number (in 1,000s)	% of Total Foreign Born
1910	New York	2,748	20.3	New York	1,944	14.4
	Pennsylvania	1,442	10.7	Chicago	783	5.8
	Illinois	1,205	8.9	Philadelphia	385	2.8
	Massachusetts	1,059	7.8	Boston	243	1.8
	Ohio	598	4.4	Cleveland	196	1.5
	Michigan	597	4.4	San Francisco	142	1.1
	Total	7,649	56.6	Total	3,693	27.4
	U.S. Total	13,516	100.0	U.S. Total	13,516	100.0
1990	California	6,459	32.7	Los Angeles	3,945	19.9
	New York	2,852	14.4	New York	3,554	18.0
	Florida	1,663	8.4	San Francisco	1,251	6.3
	Texas	1,523	7.7	Miami	1,073	5.4
	New Jersey	967	4.9	Chicago	910	4.6
	Illinois	952	4.8	Washington	484	2.4
	Total	14,416	72.9	Total	11,217	56.7
	U.S. Total	19,767	100.0	U.S. Total	19,767	100.0

Sources: U.S. Bureau of the Census, *Thirteenth Census of the United States Taken in the Year 1910, Abstracts of the* Census, Tables 14 and 210 (Washington, D.C., 1913); U.S. Bureau of the Census, *1990 Census of Population, Social and EconomicCharacteristics, United States,* Table 32 & *Metropolitan Areas,* Table 32 (Washington, D.C., 1993).

metropolitan era, while 39 percent of Asian and Pacific Islander Americans resided in the state and 18 percent in the city. The concentration of the majority of Cuban immigrants in the Miami area and many other Latino and Caribbean immigrant populations in the area have established Florida as the third largest immigrant state. It is quite natural that a significant proportion of Mexican immigrants have chosen cities in Texas as their destinations.

A more important piece of information from Table 1.2 for the purpose of this article is not the difference in the major destination states and cities between the two waves of immigrants, but the differential levels of concentration of immigrants in particular states and cities. In 1910, approximately 57 percent of the immigrant population resided in six major immigrant states and 27 percent, in six major immigrant cities. By contrast, in 1990 nearly three-fourths of the immigrant population was concentrated in the six major immigrant states and the majority of immigrants lived in six major immigrant cities. Whereas in 1990 four cities had 5 percent or more of the immigrant population, in 1910 only New York and Chicago had such a large proportion of immigrants.

Contemporary immigrants' higher level of residential concentration generally suggests that they have advantages over the earlier immigrant groups for maintaining their language and culture. Yet we need to compare two immigration periods in residential concentration by the country of origin because members of each country of origin group usually share the same language and culture. When examining settlement patterns by the country of origin, we find the differential levels of residential concentration between the two waves of immigrants to be even greater.

Contemporary Latino and Caribbean immigrant groups show extremely high levels of concentration in one or a few cities. For example, 70 percent of Guyanese, over 60 percent of Dominicans, 50 percent of Ecuadorians, and 45 percent of Jamaicans who immigrated to the United States between 1982 and 1989 chose New York City as their destination. The 1990 census shows that each of the three largest Latino groups is highly concentrated in a metropolitan area: 56 percent of Cubans in the Miami-Fort Lauderdale area, 47 percent of Puerto Ricans in the New York-New Jersey-Connecticut area, and 28 percent of Mexicans in the Los Angeles-Anaheim-Riverside area. However, with the exception of Jews in New York, the major immigrant groups at the turn of the century did not have levels of residential concentration in one or a few areas comparable to those of contemporary immigrant groups. Russian, Italian, Irish, and Hungarian immigrants composed major non-Protestant immigrant groups at the turn of the century, and all had the largest population concentration in New York City. But their New York City concentration rates in 1910 respectively were 30 percent for Russians (mostly Jews), 26 percent for Italians, 19 percent for Irish, and 16 percent for Hungarians.

Latino immigrants, who compose the largest panethnic[2] group in many cities, share a common language. Consequently, they have an advantage over both the earlier white immigrant groups and other contemporary immigrant groups for transmitting their language to their children. Already in

1990, Latinos comprised 24 percent of the population in New York City and 40 percent of the population in Los Angeles, the two largest cities in the United States, while they composed the majority of the population in three other cities, E1 Paso (69 percent), Miami (63 percent), and San Antonio (56 percent). They comprise a significant proportion of the population in many other major cities, including Houston, Dallas, San Diego, and Chicago. Latinos in these cities have access to several Spanish-language TV and radio channels. In these and other smaller cities with a large Latino population, Spanish is often used as a language for business transactions. By virtue of a large Latino population, Spanish has been adopted as the most important foreign language in American public schools for several decades. Thus, descendants of Latino immigrants can learn the Spanish language more easily than other immigrant groups.

Contemporary Immigrants' Greater Proximity to Their Home Countries

Latino and Caribbean immigrant groups have an additional advantage over the earlier white immigrant groups in transmitting their language and culture to their children partly because of their settlement in the cities much closer to their home countries. The earlier European immigrants usually chose New York and other East Coast cities—the gateways from Europe to the United States—as their destinations. Even these "Atlantic bridges" were physically so far away from Europe that the immigrants had little immediate linkage to their home countries. By contrast, the post-1965 Latino and Caribbean immigrants are generally settled in the destinations physically close to their home countries. Mexican immigrants, who compose approximately one-fourth of the total post–1965 immigrants, are heavily concentrated in the border states, such as California, Texas, and Arizona. The Mexicans settled in the former Mexican territory can visit their home cities within a matter of one or a few hours. Most Cuban immigrants settled in Miami, which is only 90 miles from Havana. For political reasons, Cubans in Miami currently do not maintain strong sociocultural ties with their home country. Yet the situation will change drastically when United States-Cuban political relations improve in the future. Other Latino and Caribbean immigrants maintain stronger ties with their home countries than both the earlier white immigrant groups and even contemporary Asian immigrant groups because of the geographical closeness between Latin America and the Caribbean Islands and such American cities as New York, Miami, and Los Angeles.

Contemporary Immigrants' Stronger Transnational Ties

As noted above, contemporary Latino and Caribbean immigrants maintain stronger sociocultural ties with their home countries partly because of their greater physical proximity. However, the major factor that contributes to contemporary immigrants' multiple linkages to their homelands is not their geographical closeness but their transnational ties, made possible by technological advances in communication, transportation, and the mass media. The turn-of-the-century white immigrants also maintained transnational ties with their home countries. They usually sent letters to their relatives and friends in their homelands. Many immigrants at that time were male sojourners who left their spouses and children at home. They sent remittances to their family members regularly. Some of the immigrants even visited their home countries to see their relatives and friends, buy land, and/or bring back their spouses.

However, by virtue of advanced technologies, contemporary immigrants maintain high levels of transnational ties with their home countries unimaginable to earlier immigrants. The only means of communication between immigrants and their relatives in the home country in Europe at the turn of the century was sending letters, which took several weeks for delivery. By contrast, contemporary immigrants can communicate with their relatives and friends in the home country almost every day, using long-distance telephone calls, fax messages, and electronic mail. The affordability of long-distance calls, in particular, has had revolutionary effects on contemporary immigrants' communication patterns with their relatives left behind in their homeland. A 1996 survey in New York revealed that about one-third of Korean immigrants talked to their relatives in Korea at least once a week while half communicated by phone once or twice a month.

The entry of steamships into the immigrant trade in the mid-nineteenth century led to a drastic reduction in the length of passage from Europe to America. Yet the trans-Atlantic voyage at the turn of the century still took approximately two weeks. Because of great expense, time, and the threat of accidents and epidemics involved in the voyage, only a relatively small minority of immigrants visited their home countries to take care of important matters. By contrast, the international air travel connecting contemporary immigrants' American destinations to their home cities in the Third World is far less expensive, far more convenient, and much faster than turn-of-the-century trans-Atlantic voyages. Most Latino and Caribbean immigrants in New York can fly to their home cities within four to six hours, while Asian immigrants in Los Angeles need to spend only seven to nine hours to visit their home cities in Asia. As a result, contemporary immigrants exchange visits with their relatives and friends at home regularly—to celebrate a parent's birthday, participate in a brother's wedding, or enjoy a vacation. In fact, some immigrants move back and forth between American destinations and Third World cities while others maintain commuter marriages, with wives and children remaining in American cities and husbands working in Third World cities.

Finally, great improvements in media technologies during the last two decades have given contemporary immigrants access to active ethnic media—ethnic dailies and weeklies and ethnic radio and TV stations. The earlier immigrants did establish a number of ethnic newspapers. Yet, as they did not have communication channels with their home countries on a daily basis, the ethnic media could not provide the earlier immigrants with day-to-day news from their homelands. By contrast, the ethnic media today tie immigrants to their homelands by supplying them with daily news from their homelands. Ethnic TV programs also offer contemporary immigrants ethnic movies and TV programs on videotape. For example, the Korean community in New York has four Korean-language dailies, all of which, as branches of major dailies in Korea, republish articles published in their headquarters in Seoul. There are also two Korean TV stations and two Korean radio stations in the Korean community in New York, which air Korean-language programs 24 hours a day. Korean immigrants in New York as well as in other major Korean communities depend mainly on the Korean-language ethnic media for news, information, and leisure activities. Their heavy dependence on the ethnic media, in turn, has strengthened their ties to the ethnic community and the home country. By virtue of contemporary technological advances, other immigrant groups have developed similarly active ethnic media, which, in turn, tie immigrants to the homeland and the origin community at multiple levels.

To sum up the preceding discussions, technological improvements in international travel, telecommunications, and the media help contemporary immigrants to maintain active and continuous contacts with the homeland and community of origin, overcoming any barriers deriving from the physical boundary. Because of the active and sustained involvement of immigrants in the home country, several source countries of United States immigrants have taken measures in recent years to strengthen their overseas residents' cultural, social, and political ties to the home country. Recently, several major source countries, including Mexico, the Dominican Republic, and Columbia, have passed laws that recognize their American residents' dual citizenship.

Strong transnational ties between host and home countries, and between destination and origin communities, help not only contemporary immigrants but also their children to maintain their ethnic subculture and identity. Second-generation children can learn their ethnic language formally through the language instruction provided by ethnic TV stations, as most ethnic TV stations offer such instruction. Moreover, as international air travel is popularized, immigrant parents send their children to their home countries during summer vacation to help them learn the language and culture. A 1989 survey showed that 80 percent of American-born Korean high school students in New York had visited Korea at least once and that 20 percent had visited Korea twice or more. Because of physical proximity, Caribbean and Latino second-generation children seem to visit their parental home countries more frequently than their Korean and Asian American counterparts. In addition, popularization of video and music tapes helps second-generation children watch ethnic-language movies and learn ethnic pop songs, even if they may not be fluent in their mother tongues.

Multicultural Policy since the Early 1970s

Multicultural policy is another factor that gives contemporary immigrant groups advantages over earlier white immigrants in transmitting their language and culture to their children. The dominant social policy in the United States up to the 1960s had been Anglo conformity, according to which immigrants and members of minority groups should replace their language with English and their cultural patterns with those of British origin. The Anglo conformity policy or ideology was most influentially expressed in the Americanization movement that tried to force immigrants and their children to get rid of their cultural traditions and to accept American culture as soon as possible. The Americanization movement reached its peak during World War I after a large number of immigrants from Eastern and Southern European countries had arrived. Squads of women were sent out "on home visits to immigrants, telling them to create a more 'American' household by preparing 'non-ethnic' foods, modifying their grooming and personal hygiene habits, and advocating the use of English in the home." The English language was associated with being "American" and "patriotic," and bilingualism was interpreted as a sign of disloyalty to the United States. In this context, one major function of public schools was to Americanize immigrant children and children of immigrants by teaching them English and inculcating American values.

However, since the early 1970s all levels of government—the federal government in particular—and local school districts have changed their policies toward minority members and immigrants from "Anglo conformity" to cultural pluralism. The policy changes were partly in response to various minority movements—the civil rights movement, the black cultural nationalist movement, the Chicano movement, and the Third World students' movement—and the women's movement, and partly in response to the influx of new immigrants from Third World countries. Probably the most noteworthy event in the United States government's multicultural policy in the early 1970s was the *Lau v. Nichols* Supreme Court decision. In 1974, the Supreme Court declared that students with limited English proficiency were to be given special remedial aid to facilitate their learning of English. Armed with the landmark Supreme Court decision, the Office of Civil Rights of the Department of Health, Education, and Welfare established a series of guidelines to require all school districts to provide bilingual education programs for "language minority children." In addition to bilingual programs, public schools have changed their curriculum by including more courses related to minority groups' language, history, and culture. They have also tried to promote cultural diversity through such extracurricular activities as ethnic festivals and symposiums on minority groups to foster ethnic pride.

Colleges and universities, too, have done a great deal to increase ethnic diversity in curricular and extracurricular activities. As a result of the influx of nonwhite immigrants and minority groups' improvement in education, colleges and universities have become racially and ethnically far more diverse than before. Employment through affirmative action programs and establishment of ethnic, area, and women's studies programs have also increased the number and proportion of minority and women faculty members. Under pressure from minority and women students and faculty members, many colleges and universities have revised the white-male-oriented curriculum by including contributions made by people of color and women in traditional liberal arts courses and adding numerous courses pertaining to the experiences of minority groups and women. Establishment of ethnic and women's studies programs on many campuses in particular has resulted in a significant revision of the traditional curriculum.

There have been some conservative reactions to multiculturalism. In response to the rapid increase in the non-English speaking immigrant population, more than a dozen states, including California and Florida, have passed laws that recognize English as the standard language. In 1998, California passed a referendum to abolish bilingual education. Conservative intellectuals have attacked multicultural education in higher educational institutions. Despite these reactionary movements and measures, both governments and schools are currently strongly committed to the multicultural policy. For example, in New York City, local officials, social workers, and teachers try actively to promote festivals and events to foster ethnic pride and glorify the city's multiethnic character. Both governments and schools are likely to strengthen rather than moderate the multicultural policy in the future, particularly because of the continuous increase in the non-white population. The children of contemporary immigrants have distinct advantages for retaining their ethnic culture over those of the earlier immigrants at the turn of the century because of the multicultural policy.

Bilingual and Bicultural Orientations

New immigrants replenish the ethnic community with the culture of the homeland and thus the continuity of immigration is essential to maintaining ethnic cultural traditions. One of the major reasons why turn-of-the-century immigrant groups have almost completely lost their ethnic cultural traditions is that their immigration almost came to an end around the early 1930s and did not revive for a long period of time. As previously noted, the current immigration flow is not likely to come to an end or even decline sharply in the foreseeable future. This is another reason why the descendants of post–1965 immigrants will be more successful than those of the earlier white immigrant groups in retaining their cultural traditions.

I have thus far examined several factors that give the children of contemporary immigrants advantages for preserving their cultural traditions over those of the earlier immigrants. However, I do not intend to suggest that the children of contemporary immigrants have disadvantages for acculturation. In fact, these children are under greater pressure to assimilate to American culture than the children of turn-of-the-century immigrants, for two major reasons. First, the media, American peers, and schools currently have a stronger effect on the behavior and attitude of children than at the turn of the century, while immigrant parents have less control over their children than before. Contemporary immigrant parents may be less effective in preventing their children from being culturally Americanized than the immigrant parents one hundred years ago, particularly because, a much larger proportion of contemporary immigrant mothers work full-time outside the home. Second, the children of today's immigrants have a greater pressure to assimilate to American culture than their counterparts a century ago partly because of the global influence of American popular culture today. Due to the presence of American servicemen, multinational corporations, and/or media in their home countries, most contemporary immigrants from Third World countries, including immigrant children, became familiar with American mass culture prior to migration.

My argument that the children of contemporary immigrants have advantages over those of the earlier immigrants for both retaining their ethnic culture and acculturating to American society may sound contradictory to many readers. But it is not contradictory because retention of ethnic culture and acculturation are not always mutually exclusive. Classical assimilationists proposed a zero sum model of acculturation, according to which immigrants' acculturation involves a gradual replacement of their ethnic culture with American culture. As indicated elsewhere, although the zero sum model may be useful as a description of the Anglo conformist policy or ideology up to the 1960s, it is not helpful in understanding the experiences of contemporary immigrants and their children. Contemporary immigrants can achieve a high level of acculturation while maintaining their ethnic culture almost perfectly, whereas their Americanized children can achieve a high level of ethnic attachment. A large proportion of the descendants of post–1965 immigrants—much larger than those of the turn-of-the century-immigrants—are likely to remain fluently bilingual and strongly bicultural because of the factors described above: their high ethnic and panethnic concentration in a particular city, their proximity to and transnational ties to their parents' home countries, and multicultural policy.

A more systematic survey study of ethnic attachment among the descendants of post–1965 immigrants is needed to test the validity of the above bilingual, bicultural hypothesis. However, both quantitative and qualitative data available at present seem to support the hypothesis. David Lopez analyzed the Public Use Sample of the 1989 Current Population Survey to examine intergenerational language maintenance and shift among Latino and Asian populations in Los Angeles. According to his analysis, 53 percent of second-generation Hispanics 25–44 years old spoke English "very well" but used their ethnic language at home, in comparison to 19 percent of their Asian American counterparts. It also showed that 47 percent of third- and later-generation Latino adults (natives of natives) and 11 percent of their Asian American counterparts were fluent in English but used their ethnic language at home.

The Latino and Asian American adults who can speak English very well but use their ethnic language at home are bilinguals. As expected, Latinos show a much higher rate of intergenerational transmission of their ethnic language than Asian Americans. But even third-generation Asian Americans include a higher proportion of bilinguals (11 percent) than expected from studies of the descendants of the 1880–1930 wave of immigrants, according to which "by the third generation, knowledge of an ethnic language beyond a few words and phrases is often lost." The earlier Japanese immigration occurred between 1885 and 1924, roughly during the European mass migration period. A major survey study of Japanese Americans conducted in the early 1960s reveals that only 2 percent of the third-generation respondents reported that they spoke Japanese fluently. The Latino and Asian American respondents (25–44 years old) included in the 1989 Current Population Survey were born and grew up before the mass influx of post-1965 Latino and Asian immigrants. Thus, they did not benefit fully from the structural factors facilitating the retention of their ethnic language discussed in this article. Accordingly, the descendants of post-1965 Latino and Asian immigrants are likely to retain their ethnic language more successfully than the sample of the 1989 Current Population Survey, the descendants of the pre-1965 Latino and Asian immigrant cohorts.

Research on the descendants of the earlier white immigrant groups and a commonsense assumption support a view that bilingualism is associated with lower-class family background and residence in an immigrant enclave. However, recent studies of the children of post–1965 immigrants suggest that fluent bilingualism is highly correlated with a professional family background. The children who have grown up in an immigrant enclave may be fluent in their ethnic language but may not be fluent in English. Yet professional families in a suburban white middle-class neighborhood have resources to make their children fluent bilinguals. Many Korean professional and high-income business families in a white, middle-class neighborhood in New York enroll their children in Saturday ethnic language schools and send them to Korea for a Korean cultural program regularly during the summer vacation. Some of them send their college-graduated children to college in Korea for a long-term ethnic education. Personal narratives by 1.5- and second-generation young Asian American professionals reveal that many, including those married to white partners, have strong bicultural and binational orientations, although all grew up in predominantly white, middle- and upper-middle-class neighborhoods and graduated from prestigious universities.

Notes

1. Born outside the United States and immigrated as children.
2. People of many different national origins who share a common trait—in this example, the Spanish language—that serves potentially to unite them; a group composed of many different ethnic groups.

CHAPTER TWO

Making a New Home in a New Land—Resettling in the United States

Introduction

Once the decision to migrate is made, the next most important decision for those on the move is to choose a destination. In the seventeenth and eighteenth centuries, migrants from Europe often made their new homes on property that was granted them by charter from the Crown to immigration and resettlement agencies such as the Plymouth Company and the Virginia Company. Colonists often selected new homes because of the abundance of available land, favorable climate, rich soil suitable for crop cultivation, and proximity to transportation arteries such as the ocean or rivers. While some Englishmen and women such as comprised the Puritan community settled in the North Atlantic coast, others chose the more moderate temperatures of the mid-Atlantic and southern regions. The waters of the mid-Atlantic region were free of ice more months of the year than those to the north, perfect for commerce. The rich lands and warm moist climate of some parts of the South attracted those who hoped to make their fortunes growing tobacco. Friends, relatives, coreligionists all followed a chain pattern of migration that would continue into the following centuries.

Virginia Yans-McLaughlin, *Family and Community: Italian Immigrants in Buffalo, 1880–1930*. (Ithaca: Cornell University Press, 1977). Copyright © 1977 by Cornell University Press. Used by permission of the publisher, Cornell University Press.

Mary Antin, *The Promised Land*. (United States of America: Houghton Mifflin Company, 1912). Public Domain.

Barry Newman, "Cultural Oases: For Asians in the U.S., Mini-Chinatowns Sprout in Suburbia—Mr. Chen's Las Vegas Mall Feeds a Growing Hunger; Comfort Zones in Heartland—Ms. Wu Eyes Pork Snouts" in *The Wall Street Journal*, April 28, 2004. Dow Jones & Company, Licensed Content Publisher. Reprinted by permission of The Wall Street Journal. Copyright © 2004 Dow Jones & Company, Inc. All Rights Reserved Worldwide. License number 1083380557061.

In the nineteenth century, migrants continued to follow family and friends to one location or another. They reestablished communities and social relationships from the old world in the new. However, there were other reasons for settlement patterns. At times, transportation opportunities determined who settled where, at least initially. During the peak period of immigration to the United States in the late nineteenth and early twentieth centuries, major shipping lines such as Cunard, the White Star Line, and the Hamburg–Amerika Line had more departures for New York than any other coastal ports such as Charleston or New Orleans. Some migrants who landed in New York, for example, disembarked and purchased train tickets for their destination, while others settled briefly in New York before heading for other locations. And still others who had no definite destination remained and found work and lodging in New York, remaining for lengthy periods, sometimes the rest of their lives.

Because such a large percentage of migrants chose the United States for reasons of economic opportunity, occupational patterns were crucial determinants of destination. In the mid-nineteenth century, Scandinavians hoping to farm selected parts of Minnesota and Wisconsin, where low cost land, good soil, and often the presence of former neighbors from their countries of origin attracted them. German artisans and craftsmen seeking to avoid employment in Europe's factories and the competition in East Coast job markets found their niche in the small but growing communities of the Midwest. The largest group of the 4.5 million arrivals between 1840 and 1860 were Irish, who were often unskilled laborers. Irish women, more marketable than males, found domestic service positions most readily in urban environments. Some Irish began their search for jobs in the streets of Boston or New York. Males found hard work but higher wages on the railroads and canals that were linking American communities. Often, Irish workers settled in communities along the route of the transportation arteries that they were helping to build. On the West Coast, Chinese workers often settled in the port of San Francisco. They, too, often worked on railroads or in mines and settled in nearby communities.

By the end of the nineteenth century, the United States needed a vast army of skilled, semiskilled, and unskilled laborers to fuel its industrial revolution. Hoping to earn enough money to return wealthy to their homelands or to enjoy their earnings in the United States, immigrants from southern and eastern Europe poured into American factories and mines, as did many Canadians moving across the northern border and Mexicans migrating north. The immigrant population of many American cities exploded. In New York City, the foreign-born population skyrocketed from 567,812 in 1870 to 902,643 in 1890, yet declined from 38 percent of the population to 36 percent. By 1910, the figure was almost 2 million, still only 41 percent of the total. Immigrants settling in American cities were competing for jobs with the native-born who were migrating from countryside to city for economic opportunity. Young African Americans, who fled webs of debt and obligation that had entrapped their parents' generation of tenant farmers and sharecroppers in the Jim Crow South, also competed with newcomers from abroad.

Because of the concentration of industry in the northeastern United States, European immigrant settlement patterns at the turn of the century formed a triangle: New England at the apex, with the southeastern point at Washington, D.C., and the southwestern point at St. Louis. Two-thirds of all European and Canadian immigrants could be found in New York, the New England states, Pennsylvania, and New Jersey, while substantial numbers also went west to Illinois and Ohio. While some Asian arrivals migrated to the same eastern states, the majority of these newcomers settled in California and other western states. The same was true for the many Mexicans who crossed the border in search of jobs. Few newcomers migrated into the South. Industry was scarce there, and job competition with low-paid white and African American labor in field and mill offered poor prospects. Fear of the South's patterns of prejudice and discrimination toward dark-complexioned individuals, including people from southern Europe, such as Italians, was yet another deterrent except for the somewhat more cosmopolitan environs of Charleston and New Orleans.

The settlement patterns of the latest newcomers, added to those who had come in the mid-nineteenth century, created cities of immigrants. According to the census records of 1910, 75 percent of the populations of New York, Chicago, Detroit, Cleveland, and Boston consisted of immigrants or their American-born children. Foreign enclaves of significant proportion evolved in other cities such as Philadelphia and Providence because they were linked to the nation's expanding industrial network by rail. The pattern was national. In the west, the port city of San Francisco was popular with immigrants, especially those from China and Japan. By 1916, over 72 percent of San Francisco's population regarded a foreign language as their primary tongue. Mexican labor was transforming Los Angeles, which had become an exporter of manufactured goods, a processor of agricultural crops, and an importer of machinery and technology.

In addition to the cities, immigrants resettled in the American countryside. Sometimes newcomers whose families had bent their backs over the land for generations purposely sought industrial jobs, especially when wages were high, but many still preferred agriculture. Governments both foreign and domestic encouraged the development of agricultural settlements in the United States to relieve urban congestion and free the immigrants from the social problems associated with cities. There were farming settlements for Italian immigrants in Texas, Arkansas, Alabama, Mississippi, and Louisiana. However, with a few exceptions these failed as the Italians eventually gravitated to cities. Mexican immigrants often began as agricultural laborers before migrating to cities. Many Mexicans were migrant laborers. Indeed, by the late 1920s, one-third of the labor force of the Imperial Valley of California was Mexican. However, those on the move continued their migration, settling and resettling several times in their search for higher wages. Sometimes Mexican workers left their families in San Antonio or El Paso, Texas while working part of the year in the steel mills of Indiana or the auto plants of Michigan or the fields of Kansas or Colorado.

At times resettlement whether in city or small town was shaped by a special industry and the skills of workers of a particular ethnic group. In Tarpon Springs, Florida, Greek immigrant John Cocoris and his brothers started a sponge business. They brought 500 Greeks from the Aegean and Dodecanese Islands in the Mediterranean Sea to dive, hook, clean, sort, string, clip, and pack. However, those who saved their money soon could afford to depart in pursuit of the economic opportunities more readily available in larger cities.

For the vast majority of newcomers in the late nineteenth and early twentieth centuries, there remained the hope of economic success sufficient to allow them to return to their home countries and live lives of content-ment and prosperity. These expectations shaped settlement patterns, as well. Many chose to settle initially in the port city where they disembarked or to journey inland only with the promise of higher wages or of reunion with family and friends, the latest links in a chain migration pattern. Permanent roots were less important than high wages, low cost of living, and mobility. After all, they believed they were going home some day.

Many of the cities where newcomers settled had never been constructed to accommodate large populations. Housing, city services, and facilities were inadequate or outdated. Streets and houses constructed before the Civil War were not adequate to the growth of population. Filthy streets and the pollu-tion of air and water supplies made cities with large immigrant populations unhealthy places. Sewage pipes were often too narrow to handle the increas-ing load. City transportation was inadequate. Some areas of cities were isolated by the absence of streetcars, while others were a chaotic mass of lines constructed by competing companies, all going in the same direction.

Newcomers resettling in cities found housing an expensive and elusive commodity. In mining towns and in cities where immigrants were working on construction projects, newcomers often lived in shacks constructed from spare parts (figure 2.1). Together, these shacks built near each other formed shantytowns. Tall tenement houses that lined the streets of many industrial cities were designed to derive large profits from small spaces. Often builders were unable to allow for adequate light and ventilation. Dumbbell-style tenements, frequently six or seven stories high, were composed of four apartments to a floor, and often only one room in each apartment received direct air and sunlight from the street. Air shafts five feet wide and sixty feet deep separated front from back apartments and were intended to bring air to interior rooms. Fire escapes on the outside of buildings were eventually mandated to allow evacuation in case of fire. Not until municipal govern-ments, pressured by urban reformers, outlawed dumbell tenements were such abuses corrected. In New York not until the 1901 state law was passed did each unit have to include its own toilet, running water, and access to fire escapes and stairs.

Immigrants who have resettled in the United States since the end of World War II have faced similar choices to those who arrived earlier. They have often selected destinations because of chains of friends and family.

Figure 2.1 While some new arrivals lived in tall dumbell tenements, other migrant families made alley shanties out of scraps of wood and metal (ca. 1890). Courtesy of the Library of Congress

And, as in the past, expectations about employment and the future have shaped their decisions.

Since the mid-1970s, large numbers of immigrants and refugees have arrived in the United States. Today, immigrants and their children number over 60 million individuals, or a fifth of the entire population. Migrants from Ireland, Germany, Italy, and Czarist Russia have been replaced at the country's ports of entry by Mexicans, Filipinos, Vietnamese, Indians, and Pakistanis.

Today's newcomers live and work in every state of the union, although they are highly concentrated in six states: California, New York, Texas, Florida, New Jersey, and Illinois. As in the past, jobs in agriculture have drawn Mexican and other Latino immigrants to agricultural states such as California, Texas, and Florida, which have a long history of Latino settlement. Others find the older industrial cities still to be places where entrepreneurial opportunities, industrial jobs, and low-cost housing are available. Refugees often resettle in communities where those organizations are located that aid them in resettlement. Hmong tribespeople from Cambodia settled in large numbers in the Minneapolis/St. Paul area because the Christian aid groups that assisted them are located there. Similarly, many Russian Jews departing the Soviet Union resettled in the greater New York area and in other major cities because the urban Jewish communities took the lead in assisting the newcomers.

The old pattern of urban ethnic enclaves is still present, but fading. A newer pattern is the growth of suburban immigrant communities. The high prices of inner city housing and the fear that their children will be victimized by the dangers of inner city urban life have caused many newcomers to find affordable housing in the suburbs. They commute to jobs on public transportation on in affordable used cars. Instead of congested urban schools, their children attend sprawling suburban schools. They shop in suburban malls, some of which are dominated by stores of their own groups. In malls that cater to Asian arrivals, there are grocery stores and restaurants that sell traditional foods and clothing stores that sell traditional garb for ceremonial occasions. Resettlement in the early twenty-first century is still often a chain pattern but the destination is often a garden apartment in a suburban development rather than a tall dumbell tenement on a narrow, congested city street.

In the main selection, Virginia Yans-McLaughlin describes the resettlement pattern of Italian immigrants in Buffalo, New York, in the late nineteenth and early twentieth century. She describes a chain migration grounded in kinship patterns that shaped settlement patterns, as well. She finds that individuals not only followed relatives to the United States, but also shared housing, engaged in neighborly relations, assisted in education, and even helped newly arrived kin to find employment and suitable spouses. Moreover, because relatives frequently preferred to live near each other, kinship bonds were crucial in shaping neighborhood patterns. Families that had lived near each other and interacted in the Old World continued to do so in the New World.

Yans-McLaughlin also observes that the extended family was less important in the towns of southern Italy than it became after migration to the United States. In Italy, the crucial individuals were the members of the same household who worked side by side in the fields. However, in the United States, dependence on the assistance of kin stretched well beyond the relatives in a single household. Other relatives such as aunts, uncles, and godparents were important sources of assistance after migration. After all, providing a job or a place to sleep for several months or longer might require the assistance of more members of a family than those in the nuclear family, especially since young husbands and sons often left their wives and children behind in the homeland when they made their first excursions to America.

The second selection is an excerpt from Mary Antin's autobiography, *The Promised Land* (1912). Antin, a noted writer and educator, emigrated with her parents from Polotzk, a city in Lithuania, to the United States, settling in Boston in the early 1890s. When the Antins lived in Polotzk, the 12,500 Jews comprised more than half of the city's total population. Boston was quite a contrast. In an earlier volume, Antin explained that "emigration fever was at its height in Polotzk" in the early 1890s. She recalled that " 'America' was in everybody's mouth. Business men talked of it over their accounts; the market women made up their quarrels that they might discuss it from stall to stall; people who had relatives in the famous land went around reading their letters for the enlightenment of less fortunate folks . . . but scarcely anybody knew one true fact about this magic land."

Mary's father had preceded the family to the United States, having been directed to Boston by "an emigrant aid society." After several unsuccessful business ventures, he had decided to establish a refreshment booth at

Crescent Beach, a nearby recreation spot. The selection describes how Mary was introduced to Boston, moving into its tenement district. However, instead of seeing a run-down slum, the young immigrant saw "two impos-ing rows of brick buildings" and "many friendly windows" that were open and seemed to be welcoming her to America. Thus, Mary and her family's resettlement in the United States was guided by American aid workers and encouraged by the opportunities for a hard worker. As for Mary, the promise of this new home lay in Boston's schools, "No application made, no ques-tions asked, no examinations, rulings, exclusions, no machinations, no fees. The doors stood open for every one of us." It was quite a contrast to the patterns of exclusion from schools to which Jews had been subjected in many parts of eastern Europe.

The final selection reflects the more recent experience of new arrivals, settling in cities spread out across the landscape with increasingly decentral-ized urban populations or in suburban communities on the perimeter of older industrial cities. In both cases, traditional ethnic neighborhoods with their stores catering to the consumer preferences of the foreign-born are being replaced by ethnic-specific shopping malls and highway strips. This article from the *Wall Street Journal* describes how some mini-Chinatowns are being planned and constructed as shopping centers in response to the needs and preferences of the tens o thousands of new Chinese immigrants arriving every year in the United States. Ethnic particular shopping malls and strips now embody opportunities for Chinese consumers and entrepre-neurs in Las Vegas, suburban Los Angeles, and many other American communities.

Suggestions for Further Reading

David Montejano, *Anglos and Mexicans in the Making of Texas, 1836–1986* (Austin: University of Texas Press, 1987).

Donna R. Gabaccia, *From Sicily to Elizabeth Street, Housing and Social Change Among Italian Immigrants, 1880–1930* (Albany: State University of New York Press, 1984).

John W. Briggs, *An Italian Passage, Immigrants to Three American Cities, 1890–1930* (New Haven: Yale University Press, 1978).

Jon Gjerde, *From Peasants to Farmers: The Migration From Balestrard, Norway, to the Upper Middle West* (Cambridge: Cambridge University Press, 1985).

Mario Maffi, *Gateway to the Promised Land, Ethnic Cultures on New York's Lower East Side* (New York: New York University Press, 1995).

Nancy Foner, *From Ellis Island to JFK, New York's Two Great Waves of Immigration* (New Haven: Yale University Press, 2000).

Peter Kwong, *The New Chinatown* (New York: Hill & Wang, 1987).

Virginia Yans-McLaughlin, "New Wine In Old Bottles: Family, Community, and Immigration"

Several brothers and cousins followed Francesco Barone when he left in 1887 for America; together they formed a chain of migration from the small town of Valledolmo. Orazio, one of the first relatives to follow Francesco, emigrated ten years later at the age of thirty-seven with his wife Frances and three children. Eleven years after that fifty-two-year-old Richard Barone settled in Buffalo with his wife and three children. By 1905, Richard had retired securely; his children could support him if need arose. Still other Barone brothers and cousins came: James, his wife, and two children arrived twelve years after the trailblazing Francesco. Another Orazio and his wife settled in Buffalo two years later. The following year Frank arrived with his wife and children. Next came John, Michael, Louis, Thomas, two Josephs, Anthony and finally, yet another Orazio; most of them chose to bring their wives and children with them rather than sending for them later.

Only two clan members, Tony and Anthony, had not been joined by their families in 1905. Tony rented in a boarding house; Anthony joined the Nonataro family, contributing his regular food and rent payments to the household budget. Working as unskilled laborers, Tony had been in Buffalo three years, Anthony, two. They were young men in their twenties, and they had not yet established roots.

Not all the Barones achieved Francesco's success. Two brothers, Joseph and Anthony, worked as unskilled laborers. These siblings helped each other considerably during the immigration and settlement period. The first to come, Joseph, encouraged his brother's family to join him, and they arrived within a year. Neither had the special skills required by Buffalo's commercial, shipping, or industrial enterprises. Each had come with a wife and two children. Within three years, Joseph and Anthony each had two more children. Both families struggled and needed help. In this strange new city, who else could be counted upon but one's own blood? The brothers cooperated, renting one of Buffalo's many two-family homes and perhaps dreaming of purchasing it together one day.

John Barone, his two married children, and their families also cooperated. They shared the same household, but for different reasons from Joseph and Anthony. Sixty-year-old John and his sons had all come to the United States together. In 1905, John was an unemployed widower, but his married sons, watchmaker Louis and grocery clerk Joseph, brought their father into their home. Another son, a musician, contributed to his support and to the joint household budget. Less fortunate families aided each other in different ways. The older Orazio Barone and his wife waited ten years before they could help their son and his family join them, but the younger Barones found an apartment reserved for them in the overcrowded tenement which housed their parents.

This extended family's history raises important questions about people on the move. Is immigration from country to city always a traumatic and disorganizing experience? Are families always severely disrupted by such an event? Or did kinship ties, as the history of the Barone clan suggests, tend to ease the adjustment to the city by supporting the families in transition?

Kin played an active part in both immigration and settlement. More sustained reciprocal relationships—sharing residences, becoming neighbors, aiding in education, and finding jobs or spouses—suggest a continued mutual support. From the beginning, economic, normative, and sentimental attachments all played a part. Economics figured more importantly in the early days; established Italian-Americans could afford the luxury of sentimental and ethical considerations. As the Italians migrated and settled in Buffalo, they developed elaborate and extended family ties. Their experience negates the conventional view of a number of historians that the "extensive family of the Old World disintegrated."

Like the Barones, many Italian families immigrated to northwestern New York to join relatives or village friends. These might be adopted relatives, or *compari*, ritual godparents whose formal functions consisted of religious guardianship for a baptized child, although the bond actually served to cement secular relationships between the child's parents and the godparents. A local immigrant who joined his grandfather and cousins in 1906 recalled: "Immigrants almost always came to join others who had preceded them—a husband, or a father, or an uncle, or a friend. In western New York most of the first immigrants from Sicily went to Buffalo, so that from 1900 on, the thousands who followed them to this part of the state also landed in Buffalo. There they joined friends and relatives who in many cases had purchased the tickets for their steerage passage to America. After they arrived, guided and assisted by their friends and relatives, they ventured out of the city of Buffalo." In 1910 Buffalo's Italian consul also emphasized the role of family and friends. "The moment an Italian immigrant arrives," he reported, "he is received by parents or a countryman who give him their support and help him get work. Generally, it is parents or very good friends who have the means to migrate here."

The Italians who had arrived in Buffalo purchased hundreds of tickets for family members still in Italy; a small number bought their tickets overseas so that by the early 1900s approximately twelve to fifteen hundred Italians, directly depending on Buffalo family contacts, were entering the city annually. Immigrant banks helped thousands to save thirty or forty dollars for each relative's fare. By the turn of the century a chain of migration from south Italy to Buffalo had been well established.

A columnist writing for *Il Corriere Italiano*, Buffalo's most important Italian-language newspaper, emphasized how these sustained migration chains also contributed to the formation of city neighborhoods: "Suppose he [the male immigrant] comes alone. Invariably, the wife, the sister, the brother, are soon to follow. Not infrequently the aged parents respond to entreaties to come to this great and glorious land. Here, then, we have the family. Bonds of kinship and the peculiarity of their language soon bring the families together into colonies, and often in our cities we find whole streets made up of Italian residents." Buffalo's Little Italy, a mosaic of provincial clusters, was composed largely of families and individuals like the Barones who chose to settle near kin and *paesani* [people from the same town of origin].

In the late nineteenth century, families from a few north Sicilian coastal towns began to dominate the important west side colony. Originating on the extreme southwest corner of Main Street, by 1922 it extended from Niagara Street's northern tip westward to the waterfront. Buffalonians designated this area "Little Italy" because the immigrant social and cultural life centered here. Less important settlements also developed. Natives of Basilicata, Calabria, and Campania occupied areas farther south and east. In the 1890s when Campobasso's children [natives of Campobasso] worked on a railroad extension to neighboring Cheektowaga, they established their own east side neighborhoods. Abruzzesi and Marchesi settled farther north. The former, gravemonument carvers, chose this convenient location on East Delevan Avenue to be near a major city cemetery. Natives of Lombardy, Romagna, Piedmont, Tuscany, and Lucca also formed settlements. Over the years as the west side colony expanded north and south, population turnover occurred just as it did in other cities. By the 1930s some of the Italians had deserted their provincial clusters for suburbia, but most remained in their inner city neighborhoods. Until mid-century, when urban renewal destroyed much of the lower west side colony, the underlying family, village, and friendship ties maintained their hold within these city neighborhoods.

Such informal social networks, combined with neighborhood facilities and economic considerations, channelled the Barones into Buffalo's Little Italy. Italian-American institutions—church, school, bank, stores, and restaurants—had their own drawing power. Limited finances forced immigrants into low-rent districts like the lower west side. Transportation costs could be saved by living near places of employment on the west side: the rail and freight yards and city docks. If more than one family member worked, the savings could be considerable. Settled relatives, *compari*, and friends who shared the newcomers' culture and language helped in many ways during immigration and settlement—searching for jobs or indicating nearby markets for pasta, red peppers, and romano cheese. Personal feelings also influenced a new arrival's place of residence. When she was reluctant to leave Italy, Marion Callendrucci's husband assured her that she could get along in Buffalo. "He told me I could get together with his sister." Settling in a provincial neighborhood made emotional and practical sense to immigrants who were confronted for the first time by loneliness and the day-to-day problems of city life.

The important role that extended families played in this settlement process can best be understood within the context of past experience. After all, immigrants left the Mezzogiorno [Italy's southern provinces] with a specific familial outlook and, while the past does not always determine future behavior, people facing a crisis like migration often seek to ascribe some familiar meaning to the world around them. In this case, immigrants put their Old World family ties to novel uses in America.

The society which these peasants left behind is frequently termed "familistic" because the nuclear and extended family, rather than the individual or the community, dominated social life to such an extent that an individual's primary social role was his or her role in the family. He or she might be mayor, teacher, or laborer, but each of these roles had to give way to that of husband, father, wife, mother, or child whenever a conflict existed. Less concerned with the larger social world or the roles within it, peasant morality placed family before communal responsibility. Family honor (*onore di famiglia*)—a sentiment which contributed significantly to kin solidarity and to clan feuds—further defined these family boundaries. South Italians resolved the potential conflicts between family and other personal ties by means of the institution of *comparraggio*, which incorporated friends into the family by making them ritual god-parents (*compari*).

Kinship ties were extremely significant in the Mezzogiorno, but there immediate family loyalties often took precedence. When the situation demanded, the original family unit kept to itself and governed its own affairs. A proverb expressed the southern attitude well: "Christ minds His own business." The extended family, a loosely structured constellation, occupied itself more with social functions. Its obligations were typically (although not always) limited to defense of family honor and attendance at baptisms and other family rituals. In Niccopurto, Sicily, for example, it played no part in major decisions except to give advice on proposed marriages. The decisions to emigrate, to educate, or to seek employment were all made by immediate family members.

The southern hill-town homes, usually one- or two-story structures shared with animals, housed only the conjugal unit. In the Mezzogiorno as in many other peasant societies, scattered holdings, divided inheritance, and insecure land tenure offered little incentive for extended family households. Instead of incorporating relatives into their homes, overburdened peasants hired laborers when extra work had to be done. The heavy emphasis upon single crop production made seasonal hands more economical than a permanent labor force composed of related kin in one household. These circumstances explain why the nuclear family household typically prevailed in the South. The infrequency of expanded households deserves emphasis simply because historical myths claim that immigration destroyed them. This could not be true if they had rarely existed to begin with.

The extended family, then, performed social, not economic functions; and even its social obligations were minimal. There were some exceptions. In Reggio Calabria [sociologist John S.] MacDonald observed "nuclear family solidarity plus relatively strong identification with and participation in cliques of certain relatives . . .[and] friends (especially *compari* [godfathers] and *comare* [godmothers])." These cliques cooperated to form chains of migration to foreign locations. In such communities helping relatives to migrate became a family obligation.

If in most instances the extended families concerned themselves only with ritual and social obligations, why did they expand their operations during immigration and settlement periods? The successful migration chains, frequently offering material help as well as advice and encouragement, are best understood as elaborations of already established family connections. The process involved was complex; the suggestion that immigrants packed kinship ties along with their meager belongings and shipped them to America is too crude. Yet economic aid and other favors did not emerge as something entirely new, instituted after the immigrants' arrival in the city. Because the quality and kinds of commitment to kin varied regionally, general explanations referring to past experiences are suspect. Some villages already had active kin networks engaged in a variety of tasks; these were easily adapted to support migration chains. In other instances, the immigration crisis pushed more restricted social networks in new directions and assigned them new functions. In both cases, the links that already existed between relatives or *compari* were now expanded to include other kinds of aid.

Anthropological studies indicate that kin bonds based upon blood or ritual adapt readily to particular historical contexts. The original religious basis of godparenthood, for example, expands to secular areas—to enhance relationships between parents and godparents, to provide social and economic aid, and to ensure social controls. In times of rapid change such as immigration, these adaptations seem to represent a "community's unconscious effort to answer new problems." If the New World the immigrants confronted seemed hopelessly confusing, these informal social networks provided stability and security by strengthening social ties outside the immediate family. Whereas community involvement in Italy might have been insignificant, in the New World the creation of such networks involved relatives, friends, and neighbors in interdependent relationships which frequently permeated entire Italo-American neighborhoods.

Once immigrants settled in Buffalo, the extended family ties expressed themselves in several new ways. Such cultural adaptations could not have survived unless they continued to fit New World conditions and fulfilled some vital need. For example, while joint residence rarely existed in the Mezzogiorno, Buffalo immigrants used it as a form of reciprocal aid. In 1905, twenty years after the heavy in-migration had begun, more complex family units existed, although most of the households were still nuclear. Of more than two thousand families, 88 percent were simple nuclear families living alone. So high a percentage is not unusual, as an independent unit of this type would more readily adapt to geographic mobility. The remaining 12 percent of all households were expanded: 9 percent of the first-generation households included some relative of the husband or wife, usually a widowed parent or an unmarried sibling; 2 percent were stem households containing parents and their married children; 1 percent were joint households consisting of married siblings and their families.

The proportion of complex households was not large. A surprising number of studies indicate that it was the norm in both urban and rural communities. But a sensitive reading of the census data should warn us against drawing conclusions too hastily. Even a normal percentage of extended households, depending upon the form they take, is impressive in a new immigrant community. Few immigrant households contained aging parents because old age and poverty forced many relatives to remain abroad.

Middle-aged adults approaching the autumn of their lives abandoned their Italian homes only hesitantly to begin life anew in Buffalo. Like many immigrant communities, this one had more than its normal share of young couples in their twenties and thirties just beginning married life, many of whom had not yet produced children. These demographic peculiarities explain why three-generation households including grandparents and grandchildren were rare.

Additional evidence suggests that the new situations encouraged new and longer-term commitments to kin, which extended beyond the initial crisis of settlement. Some immigrants, for the first time in their lives, had enough money for survival, perhaps even money to invest. They involved themselves in economic relationships with relatives that required sustained obligation. The emotional values in which some immigrants could now afford to indulge determined their relationships to kin. A few examples will illustrate these points. Relatives who were employed could contribute their wages to a scanty household income, thus permitting some families to save. Although few achieved such dreams before the 1920s, homeownership and the inheritance of a house were now real possibilities for these families. And they adapted their kin ties accordingly. The Ferranti family is a case in point. Explaining how his family acquired their own home, Richard Ferranti said: "Two brothers-in-law bought the house; the two families cooperated." Even when the chance of owning a home remained remote, other living arrangements bound families together. A dwelling or apartment shared with relatives spread the family expenses. Mr. and Mrs. Angelico shared a flat with her parents from the time of their marriage. "No trouble. No arguments," said Mrs. Angelico. "It was hard to get a house."

Other considerations were also operating, of course. Providing a home or a job for an unemployed relative—perhaps the aged, widowed parent whom a son had encouraged to immigrate—added to the economic strain, but such close kin could not be expected to fend for themselves in a strange land. Again the Ferranti family gives an illustration of family help patterns. Richard Ferranti, owner of a soda-bottling business, employed his own relatives. "We were all friends," he said, "and helped each other in business." Ferranti's mother initially financed his business, "to help her son," he said. "A lot of people tried to help their children in this way." By hiring relatives, Ferranti recognized his mother's generosity and attempted to repay her favor.

In this way, family ties supported the Ferranti family business activities.

Although many Italians still expected to return home in 1905, individual and *padrone*-[labor broker] sponsored migration by then had dwindled in importance. The census listed only 9 percent (651) of first-generation Italian men as "roomers" or "boarders," most of them unskilled laborers. Almost always recent arrivals, many had not yet committed themselves to sending for a family or establishing an American-based household. "Sometimes," immigrant housewife Mary Sansone recalled, "the boarders would stay for a very short time, sometimes for two or three years. Then they would send for their wives. The boarders were men seeking work where they could find it, so they would go from place to place. Sometimes they would go to *paesani* who would help them find work." But these men were more than marginally attached to the local community. Three-quarters (507) lived with a family, in many instances with relatives or *compari*. "Many people," Mrs. Sansone tells us, "had boarders in their house at one time or another. They came from the same town. They didn't want to get in with the wrong kind of people."

If a family could not ask newly arrived relatives into its already overcrowded household, it referred them to friends with more living space. In turn, such references provided the host families with a security that would have been unobtainable in more anonymous neighborhoods lacking personal ties. Because most boarders were single men in their teens and twenties or married men not likely to remain long, their presence was tolerable to host families. Although an alternative—the urban boarding house—existed, even the young and unattached rarely opted for it. Very few families found it necessary to live in boarding houses until they had established roots. The fact that so many could bypass rooming houses again indicates how strongly personal ties between adults used in novel ways cemented this community together. By 1905 these Italians had established a personal, familial community. They intended to settle down and get on with their lives.

Household formation patterns tell us more about both the nuclear and the extended family style of migration. About half of all family households (1,135) had one relative who preceded the others to America. A few of these households formed after all members had immigrated, but the remaining cases say much about the methods relatives used to help one another. Because most Italians lived in nuclear households, we can learn a great deal about their genesis, but a study of the more complex households shows how and why more distant relatives got help.

Who were the first Italian-born household members to come to America and what sort of person helped others to migrate? Eighty-one percent (916) of the earliest migrants were husbands and fathers in their twenties and thirties who by 1905 had established or sent for their families. The wives of family heads represented the next largest group, 12 percent (139). Because Italian mores forbade it, few women traveled and settled in America without their husbands or a chaperone. So deeply engrained was this attitude that it found lyrical expression in a popular Italian folk song:

> "Mother, mother, give me a hundred lire
> For to America I want to go."
>
> "I won't give you the hundred lire
> And to America no, no, no!"
>
> "If you don't let me go to America,
> Out of the window I shall jump."
> "I won't let you go to America,
> Better dead than dishonored."
>
> Her brother is at the window:
> "Mother, mother, let her go."
>
> "Go ahead, evil daughter,
> May you drop in the deep, deep sea!"

The girl eventually left for America and drowned at sea. Perhaps heeding this song's warning, less daring single girls tended to emigrate to Buffalo only to marry a particular young man. Most of these women who had lived in America longer than their husbands had not actually initiated family migration. They had either arrived with first husbands who had since died or, more likely, they had come with their own original families. Unmarried or widowed relations—sisters, brothers, aunts, uncles, and various in-laws—rarely began households; rather, established families welcomed them as homeless newcomers and as lonely relatives temporarily separated from their loved ones.

Immigrant families admitted kin into their homes, whether permanently or temporarily, for several reasons. Many new arrivals got temporary help until they became oriented to their new life. This does not explain the presence of some 15 percent of relatives who were born in the United States; however, 61 percent of all Italian-born relatives had been in the United States two years or less. Probably only some 39 percent, then, were taken into these households on a long-term basis. Feelings of charitable obligation explain why some families offered their relatives homes—a large number of unemployed women who made no financial contribution to their host families fell into this category. Employed people who had been city residents for some time but without immediate families of their own helped to defray household expenses; but a charitable impulse toward unattached relatives also explains their presence. Several motivations, then, among them social obligation, charity, sentiment, and economic considerations, explained the continuation of expanded households long after migration.

Did the host families wish to help relatives, to be helped, or to engage in a relationship of mutual benefit which might continue on a permanent basis? In households containing relatives who had migrated after the head, aid in migration and settlement undoubtedly constituted an important consideration. But relatives who came before the household head obviously did not receive this type of aid; they either donated money toward the household expenses or relied upon their hosts for support. Those who came to the United States at the same time as the household head could have represented a mixture of these motives. Any working relative, regardless of years spent in America, could contribute to the household budget; but recent arrivals were more likely to receive financial or other aid than any other group. The largest group of foreign-born relatives (48 percent) entered the United States after the foreign-born head of their household; 24 percent entered before; and 28 percent at the same time. These migration sequences confirm the earlier impression that chain migration and aid in settlement played a major part in shaping the expanded household patterns.

Relatives without families (usually brothers or brothers-in-law in their teens and twenties) received help in immigrating and settling and joined their hosts primarily for this reason. These men, like the single boarders, were considered visitors. Other relatives lacked the resources to increase the family budget; indeed, many unemployed and widowed mothers and older female relatives added to the family burden. Some provided child care, but since Italian mothers rarely left the home to work, such help was not usually necessary. Most complex households expanded to provide homes for needy relatives, and the most likely candidates for help were the very young and inexperienced and the very old and poor. The former stayed only temporarily, while the latter indicated a more serious commitment.

Most expanded households had been involved in the immigration process in some important way, yet the census data provide only a snapshot of family patterns at one historical moment. Set the image in motion and a panoramic view of Italian neighborhoods laced together by hundreds of personal bonds and mutual experiences emerges. If kinship ties strengthened the formation of ethnic neighborhoods, coresidence with relatives, *compari*, or *paesani* added another level of interaction. Its effects continued even after separate residences were established. Other personal negotiations reinforced the sense of interdependency as this immigrant community matured. The earlier immigrants often assisted their friends and relatives to find employment in construction and dock work, where jobs were frequently obtained through personal contact. Their help also included such simple intangibles as advice, encouragement, and companionship.

Mary Antin, *The Promised Land*

Passover was celebrated in tears that year. In the story of the Exodus we would have read a chapter of current history, only for us there was no deliverer and no promised land.

But what said some of us at the end of the long service? Not "May we be next year in Jerusalem," but "Next year—in America!" So there was our promised land, and many faces were turned towards the West. And if the waters of the Atlantic did not part for them, the wanderers rode its bitter flood by a miracle as great as any the rod of Moses ever wrought.

My father was carried away by the westward movement, glad of his own deliverance, but sore at heart for us whom he left behind. It was the last chance for all of us. We were so far reduced in circumstances that he had to travel with borrowed money to a German port, whence he was forwarded to Boston, with a host of others, at the expense of an emigrant aid society.

I was about ten years old when my father emigrated. I was used to his going away from home, and "America" did not mean much more to me than "Kherson," or "Odessa," or any other names of distant places. I understood vaguely, from the gravity with which his plans were discussed, and from references to ships, societies, and other unfamiliar things, that this enterprise was different from previous ones; but my excitement and emotion on the morning of my father's departure were mainly vicarious.

By the time we joined my father, he had surveyed many avenues of approach toward the coveted citadel of fortune. One of these, heretofore untried, he now proposed to essay, armed with new courage, and cheered on by the presence of his family. In partnership with an energetic little man who had an English chapter in his history, he prepared to set up a refreshment booth on Crescent Beach. But while he was completing arrangements at the beach we remained in town, where we enjoyed the educational advantages of a thickly populated neighborhood; namely, Wall Street, in the West End of Boston.

Anybody who knows Boston knows that the West and North Ends are the wrong ends of that city. They form the tenement district, or, in the newer phrase, the slums of Boston. Anybody who is acquainted with the slums of any American metropolis knows that that is the quarter where poor immigrants foregather, to live, for the most part, as unkempt, half-washed, toiling, unaspiring foreigners; pitiful in the eyes of social missionaries, the despair of boards of health, the hope of ward politicians, the touchstone of American democracy. The well-versed metropolitan knows the slums as a sort of house of detention for poor aliens, where they live on probation till they can show a certificate of good citizenship.

He may know all this and yet not guess how Wall Street, in the West End, appears in the eyes of a little immigrant from Polotzk. What would the sophisticated sight-seer say about Union Place, off Wall Street, where my new home waited for me? He would say that it is no place at all, but a short box of an alley. Two rows of three-story tenements are its sides, a stingy strip of sky is its lid, a littered pavement is the floor, and a narrow mouth its exit.

But I saw a very different picture on my introduction to Union Place. I saw two imposing rows of brick buildings, loftier than any dwelling I had ever lived in. Brick was even on the ground for me to tread on, instead of common earth or boards. Many friendly windows stood open, filled with uncovered heads of women and children. I thought the people were interested in us, which was very neighborly. I looked up to the topmost row of windows, and my eyes were filled with the May blue of an American sky!

In our days of affluence in Russia we had been accustomed to upholstered parlors, embroidered linen, silver spoons and candlesticks, goblets of gold, kitchen shelves shining with copper and brass. We had featherbeds heaped halfway to the ceiling; we had clothes presses dusky with velvet and silk and fine woollen. The three small rooms into which my father now ushered us, up one flight of stairs, contained only the necessary beds, with lean mattresses; a few wooden chairs; a table or two; a mysterious iron structure, which later turned out to be a stove; a couple of unornamental kerosene lamps; and a scanty array of cooking-utensils and crockery. And yet we were all impressed with our new home and its furniture. It was not only because we had just passed through our seven lean years, cooking in earthen vessels, eating black bread on holidays and wearing cotton; it was chiefly because these wooden chairs and tin pans were American chairs and pans that they shone glorious in our eyes. And if there was anything lacking for comfort or decoration we expected it to be presently supplied—at least, we children did. Perhaps my mother alone, of us newcomers, appreciated the shabbiness of the little apartment, and realized that for her there was as yet no laying down of the burden of poverty.

Our initiation into American ways began with the first step on the new soil. My father found occasion to instruct or correct us even on the way from the pier to Wall Street, which journey we made crowded together in a rickety cab. He told us not to lean out of the windows, not to point, and explained the word "greenhorn." We did not want to be "greenhorns," and gave the strictest attention to my father's instructions. I do not know when my parents found opportunity to review together the history of Polotzk in the three years past, for we children had no patience with the subject; my mother's narrative was constantly interrupted by irrelevant questions, interjections, and explanations.

The first meal was an object lesson of much variety. My father produced several kinds of food, ready to eat, without any cooking, from little tin cans that had printing all over them. He attempted to introduce us to a queer, slippery kind of fruit, which he called "banana," but had to give it up for the time being. After the meal, he had better luck with a curious piece of furniture on runners, which he called "rocking-chair." There were five of us newcomers, and we found five different ways of getting into the American machine of perpetual motion, and as many ways of getting out of it. One born and bred to the use of a rocking-chair cannot imagine how ludicrous people can make themselves when attempting to use it for the first time.

We laughed immoderately over our various experiments with the novelty, which was a wholesome way of letting off steam after the unusual excitement of the day.

In our flat we did not think of such a thing as storing the coal in the bathtub. There was no bathtub. So in the evening of the first day my father conducted us to the public baths. As we moved along in a little procession, I was delighted with the illumination of the streets. So many lamps, and they burned until morning, my father said, and so people did not need to carry lanterns. In America, then, everything was free, as we had heard in Russia. Light was free; the streets were as bright as a synagogue on a holy day. Music was free; we had been serenaded, to our gaping delight, by a brass band of many pieces, soon after our installation on Union Place.

Education was free. That subject my father had written about repeatedly, as comprising his chief hope for us children, the essence of American opportunity, the treasure that no thief could touch, not even misfortune or poverty. It was the one thing that he was able to promise us when he sent for us; surer, safer than bread or shelter. On our second day I was thrilled with the realization of what this freedom of education meant. A little girl from across the alley came and offered to conduct us to school. My father was out, but we five between us had a few words of English by this time. We knew the word school. We understood. This child, who had never seen us till yesterday, who could not pronounce our names, who was not much better dressed than we, was able to offer us the freedom of the schools of Boston! No application made, no questions asked, no examinations, rulings, exclusions; no machinations, no fees. The doors stood open for every one of us. The smallest child could show us the way.

This incident impressed me more than anything I had heard in advance of the freedom of education in America. It was a concrete proof—almost the thing itself. One had to experience it to understand it.

It was a great disappointment to be told by my father that we were not to enter upon our school career at once. It was too near the end of the term, he said, and we were going to move to Crescent Beach in a week or so. We had to wait until the opening of the schools in September. What a loss of precious time—from May till September!

Not that the time was really lost. Even the interval on Union Place was crowded with lessons and experiences. We had to visit the stores and be dressed from head to foot in American clothing; we had to learn the mysteries of the iron stove, the washboard, and the speaking-tube; we had to learn to trade with the fruit peddler through the window, and not to be afraid of the policeman; and, above all, we had to learn English.

The kind people who assisted us in these important matters form a group by themselves in the gallery of my friends. If I had never seen them from those early days till now, I should still have remembered them with gratitude. When I enumerate the long list of my American teachers, I must begin with those who came to us on Wall Street and taught us our first steps. To my mother, in her perplexity over the cookstove, the woman who showed her how to make the fire was an angel of deliverance. A fairy godmother to us children was she who led us to a wonderful country called "uptown," where, in a dazzlingly beautiful palace called a "department store," we exchanged our hateful homemade European costumes, which pointed us out as "greenhorns" to the children on the street, for real American machine-made garments, and issued forth glorified in each other's eyes.

With our despised immigrant clothing we shed also our impossible Hebrew names. A committee of our friends, several years ahead of us in American experience, put their heads together and concocted American names for us all. Those of our real names that had no pleasing American equivalents they ruthlessly discarded, content if they retained the initials. My mother, possessing a name that was not easily translatable, was punished with the undignified nickname of Annie. Fetchke, Joseph, and Deborah issued as Frieda, Joseph, and Dora, respectively. As for poor me, I was simply cheated. The name they gave me was hardly new. My Hebrew name being Maryashe in full, Mashke for short, Russianized into Marya (*Mar-ya*), my friends said that it would hold good in English as *Mary*; which was very disappointing, as I longed to possess a strange-sounding American name like the others.

I am forgetting the consolation I had, in this matter of names, from the use of my surname, which I have had no occasion to mention until now. I found on my arrival that my father was "Mr. Antin" on the slightest provocation, and not, as in Polotzk, on state occasions alone. And so I was "Mary Antin," and I felt very important to answer to such a dignified title. It was just like America that even plain people should wear their surnames on week days.

As a family we were so diligent under instruction, so adaptable, and so clever in hiding our deficiencies, that when we made the journey to Crescent Beach, in the wake of our small wagon-load of household goods, my father had very little occasion to admonish us on the way, and I am sure he was not ashamed of us. So much we had achieved toward our Americanization during the two weeks since our landing.

Crescent Beach is a name that is printed in very small type on the maps of the environs of Boston, but a lifesize strip of sand curves from Winthrop to Lynn; and that is historic ground in the annals of my family. The place is now a popular resort for holiday crowds, and is famous under the name of Revere Beach. When the reunited Antins made their stand there, however, there were no boulevards, no stately bath-houses, no hotels, no gaudy amusement places, no illuminations, no showmen, no tawdry rabble. There was only the bright clean sweep of sand, the summer sea, and the summer sky. At high tide the whole Atlantic rushed in, tossing the seaweeds in his mane; at low tide he rushed out, growling and gnashing his granite teeth. Between tides a baby might play on the beach, digging with pebbles and shells, till it lay asleep on the sand. The whole sun shone by day, troops of stars by night, and the great moon in its season.

Into this grand cycle of the seaside day I came to live and learn and play. A few people came with me, as I have already intimated; but the main thing was that *I* came to live on the edge of the sea—I, who had spent my life inland, believing that the great waters of the world were spread out before me in the Dvina [River]. My idea of the human world had grown enormously during the long journey; my idea of the earth had expanded with every day at sea; my idea of the world outside the earth now budded and swelled during my prolonged experience of the wide and unobstructed heavens.

Barry Newman, "For Asians in the U.S., Mini-Chinatowns Sprout in Suburbia"

LAS VEGAS—The inspiration for building his Chinatown on a vacant lot a mile from the Strip came to James Chih-Cheng Chen at the end of a weekend's gambling. He and a friend had driven in from Los Angeles with the friend's mother, who was visiting from Taiwan.

"She was a religious person," Mr. Chen says. "Buddhist. A vegetarian. She was quiet the whole trip—just watching. As we were leaving, she finally said, 'I guess this is what heaven is like.' "

Except for one qualm: the nothing-she-could-eat casino buffet. If the roulette wheel was heaven, the turkey-roll was hell. Mr. Chen couldn't get his friend's mother an honest Chinese meal.

He knew how to satisfy a need for bok choy and bean sprouts in older American cities. "You get in a cab and say, 'Take me to Chinatown.' " But here, he says, "I asked people, looked at the map, checked the phone book. No Chinatown in Las Vegas."

That's why Mr. Chen had to invent one. Nine years ago, he built what he calls America's first "master-planned Chinatown"—and, on the way, helped take immigrant enterprise into new territory. Mr. Chen and a few others, mostly East Asians with capital, have come up with an angle that lets middle-class immigrants move away from the coasts and into America's inland car culture without leaving their own cultures behind.

These investors have brought to life what might be called the ethnic commercial enclave, a cross between the regional mall and the corner store. Because their customers live scattered in unsegregated subdivisions, instant-Asia shopping centers can park anyplace where the rent is low and the drive-time reasonable. These commercial spaces are taking on all the intimate social functions of the old immigrant neighborhood. The neighborhood is the only thing missing.

Rice-loving shoppers from the suburbs are driving to about 70 stand-alone Asian shopping centers on the coasts—not only in New York and Los Angeles, but Seattle, Baltimore and Miami—and to about 50 in such mid-American cities as Denver, Minneapolis and Phoenix.

"When I lived in Baton Rouge, I drove five hours to the Chinese mall in Houston," says Min Zhao, a Chinese-born sociologist at the University of California, Los Angeles. "Now Baton Rouge people don't need to drive to Houston. They have Chinese malls in New Orleans."

One Chinatown Plaza knockoff is even going up as a downtown-revival project in New York's upstate capital of Albany.

"There's no Chinatown there," says Raymond Xu, president of a non-profit group who put the deal together. "That's what we're creating."

Capital flowing in from East Asia, itself already full of giant malls, is the main force at work here, along with masses of well-paid immigrants. The U.S. now has 12 million Asians. Their buying power, pegged by the Selig Center for Economic Growth at the University of Georgia, is $344 billion.

In 20 states, Asians make up between 2% and 6% of the population: too few to congregate, perhaps, but enough to ignite a demand for very fresh fish.

Mr. Chen learned that early on. His Las Vegas Chinatown Plaza opened for business in 1995. By 1998, it was complete: an imperial arch on Spring Mountain Road; a golden statue of Xuan Zang's "Journey to the West" in the parking lot; and a two-tiered shopping center under tiled roofs with dragons at every tip. By mall measures, the plaza is an 85,000-square-foot mini. But it has nine restaurants, shops with Asian goods from jade to ginseng, and an anchor supermarket where tree-ear fungus outsells Cheez Whiz. The place is usually jammed with Asians. In a desert city fixated on fantasy, Chinatown Plaza has matured into an oasis of authenticity.

At the University of Nevada here, Prof. Gary Palmer sends his students there on anthropology field trips. "The Asian people in the stores weren't just looking, but instead buying these products," one wrote in a term paper. "For the first time, I saw something in this town of billion-dollar mega-resorts that impressed me."

Like Bugsy Siegel's Flamingo, the casino that first lit up Las Vegas in 1946, Mr. Chen's Chinatown didn't come out of nowhere. Long before his brainstorm hit, he had been thinking about moving "inland."

"If you stay in Southern California, you're not mixing, you're isolated," he said during a spring-onion-pancake breakfast at the Emperor's Garden on the plaza's second floor. He is 56 years old, in a white shirt and a gold watch. In 1948, his father fled China for Taiwan; in 1971, Mr. Chen left for Los Angeles.

He studied finance and washed dishes. With Henry Hwang, a buddy back home, he exported medical equipment to Taiwan and imported mother-of-pearl carved birds for Native American necklaces. Then he bought 30 acres, hired 60 Mexicans and started a Chinese-vegetable farm. To sell the vegetables he opened a grocery, and in the grocery he opened an early video-rental service, with rights from 23 Hong Kong movie houses and three Taiwanese television stations.

"I like pioneer things," Mr. Chen says.

So he moved to Las Vegas. In 1990, Nevada's entire Chinese population was just 6,618. To test the market for his shopping center, he opened another Chinese-video service there. Customers supplied their zip codes, and that gave him a map of where Las Vegas Asians lived. Video rentals were understandably sluggish. "It was very risky," he says. "People warned us." But like all Chinatowns, he reckoned his would draw tourists—especially in the shape of hungry Asian gamblers.

"Do you want population before you build, or do you build to attract population?" says Mr. Chen. "You don't want to be late. You want to be early. That's the game."

With Mr. Hwang (who immigrated on an investor's visa) and a second friend who owns a button factory in China, he acquired eight acres on Spring Mountain Road for a project that would cost $10 million. It was a rough district of wholesalers, small factories, topless bars and no Chinese people.

That's where Mr. Chen wanted to build. But first, he went after the one anchor tenant that he knew would make a desert Chinatown work: 99 Ranch—America's biggest Asian supermarket chain with 26 west-coast stores and franchises in Phoenix and Atlanta. The number 99 is lucky to Chinese, and "ranch" sounded trendy to another Chen from Taiwan— Roger Chen—who founded the chain in 1984.

Since it opened in Las Vegas, and perfected an ability to truck swimming fish over long distances, the 99 Ranch here has turned into a gold mountain. "I thought the population growth would slow down," says Jason Chen, Roger's nephew and the Las Vegas franchisee. "It went the other way. It keeps going and going."

The nation's fastest-growing state, Nevada had two million people in 2000. Of them, 90,000 were Asian, a 250% increase in 10 years. Yet Las Vegas census maps show them lightly sprinkled. Fewer than 2,000 live in Chinatown Plaza's immediate surrounds.

In suburban Los Angeles or New Jersey, and the old urban enclaves of New York or San Francisco, Asian districts encircle Asian malls. In Las Vegas and young cities like it, the ghettos are gone. Hispanics, more numerous and less affluent, still cluster, but Asians often migrate from the coasts and integrate economically before they arrive. Along with the many others who move to Las Vegas each year, Asians are buying houses in the developments that are advancing into the desert like pink-stucco lava flows. Still, they're rarely more than 10 miles from Chinatown Plaza.

"We don't go to the neighborhood," says James Chen's son, Alan, who was born in Los Angeles. "The neighborhood comes to us."

Some of the neighbors were taking numbers at the fish tanks on a Saturday morning: Filipinos, Koreans, Vietnamese and Chinese, pushing cart loads of sausages, taro root, bean curd. The Chinese who move here often work as blackjack dealers, but Wendy Wu came because her husband got an engineering job. She was at the cold-cut counter, eyeing the pork snouts and beef feet (hooves included).

"We didn't know that in Las Vegas there's a Chinatown," said Ms. Wu. She came to the U.S. from China in 2001, lived in Texas and Florida, and has only just arrived here. "We're going to look for a house," she said, tossing a shrink-wrapped package into her cart. "I never thought I would get pork snouts in Las Vegas."

Once James Chen corralled 99 Ranch, Sam Woo Barbeque signed on, as did a string of other California restaurants. Then came the hair salon, jeweler, florist and optometrist; the travel, real-estate and insurance agencies; the pharmacy, bakery and bookstore; the offices of the Las Vegas Chinese Daily News, and the art gallery that sells shimmering backlit pictures of waterfalls.

Chinatown Plaza feels snug and homey. In contrast to kitschy casino shows for Asian gamblers, it began a parking-lot Chinese New Year's festival. Politicians came. Signs went up on Interstate 15: "Chinatown Next Exit." Mr. Chen founded a Chinese-American Chamber of Commerce and printed up a directory. He puts on a Miss Chinatown beauty pageant, holds open-houses for school kids, arranges free flu shots for the elderly and offers help with their tax returns.

"My father can't stop," says Alan Chen, who is 25 and his father's property manager. "He can't sit still." Mr. Chen says: "People come here because they feel comfortable."

Comfort, as Prof. Zhao at UCLA sees it, is what Chinatown Plaza and places like it are about. She calls the Asian shopping center a new form of social organization for America's migrating immigrants. "When people have to drive for miles, they want to spend a day," she says. "Nobody lives in it, but it becomes the meeting place, the center of a community."

It didn't take long for other entrepreneurs to get the picture. Now Chinatown Plaza is expanding into a Chinatown strip. In 1999, the contractor who built it put up a satellite, Great China Plaza, right next door. Then Harsch Investment Properties, an Oregon developer, acquired an old shopping center one block east. It had a few Asian shops already and more wanting in.

"Asians were knocking on our doors," says Jordan Schnitzer, president of Harsch. Mr. Schnitzer isn't Chinese, but he has become one of the few non-Asians to see the possibilities. "So we said, let's do the whole thing Asian. Look, this is a themed town. Our other tenants wouldn't mind at all."

Mr. Schnitzer hired a feng shui master and spent $8 million dolling up the Center at Spring Mountain with red and gold Chinese roofs. The tenants include Chung Chou City Dry Seafood, the D Bar J Hat Company, Wing Chung CPA, and the Detox Massage Center.

Joy Yu and Sean Chung have also paid James Chen the compliment of cloning his concept. They will soon open Pacific Asian Plaza a mile up Spring Mountain Road. Both Taiwanese, Ms. Yu made her money developing software for Cisco, Mr. Chung as a Las Vegas contractor. They won't say how much it cost to build, but their plaza has indoor parking, floors of polished granite, and dark-blue roofs reminiscent of Japan.

Its supermarket is called Shun Fat. It will be double the size of 99 Ranch. The owner, a Chinese seafood wholesaler originally from Vietnam, decided to build big, Mr. Chung says, "after standing in the Chinatown Plaza parking lot for 45 minutes."

Hearing this, James Chen said, "That means we did good. Our vision was correct." The competition has gratified him. He stood on his second-floor walkway, another Las Vegas pioneer looking past a full parking lot to the desert's hills. "Chinese people go to the Strip, see the casinos," said Mr. Chen. "Then they come here. They can think, wow, American Chinese are pretty good, too. We also can make something from nothing."

CHAPTER THREE

Transnational Ties: The Immigrants' Continuing Relationships with Their Homelands

Introduction

It has always been tempting to see immigration as a one-way, irrevocable step, which is best understood in terms of its finality. This way of seeing immigration makes for a particularly compelling and dramatic narrative, for it frames the immigrant's life in terms of adjustments to wholly new cultural, social, political, and economic circumstances that may be conceived as challenging ordinary people to the core of their being. Individuals are seen as needing to solve a large number of practical problems in daily life, such as finding a new place to live and a new job and learning bus routes, banking and shopping practices, and mastering the habits and manners that govern public behavior. All of us can identify with such challenges, because each of us has faced them, if perhaps less dramatically, to one extent or another in our own lives. For different reasons, governments in host societies, too, have been led to see immigrants only in terms of the lives they must make for themselves in the places that receive them. The presence of large numbers of foreign-born residents has usually prompted fears among the citizens of host societies. Immigrants appear to constitute a challenge to the usual ways

Johanna Lessinger, "Investing or Going Home? A Transnational Strategy among Indian Immigrants in the United States" in *Towards A Transnational Perspective on Migration: Race, Class, Ethnicity, and Nationalism Reconsidered*, edited by Nina Glick Schiller, Linda Basch, and Cristina Blanc-Szanton, *Annals of the New York Academy of Sciences*, v. 645 (New York: New York Academy of Sciences, 1992), pp. 53–74. Reprinted by permission of the New York Academy of Sciences.

Lawrence J. McCaffrey, *The Irish Diaspora in America* (Bloomington: Indiana University Press, 1976), pp. 108–111, 117–123. Rights now owned and permission granted by Catholic University Press, Washington, D.C.

Silvio Torres-Saillant, "Nothing to Celebrate" in *Culturefront*, v. 8 (Summer, 1999): 41–44. Reprinted by permission of Silvio Torres-Saillant and the New York Council for the Humanities.

in which people understand one another, even if they are strangers to one another. They speak different languages and manifest different behaviors. There is always the fear that they might organize, gain political power, and force unwelcome changes on their new societies. It is no wonder that the assimilation model, which sees immigrants exclusively in terms of how they might fit (or might not fit) into their new society, has been the principal way of conceiving of immigrants. It is a useful vehicle for dealing with the hopes and fears that immigration inspires.

But there have been other reasons for the popularity of the assimilation model. The University of Chicago sociologists who began almost a century ago, in response to massive European immigrations, to advance various formulations of how immigrants assimilate were led to their views by an interpretation of the workings of modern society itself. They saw the social and economic processes of modern society as working to create uniformity at all levels of daily life. In this view of modernization, the differences among people were destined to decline before the overwhelming force of the processes that created a homogenized citizenry. Whether immigrants or native-born citizens desired it or not, this perspective said, over the course of several generations they were going to end up more alike than different.

In recent years, this understanding of the destiny of immigrants has been challenged from several different perspectives. One of the most significant of these is associated with the understanding of today's immigrants' *transnationality*—the ability and willingness of immigrants to participate simultaneously in their homelands and in their receiving societies. Analysts who advance this idea are struck by the ways in which contemporary transportation and communications make it possible for immigrants to continue to be engaged with life in their homelands. Jet transportation enables people to get anywhere in the world within a day or two, while electronic communications allow for instantaneous contact. Moreover, many homeland governments today encourage immigrants to remain politically and economically involved with their homelands. Immigration may drain the homeland of workers, but homeland economies cannot employ these workers, anyway. Immigration is a safety valve for large numbers of people, especially highly educated professional and technical workers, who might become discontented because of unemployment in homeland economies that are not able to absorb their skills and pose political challenges to the state. The money immigrants send home is seen as helping relatives surmount poverty, and, thus, provides another safety valve by helping those who do not immigrate to survive. Immigrants are also encouraged to invest in businesses and industries in their homelands, which serves to stimulate national economic development. Homeland political parties and factions, furthermore, compete for the loyalty and, depending on the laws, even the votes of immigrants, though they might live thousands of miles away.

While there is no denying the relative ease of international travel and communications today, there are many examples from the distant past of transnationalism among immigrants, when travel and communication were more challenging. There is also evidence of the continuing interest among immigrants in the past, not only in maintaining ties with family, kin, and friends in their homelands, but also in being involved in homeland politics and social affairs. Immigrants in the past did not have access to fax machines and the Internet, let alone (before the 1920s) international long-distance telephone service. But they wrote letters, and the tremendous volume of mail they produced actually was a particularly significant source, alongside the increasing internationalization of business transactions, for the rise of international postal services. As needed, they sent money to or received money from relatives in their homelands. When they could afford to do so, they returned for visits, which were easier and cheaper after transoceanic steamship travel became common in the mid-nineteenth century. Also, some permanently re-emigrated to their homelands. These earlier immigrants, too, were vitally engaged by homeland politics, especially in those cases in which the lands of their birth were oppressed by foreign occupation or unpopular governments. From the viewpoint of what we all know about human psychology, none of this should be too much of a surprise to us. Our personal identities depend on there being continuity between our past and our present. It is a rare person who can completely break with the past and banish familiar relationships and memories from the heart or mind.

The readings in this section demonstrate the extent of, as well as the limits of, transnationalization, past and present, and give us insight into the roots of transnational behavior from the standpoint of immigrants, governments, and international political movements. The first reading sets out the contemporary example of Indian immigrant investment in the economy of India against the backdrop of the motivations of both the Indian government and the immigrants themselves. For the immigrants, such investments are, of course, from one perspective a chance to make money, but there is more to it than that, as Johanna Lessinger makes clear. The government of India, which actively pursues such investments because it trusts Indian immigrant capitalists more than foreign ones, has proven very successful at soliciting such investments among "NRIs," (Non-Resident Indians) on the basis of appeals to their strong and emotional homeland ties. These investments allow Indian immigrants to relieve some of the tensions they feel about leaving the land of their birth, compromising their Indian identity, and making comfortable lives for themselves outside their homeland, at a time in which India, though an increasingly developed society with a strong middle class, continues to have a large population of impoverished people.

The second selection takes us back in time to the transnational world of nineteenth-century Irish immigrants to the United States, where we discover some of the same emotions among immigrants in regard to their homelands that we find among contemporary Indian immigrants. Irish immigrants felt a deep sense of obligation to their homeland, which was then a reluctant part of Great Britain. Many rejected thinking of themselves as "West Britons" rather than as Irish, and looked at Britain as a foreign occupying power, which was responsible for Ireland's severe poverty and economic underdevelopment, and hence for the necessity of their emigrating from their homeland in order to survive. These feelings, according to

Lawrence J. McCaffrey, did not decline in the United States, but instead grew more intense, because of the poverty, ghettoization, and prejudice Irish immigrants found waiting for them here. Alienation from their American lives, in this view, increased their identification with and commitment to Ireland, and their bitterness about its national oppression. Many Irish in the United States contributed money to and were willing to serve as soldiers in radical nationalist movements bent on liberating their homeland.

The third selection in this chapter reminds us that even today, in the context of contemporary electronic communication and jet travel, transnational ties may be difficult to sustain for the majority of immigrants. The very large population of migrants from the Dominican Republic in New York City should find it easy to be transnational, for their homeland is only a relatively short plane ride away. Yet, as Silvio Torres-Saillant makes clear, many Dominicans in New York City are poor, and face painful choices when they want to travel to their homeland to see their families. In effect, they can only maintain such ties at the expense of the material resources they need to gather to build secure lives for themselves in the United States. For many contemporary immigrants, it would seem as if it is too expensive to be transnational. The situation Torres-Saillant describes is probably true of many contemporary immigrants, including Indians, not all of whom, of course, have the savings necessary to invest in their homeland, let alone travel there or maintain regular e-mail, telephone, or fax contact. The experience of sending letters home, the cheapest way to maintain regular contact, therefore, seems to unite immigrants across the centuries, whatever their point and time of origin.

Suggestions for Further Reading

Arthur and Usha M. Helweg, *An Indian Success Story: East Indians in America* (Philadelphia: Temple University Press, 1990).

Johanna Lessinger, *From the Ganges to the Hudson* (Boston: Allyn and Bacon, 1995).

Linda Basch, Nina Glick Schiller, and Cristina Szanton Blanc, *Nations Unbound: Transnational Projects, Post Colonial Predicaments and Deterritorialized Nation-States* (Amsterdam: Gordon and Breach Science Publishers, 1994).

Michael Jones-Correa, *Between Two Nations: The Political Predicament of Latinos in New York City* (Ithaca: Cornell University Press, 1998).

Peggy Leavitt, *The Transnational Villagers* (Berkeley: University of California Press, 2001).

Thomas N. Brown, *Irish-American Nationalism, 1870–1890* (Philadelphia: Lippincott, 1966).

Johanna Lessinger, "Investing or Going Home? A Transnational Strategy among Indian Immigrants in the United States"

This paper examines a particular transnational economic strategy which developed among immigrants from India from the early 1980s to 1991, when laws pertaining to all foreign investment in India were liberalized. Some recent Indian immigrants now settled in the United States, Europe, Southeast Asia, and the Middle East are returning as capitalist investors to the land of their birth. They are attracted by the potential for profit in India's cheap, skilled labor force and its growing middle-class consumer market.

These investors are emerging as a new transnational business class which is attempting to carve out a role for itself, both in India and globally. The presence of these expatriate investors has already had political repercussions in India and has fed an ongoing debate there about national identity and about the role of the state in development. Since common culture was the basis for immigrant investors' privileged economic relationship with India as well as for their unique role within the society, there also developed a wide-ranging cultural debate in India and in Indian immigrant communities around the world about national identity and the definition of "Indianness." Although a sudden opening of India to foreign investment in the summer of 1991—a response to economic and political crisis—may eventually undermine the competitive advantage of expatriate Indian investors, the cultural debate will continue.

This form of investment by departed immigrants is very recent in India; it has been made possible by the last decade's restructuring of the global economy, by Indian government efforts to adjust to that restructuring through recourse to foreign investment, and by pressure from indigenous Indian capital for greater contact with world markets. In the last eight years India has abandoned its "inward-oriented" development policies in favor of a search for foreign investment. As former socialist societies have abandoned their planned economies, India has been under increasing pressure from international capital to jettison its own protectionist economic policies. Significant numbers of first-generation Indian immigrants, primarily residents of the United States and Britain, and to a lesser degree of Europe, Southeast Asia and the Middle East, have become investors in India's newly opened economy. These expatriates, known as Non-Resident Indians or, more popularly, NRIs, invest their savings—accumulated overseas from professional salaries, business enterprises and profitable domestic investments—in Indian industrial ventures and Indian banks. In the process, immigrant investors themselves are altering their class relationships. They have seized a unique historical moment in order to move from the ranks of the professional and entrepreneurial bourgeoisies of their adopted countries into the ranks of transnational capitalists. As NRI investors become aware of their distinct interests, they are beginning to organize internationally to pursue them.

Initially a response to urgings and incentives offered by the Indian government in the early 1980s as part of its own push for industrial modernization, this form of investment from within the Indian immigrant community quickly took on a life of its own. As the investors organized to further their economic and political interests, they have exerted mounting pressure on the Indian government to facilitate still more investment, provide more incentives, and to grant investors an overt political role. Within India, however, there is growing unease about immigrant entrepreneurs as polluters, union-breakers, and recipients of vast amounts of state subsidy. Their bids for political representation are rejected as yet another effort at outside domination of India.

The phenomenon of immigrant investment has other implications as well. The process touches on India's changing path of economic development, and is closely involved in the polarization of class relations within India, a country where extreme social stratification is already a source of political instability. The overseas investment process has also played a role in the development of class stratification within the Indian immigrant community here in the United States.

One of the most important steps paving the way for Indian immigrant investors was the decision of the Indian government in the late 1970s to make foreign investment an active priority, the centerpiece of a new industrialization drive. The economic ascendancy of various Southeast Asian countries like Taiwan or South Korea, which already outstrip India in productivity, access to foreign investments and foreign markets, and standard of living, gave real urgency to India's efforts to do likewise. The turn toward greater foreign investment and the abandonment of 25 years of Indian "self-reliance" was the culmination of years of internal ideological struggle within the Indian elite. By the time Rajiv Gandhi was elected in 1985, the modernizers were in the ascendancy, rallying under Rajiv's slogan, "Forward to the Twenty-first Century." In July 1991 the newly elected Congress Party government of P.V. Narasimha Rao made one of its first acts the relaxation of foreign investment regulations. For the first time since the mid-1970s, foreign firms will be able to hold a controlling 51% interest in companies in India. Real estate, the stock market and even certain "strategic" industries will no longer be off-limits to foreign investors. These changes may eventually undermine the privileges, and the competitive advantages over foreign competitors, NRIs have enjoyed so far.

The proponents of a self-contained and highly regulated economy, whose stance was forged in India's long anticolonial struggle, are not wholly defeated, however. Against this backdrop, discussions about NRI investment become, automatically, part of a nationalist discourse about Indian economic autonomy.

As India made cautious overtures toward foreign capital in the early 1980s, however, planners and economists advocating economic "liberalization," were chagrined that no eager flood of foreign investors materialized, clamoring to invest money in Indian industry as they did in Taiwan, South Korea, Singapore, or Hong Kong. In this situation, the NRIs seemed appealing as a kind of "third force," combining the advantages of foreign capital with a native's tolerance of Indian society. India's expatriate immigrant population—an estimated 10 million people worldwide, with perhaps 650,000 of them living in the United States—seemed to offer a reservoir of capital, skills and entrepreneurial zeal which might be of great benefit to India. The government singled out NRIs in North America and Europe precisely because of the ways these immigrants in particular are situated within Western economies and institutions. The employment histories of Indian immigrants in the United States have given them money to spare, technical and management expertise, and important networks within scientific, industrial and financial institutions. In contrast, many within Britain's large Indian immigrant population are lifelong entrepreneurs skilled in running small industrial firms. These skills also foster NRI investment in India.

As part of its outreach to NRIs, the government offered to treat these investors as a special, favored subcategory of foreign investor, exempt from some—but not all—of the tight restrictions which applied until the summer of 1991 to non-Indian investment from abroad. The new allocation of privileges was designed to spur investments—in sought-after Western currencies—from individual immigrants or from groups of immigrants. Yet this influx of NRI capital, technology, skills, and perhaps personnel was to be carefully regulated and controlled by the Indian state in accordance with its own nationalist agenda.

NRIs—defined in the text of a Citibank advertisement soliciting NRI deposits as "Indian nationals and foreign passport holders of Indian origin. They include even wives of Indian citizens and those whose parent/s or grandparent/s was/were resident in undivided India"—were given wide-ranging government assistance in setting up new industries, in becoming partners in existing firms, (and) in investing savings in Indian banks. NRI industrial investors got help from state and federal governments in planning and siting an industry, in acquiring raw materials, in borrowing start-up money and in finding the necessary Indian co-investors (since NRIs who planned to repatriate profits could not be the sole shareholders in a venture). In some cases state governments themselves became partners in NRI ventures. Tax concessions were offered along with special rights to import equipment, move currency in and out of the country and to repatriate profits. Much assistance available to NRI investors was not available to local Indian capitalists. Some of it was not available to non-NRI foreign investors either. It is this competitive edge which the new regulations may have eliminated.

The impetus for NRI investment does not come entirely from the Indian government, of course. In larger terms it coincides with the push for the internationalization of capital and labor which emanates from the very Western capitalist centers where NRIs are now concentrated. The preponderance of investments from North American and British NRIs suggests that these immigrant investors are propelled by capitalist strategies current in their adopted countries.

From the viewpoint of the Indian government NRIs, particularly those in the United States, are attractive as investors because of their unique class position; they are especially well-positioned to become investors and active participants in the kind of high-tech, export-oriented industrialization which India must pursue if it is to compete with Singapore or South Korea. The clear recognition of the social and economic ramifications of the immigrants' class position has obviously shaped the Indian government's decision to pursue NRI investment actively. What is sought is not just the money which NRIs might put into fledgling industries in India, but also NRI technical and managerial expertise garnered abroad, and NRI social networks within the scientific, business and financial worlds of the West. At the same time, Indian government planners clearly see NRI investment, with its cultural nationalist overtones, as more manageable, less disruptive and threatening than investment from wholly foreign investors and firms.

In cultural terms, the process has intensified the kind of debates common among all immigrants and the societies that send them: debates about post–migration identity and cultural change. Both Indians and Indian immigrants in the United States are involved in endless discussion about what it means to be Indian as India itself changes, what constitutes Indian-ness, and whether one can remain truly Indian outside of India. There is an ongoing attempt on the part of those groups involved in NRI investment to break with a narrow, nationalist definition of "Indian" and to recast that identity in new, global terms. Meanwhile people in India tend to see NRIs as no longer fully Indian, and to blame them for the social and spiritual dislocations inherent in the modernization process itself. In some ways NRIs have come to stand for a whole category of India's urbanized, superficially Westernized "new rich" who have flourished with modernization.

The Indian Migration to the United States

The post–1965 immigration of Asian Indians to the United States has been a selective one, characterized by the arrival of large numbers of highly educated, urban, middle-class people. It is also a migration spurred by the forces of modernization within India itself. Unlike many other U.S. immigrant groups, Asian Indians have been able to maintain their bourgeois status after arrival here, via the professional jobs they have obtained. If the "traditional" immigrant road to success in the United States is a slow, painful climb into the professions via education in the second generation, many Indian immigrants have been able to capitalize on their knowledge of English, advanced education, skills and/or comparative wealth to insert themselves into U.S. professions at a time when this country has perceived itself as having a shortage of both skilled professionals and of investment capital.

Thus Indian students come to the United States to specialize in science, technical fields, medicine, business or management, and then arrange to stay on permanently; professionals trained in scientific, technological or medical fields immigrate under professional preference quotas; large-scale entrepreneurs are able to immigrate by virtue of the capital they have available to invest here.

Illsoo Kim, in his study of Korean immigrants to New York City, notes some of the ways in which the Korean urban middle class as a whole has been primed to migrate to the United States, long before individuals actually decided to leave, by the penetration of U.S. capital and U.S. cultural influences there. In fact a similar pattern is observable in India as well. There a Western-style, technically oriented system of higher education has played a major part, as have the numerous foreign firms in India which hire Indian professionals. Moreover the immigrant network itself is now a prime source of inspiration for young people planning to leave; quantities of information about the educational and employment strategies for migration now circulate within the middle-class kinship circles of every large Indian city. Virtually every family at a certain social level has at least one member living abroad in Europe, North America or the Middle East; the younger generation, faced with a shortage of good jobs at home, is aching to follow and is willing to pursue any path to get the treasured visa to a Western or Middle Eastern country.

Needless to say this "brain drain" has been of considerable concern to the Indian government for some time, but few effective measures have been found to stem it. The graduates of India's premier science, technology and medical schools are flocking West after receiving a publicly funded education in India yet India still lacks enough doctors and claims that it needs scientific and managerial talent. Meanwhile India's own lagging industrial growth has made jobs scarce and working conditions poor for highly trained graduates.[1] Many universities, scientific laboratories, clinics and hospitals lack essential equipment. Certain research institutions are acquiring unsavory reputations as petty fiefdoms where jealous, incompetent older scientists deny opportunities to younger people. Jobs in large "modern" firms or in multinationals are fiercely sought-after, not only for their better pay but because the job experience is highly valued abroad and company transfers overseas facilitate permanent migration. Yet even the most able graduates need patronage and influence to secure any employment. It is no wonder that so many Indian professionals, having made the move to the United States, talk about the sense of freedom, autonomy and accomplishment they find in working here. In addition, of course, immigrants can also attain a level of material comfort which is becoming increasingly elusive for many segments of India's urban middle class.

In 1988 almost 43% of Indian immigrants in the United States held managerial or professional positions, and another 36% held technical, sales and administrative support jobs. In 1988 almost 46% of the adult foreign-born Indian immigrants in the United States earned $25,000 a year or more, 30% of them earning $35,000 or more annually. These relatively high individual incomes, combined with a two-earner family structure common among Indian professionals in the United States and a culturally conditioned frugality, mean that many Indian immigrants have considerable savings available for investment. NRIs were, in fact, the answer to a planner's prayer.

At the same time, NRIs seemed attractive investors in the eyes of Indian government experts precisely because the immigrants retain tremendous cultural identification with India and an ongoing involvement with Indian society which allows them to operate within it more like natives than like foreigners. The ambivalence, even guilt, NRIs feel about having left India make them receptive to Indian government pleas for investment. These pleas combine moral and emotional appeals to nostalgia and to (India's) national interest with appeals to NRIs' frank interest in making money. In government advertising NRIs are reminded of how much they can do for themselves while bringing jobs, prosperity and modernity to the struggling, beloved country they once called home. Private advertisements soliciting NRI investment sound a similar call. "If your heart misses a beat for India . . ." begins a full-page advertisement in the New York-based *News India* of October 19, 1990 which solicits NRI doctors to invest in, and eventually return to practice in, an elaborate new medical center being constructed by the Apollo Hospitals Corporation and the Sterling Group in Ahmedabad.

Immigrant guilt and ambivalence is on weekly view in the United States in the Indian immigrant press, a tremendously important forum for debate and soul-searching within the community. Articles, letters and opinion columns express, with startling frankness, the agonies of assimilation, divided cultural loyalties and the question of "what does it mean to be Indian?" Writers compare the luxury of life in the United States with India's extreme poverty, India's interpersonal warmth and American coldness, the dangers of American dating versus arranged marriages. They reflect on the care of their aged parents and the kind of old age they themselves face in an alien land hostile to the elderly. They debate the virtues of staying, of going home, or of trying to create some kind of bicultural, bicontinental existence for themselves.

The majority of Indians in the United States maintain close links with friends and relatives at home. Modern technology makes it possible for this generation of immigrants to maintain a kind of intimate contact with the social system they left behind which was impossible for earlier generations. It is the wealthiest and most successful Indian immigrants who are able to maintain the closest links with India—despite their greater Westernization—while the less successful tend to cut all ties. At one extreme is the rich young woman who calls her mother in Delhi every day and the wealthy business-man who flies home on mixed business and pleasure trips three or four times a year. At the other extreme is the modest couple (he has a civil service job, she runs a newsstand) who migrated in 1971 and have returned only once, to marry their daughter to a doctor within their narrow village marriage cir-cle. They swear they will never go back. A more usual pattern is for families to make weekly or biweekly phone calls, and to take their children to visit every year or two years, in combination with a regular exchange of letters, photos and videos chronicling life crisis events. Much of the visiting and the constant contact is described in terms of love for family (itself a hallmark of Indian-ness) but also explicitly in terms of maintaining one's own, and one's childrens', cultural identity.

Ties within the kin network, as well as Indian-based political alliances, are maintained through exchanges of gifts and a strenuous round of visits when people go home. Sometimes local political ambitions are nourished through the sponsorship of extravagant rituals in India. An acquaintance who is considering running for political office in India returned one summer to spend two months organizing an elaborate three-day wedding for a younger brother's child. The man and his American wife took on all the heavy administrative and financial responsibilities traditional to the oldest brother, in a wedding to which 1000 guests were reportedly invited.

The overall impression, therefore, is of an immigrant population in the United States of which a sector is still closely tied to daily life "at home" and maintains a stake in Indian society. For some NRIs, of course, investment in India is just a convenient way to make a profit off a country offering cheap labor, expanding industrial opportunities and booming consumer markets. For many others, however, NRI investment is a more complex process. It offers a welcome profit alongside a way to help those who stayed behind, a way to remain connected to India, an excuse to visit more often, or even a pathway to permanent return—perhaps with higher status. For a smaller number it may facilitate a truly bicultural life lived in both social arenas.

Culture and Identity

The rhetoric and the sentiments of Indian nationalism and cultural identity are central to the discourse about NRI investment. Both the Indian government and NRIs themselves use appeals to would-be investors' love of their "motherland." Immigrant cultural events which symbolize both Indian-ness and regional/linguistic identity within India are favored venues for what are essentially sales pitches for NRI investment. The events lend themselves to elevated and emotional language which temporarily obscures the profit motif. The impediment to such a cultural approach is the universal assumption among both Indians and Indian immigrants that emigration inexorably involves loss of culture, a lessening of one's essential Indian-ness. Central to the whole question, therefore, is the contradiction inherent in NRI identity as simultaneous "insiders" and "outsiders."

The most sophisticated NRI investors are responding to this contradiction as part of their own efforts to develop a class cohesion permitting concerted political action. Part of their effort involves construction of a global, pan-Indian identity. This identity, far from universally recognized yet, nevertheless attempts to accommodate the facts of transnational identity. At the core of this discourse is, of course, Indian society's profound xenophobia and intense conviction of superiority.

Historically, Indians have rejected foreign ways and foreign people as profoundly corrupting, even polluting, as they endured centuries of foreign domination. In the 19th century, Indians who went abroad were obliged to undergo elaborate purification rituals when they returned. Today the problem is identified not as loss of ritual purity but as loss of culture. Immigrants, by leaving the motherland and immersing themselves in an alien cultural context, have lost their Indian-ness. Overseas Indians are thought to have lost their language, their manners, their morals, their religion, their sense of community, and their connectedness to India. In pursuit of foreign wealth they have adopted the soul-less, anomic, and licentious ways of the alien. Immigrants several generations away from India, such as Indo-Caribbeans, Indo-Fijians or the long-term Sikh population in California, are simply rejected (both in India and by first-generation Indian immigrants in the United States) as "not real Indians." The yearnings of many groups within the Indian diaspora to retrieve an Indian heritage are derided. First-generation immigrants occupy an intermediate position in the eyes of those remaining "at home." Their cultural loss can sometimes still be remedied by return to the motherland.

In their internal discourse, overseas Indians often agree with aspects of this loss-of-culture critique and the essentialist view that a person can only hold one, unmixed cultural identity. However, the phenomenon of NRI investment, whose legal framework has spotlighted a mixed insider/outsider identity and whose practice has helped reinforce dual cultural allegiances, has created resistance to the dominant ideology. NRIs are beginning to assert that they are, indeed, still Indian and to insist that it is possible to hold dual identities: Indo-American, Indo-French, Indo-Fijian. First- and second-generation immigrants in the United States indignantly deny that they are any less Indian than they were. They stress their retention of food habits and family solidarity, their creation of musical, literary and regional associations, the continued construction of temples, *gurdwaras* and mosques abroad in the face of Christian bigotry. Immigrants feel India should be proud that they carry the flame of Indian high culture to foreign shores. Furthermore NRI investors feel India should be grateful for the effort and money they pour into its modernization.

This never wholly convinces Indians who did not migrate. Immigrants visiting relatives for the holidays are scrutinized, their barbarous foreign demeanor and ideas noted. During marriage negotiations prospective bridegrooms sniff that the immigrant girls are "too bold, too American" to make good wives. Immigrants are fully aware of the covert criticism. The international arrivals lounges in Indian airports are full of women nervously adjusting saris they have not worn for several years, teenagers being admonished to throw away their chewing gum, to stop slouching, and to touch Grandmother's feet when she arrives. Whenever NRI enterprises languish, the local competition not only gloats but blames the failure on NRI inability to understand local conditions and local sensibilities. NRIs make the mistake, it is said, of operating as if they are still in the West; the implication is, "They cannot understand us because they are no longer Indian."

It is no surprise, therefore, that NRIs are beginning to assert their essential Indian-ness in an organized way, often in conjunction with efforts to organize NRIs internationally as an effective political force. A recent event provides an interesting example of such an effort, framed largely in terms of the continuity of Indian culture throughout the world. The First Global Convention of People of Indian Origin was held in New York City in the late summer of 1989. A year of planning had taken United States-based

Indian immigrants on organizing visits to Indian immigrant communities in Europe and the Caribbean and brought representatives of the immigrant communities in the Middle East and the Philippines to New York for planning discussions. Many of the organizers were NRIs with political ambitions or economic interests in India. Much of the funding was raised from United States-based entrepreneurs—both NRI investors and potential investors. There was also major financial support from two major firms in India and from the State Bank of India (which is heavily involved in promoting NRI bonds and savings accounts). The event was sponsored by the Federation of Indian-American Associations, a national umbrella group of Indian immigrant associations in the United States.

The actual event was complex and multilayered. Attendees came from the immigrant communities of the United States, Canada, Europe, the Caribbean, Fiji, Sri Lanka, South Africa, Southeast Asia, and the Middle East. High-ranking representatives of the Indian government spoke—indeed their participation was essential both in authenticating the event as an item of Indian cultural identity, in offering a channel for NRI contact with the Indian government, and in forming an audience for the event's assertion of a global Indian identity.

A great many different issues were discussed among the several hundred people who attended each day: discrimination against Indian ethnic minorities in various countries and India's moral obligation to protect minority populations of Indian origin in countries like Fiji, Guyana and South Africa; the importance of political participation in one's adopted country; the transcultural dilemmas of Indian immigrant youth; the power of Indian spirituality, and, in various forms, the eternal question "What is an Indian?" There were music and dance performances and a day devoted to intense discussions of NRI investment which brought together in sometimes heated discussions investors, potential investors and representatives of various government departments in New Delhi.

One of the underlying themes elaborated by the event was the existence of a single Indian identity among immigrants separated from India by thousand of miles, and in some cases by several generations. Perhaps this shone through most vividly in the evening cultural performances in which established artists from India appeared alongside largely amateur groups from Canada, the Caribbean, and the United States. The works they performed were drawn from a common repertoire of music, dance, dance-drama and religious ritual. The clear message, articulated by many conference participants in subsequent days, was the tangible existence of a single, unifying Indian identity, persisting over time and space, which ties the overseas Indian community together, and links it firmly with India. Furthermore, the clear message of the entire event was that this common heritage gives the overseas Indian community moral claims to Indian-ness, and thus on India itself. For NRIs the moral claim bolsters their demand for freer access to the Indian economy.

Obviously this question of Indian immigrant identity can have two resolutions. One is that posed by many immigrants—an insistence that it is possible to be Indian even abroad, amid some kind of pan–Indian identity which the transnational migrants can inhabit. The other resolution, and one which the Indian government clearly favors, is to bring the immigrants, their talent, and their money, home for reintegration into India. Certainly some immigrants do eventually return permanently to India, but a larger number clearly want to remain part of two cultures.

Note

1. Since 1992, when this essay was published, the Indian economy has become one of the most dynamic in the world. To the extent that the investments of Indians living abroad have helped to make this possible, however, no Indian government is likely to reverse the policy of encouraging transnational investments.

Lawrence J. McCaffrey,
The Irish Diaspora in America

When the Irish came to the United States they brought their townland, parish, county, regional, and clan loyalties with them, but the common ghetto experience and Anglo-American Protestant hatred contributed to the creation of a larger Irish identity. Men from all parts of Ireland worshipped together in the same Catholic churches, voted as a bloc for Democratic Party machines, and worked side by side on the railroads and in the mines and factories. Anglo-American contempt for all things Irish deepened an already festering Irish inferiority complex, necessitating a search for pride through identity. Irish-Americans soon cultivated their own "racial" myths to match those of their persecutors, rejecting what they considered to be "West British" patriotism and turning to the poems, essays, and doctrines of Young Ireland as the source of their cultural and revolutionary nationalism. Young Ireland refugees from the 1848 comic-opera, cabbage patch revolution left Ireland as dismal failures; they arrived in America as heroes. Emigration and the development of an Irish identity among American immigrants speeded the progress of Irish nationalism on both sides of the Atlantic.

Throughout the nineteenth century Irish-Americans read literature that created and sustained cultural and revolutionary nationalism. In the immediate postfamine period, Thomas Davis, Charles Gavan Duffy, James Clarence Mangan, and John Mitchel were the evangelists of cultural nationalism. Late in the nineteenth century, T. D. Sullivan's edited collection *Speeches from the Dock* inspired the American Irish with the eloquence so many Irish rebels seem to express on the way to the gallows. Many a second-generation Irish-American lad listened in awe, reverence, and pulsing anger as his Irish-born father or grandfather recited Robert Emmet's defiant speech from the dock.

In the United States the American Irish formed societies to study and preserve the Irish language, and in Catholic parish halls they attended concerts featuring Thomas Moore's *Irish Melodies*. They read and memorized passages from Charles Kickham's *Knocknagow* (1879), a novel that reinforced their romantic image of Ireland and the courage, generosity, spirituality, and purity of her people. In another Kickham novel, *Sally Cavanagh* (1869), Neddy Shea expressed the Irish-American messianic determination to liberate Ireland from British tyranny. As a one-armed veteran of the American Civil War, Neddy returned to Ireland to mark the grave of his mother, a victim of landlord greed and cruelty. With eyes flashing anger, he shouted out his hatred of English and landlord oppression, proclaiming that although he was maimed fighting for the United States, he still had one "arm left for Ireland."

Irish-American nationalism was saturated with hate; many Irishmen harbored a deeper hatred of England than love for Ireland. Despising England was a catharsis for Irish-American tensions and frustrations, a way of expressing and explaining Irish failure, a way of striking out at real and imaginary enemies. Britain had to be punished and humiliated, not only as a step toward Irish freedom but as an atonement for her sins against the Irish. British laws, cruelty, religious bigotry, insensitivity, and indifference to Irish needs had contributed to the deaths and exile of millions of Irish people.

To the American Irish, Britain was the source of Irish disgrace and humiliation at home and abroad. And during his American exile, John Mitchel, the most passionate and unforgiving of the Young Irelanders, analyzed the motives underlying his nationalism:

> I have found that there was perhaps less of love in it than of hate—less of filial affection to my country than of scornful impatience at the thought that I had the misfortune, I and my children, to be born in a country which suffered itself to be oppressed and humiliated by another . . . And hatred being the thing I chiefly cherished and cultivated, the thing which I specially hated was the British system . . . wishing always that I could strike it between wind and water, and shiver its timbers.

There were those who never reconciled themselves to physical or spiritual exile from Ireland or whose need for a scapegoat to explain their lack of success in the United States formed the core of a paranoid Irish nationalism. But other Irish-Americans, people who had achieved social and economic mobility, worked for an Irish nation-state that could earn them respectability in the general American community. They believed that an independent Ireland would help them be assimilated in the United States. These searchers for status and respectability argued that an Ireland wearing the British collar and leash was a symbol of Irish inferiority and degradation, encouraging the contempt of Anglo-Americans. But a free Ireland "numbered among the nations of the earth" would elevate her exiled children in the eyes of other Americans. The Irish may have been the first but they were certainly not the last minority group in the United States to link their destiny to the sovereignty of their homeland. Contemporary Jews, blacks, and Slavs insist respectively on the continued existence of Israel, African freedom, and the independence of Poland and other countries in eastern Europe for the same reasons that nineteenth-century Irish-Americans became involved in Irish nationalism.

Because respectability was such a strong motivation in Irish-American nationalism, the middle class tended to be more active in Irish freedom movements than the lower class. The latter group was more concerned with the bread-and-butter issues of American politics. With the tremendous improvement in the quality of Irish immigrants after 1870 and the rapid occupational and economic mobility of first, second and third-generation Irish-Americans, increasing psychological needs for recognition and social status aided the forces of nationalism.

During the 1850s, Irish-American nationalists worked out a revolutionary strategy that remained consistent for much of the nineteenth and twentieth centuries. They decided to use the United States as an arsenal for Irish freedom by providing money and guns for liberation movements in Ireland and by using Irish political power to shape American foreign policy in an anti-British context. During the 1844–1846 dispute between America and Britain over the Oregon boundary, the American Irish were in the front ranks of the war hawks. They constantly tried to promote armed conflicts between Britain and her Continental enemies, emphasizing the slogan "England's difficulty is Ireland's opportunity." For example, during the Crimean War of 1853–1856, Irish-American agents tried to persuade the czar to ally Russia with the forces of Irish nationalism. And they offered their support to Spanish government efforts to recover Gibraltar from Britain, hoping in turn to win a pledge from Spain to aid revolution in Ireland. Throughout the 1850s and 1860s, Irish-Americans hoped and prayed that Napoleon III would dispatch an army of liberation to Ireland.

While most Irish-American nationalist plans had a fantasy-land quality, Fenianism was something more; it was a tough, hard-nosed commitment to revolution. Fenianism emerged in 1858 from the Emmet Monument Association, a New York-based organization dedicated to fulfilling an obligation to nationalist Robert Emmet: they wanted to write his epitaph in an Irish nation-state. Two Young Ireland veterans of 1848, John O'Mahony and Michael Doheny, the latter the author of *The Felon's Track* (1849), were directors of the Emmet Monument Association. They, along with another rebel, James Stephens, escaped a British dragnet in 1848 and managed to get to Paris. Doheny then crossed over to New York, but O'Mahony and Stephens, working as a translator and an English teacher respectively, stayed on in the French capital, absorbing revolutionary conspiracy tactics from a variety of political refugees.

Responding to an appeal from Doheny, O'Mahony left Paris in 1854 for New York to enlist Irish-Americans in revolutionary conspiracy. Stephens, on the other hand, decided to concentrate his recruiting efforts on the Irish in the United Kingdom. In 1858 he launched the Irish Republican Brotherhood (IRB), the same year that Stephens organized the IRB in the United Kingdom, O'Mahony transformed the Emmet Monument Association into its American wing. But since he was a Gaelic scholar who admired the "Fianna" sagas of ancient Irish literature, O'Mahony decided to name the American organization the Fenian Brotherhood. Because of its romantic allusions to the Gaelic past, Fenianism became the popular designation for republicanism in Ireland, Britain, and America.

In order to preserve a maximum of secrecy and security, O'Mahony and Stephens employed Continental conspiracy tactics, organizing the Fenians into "circles" commanded by a "centre," and each circle was divided into smaller cells led by "captains," who had authority over "sergeants," who supervised the work of "privates." Republicans in the lower ranks knew only their immediate cell comrades. Stephens was head centre for the United Kingdom; O'Mahony held that post in the United States. Recruits took oaths of secrecy, obedience to officers, and loyalty to the Irish republic. One Fenian leader, John Devoy, concentrated on enlisting Irish soldiers already in the British army, hoping to create a fifth column in the ranks of the enemy.

But then the American Civil War interrupted the normal evolution of the IRB. Republican emotions were divided over the sectional conflict between North and South. Many feared that the war would divert the attention of Irish-America from its main goal of Irish freedom, but most Fenians enthusiastically supported the Union because they wanted a strong, unified American foe of British power and imperialism. A number of Irish-Americans hoped, even believed, that pro-Southern, British opinion would result in a military confrontation between Britain and the United States, resulting in Irish freedom. Many Irish-Americans took advantage of the war to enlist in either the Union or Confederate armies as a means of acquiring military expertise which they hoped someday to use against British imperialism. In addition, Fenian recruiters were busy in both camps enlisting talent for the republican cause. During national Fenian conventions, a large number of delegates appeared in uniforms of Union blue.

Following the Confederate surrender at Appomattox, republicans in Ireland and America began to plan for revolution. By then there were almost 50,000 Irish-Americans enrolled in the brotherhood, and thousands more contributed dollars to the effort. In 1865, the American Irish provided the Fenian treasury with $228,000; the next year they increased their contributions to almost $500,000. According to the revolutionary blueprint, Irish-Americans would participate in an Irish insurrection and would provide money and equipment for the venture. Once the fighting started, republicans in the British army would mutiny, paralyzing British efforts to crush the Fenians.

Immediately after the conclusion of the Civil War in their own country, combat-trained Irish-Americans began to drift over to Ireland to begin drilling the Irish for rebellion. But before a revolution could begin, dissension and factionalism split the ranks of American Fenians, halting plans to attack British power in Ireland. In 1865, a national convention of the Fenian Brotherhood in Philadelphia had adopted a new constitution changing the organizational structure of the American branch to harmonize with the country's political system. The constitution abolished the head centre, substituting a president responsible to a general congress, itself divided into a senate and house of delegates.

Disagreement over this new structure was only one aspect of dissension within the republican movement. Col. William R. Roberts, the dominant personality in the Fenian senate, disagreed with the Stephens–O'Mahony strategy for revolution. He insisted that Irish-Americans should strike at British imperialism in Canada rather than concentrate their resources on revolution in Ireland. Roberts reasoned that a captured Canada could be held as hostage for a free Ireland. This conflict in strategy between Pres. O'Mahony and the senate prevented the shipment of an adequate supply of guns and ammunition to Ireland. Faced with a shortage of weapons and the split in the American Fenian organization, Stephens postponed revolution in Ireland, refusing to reenact the farce of 1848.

While Fenians were quarreling over leadership and strategy, British agents were successfully penetrating the leaky IRB structure on both sides of the Atlantic. After a spy in the office of the Fenian newspaper in Dublin, *The Irish People*, provided the government with incriminating documents, officials shut down the paper and arrested its staff, along with Stephens, the international head centre. At the same time that British agents infiltrated the IRB, however, Fenians were operating within the ranks of the police. Through the efforts of John Devoy and republicans in the police, Stephens managed to escape from prison and immediately left for the United States.

In May 1866, American Fenians invaded Canada with a force of about six hundred men, defeated a company of Canadian volunteers and then retreated before the regular army advanced on them. Instead of discouraging raids across the borders of a friendly neighbor, the United States government used the Fenian threat against Canada as a diplomatic weapon in negotiations with the British. The United States at that time was insisting that Britain pay millions of dollars in reparation for the damage to Union shipping inflicted by the Alabama, a Confederate cruiser built in British shipyards. And the United States also wanted Britain to accept the naturalization process when applied to former citizens of the United Kingdom. Fenianism could particularly benefit from the last demand. Many Fenians captured and imprisoned by the British were naturalized American citizens and appealed to the United States for support. Links between United States government officials and Fenians are evidenced by the fact that the Irish republicans invading Canada were equipped with American army surplus guns and ammunition, and the government arranged the moving home of those Fenians who retreated south of the Canadian border after the attack in 1866.

Silvio Torres-Saillant, "Nothing to Celebrate"

Academic observers of the migratory experience of Dominicans have lately marveled at its bi-directionality, the apparent interdependence of the immigrant community in the host country (the United States) and their compatriots in the sending society (the Dominican Republic).

Political scientist Pamela Graham, for example, has pointed to effective cross-fertilization in the political realm. Dominicans in the United States have influenced legislative reform in the Dominican Republic while political parties from the island have helped send one Dominican to the New York City Council and another to the State Assembly. An emphatic proponent of Dominican bi-directionality, sociologist Luis E. Guarnizo, has also credited the émigré community with playing a major role in the home country's politics. For Guarnizo, this is illustrated by the election in 1994 of New York-based José Fernández as a Partido de la Liberación Dominicana candidate to the lower house of the Dominican Congress. Guarnizo contends that we should no longer see the Dominican Republic and the United States "as separate, isolated national domains, but [rather] as part and parcel of a single (unevenly developed) sociocultural, economic, and political field."

Sociologist Peggy Levitt, on the other hand, takes a less sanguine position. Levitt suggests that the Dominicans in at least one area of Boston might be stagnating because of their concentrated attention on social and political developments in their native village of Miraflores. Her research raises doubts about the possibility of migrants participating fully in two political systems at once.

According to the theory of transnationalism, migration produces new forms of identity that transcend traditional notions, of physical and cultural space. Nina Glick Schiller, Linda Basch, and Cristina Blanc-Szanton define this new "paradigm" in immigration studies as the process by which immigrants "link together their country of origin and their country of settlement."

The transnationalists explain the current state of affairs by looking at changes in the global economy. They point to the new information technologies that, over the past two decades, have magnified the speed and fluidity with which capital can now be moved across vast distances, thereby transforming banking, media, and commerce. It seems fitting to ask, though, whether these technological developments have so radically transformed the reality of ordinary Dominican migrants that we should regard them as a group "whose territory is a borderless, transnational space."

Supporting his view of the bi-national structure of contemporary Dominican society, Guarnizo opens a recent article on return migrants with two vignettes that evoke a picture of Dominicans as quintessential transnationals. One introduces sixty-four-year-old migrant worker Carlos Avila, who, though returning to the Dominican Republic for good after twenty-five uninterrupted years of living in New York City, makes sure to keep his Washington Heights apartment—just to be on the safe side. The other, describing the bi-national life of the current Dominican president, reads as follows:

> Leonel Fernández, the son of a Dominican nurse who emigrated to the United States in the 1960s, lived for over a decade in New York City, where he went to primary school and high school in Washington Heights. Upon returning to Santo Domingo, he graduated from law school. He went back to New York to pursue graduate studies and to coordinate the political activities of the Partido de la Liberación Dominicana there. After graduating, the 42-year-old Mr. Fernández returned again to Santo Domingo. On June 30, 1996, he was elected president of the Dominican Republic. A legal U.S. resident, President Fernández has since been encouraging Dominican migrants to naturalize as U.S. citizens and become active in local politics while maintaining their ties with their homeland. Recently, he stated that he intends to live in the United States after serving as president. He will then be joining his mother and other relatives who still reside in the same apartment in the Big Apple.

Though both cases are used by Guarnizo to exemplify the modern Dominican migrant, neither Avila nor Fernández qualifies as an ordinary or typical member of the community. Given the skyrocketing cost of rents, it's unlikely that an average Dominican worker could continue to finance a Manhattan apartment after retiring to his native land. Similarly, the Fernández case seems anecdotal and ill-suited to generalizations. Although it does happen, émigrés have a slim chance of becoming heads of state in their homeland. Fernández's political ascent today is as exceptional as that, almost a hundred years ago, of Cuban émigré Tomás Estrada Palma, who served as principal of the Central Valley School for Boys in Orange County, New York, before becoming president of the Republic of Cuba in 1902.

Guarnizo's second vignette also exhibits some troubling inaccuracies. For instance, Fernández returned to his homeland *prior* to completing high school; he did not return to New York to pursue graduate studies, and he did not coordinate the Partido de la Liberación Dominicana's activities in New York. Also, his mother does not reside in the Big Apple, but is comfortably settled in the city of Santo Domingo. Fernández did not participate in his country's politics as a bi-national. He paid his dues as a thoroughly native Dominican politician, serving twenty years as the unconditionally loyal disciple of Juan Bosch, his party's founder. In fact, Fernández's New York experience long remained submerged, only surfacing in his or his party's public statements after he became the party's presidential nominee. These corrections obviously decrease the value of the Fernández example as proof of Dominicans' quintessential bi-nationalism.

The more radical advocates of transnationalism typically fail to take into account the arguments put forward by proponents of community-building. They shun or ignore those scholars who have documented Dominicans' efforts to establish a permanent presence in the United States.

This explains, for example, the characterization one finds in "The New Immigrant Tide: A Shuttle Between Worlds," an article that appeared in the *New York Times* on July 19, 1998. Coauthored by Deborah Sontag and Celia W. Dugger, this was the first installment of a three-part series that aimed to explain how modern migrants differed from their counterparts in generations past. The article begins by focusing on Dominicans, whom the journalists regard as the epitome of the new immigrants. Dominicans are depicted as straddling two worlds, shuttling between the United States and their Caribbean homeland. To read this article, the impediment of geographic distance has practically been obliterated and the tension often associated with the choice of being here instead of there has nearly been nullified. The present circumstances supposedly allow large national groups to move freely about, traversing the borders of cultures and nation-states.

This perception of the new migrant's limitless mobility would seem to have transformed the metaphor of the *guagua aerea* (the flying bus) into reality. Writer Luis Rafael Sánchez developed this concept to describe the commuter-nation status of Puerto Ricans. Though he does not wallow in despair, Sánchez specifically locates the rise of his "airbus" in the specific details of Puerto Rico's traumatic history. In contrast, Sontag and Dugger apply their benign vision of the commuter-nation to a global spectrum: "As the world has grown smaller," they write, "the immigrant experience has inevitably changed."

The journalists use well-known New York Dominican businessman Fernando Mateo to illustrate their claims. A front-page photograph accompanying their article shows Mateo and his wife flying first-class between their Dominican homeland and their New York abode. "Many a day," the authors inform us, "he and his wife, Stella, start out in blaring traffic on the Grand Central Parkway and end up on horseback in the verdant Dominican countryside, cantering down to a river to feast on rum and goat." The journalists portray Mateo as the embodiment of the typical modern immigrant:

A dual citizen of the Dominican Republic and the United States, he wears a custom-made lapel pin that intertwines the Dominican and American flags. He is fluent in Spanish and English, in the business handshake and the business hug, in yucca and plantains, bagels and lox. But there is nothing fractured about his existence.

Their article, however, does not connect Mateo's atypical wealth with his ability to "commute" in this way. Instead, it uses this exceptional case to represent the overall condition of Dominican migrants.

The realities faced by the Dominican community are far more dismal. According to University of Massachusetts sociologist Ramona Hernández and Columbia University economist Francisco Rivera-Batiz, 36% live below the poverty line and 18% are unemployed. While the *New York Times* journalists acknowledged the difficulties many Dominicans face, the community's socioeconomic circumstances did not lead them to modify their analysis. Rather, they affirmed unequivocally that "Dominicans, regardless of class, are probably the most transnational of all New York immigrants. The city's largest immigrant group, they have transformed their nation while laying claim to whole New York neighborhoods."

Many "bi-nationals" cannot afford even commonly available solutions to problems associated with the wrenching division of their families. Often, they must bear terrible personal anguish. Take, for example, the case of my friend Juan, an illegal alien during the 1980s. When news of his father's death in the northern Dominican city of Santiago de los Caballeros reached him in New York, Juan was unable to travel back home to mourn with other relatives. To do so would have jeopardized the life he was building in this country. He would have been barred from reentering the U.S., thus forfeiting the college degree he was about to complete, the job he held, and the social network he had created. Juan subsequently legalized his immigration status, becoming a card-carrying documented alien. But in the mid-1990s he was unemployed for several months; when his mother died, he again had to endure the trauma of not being able to travel. The impediment this time was not his legal status but his lack of funds to pay for the airfare, the financial assistance required (and expected) by needy relatives back home, and the exorbitant fees charged by Dominican authorities to renew a passport—fees that are many times higher than those charged by any other foreign consulate. The benefits of unencumbered mobility are, in short, illusory without the financial means to take advantage of them.

In telling the story of the Dominican exodus, one could sing a myriad of dirges for every happy lyric. I find it productive to think of Dominicans in the U.S. as a diasporic settlement. This concept captures the nuances of the modern Dominican immigrant experience better than transnationalism does. It also takes note of the darker aspects of this great human flow. The very idea of a diaspora, with its Hebrew, Greek, and Armenian antecedents (and its more recent adoption by those of African descent), can help moderate the unwarranted sense of novelty that scholars have been all too ready to attribute to contemporary population movements. Finally, whereas transnationalism is indifferent to community-building activities in the host country, the determination of a transplanted people to grow new roots emerges quite naturally from the diasporic perspective.

Many scholars nowadays make a fetish of globalization, hybridity, multiple identities, and borderlessness. Major newspapers and scholarly articles declare the nation to be a thing of the past, an atavism inherited from our benighted ancestors, which our resourcefulness has enabled us to transcend. This despite the fact that the United States is experiencing a great burst of zeal about controlling its borders, restricting immigration and increasing deportations. Furthermore, we tend to assume widespread agreement with our "advanced" view of the nation, as though our American privileges—education, employment, cultural capital, political empowerment, and personal security—were shared by all.

Upon closer examination, however, we find that the "us" in the scholarly literature covers only the relative minority that can indeed reap benefits from the rapid, almost hallucinatory movements from country to country of capital, people, consumer products, and telecommunications. In fact, for the majority, spatial dislocation remains a heart-rending plight, one the disen-franchised have always had to endure. It accentuates the weakness of the lowly, whether on one shore or another.

What was true throughout history remains true today: people want to be at home. They do not want to be foreign, much less alien. All too often, transnationality points to the tragic situation of people without a place they can call their own on the surface of this good Earth. For only the well-off can achieve multilocality without sorrow; the rest of humanity normally craves roots. Poor people do not willingly or gleefully choose to go places where they cannot speak and are treated like children. Nor do they enjoy situations in which their children speak one language and they another.

The fact that people have to travel vast distances and surmount language and cultural barriers to make a living speaks more of receding job markets than of expanded visions of national identity. Irrespective of the social, cul-tural, or ideological changes that migrants might undergo, it is the need for material survival rather than an impulse for spiritual renewal that drives them to leave their places of birth. This quest does have a favorable outcome for many people, but for many more that kind of mobility plays out as a drama of displacement, destitution, and ultimate homelessness.

CHAPTER FOUR

Ethnicity and Ethnic Identification

Introduction

While immigrants continue to be psychologically and practically involved in their homelands and develop the transnational ties to make that possible, they also must make lives for themselves in the host societies they have entered as newcomers. One of the most important mechanisms that exist for facilitating these adjustments is the ethnic group, which brings people together on the basis of common origins, memories, and such common cultural traits as language. Ethnic groups are not simply based on the past, however, for they are creations of present needs in a new society, in which immigrants often face prejudice, poverty, social isolation, and confusing cultural differences. There is nothing stable, let alone inevitable, about the ethnic group. Different groups of immigrants have produced ethnicities that are characterized by wide varieties of intensity and densities of organiza- tion, which may include houses of worship, newspapers, schools, insurance societies, and fraternal organizations, but may not have any of these institu- tional structures at all. What seems necessary, moreover, for the immigrant generation is not necessarily needed by its more assimilated children. If they want to retain ethnicity at all, the second and later generations may take the ethnic group in other directions that represent needs and goals more appro- priate to the lives of those who are not foreign to, but instead at home in, a new society.

Ethnic *identification*—in other words, identifying with an ethnic group— is not the same as having an *identity*, though the two may be closely related to one another. Personal identity is best thought of as the individual's self- understanding as the same person throughout time and space. Personal

Kathleen Neils Conzen, David A. Gerber, Ewa Morawska, George E. Pozzetta, and Rudolph Vecoli, "The Invention of Ethnicity: A Perspective from the USA" in *Altreitalie*, v. 3 (April, 1990): 37–62. Edizioni della Fondazione Giovanni Agnelli, Turin, Italy. Copyright © 1989 Edizioni della Fondazione Giovanni Agnelli. Reprinted with permission of the Giovanni Agnelli Foundation and Altreitalie.

Claire S. Chow, *Leaving Deep Water: The Lives of Asian American Women at the Crossroads of Two Cultures* (New York: Dutton, 1998), pp. 187–189, 191–193, 193–194, 197–199. *From Leaving Deep Water* by Claire S. Chow, Copyright © 1998 by Claire S. Chow. Used by permission of Dutton, a division of Penguin Group (USA) Inc.

identity is what allows us to know that we are the same person in the present as we were yesterday, last month, and throughout our lives, no matter how much we might relocate our home or change our social circumstances, or how much our bodies may age. It provides individuals with a feeling of continuity throughout the full cycle of their lives. Ethnicity can be a convenient source for personal identity, because it may provide individuals with an understanding of their origins among a certain people, with a particular history, historical memory, and language, and those origins can frame an individualized organization of the narrative of their lives. In other words, people may choose to understand the story of their lives, from birth to old age, in ethnic terms, as a member of an ethnic group, related in a variety of ways of fellow ethnics. But there are certainly other ways to understand the story of one's life—through family and other long lasting personal relationships and to places that have been one's home, though these elements of life themselves may be placed in an ethnic wrapper and partly understood in ethnic terms. What makes ethnicity such a powerful source for our self-understanding is not only the diversity of American society that almost seems to require that people think of themselves in ethnic terms, but also the ways in which ethnic identification may help to fulfill the psychological needs of individuals for identity.

The selections in this chapter are intended to illustrate the complex nature of the ethnic group and ethnic identification and the relationship of both to personal identity. Based on case studies of greatly different European groups in different time periods in American immigration history, the first selection demonstrates the variable and durable nature of ethnic groups. The authors understand ethnic groups as *inventions*, by which they mean that ethnic groups are capable of being molded by those claiming ethnicity to meet their needs in certain times and places. These case studies of ethnicity illustrate in particular how ethnicity simultaneously may serve to provide people with both a source of personal identity based on their common ancestry and homeland origins and a way of relating positively to their present circumstances as immigrants and ethnics in American society. In these examples, we see that ethnicity is not intended to distance people from American society, but rather to be a vehicle for proving just how American are members of the ethnic group. A marker of difference from the mainstream, ethnicity also may be a means for affiliating with the mainstream.

The second set of readings examines the dynamics of ethnicity from the perspective of the testimonies, in oral history interviews done by Claire S. Chow (and including Chow's own testimony), of contemporary individual Asian American women. These testimonies provide us with a look at the inner workings of ethnic identification, because the women tell us a great deal about the ways in which ethnicity assists them in resolving some of the difficulties presented by their needs for coherent personal identities. Racial difference may appear to be a complicating factor in any effort to think through the problem of how these present-day testimonies might resemble the testimonies about ethnic identification among European immigrants of a century or more ago. As we shall see in a later chapter, however, understandings of *race* have changed greatly over time. European immigrants, such as the Irish, Italians, and Jews, were often conceived as being of different races than native-stock white Americans. Understanding them in racial terms seemed a way of making sense of their different facial features, slightly different tones of skin color, and different cultural traits, including different clothing. Over time, of course, these same peoples came to be considered "white" people. What is really likely to be most different about these testimonies, relative to those we might have solicited from immigrants of a century ago, is the ease with which these women speak in very personal terms about themselves. This represents a larger cultural change, seen throughout American society during the late twentieth century, in which ordinary people have developed a language for talking about *self* and feel comfortable revealing intimate details of troubled relationships and struggles with personal confusions. In these selections, Chow herself writes of the painful process by which she came to see a relationship to other Chinese Americans and feel comfortable with that identification. Cathy, who provides the next testimony, tells us how her identification with other Korean Americans resolves certain psychological needs she has at the same time as it creates quandaries about such matters as the choice of whether she should seek a marriage partner who is a Korean American or one who is of another background.

The final two testimonies are both from Japanese American women, who also are negotiating the problem of the dual nature, Asian and American, of their identities. Central to both testimonies, however, is a historical memory that is unique to the history of Japanese Americans. Every Asian American group has had to confront racism in its residence in the United States, but the consequences of anti-Asian immigrant racism were especially extreme in the case of Japanese Americans. At the start of American involvement in World War II, soon after the Japanese air force attack on Pearl Harbor, Hawaii of December 7, 1941, the majority of American citizens of Japanese ancestry in the continental United States lived in California, Oregon, and Washington. They were forced by the federal government to leave their homes, farms, and businesses, and were interned in concentration camps, an experience many contemporary adult Japanese Americans remember, because they spent some childhood years behind barbed wire in camps guarded by armed men. The reasons stated for this policy, a particularly blatant violation of the rights of American citizens, were somewhat contradictory. It was feared that the Japanese would cooperate with America's enemy, *and* it was claimed that the Japanese needed protection against their neighbors, who were angry about the attack on Pearl Harbor. (The larger Japanese American population in Hawaii was not interned, though Hawaii was much more vulnerable to attack. There were simply too many Japanese in Hawaii to make internment there a feasible project.)

The memories of ethnic group and individual trauma caused by racism and internment pervade these two testimonies, but these memories are not restricted to acknowledging public circumstances, for such memories haunt both women's personal lives and relationships.

Suggestions for Further Reading

Alejandro Portes and Rubén Rumbaut, *Legacies: The Story of the Immigrant Second Generation* (Berkeley: University of California Press, 2001).

Elizabeth Pleck, *Celebrating the Family: Ethnicity, Consumer Culture, and Family Rituals* (Cambridge: Harvard University Press, 2000).

John J. Bukowczyk, *And My Children Did Not Know Me: A History of Polish Americans* (Bloomington: Indiana University Press, 1987).

Mary C. Waters, *Ethnic Options: Choosing Identities in America* (Berkeley: University of California Press, 1990).

Milton Gordon, *Assimilation in American Life: The Role of Race, Religion, and National Origins* (New York: Oxford University Press, 1964).

Richard Alba, *Ethnic Identity: The Transformation of White America* (New Haven: Yale University Press, 1990).

Stephen Cornell and Douglas Hartman, *Ethnicity and Race: Making Identities in a Changing World* (Thousand Oaks: Pine Forge Press, 1998).

Kathleen Neils Conzen, David A. Gerber, Ewa Morawska, George E. Pozzetta, Rudolph J. Vecoli, "The Invention of Ethnicity: A Perspective from the USA"

Since the United States has received recurring waves of mass immigration, a persistent theme of American history has been that of the incorporation of the foreign born into the body politic and social fabric of the country. The dominant interpretation both in American historiography and nationalist ideology had been one of rapid and easy assimilation. Various theories which predicted this outcome, that is, Anglo-conformity and the Melting Pot, shaped the underlying assumptions of several generations of historians and social scientists.

Historical studies in the United States over the past two decades have called these assumptions into question. Scholars have increasingly emphasized the determined resistance with which immigrants often opposed Americanization and their strenuous efforts at language and cultural maintenance. They no longer portray immigrants as moving in a straight-line manner from old-world cultures to becoming Americans. At the same time recent studies agree that the immigrants' traditional cultures did not remain unchanged. Rather immigration historians have become increasingly interested in the processes of cultural and social change whereby immigrants ceased to be Europeans and yet did not become One Hundred Per Cent Americans. From immigrants they are said to have become *ethnic Americans* of one kind or another.

Ethnicity has therefore become a key concept in the analysis of this process of immigrant adaptation.

Classical social theories as applied to the study of immigrant populations as well as indigenous peoples had predicted the inevitable crumbling of traditional communities and cultures before the forces of modernization. However, from the 1960s on, the rise of ethnic movements in the United States and throughout the world have demonstrated an unexpected persistence and vitality of ethnicity as a source of group identity and solidarity. These phenomena stimulated an enormous amount of research and writing on the nature of ethnicity as a form of human collectivity. Although there are many definitions of ethnicity, several have dominated discussions of immigrant adaptation. One, stemming from the writings of anthropologists Clifford Geertz and Harold Isaacs, has emphasized its primordial character, originating in the basic group identity of human beings. In this view, persons have an essential need for belonging which is satisfied by groups based on shared ancestry and culture. For some commentators, like Michael Novak, such primordial ethnicity continued to powerfully influence the descendants of the immigrants even unto the third and fourth generations. Others, like sociologist Herbert Gans, have dismissed the vestiges of immigrant cultures as symbolic ethnicity, doomed to fade away before the irresistible forces of assimilation.

A different conception of ethnicity, initially proposed by Nathan Glazer and Daniel Moyhnihan, deemphasizes the cultural component and defines ethnic groups as interest groups. In this view, ethnicity serves as a means of mobilizing a certain population behind issues relating to its socioeconomic position in the larger society.

Given the uneven distribution of power, prestige and wealth among the constituent groups in polyethnic societies and the ensuing competition for scarce goods, people, so the argument goes, can be organized more effectively on the basis of ethnicity than of social class. Leadership and ideologies play important roles in this scenario of emergent ethnicity. While primordial ethnicity both generates its own dynamic and is an end in itself, interest group ethnicity is instrumental and situational.

The authors of this paper propose to explore a recently formulated conceptualization: the invention of ethnicity. With Werner Sollors, we view ethnicity neither as primordial (ancient, unchanging, inherent in a group's blood, soul, or misty past), nor as purely instrumental (calculated and manipulated primarily for political ends). Rather ethnicity itself is to be understood as a cultural construction accomplished over historical time. Ethnic groups in modern settings are constantly recreating themselves, and ethnicity is continuously being reinvented in response to changing realities both within the group and the host society. Ethnic group boundaries, for example, must be repeatedly renegotiated, while expressive symbols of ethnicity (ethnic traditions) must be repeatedly reinterpreted. By historicizing the phenomenon, the concept of invention allows for the appearance, metamorphosis, disappearance, and reappearance of ethnicities. Much of this paper will be devoted to illustrating the processes which we believe account for periods of florescence and decline, for continuities and innovations, for phases of saliency and quiescence, in the histories of particular ethnic groups.

The invention of ethnicity furthermore suggests an active participation by the immigrants in defining their group identities and solidarities. The renegotiation of its traditions by the immigrant group presumes a collective awareness and active decision-making as opposed to the passive, unconscious individualism of the assimilation model. In inventing its ethnicity, the group sought to determine the terms, modes, and outcomes of its accommodation to others. We conceive of this as a process of negotiation not only between immigrant group and dominant culture, but among various immigrant groups as well. One of the virtues of this research strategy is that it focuses upon *relationships* among specific immigrant groups and between them and the dominant ethnoculture, in this case, the Anglo-American. These interactions, competitive, cooperative, or conflictual, and perhaps a combination of all three, are seen as essential components of the process of ethnic group formation and definition.

Immigrant groups themselves were by no means homogeneous; they were divided by varying combinations of regional origin, dialect, class, politics, and religion. Internal debates and struggles over the nature of the group's emerging ethnicity were inevitable. One of the purposes of invented traditions was to provide symbols and slogans which could unify the group despite such differences. The symbolic umbrella of the ethnic culture had to be broad and flexible enough to serve several, often contradictory, purposes: provide the basis for solidarity among the potential members of the group; mobilize the group to defend its cultural values and to advance its claims to power, status, and resources; and, at the same time, defuse the hostility of the mainstream ethnoculture by depicting the compatibility of the sidestream ethnoculture (to use Joshua Fishman's term) with American principles and ideals. On the level of individual psychology, the invention of ethnicity sought to reconcile the duality of the foreignness and the Americanness which the immigrants and their children experienced in their everyday lives.

The concept of the invention of ethnicity also helps us to understand how immigration transformed the larger American society, engendering a new pluralistic social order. Once ethnicity had been established as a category in American social thought, each contingent of newcomers had to negotiate its particular place within that social order. Anglo-Americans had to assimilate these distinctive groups into their conception of the history and future of their country, and to prescribe appropriate social and cultural arrangements. Inevitably all Americans, native born and immigrant, were involved in a continual renegotiation of identities. Further a process of syncretism occurred by which much of ethnic cultures was incorporated into changing definitions of what was American and what it meant to be an American. Without corresponding to either the Anglo-conformity or Melting Pot models of assimilation, the interaction of mainstream ethnoculture and sidestream ethnoculture wrought major changes in both.

Ethnicization: Three Case Studies

To this point, our discussion both of the rise of the conceptions of ethnicity that established its cultural and ideological legitimacy and of the contextuality and periodicity of the rise of ethnicities has been intended to counter the ahistorical, reified notion of the ethnic group as an unchanging, primordial solidarity. Historicizing ethnicity implies an understanding of the ethnic group not as a thing, complete in itself and unchanging, but as a process that is characterized by the constant interaction of centripetal and centrifugal forces. From this perspective, we must conclude that as far as individual ethnicities are concerned, the process of ethnicization—ethnic group invention and formation—in American history does not necessarily ever end nor, for long, even reach a steady state. In fact, accommodation to these forces requires constant invention, innovation, negotiation, and renegotiation on the part of those seeking to organize identities, patterns of daily life, or the competitive struggle for social resources around ethnic symbols. Nothing seems more to highlight the contingent, historical nature of this process than the creation of newly minted traditions to serve as ethnic symbols.

We have chosen to illustrate the explanatory potential of this conceptualization through three case studies of ethnicization in different contexts and periods. The first focuses on Buffalo, New York during the 1840s and 1850s, the decades of the first mass immigration of American national history. Here, among three distinct, yet long interacting, immigrant groups (Irish Catholics, Scots, and English) an annual round of public festivals and banquets became the emergent traditions of new ethnicities. The second analyzes the shifting discourse among Eastern European ethnics on the conceptualization of pre-immigration, old-world experience. Here we find an example of evolving efforts at self-representation that centered around the concept of *Vaterland*. *Vaterland* was a symbol that provided a basis for continuity amidst dislocation and unity beyond customary local attachments, but also ultimately it became a symbol of a backward, unprogressive Old Country that emerges as distinct from a new, American reality. The third case study depicts Italian American efforts at self-definition over many decades, and in particular during the ethnic revival of the 1960s and 1970s. Just when the disappearance of the groups conceived out of the second mass immigration of the early twentieth century was confidently anticipated by American social science, Italian Americans were again engaged in renegotiating their identities and the terms of their social and cultural integration.

Symbolic Occasions, Invented Traditions and Ethnicization in the 1840s and 1850s: Scots, English, and Irish in Buffalo, New York

Located at the terminus of the Erie Canal and the headwaters of the continuously navigable portion of the Great Lakes, Buffalo was America's principal inland port and the world's largest grain shipping center in the mid-nineteenth century. Its dynamic economy served as a magnet for both internal migrants and foreign immigrants. By 1860, when it was the nation's tenth largest city, approximately 75% of its people were recently arrived immigrants. About half the foreign-born population were German-speakers, and another 30% were from the British Isles, including Ireland.

The Scots and English in Buffalo were relatively small in number—at most, some 2,000 by 1860. They were concentrated in no particular neighborhood, and were too small to contend effectively for power and recognition as groups. They lived, worked, voted, prayed, intermarried, and took their leisure with higher status, native white American Protestants, who welcomed them into their ranks on the basis of common standards of living, skills, levels of education, language, religions, and habits of daily life. They had no organized group life other than two voluntary associations, the Scottish St. Andrew's and the English St. George's societies, both of which engaged in some informal charity, but existed principally to sponsor annual dinners to commemorate the birthdays of the patron saints of their respective homelands in the British Isles. In contrast to the classic large ethnic groups of American immigration history, which had long careers between arrival and the attainment of a high degree of assimilation, these groups, with their tenuous *groupness*, had sharply truncated histories. With a short time in their American careers, they had entered what Richard Alba called "The Twilight of Ethnicity," in which ethnicity is no longer the central element in efforts to organize important areas of life, but a peripheral, if— especially in the case of the Scots—long abiding characteristic, with episodically articulated and almost exclusively symbolic roles.

Scottish and English immigrants, however, did seek to retain some sense of themselves as Scottish or English, though very probably this retention was not a pressing or daily emotional requirement of their lives. They continued to feel a part of the political narratives of their homelands. In the case of the Scots, Scotland's relative poverty as a part of England's colonized Celtic fringe, its famine-inducing crop failures, and its struggles between established and dissenting churches, all were matters on which Scottish immigrants not only wanted to be informed, but wished to express themselves publicly. In the case of the English, they retained interest in defending Britain's behavior in Ireland against constant Irish and Irish American criticism and in supporting the popular struggles in Britain for social and political democracy within the framework of monarchy.

Under these circumstances, the annual celebratory banquets commemorating the two saint's days (April 23 for St. George; November 30 for St. Andrew) were heavily freighted with emotional and political significance. In both England and Scotland, these saint's days had been marked, but they were more acknowledged than celebrated, and nothing near as central in the existential patterning of life as they would be in the British diaspora. The principal expressive symbol of this new tradition was the seemingly endless toasting, by which the evening progressed into inebriated fellowship, and more specifically, the subjects of the toasts themselves. By turns maudlin and nostalgic, militant and ideological, the toasts invited the celebrants to recall the happy (and much idealized) village scenes of their youth and to defend their homelands in the face of unjust criticism or oppression. Hours were spent in this activity, and everyone among the dozens of men present was expected to raise his glass and propose a toast.

When an American, after reading in a newspaper that Queen Victoria had been toasted before the American president at a St. Andrew's Day Banquet, angrily criticized the local Scots for a lack of concern for their new, American homeland, the paper's editor, who was himself a St. George's Society member, explained that there was no need to make something threatening of the proceedings. The Scots on their saint's day and the English on theirs, he said, in effect became Scots and English, but when the day was over, they were again ordinary Americans. Here we find a new ethnic tradition emerging that functioned as an emotional safety valve, a source of episodic communalism, and a forum for political expression in the life of weak groups, which were faltering even as they were being invented.

The Buffalo Irish were much larger in number (about 18,000 by 1860). They were lower in social status and mired in poverty, but they attained considerably greater solidarity and a high degree of institutional completeness, and they did so early in their American career. Although this solidarity is one of the characteristics by which Irish Americans have come to be understood in American historiography, it may not be taken for granted simply as the heritage of European experience. Though the circumstances of colonization and oppression by a vastly more powerful people of a different culture did undoubtedly lead to expressions of national solidarity, such as the rebellions that episodically occurred in Ireland against British repression of native Irish culture and the Catholic religion, the Irish in Ireland were a divided people. City against countryside, clergy against laity, class against class, and region against region were sources of tension that weakened the national liberation struggle. Impoverishment, too, impaired the capacity for unity and political action.

Irish American leadership faced the task of overcoming these well-established divisive forces, while simultaneously meeting a number of other pressing, practical challenges, the overcoming of which also seemed to require unity. First, there was the problem of the liberation of the homeland, which became all the more critical an issue after the socially devastating potato famine of the 1840s. Second, there was the crushing burden of prejudice and discrimination they faced in America, and the threat that loomed over the security of the American Catholic church. Preoccupation with homeland affairs and unswerving devotion to the Catholic church led to charges that the Irish had no loyalty to the United States and were a subversive force that would assist the Pope in destroying the American republic. Third, there was the poverty experienced by a largely unskilled people, almost exclusively engaged in the secondary labor market and frequently underemployed.

The synthesis of ideas and strategies Irish American ethnic leaders in Buffalo and throughout the United States created to confront these challenges was a powerful work of invention that simultaneously placed group formation in the service of obligations to Ireland and aspirations in America. Given Irish numbers, Irish unity could translate into power in American politics. Political power would provide a means for speaking authoritatively from America on behalf of Irish national liberation and self-rule, creating legal guarantees for the security of the American Catholic church, and obtaining the material resources in the form of patronage, public employment, and payoffs to combat chronic poverty and subsidize the Irish American quest for respectability. The artfulness of this synthesis was that Irish leadership could argue that nothing more proved the loyalty of the Irish to their new homeland than their republican aspiration to participate in the tasks of self-government. Also said to prove their Americanness was their frequently articulated commitment to work toward the day when Ireland, after a revolution modeled on the American Revolution, would be a republic, with a political system itself modeled on American democracy. Their defense of the Catholic church was cast in the ideological terms of fair play and religious tolerance that informed the spirit of American laws.

This synthesis emerged in the 1840s and 1850s among the Irish throughout the U.S. The central, localized occasion for its formulation and articulation was St. Patrick's Day (March 17). As the Irish came to commemorate it in America, St. Patrick's Day was a cultural invention. In Ireland the day had been marked as a holy day, not celebrated as a holiday. In America, it came to be a vast, largely secular celebration of ethnicity with parades, dances, banquets, and communal liquor drinking as well as a high mass, and nearly every activity was accompanied by oratory that iterated and reiterated this ethnic synthesis.

The banquet was the highpoint of the day for the higher status Irish, among whom ethnic leadership was recruited. The principal symbolic and most time-consuming activity at this new tradition, the banquet, was the toasting. Here, too, toasting offered a forum for the formulation of goals and of a self-concept for the emergent group. In analyzing the toasting, we may trace the formulation, from year to year, of the ideological synthesis that guided Irish ethnicization. Toasts alternated between militant declarations of hostility to British rule, tributes to the social utility of the Catholic church and the selfless dedication of its clergy, and expressions of loyalty to the United States. Heroes of Irish rebellions and protest mobilizations were compared to the American Founding Fathers in an effort to tie together into one set of ideals loyalty to Ireland, to Catholicism, and to the United States. Like the Scots and the English, but even more so, the Irish had so arranged their conception of themselves through this new tradition of public self-representation that the more Irish they were, the more American they became and the more their self-interested, American group behavior became, in their own eyes, historically legitimate.

Changing Images of the Old Country and the Development of Ethic Identity among East European Immigrants, 1880s–1930s

This analysis rests on two related assumptions. One is that representations of the Old Country constitute an important component in the development of ethnic consciousness among immigrants. Another is that these images serve manifold functions that are characterized by varying degrees of significance. Within the group, these representations provide both a sense of collective historical continuity in a drastically altered sociocultural environment and a foil against which the immigrants define themselves and their new situations. Presented to the outside world, these images symbolize both the respectability and the ethnic distinctiveness of group members.

Because of space limitations, this discussion combines under the term East European six immigrant groups: Poles, Ukrainians, Rusyns, Slovaks, Hungarians, and Lithuanians. Such joint treatment seems justified inasmuch as the evidence, which has been gathered from documents and testimonies created by the immigrants themselves, suggests that both the construction and the trends in these groups' old country representations displayed important underlying similarities. Unavoidably, however, a focus on what is shared among them omits many of the singularities of the experiences of individual groups.

The immigrants' old country imagery functioned at two analytically distinguishable levels, private and public: the former was created, sustained, and reconstructed in immediate, personal relationships; the latter, in immigrant popular culture and social institutions. This report discusses these representations in the public sphere of the immigrants' lives.

The distinction between *Heimat*, the local homeland, and *Vaterland*, the ideological fatherland or *Patria*, used by the Polish sociologist Stanislaw Ossowski in his discussion of the emergence of modern nationalism, can also be applied to an analysis of the ethnicization of immigrant groups in America. The overwhelming majority of non-Jewish East Europeans, over 90% of whom were from rural backgrounds, came to the United States with a group identity and a sense of belonging that extended no further than the *okolica* (the surrounding countryside). In turn-of-the-century East Europe, the peasants usually replied to the question "Who are you [people]?" with the reply, "We are from around here," which was then followed by the name of the area. It was only after they settled in America, and went about developing organized immigrant networks for assistance and self-expression, and establishing group boundaries in the encounter with an ethnically pluralistic environment, that East European immigrants developed a translocal, national identity as Poles, Ukrainians, Slovaks, Lithuanians, etc. The Lithuanians refer to the United States as the second birthplace of their nationality—and the same may be said of the others as well. In this process of ethnicization *qua* nationalization, the concept and symbols of *Vaterland* played an essential role in transcending local attachments and loyalties.

By the turn of the century, only in Poland and Hungary was ideological nationhood anchored in well-developed systems of traditional historical symbols, created and preserved by the native upper classes, the gentry and the urban intelligentsia. Somewhat paradoxically, Polish and Hungarian peasant immigrants included themselves in these national, to use Benedict Anderson's phrase, imagined communities by leaving their societies, and, as they defined themselves in America, by appropriating the emblems and metaphors the culturally dominant classes in their European homelands had traditionally considered their own property.

The mediators in this process were often émigrés of the lower strata of the East European intelligentsia, petty déclassé gentry active in immigrant cultural forums, for whom passionate nationalism was the main, if not the only, demonstrable link with the homeland elite. The remaining groups in East Europe (Slovaks, Rusyns, and Lithuanians), whose homelands did not possess long established native upper-class elites in the last decades of the nineteenth century, were only just beginning to experience their various national awakenings and to construct ideological *Vaterlands*. In cooperation with their fellow nationals who remained in Slovakia, Carpatho-Ruthenia, Lithuania, and Ukraine, the immigrants in America took an active and, indeed, constructive part in this development, which was unfolding, as it were, from the bottom up. Among the variety of sociocultural agencies created by East European immigrants between the 1880s and the 1910s to assist them as they confronted the new environment, the foreign-language press played an important role in defining ethnic group boundaries and fostering solidarity by forcefully propagating identification with and commitment to the *Vaterland*. In addition to current news from the homeland, virtually all these newspapers regularly carried sections devoted to their group's national history. These emphasized the bravery and noble deeds of famous kings, queens, and princes out of the past and the achievements of other illustrious warriors or cultural heroes. These images of a glorious past were then contrasted with depictions of the undeserved present sufferings of *Nas Narod v jarmo* (Our Nation under the yoke), fallen prey to its enemies. (Except for the Hungarians, who were linked to Austria in the Dual Monarchy, the other East European peoples under consideration here were subject to rule by imperial states prior to World War I). The immigrant press regularly reprinted (and advertised) novels and poetry by writer-heralds of nationalism and patriotism in their respective countries, in which similar themes figured most prominently. So intense was this preoccupation with the old country *Otcestvo* (Fatherland) that the American church hierarchy and educational institutions, with whom East European leaders battled over language rights in parish and classroom, were commonly depicted as Prussian policemen, Muscovite spies, etc.—that is, as extensions of the oppressors in Europe.

The symbols and representations of the *Vaterland* were also conspicuous in the activities of immigrant associations, which mushroomed wherever a group of East Europeans settled. The very names of these organizations reflected the prominent role of the ideological Fatherland in fostering group ethnic identity. Virtually no growing immigrant community was without, to take the Polish example, societies named after such national heroes as King Kazimierz Wielki, King Jan Sobieski, Queen Jadwiga Jagiello, or the renowned author of historical-patriotic novels, Henryk Sienkiewicz. Much of the social activities of ethnic associations centered around celebrations of the traditions of the *Vaterland*: national parades, festivals, commemorative anniversaries, banquets with patriotic speeches, and recitations. Among Lithuanian immigrants, according to contemporary observers, national societies spread the love of the faraway country and the cult of the national traditions. Among Slovaks, it was backwardness and poverty. These were contrasted with the opportunities existing in America, and with the immigrants' achievements here. "How men live in these modern United States of America, does not even compare to the Old Country," editorialized the Polish paper *Zgoda* in 1933, during the depth of the Great Depression. "Even when it is the worst, we eat better white bread here than at home." Interestingly though, such contrastive, deprecatory representations of the Old Country were reserved for the internal public, which was able to appreciate success as measured by the quality of bread put on immigrant tables. In collective self-presentations directed at the outside American world, the East European communities, unable to demonstrate group status achievement commensurate with the standards of the dominant society but anxious for respect, offered an unspoiled laudatory image of their old country's Great Tradition with themselves as heirs to its national glories.

Italian Americans: The Ongoing Negotiation
of An Ethnic Identity

Whether as artisans and peasants in Europe or as immigrants in the United States, Italian workers at the turn of the century confronted a range of competing ideologies and movements seeking to shape their identities and loyalties. Given the *mentalità* of the typical Italian immigrant, the spirit of *campanilismo* initially defined their dominant sense of peoplehood. Their feelings of solidarity and identity were largely circumscribed within the boundaries of the *paese*. Once in America, they maintained this spirit of *campanilismo* principally through the cult of the saints, the veneration of the patrons of the particular villages, embodied in elaborate feast day celebrations. The first mutual aid societies, usually named after the local dieties, San Rocco, San Gennaro, San Antonio, and so on, devoted great effort and expense to ensure the authenticity of the *festa*.

Immigrants brought statues of the saints and madonnas, exact replicas of those in the *paese*, to America, and attempted to reenact the processions and acts of piety and veneration that were parts of the traditional *feste*. However, changes began to creep into the observances from the beginning. The pinning of money, of American dollars, on the robes of saints, for example, was an innovation. Moreover, the *festa* in the streets of Chicago or Boston did not have the unquestioned claim to public space it did back in the *paese*. Non-*paesani* and even non-Italians attended the *feste*, sometimes to mock and jeer. The outcome was that despite every strenuous effort, the *festa* could not be celebrated strictly in the traditional manner. Inevitably the campanilistic basis of the celebration became diluted, elements from the new-world setting were incorporated, and it became over time itself an expression of an emerging Italian American ethnicity. Challenging the campanilistic-religious culture of the *paese* was a new military-patriotic form of Italian nationalism. Many mutual aid societies took on this character under the tutelage of *prominenti* [leaders] who used them as a means of controlling their worker-clients. These societies espoused the invented symbols and slogans of the recently unified Kingdom of Italy. Named after members of the royal family (*Principe Umberto*) or heroes of the Risorgimento (Garibaldi was the favorite), these societies sponsored rounds of banquets, balls, and picnics which celebrated national holidays (Constitution Day, *XX settembre*, etc.). When they marched in parades, society members donned elaborate uniforms, with rows of impressive medals. A colonial elite of businessmen and professionals abetted by the Catholic clergy promoted this nationalist version of ethnicity as a means of securing hegemony over the laboring immigrants.

Both of these definitions of Italian immigrant identity were vehemently opposed by the *sovversivi*, the socialists and anarchists. Espousing oppositional ideologies which were antireligious, antinationalist, and anticapitalist, they sought to inculcate class consciousness as members of the international proletariat among Italian workers. The radicals utilized newspapers, songs, drama, clubs, and their own holidays to evangelize their gospel. Rather than celebrating saints' days or national holidays, they marked the fall of the Bastille, the Paris Commune, and, of course, May Day. On *Primo Maggio* they held balls, picnics, and parades, at which they sang the revolutionary hymns, recited poetry, and held presentations of Pietro Gori's play, *Primo Maggio*.

Each of these forms of ethnicization sought to define the essential character of the immigrants in terms of a collectivity: the *paese*; the nation; the proletariat. Each used a constellation of symbols, rituals, and rhetoric to imbue a sense of identity and solidarity among its followers. In succeeding decades other versions of peoplehood offered the immigrants alternative self-concepts and collective representations. As Italian immigrants became more rooted in America, and the immigrant generation itself began to wane, the necessity of creating an Italian American identity assumed primacy. The formation of the Sons of Italy in America in 1905, for example, was one effort to reconcile, with appropriate language and symbolism, the duality of being Italian American. Similarly Columbus Day served as the symbolic expression of this dual identity *par excellence*. By placing the Italians at the very beginnings of American history through their surrogate ancestor, the anniversary of the discovery of the New World served to legitimize their claims to Americanness at the same time that it allowed them to take pride in their Italianness.

In the 1920s Benito Mussolini's Fascist regime added to the contestation present within Italian America by attempting to win over immigrants and their progeny to its cause. A new cluster of festivals, heroes, and slogans emerged to this end. Fascist elements sought to dominate distinctly Italian American celebrations, such as Columbus Day; lay claim to the symbols of Italian patriotism and nationalism; and insert their own holy days (e.g., the anniversary of the March on Rome into the calendar. Oath taking to Mussolini and the King, playing *Giovinezza* (the Fascist official hymn) and the *Marcia Reale*, singing Fascist battle songs unfurling banners with Mussolini's commands and wearing black shirts provided the necessary iconography and pageantry. Sensitive to the generational transition, the Fascists also supplied English-language publications, as well as films and radio programs, for the children of immigrants who could not understand Italian.

Antifascist Italians contested these initiatives with counter demonstrations and contrasting values and symbols. Composed of an unlikely mix of Italian American labor activists, leftist radicals, liberal progressives, and educated Italian exiles, antifascists found it difficult to agree upon a united front. Despite these internal divisions, their demonstrations typically attempted to link Italian Americans with the republican legacy of Italy and its champions of freedom, such as Garibaldi and Mazzini. Memorials to Giacomo Matteotti, the martyred socialist deputy, accompanied by renditions of *Bandiera Rossa* and *Inno di Garibaldi*, became fixtures of antifascist festivities. After the Italian invasion of Ethiopia in 1935, opponents of Mussolini added antiimperialism to their cause.

World War II resolved the question of Fascism by making the maintenance of dual loyalties impossible, and the ensuing Cold War further eroded the position of radicals in the Italian American community. The war crisis and subsequent anticommunist crusade placed a high premium on conformity, loyalty, and patriotism to the United States. To many observers in the 1940s and 1950s it appeared that Italian Americans were comfortably melding into the melting pot as particularly the second generation realized increased social mobility, adopted middle-class values, and joined in the rush to mass consumerism.

By the 1960s, however, third- and fourth-generation Italian Americans unexpectedly began to assert their distinctiveness as part of a wider ethnic revival sweeping America. Italian Americans joined with other ethnics to renegotiate their ethnicities in the midst of a national political crisis during which dominant societal values and identities came under increasing assault. Once again, the self-conscious crafting of symbols, rituals, and images became heightened as Italian Americans attempted to generate as much internal unity as possible, lay claim to being fully American, and inscribe a more dignified place for themselves in the dominant narrative of American history. Since the Italian American population was increasingly segmented by generation, class, occupation, education, and residence, there was substantial disagreement over the proper rhetoric and cultural forms to use in expressing Italian American ethnicity. This diversity of opinion was further sharpened by the proliferation of Italian American organizations of all kinds during the sixties and seventies. Upwardly mobile and social climbing individuals, for example, attempted to fashion a more positive image by focusing on the glories of old country high culture, seeking to connect Italian Americans with the accomplishments of Dante, DaVinci, and other renowned Italians. In a variant of this strategy, other Italian Americans sought to cash in on the cachet of contemporary Italian design and style, by consuming Gucci, Pucci, Ferrari, and so on. Status anxieties engendered by negative stereotypes inherited from the era of peasant immigration generated intensified efforts to highlight the contributions of Italians to the development of America. Seeking to compensate for insecurities, filiopietists campaigned for the issuance of commemorative stamps to Filippo Mazzei and Francesco Vigo; recognition of exceptional immigrants such as Constantino Brumidi, Father Eusebio Kino, and Lorenzo da Ponte; and erection of monuments to other overlooked notables. Perhaps the most vigorously fought struggle was the successful effort to have Columbus Day declared a federal holiday. Such a strategy, common to all ethnic groups, challenged the standard rendition of American history—indeed, often stood it on its head—by showing how the group's values and heroes were instrumental in shaping national development.

These filiopietistic initiatives have frequently clashed with the recent work of academics, often themselves Italian Americans, who have portrayed the common experiences of millions of peasant immigrants as representing the key elements of the Italian American saga. Such historical studies have also questioned the assimilationist interpretation of the Italian American past, by stressing the ability of ordinary people to preserve aspects of their cultures and to change the dominant society by their presence. This opening up of Italian American history in all its dimensions for public discussion, including such unpalatable aspects as crime, radicalism, and peasant culture, has led to friction with those interested in concentrating solely on the achievements and contributions of Italian Americans.

Meanwhile, the mass of working- and lower-middle-class Italian Americans continued to draw upon their heritage of peasant and proletarian values and traditions to shape their ethnicity. The ethnic revival by sanctioning cultural difference brought a renewed vitality to street festivals, parades, and celebrations in Italian American settlements across the nation. Whether refurbished feast days of saints or newly created rituals, these events often highlighted the virtues of close family networks, intimate neighborhoods offering stability and security, and smaller value structures. A recurrent theme emerging from the rhetoric and ritual of these occasions was a bootstraps interpretation of the past, focusing on the immigrant work ethnic, sacrifice, family, and loyalty. A nostalgia for the Little Italies of the past which allegedly embodied these values offered a psychological defense against the perceived materialism, faceless anonymity, and moral chaos of America.

The new Italian American ethnic activism also took the form of an aggressive antidefamation campaign designed to counter prejudices and negative stereotypes through pressure group tactics. A major target of this campaign was the pervasive characterizations of Italian criminality in the mass media. Various Italian American organizations brought intense public pressure against the U.S. Department of Justice, the *New York Times*, and other media to discontinue references to the Cosa Nostra and the Mafia. Similar motivations underlay attempts to halt derogatory Italian jokes as well as commercials and media representations which depicted Italian Americans as coarse, uneducated boors. After submitting passively for decades to stereotyping and defamation, Italian Americans had mobilized to renegotiate their ethnicity with mainstream institutions. Their considerable success in doing so demonstrated that they had attained a level of economic and political power which enabled them to bargain from a position of strength. Curiously at a stage of their history which has been characterized as the twilight of ethnicity, the Italian Americans have demonstrated a greater unity, creativity and effectiveness in defining their position in the larger society than ever before.

This selective refashioning of Italian American ethnicity no doubt will continue as individuals dip into their cultural reservoirs and choose aspects that suit their needs at particular moments in time. What emerges as important in this process is not how much of the traditional culture has survived, but rather the changing uses to which people put cultural symbols and rituals. The problems inherent in arbitrating complex ethnic identities ensure that there will also be ongoing internal group conflict over which aspects should be selected and used. The patterns of accommodation and resistance that have characterized the invention of Italian American identity speak to the tensions and contradictions that form a critical component in the American ethnic group experience.

Conclusion

The concept of invention offers an optic of power and subtlety for the analysis of ethnicity, this social phenomenon which has demonstrated such unanticipated resilience in the modern world. Since in this conception ethnicity is not a biological or cultural given, it is restored to the province of history. We trust that our paper has suggested how the idea of invention or construction, of group identities can be applied to reveal the inner workings of social and cultural processes. For the study of immigrant adaptation, this approach, we believe, has significant advantages over preceding theories. It shifts the focus of analysis from the hackneyed concern with individual assimilation to a host society to the sphere of collective, interactive behavior in which negotiations between immigrant groups and the dominant ethno-culture are open-ended and ambivalent. It further calls into question the assumption that the host society unilaterally dictates the terms of assimilation and that change is a linear progression from foreignness to Americanization. Rather it envisions a dynamic process of ethnicization, driven by multiple relationships, among various side-stream ethnicities as well as between them and the mainstream ethnicity, and resulting in multidirectional change. Everyone is changed in this dialectical process. Since such relationships are often competitive and conflictual, contestation is a central feature of ethnicization. Thus power and politics, in the broadest sense, both internal to the groups and in their external relations with others, are basic to the formation and preservation of ethnicities.

   The invention of ethnicity, therefore, offers promising alternatives to the single-group approach which threatened to bog down immigration studies in a sterile parochialism. It further facilitates, we believe, a fresh strategy for addressing the question, "What is American?" Rather than positing a hegemonic Anglo-American core culture, this conceptualization entertains the notion that what is distinctively American has been itself a product of this synergistic encounter of multiple peoples and cultures.

Claire S. Chow, "Ethnicity and Identity: What It Means to Be Asian American"

1. One fine autumn day when I was in seventh grade, my civics teacher called me to the front of the classroom. I assumed he wanted me to say something about the day's lesson, which I was more than prepared to do. Instead, he pulled out a yellow piece of construction paper and asked me to lay my arm against it. "See, class," he explained, "her skin isn't really yellow at all, it's more like an ivory color." He made his point and then dismissed me to my seat. Walking back to the fifth desk, first row nearest to the door, I could not have been more stunned. I was not angry with him. I knew this was his way of trying to confront racial stereotypes. Instead, I experienced a wave of self-loathing and shame that still crashes at the edge of my consciousness some thirty years later. The teacher was not at fault—it was *me*, with my ivory skin, my slanted eyes, my high cheekbones and foreign last name that was responsible for this situation. I have no idea how my classmates actually related to the civics lesson they were witnessing, but in my heart and in my memory, I still hear the giggles, the snickers, the jokes. They cannot be erased.

My sister and I used to fantasize about how our lives would be different if we could wake up one morning with blond hair and blue eyes. We would be popular. Boys would pay attention to us. Girls would not giggle and whisper when we walked into the room. In other words, we would be just like everyone else.

But for me, the desire to be white went a step further. What I did not fully understand at the time, what I kept to myself, was that I hated being Chinese. I was embarrassed about how I looked. I believed Chinese were rightfully second-class citizens, less worthy or valuable than whites. I did not want any Chinese friends because looking at their faces provided an unsettling and undesired reflection of my own countenance. I dated only white men and vowed to marry one. And when I did, I found myself feeling grateful to this man—who could trace his ancestors to the *Mayflower*—for marrying me despite my ethnicity. It is not just that I wanted to be white, or that I hated being different, it is that I hated *myself* because I was Chinese.

And yet, at the same time, I had very little real understanding of what being Chinese meant. As far as I was concerned, my language, my values, my dreams were no different from those of my white classmates and peers. I thought it was only my physical appearance that made me Chinese, and so I lived with a sense of despair that things would never change. I could be sixty years old, living in California or Texas or Lithuania, and would still be identified as Asian. Whatever was inside me would always be tempered by the fact of my facial features. The best I could hope for was to act as white as possible, and perhaps those around me would forget my ethnicity.

Today I am at a point in my life where I no longer wish I were someone other than who I am. Now I know that, for better or worse, I have more Chinese in me than just the genes for black hair or short stature. My mother may have baked brownies for us to take to school, but *her* grandmother struggled to walk from room to room with bound feet. I am *both* Chinese and American, a product of history and present circumstance, and if I choose to devalue or reject either side, I will never be able to experience myself as a whole person. Now, because I have had a taste of wholeness, because I feel like a woman who has taken secrets out of their ancient hiding places and exposed them to the clear pure light of day, I recognize that there is no turning back.

The quest to integrate ethnicity and identity is not an easy one, or a singular event, but a process. I will probably always have questions and doubts. I may never be able to fully eradicate the shame I felt as a child, but each new bit of information or shared connection is one more piece of the puzzle in place.

Part of the journey for me has involved discovering what it is about me that I can attribute to being Chinese. This is probably a question with no definitive answer, but there are certain things I know to be true about myself that feel more Asian than Western. This intuition has been confirmed in my conversations with women of similar backgrounds. For example: my relationship with my mother. My elitist attitudes about education and occupation. My work ethic. My discomfort with promoting myself or my work. My deference to authority. My need to excel. My reserve. My ability to save money and defer gratification. My self-control and my discomfort with others who do not censor strong displays of emotion in public. Some of these traits have been helpful, others have probably held me back; but they are still part of who I am, where I come from. And in the act of making this discovery I have experienced the joy of recognition: "Oh, you mean you also have a hard time expressing affection? It isn't just me? Maybe it's one of those Asian things." I feel less alone, less strange, and in me a deep human longing for connection and twinship is satiated.

I have also had to come to terms with being different. Several years ago, a Caucasian friend told me that he didn't think of me as Asian, simply as Claire. That statement was something I had been longing to hear all my life. What surprised me, however, was that it didn't have the kind of magic I thought it would. In a way, I no longer want this. I felt like saying to him, "Well, the fact is, I *am* Chinese. I'm not exactly like you and I wish you could see that. Otherwise, I feel denied and unacknowledged." In fact, I realize that I have lived with differentness for so long that it has become part of who I am. Some of my self-esteem derives from being set apart from the crowd; I'm starting to feel a little threatened when I see all these other Asian American women wanting to become therapists. You mean I'm not the only one anymore?

2. For Cathy, ethnicity is very much a part of her identity. The dilemma she faces is how to keep her cultural legacy alive through the generations, how to pass it on.

"I feel I have a very strong Korean American identity. I grew up primarily with Caucasians in a rural community in northwest Washington state, but my first language was Korean and I spoke it until I went to kindergarten. I am concerned that, in a few generations, the Korean part of our family will just fade away, that my grandchildren won't even know how to use chopsticks—or that's the *only* Asian thing they'll be familiar with. To me, being Korean American means that I could never go back there to live, but I'm not entirely American either. I'm somewhere in between. And that is a place of identity for me.

"My dad came to the U.S. to get his Ph.D. Because there were so few other Koreans at the time they arrived in Pullman, my parents felt it was important for us to assimilate as quickly as possible. They knew no English when they came, but by the time my brother, two years younger, was ready for school, he already spoke the language quite well. I learned English easily, but I never had the sense of not wanting to speak Korean. In fact, we still speak a mix of the two languages at home. Some concepts are just better expressed in one language or in the other, and I feel lucky to have access to both.

"As an adolescent, sometimes I felt my life would have been easier if I were white. I think all Asians go through that to some degree. Things would have been less complicated if my parents were more like the parents of my friends. For example, if their English was perfect. Or if they weren't always making people take off their shoes every time they came into the house. Stuff like that. But it wasn't a major issue. I never disliked myself or felt others disliked me for being Korean American.

"I was aware that some things about our family set us apart from many of my peers. Definitely grades and school. Even though many of my classmates were also the children of professors, they seemed to have much more leeway. Getting A's wasn't the big celebratory thing it was in our house. But then again, they didn't think a B+ was a bad grade. My two best friends were very social. To them, it was a good semester if they didn't' get too many C's. Part of what kept our friendship intact was that we never compared report cards. I do remember occasionally getting less than an A in math (my father has a Ph.D. in that subject) and wishing my parents wouldn't make such a big deal about it, but mostly, I wanted the good grades for myself. Now, in grad school, where everyone else also works really hard, I feel right at home.

"I also know that my parents have a pretty traditional Korean marriage and that they put up with a lot in each other. Dissolving the marriage is never an issue. My mother is a feminist in some ways and she has confided in me that she doesn't feel she has fulfilled her potential because her culture relegated her to the role of wife and mother. I want something different for myself. That's why, at this point, I'm not sure I want children. I don't want to face that conflict. Of course, my mother tells me I'll change my mind, as she did.

"I am dating a Caucasian man right now. He's interested in Asian issues, does environmental work in Vietnam. No one in my family has yet married Korean. But in a reversal of how I felt as a teenager, I believe it would be simpler if *I* married a Korean American man. Sometimes I think to myself,

'Oh, my God. If I marry this Caucasian man, my family is no longer going to be Korean from *here on out*.' I know I am putting this pressure on myself, but it is a real conflict."

3. Meg is a Japanese American woman who has given a lot of thought to her own struggles around the issue of identity.

"For me, the question of ethnicity and identity is very important, but also very complicated. So much of me is American, but at the core, I am really Asian. This makes for a lot of confusion in my life and brings up questions I can't answer. For example, I observe a number of Japanese customs, such as tea ceremony. I value these traditions, they enrich my life. Yet, at the same time, knowing that Japanese have the highest rate of out-marriages of all the Asians, I foresee that in a few generations, our culture will be lost, indiscernible. On the one hand, this is a loss, but on the other, I have a Zen orientation and believe that, fundamentally, we are all one. Part of me also believes that when people attach to their differentness it is part of the process of gaining self-esteem, but that it may not ultimately be what we should be seeking. I feel torn.

"My parents were both interned, and I was born in camp. However, I didn't really find out anything about my parents' experience until I was seventeen. They just did not talk about it. Same with Hiroshima. My grandmother was killed in the bombing, but for months afterwards, my mother couldn't get any word on whether her mother had survived or not. Finally, she did get some sort of communication saying that my grandmother had died. She didn't talk about that either. My parents and others like them were experiencing a kind of amnesia about the facts of war, life in the camps.

"I think that for them, and for myself, one of the primary effects of these experiences has been the abiding need to prove myself, to overcompensate. So if my brother goes into Boy Scouts, he's got to be an Eagle Scout. Good is never good enough. That's partly why I dropped out of grad school almost thirty years ago and am just now able to return to work on my doctorate. The Japanese part of me was very uncomfortable speaking up in class, raising my hand, being recognized. I had a very hard time being successful in that environment.

"I also feel that some of my Japanese attitudes or beliefs are not helpful in the work I do (social work). I grew up believing in the value of stoicism, 'pulling yourself up by your own boot-straps,' etc., but I don't think I should impose those values on people who come from a different culture than I do. So I try to be aware of them, to rein them in.

"This has been such a thorny issue for me. In the sixties, I went to see a therapist. The question I was trying to ask was 'Who am I, really?' I don't think the therapist, who was white, could help me. I wasn't able to articulate how I felt as a marginal person, a 'hyphenated' person. What it means to live day after day, twenty-four hours a day, as an identifiable minority."

4. The first time I interviewed a woman from Hawaii, it was a real shock. I couldn't imagine being American but growing up in a part of the country where Asians are part of the dominant culture and where ethnicity is really

not an issue. Annette shared her views on growing up Japanese in Hawaii. Like others in her situation, it was not until she traveled to the mainland that she got a taste of what life as a minority might feel like. But because she was grounded already in a solid sense of self and culture, this experience did not fundamentally alter her view of herself.

"I was born and raised in Hawaii and I think that really colors my perception of how I see myself as Asian or, more specifically, as Japanese. There is such a large Asian population there—Asians in political office, as the superintendent of schools, etc.—that in a sense, there was almost a form of reverse discrimination against whites. They call Hawaii the 'melting pot' and I think it's true; the races really do get along. So I grew up feeling comfortable about who I was. I never felt excluded in any way.

"My mother was raised in Japan and my dad was a Kibbei (born in the U.S. but educated in Japan). In some ways, he was a traditional Japanese man, stoic and quiet. For example, my sister and I recently discovered some clippings, papers in an old scrap album that indicated my father had had to go through the courts in order to get his citizenship back because he was studying at Meiji University (in Japan) at the time of the war. He never said a thing about this before, and he still doesn't talk about whether he was angry that it happened. But my mom is different—she speaks her mind, is very outgoing, and sort of 'wears the pants' in the family. In my marriage now, I also have a lot of say in how things are run. That's part of the reason I have no real burning interest to go back to visit Japan anytime soon; I think it would be hard to be in an environment where women are expected to be so deferential to men.

"My sister is much more into Japanese cultural issues and traditions. I'm kind of spending my time working on my business and professional connections. Sometimes I feel bad that I don't share her drive to reestablish our cultural roots.

"Last year, we went on a pilgrimage to Tule Lake [California], one of the internment camps. I remember a certain building, kind of a prison for the more unruly detainees, bare cement floors, two or three levels of beds. Much of the rest you just had to imagine. It was interesting, but I have to say I probably wouldn't have made the time to go there if my sister wasn't so interested. We're very close, so I felt I'd like to accompany her. I think that because I didn't actually know anyone who went to camp, not even relatives, it doesn't have a real or personal significance for me. Simply the fact that Japanese men and women were detained there is not enough to make that connection.

"At the same time, I do notice I feel more comfortable around Asians. If I'm at a sales function, I guess I naturally gravitate toward the other Asians in the room, even if they only make up 1 percent of the people there. I've dated Caucasian guys, but I knew I'd prefer an Asian man; there would be a comfort level there that would just make life easier. For example, when I was invited to a boyfriend's home, I liked to observe the traditional Japanese custom of bringing a gift. The white men I dated were always like 'Why do you bother?' Or, 'You don't need to do that, don't get so stressed out about it.'

They didn't understand that it made *me* feel more comfortable. I also think we are in fact more repressed, don't share as much of ourselves. Because of this, whites see us as uncommunicative. You don't run into this issue as much with an Asian partner.

"I have not experienced much racism. Growing up as I did, I expect equitable treatment—both in business and interpersonal relationships. Even coming to the mainland, *I* didn't feel like a minority. But I experience, while traveling for my job, being on the receiving end of racism. My husband and I were leaving New York, standing in a long line waiting to get our bags checked. We were tired, eager to be on our way, when this lady pushes ahead of us. I said, 'Excuse me, but there is a line here.' She took one look at me and suggested I 'go back where I came from.' I was shocked. I hate to admit this, but I turned right around and told her she should shut up. I'm sure she expected me just to be quiet, mousy, not say anything. She didn't say another word. Walked off to another line.

"When we have children, I hope they will feel as comfortable with their identity as I am with mine. If they experience some type of discrimination because they are Asian, I would tell them they are worthwhile, special people, and they should be proud of themselves. I want to pass my self-confidence and belief about fairness on to them. But of course, I realize it's easy to say this when it hasn't actually happened yet. I just hope it works out that way."

CHAPTER FIVE

Generations

Introduction

In a now famous 1937 talk at Augustana College, "The Problem of the Third Generation," pioneering immigration historian Marcus Lee Hansen described the perspective of different generations both on the experience of migrating to the United States and on each other. He observed, "What the son wishes to forget, the grandson wishes to remember." This oft-quoted line refers to the very different feelings that members of the same family may have about immigration because of the distance each generation has from the wrenching experience of leaving a homeland, traveling to the United States, and adjusting to a new place and new neighbors.

While scholars continue to debate whether different eras and circumstances qualify Hansen's generalization, at some level Hansen has described what many newcomers experience in the context of their own families and communities. The first generation must make concessions to American society in order to survive economically, live day to day in a strange culture, and master the skills required to take advantage of life in a democracy. The second generation (a child born in the United States or arriving with parents at a very young age) almost invariably lives in two worlds at the same time. The child of an immigrant is raised by parents who may speak a foreign tongue, prefer the music and cuisine of their homeland, and cherish values, attitudes, and beliefs that reflect the heritage of their home country. However, the child of immigrants raised (and most often born) in the United Sates must do what is required to prosper in the community where their parents have resettled and thrive in the American cultural environment. The problem of the third generation (whose parents as well as themselves are American born), then, is to understand and interpret the experiences of the two previous generations. Members of the third generation of every group arriving in the United States must reconcile whatever material comfort and cultural acceptance they may feel with the stories of struggle told by the generations that preceded them. They must honor the memory of earlier generations' experiences even as they live their lives as full members of American society, who are separated from migration by several generations.

In addition to interacting with American society in the era in which they live, each individual of immigrant stock must deal with the generations representing both the past and the future. Members of the first generation often feel a sense of loss when they leave their home country for the United States. Should they attempt to impose their familiar language and cultural ways upon their children or encourage them to abandon old ways for new? What are the responsibilities of the children of immigrants to their parents? What kinds of tensions develop when the second generation finds that it understands American society and culture better than the first generation? In such cases as the latter, the child and parent frequently reverse roles. In many Eastern European Jewish families, for example, Yiddish-speaking parents had to ask their bilingual children to translate documents for them or to read English language newspapers to them at the dinner table so they could inform themselves about what was happening in their adopted country. Such role reversals are not exceptions, but have been typical of intergenerational relations throughout the history of migration to the United States.

Tensions developed when children offered advice to their parents on how to conduct themselves in the United States. Italians quoted to each other folk wisdom from southern Italy's villages, "Never make your child better than yourself." In other words, never shatter the time-honored structure of family life by permitting education and prosperity to become barriers between parental authority and children. Chinese fathers could not understand why their American children objected to arranged marriages, as occurred routinely in the old country. After all, parents and other elders were expected to have a wisdom that came with age and experience.

Religion was often a source of intergenerational disagreement. The traditional piety that sustained immigrants in their countries of origin seemed old fashioned to children who were adjusting to the secular ways of American society. Irish Catholic immigrants who attended mass every Sunday and went to confession regularly could not understand children who neglected such duties. Italian Catholics in New York's Harlem who prayed to the Madonna of Mount Carmel for their family's health were puzzled and irritated by children who trusted the therapies of physicians instead of prayer in church or the amulets and incantations of traditional healers. In the 1950s and 1960s, Eastern European Jewish parents who had arrived earlier in the century often felt shattered when they observed their children decorating Christmas trees in their home and their grandchildren going off to a department store to see Santa Claus. They found it difficult to accept the argument of their astonished children that there was nothing to get excited about because Christmas in America is a secular holiday, or that dubbing a Christmas tree a "Chanukah bush" made the tree innocuous with respect to Jewish belief.

The literature of the immigrant experience is replete with examples of generational conflict between first and second generations, especially between fathers and daughters where gender differences are also at issue. In her 1925 autobiographical novel, *Bread Givers*, Eastern European Jewish writer Anzia Yezierska recalls her religious father, an inadequate wage-earner persuaded that his daughters ought to support him so he could continue his study of Torah and Talmud, as an obstacle to her own upward mobility. She leaves home, acquires an education, and becomes a teacher, a model of the modern American woman, but returns to care for her father, widowed, alone, and impoverished in his old age. A more recent novel, *How the Garcia Girls Lost Their Accent*, by Julia Alavarez, describes the experiences of four daughters from an upper-class Dominican family who flee the politically tumultuous Dominican Republic with their parents only to find that readjustment in the United States brought its own set of generational disputes. In the Dominican Republic, young women of wealthy families went nowhere without a male escort. In the United States, young women went where they chose when they chose and pursued careers of their choosing. Their father, a physician in the Dominican Republic, must readjust to not being licensed as a physician in the United States and learning that here his daughters will not always do what he tells them. The theme of parents losing control of their children and feeling betrayed was so popular with immigrant audiences that in Yiddish theaters where Shakespeare's plays were performed, *King Lear*, the story of a king whose children treat him badly, was a perennial favorite.

And what of the third generation? Much of the revival of interest in ethnic identity that began in the 1970s and has continued is grounded in the search of the immigrants' grandchildren for their roots. In the past three decades, the grandchildren of immigrants who arrived at the turn of the twentieth century have sought to discover the language, customs, cuisine, and values of their grandparents. At times this search takes the form of pursuing elaborate genealogies or family trees constructed with the latest computer software package. At other times, it is in evidence by the increasing popularity of language courses at college or in adult education classes. Yiddish and Italian are popular choices of those who want to speak to their immigrant forbears across time and space by speaking the language they spoke or reading their letters without a translator as intermediary. Even the grandchildren of more recent immigrants from China, India, Mexico, or the Philippines seek to uncover the cultural treasure trove that they believe will enrich their materially prosperous lives as Americans. They seek recipes for the cuisine their grandparents ate daily or choose to celebrate their wedding in a manner that observes all of the traditions of their forebears.

The greater the difference between the home culture and American society, the greater the generational divide. Contemporary immigrants from Mexico and Latin American countries often insist that their children speak

Spanish at home. They hope that language continuity will keep their children loyal to traditional values and to them. As did earlier generations, they fear the loss of their loved ones to America. Some groups such as the Koreans organize schools that have classes meeting after the American public school day ends so that the second generation can be tutored in language and customs of their parents' homeland. The end is to retain Korean ethnicity while not relinquishing the opportunity to achieve economic prosperity in the United States.

The first selection by historian of immigrant culture Victor Greene, addresses the generational divide in terms of the music that each generation appreciated. Few children, immigrant or native born, ever completely agree with their parents' tastes in music. However, Greene observes that folk dancing and ethnic music often brought the generations together, serving as a bridge that transcended intergenerational conflict. Rather than despise their parents' tastes, members of the second generation often embraced their parents' music and some even brought it to a wider American audience.

The second selection is an excerpt from Jane Addams's 1910 classic, *Twenty Years at Hull House*. Jane Addams was one of the leaders of the settlement house movement. Settlement houses were institutions begun by social reformers to offer material assistance and education to the urban poor, especially to immigrants struggling to adjust to life in the United States. In 1889, Addams and Ellen Gates Starr founded Hull House in the section of Chicago where many Italian immigrants had settled (figure 5.1). Addams, Starr, and the other social workers who joined them at Hull House were concerned that intergenerational conflict would magnify the cultural shock

Figure 5.1 Settlement Houses in Chicago's Hill House and ethnic fraternal organizations, traditional dances brought the generations together and preserved ethnic customs (courtesy of the Library of Congress).

that immigrants felt as they experienced alienation from their children. Such disordering of familial relationships might also lead to juvenile delinquency in the second generation, damaging the individuals, but also besmirching the group's reputation among native-born Americans. While some immigrant parents, in Addams's view, held their children in a "stern bondage which requires a surrender of all their wages and concedes no time or money for pleasure" in order to ease the burden on themselves and other family members, others were compassionate. Their struggles aroused the fidelity of their children. Addams cites one case of a daughter who might actually earn more money as a stenographer than as a seamstress, but would then not be able to quit work on the Jewish Sabbath. Knowing that her labor on Saturday would displease her father far more than he would be pleased by the extra income, the young woman made the sacrifice and remained a shop worker.

In another case, the child became the teacher of the parent. After attending classes at Hull House, an Italian child had to teach her mother that the reason that babies in Italy were healthy and those in Chicago were often sickly had nothing to do with the Italian children getting goat's milk rather than cow's milk, but rather it was the difference between the clean healthy milk of the Italian countryside and the contaminated milk available to the poor children of Chicago.

Addams hoped that she and her staff could be intermediaries between immigrants and their children to preserve and strengthen the immigrant family. The Labor Museum that they organized at Hull House was designed to make first-generation parents feel good about their lives by engendering pride in their trades and crafts. Explaining and lauding the skills of the parents was also intended to enhance the respect and affection with which immigrant children regarded their elders. Their pasts had something praiseworthy to offer them. It was a strategy designed to make first- and second-generation newcomers feel good about their heritage and each other.

While generational conflict often occurred between first and second generations, such clashes were hardly inevitable. Indeed, very often the second generation expressed love for their parents and appreciation of their parents' values by echoing those values in their own life choices. The final selection describes just such a scenario. The selection is a marriage notice from *The New York Times*. Every Sunday, one wedding is featured in this newspaper in greater detail than the usual wedding announcements. This wedding joined two Indians of the Sikh faith. The bride, Rakhi Dhanoa, an immigration attorney at a New York law firm, was born in India, but emigrated with her parents when she was quite young. Thus, for all practical purposes she was raised as a second-generation newcomer. The groom, Ranjeet Purewal, a recruiter for a corporate staffing agency in New York, is thoroughly second generation, born in the United States, growing up in Eltingville, Staten Island. Although the groom was not aware of it, his mother had hired a Sikh matchmaker who had Ms. Dhanoa in her sights as a good prospect. Neither the young woman nor the young man approved of being forced to marry someone they did not love, but when they met at

Dhanoa's graduation party, an invitation to Ranjeet engineered by the matchmaker, love took a hand. Now rather than rebelling against tradition and their first-generation parents, the couple insisted upon a very traditional Sikh wedding. Indeed, the bride, an ardent feminist, proud of her strength and independence, wanted it even more than her American-born groom. The reason she gives is a desire for stability, which she perceives to be grounded in religion and family. And generation plays a role because, as Ms. Dhanoa told the *Times*, "When you are growing up as the first generation in America, it's important to have that identity."

Suggestions for Further Reading

Alejandro Portes, ed. *The New Second Generation* (New York: Russell Sage Foundation, 1996).

Alejandro Portes and Ruben G. Rumbaut, *Legacies, The Story of the Immigrant Second Generation* (Berkeley: University of California Press and New York: Russell Sage Foundation, 2001).

Anzia Yezierska, *Bread Givers* (New York: Persea Books, 1975; orig.1925).

David K. Yoo, *Growing Up Nisei: Race Generation, and Culture Among Japanese Americans of California, 1924–1942* (Urbana: University of Illinois Press, 2000).

Deborah Dash Moore, *At Home in America, Second Generation New York Jews* (New York Columbia University Press, 1981).

Julia Alvarez, *How the Garcia Girls Lost Their Accents* (Chapel Hill: Algonquin Books, 1991).

Mary C. Waters, *Ethnic Options: Choosing Identities in America* (Berkeley: University of California Press, 1990).

Mary C. Waters, *Black Identities, West Indian Immigrant Dreams and American Realities* (Cambridge: Harvard University Press, 1999.

Min Zhou and Carl L. Bankston III, *Growing Up American: The Adaptation of Vietnamese Adolescents in the United States* (New York: Russell Sage Foundation, 1998).

Selma Cantor Berrol, *Growing Up American, Immigrant Children in America Then and Now* (New York: Twayne Publishers, 1995).

Victor Greene, "Old-time Folk Dancing and Music among the Second Generation, 1920–50"

Folk Dancing

The first ethnically induced modification of our national culture was the emergence of an international folk-dance movement, popularized when immigrant dancers and others displayed traditional steps at large urban festivals and parks. This transfer of ethnic dance from the communities to intergroup functions began at the start of this century and became common in American metropolitan centers by the end of the 1930s.

Nongroup, native-born Americans initially promoted ethnic folk dancing beyond the individual groups. They saw the activity as being for all Americans, or at least all female Americans. Before 1914, these promoters were Progressive reformers like Luther Gulick, head of the Playground Association of America, and his aide, Elizabeth Burchenal. They and their playground reformers believed that there were considerable moral and physical advantages for young women and young men in learning the polka, cardas, and tarantella in public school.

Additional support for dance exercise came from the YWCA. The person most responsible for encouraging the dances there was Edith Terry (later Edith Terry Bremer). Reacting to the mounting nativist pressures on immigrant newcomers, she sought to show the value of their arts and crafts by display and performance. Her efforts in the 1920s were modestly successful even though intolerance continued to grow. By the end of the decade the YWCA had created more than fifty International Institutes around the country to foster the ethnic arts at various metropolitan festivals.

In that postwar decade two other reasons for promoting these metropolitan events appeared: the desire to boost civic sentiment and to combat . . . the alienation of the second generation. Probably the best example of the former was the serious effort of a Cleveland daily newspaper to display that city's cosmopolitan character in a very successful Festival of Nations. With the depression's deleterious impact on the American family, social workers reemphasized the need for community sanction of the ethnic arts as a way to ease the generational conflict in the immigrant home. They sought to build the children's respect for their parents' traditions. As a YWCA publication entitled *Second Generation Youth* put it, foreign-born parents would be less authoritarian and their American-born children more considerate of their parents when the total community recognized the artistic expression of the parents' ethnic group.

This concern of social workers about generational alienation might have been lessened had they been aware that certain ethnic group leaders were laying the groundwork for an international folk-dance movement. These ethnic dance leaders would later join the social workers in a more formal framework and establish the symbolic birthplace of international folk dancing—the American Common—at the 1939 New York World's Fair.

Probably the earliest major group dance leader to instruct young people in dances of their own and of other nationalities and one of the most important founders of international dancing in America was the young Lithuanian immigrant, Vytautas Beliajus of Chicago. Having arrived as a youth with his grandmother in 1923, he conveyed his enthusiasm for Lithuanian and other ethnic dances to his group's young people—the American-born. By 1930, he was teaching Lithuanian adolescents a variety of folk dances in Chicago's Lithuanian center, the Bridgeport neighborhood. After officials of the Chicago World's Fair of 1933 invited him and his dancers to perform at the exposition, he organized students into a dance ensemble called the Lithuanian Youth Society. Later the Chicago Park District engaged Beliajus to conduct folk-dancing classes at parks around the city. For the next ten years he edited a newsletter on ethnic folk dance, helped form a confederation of ethnic dance groups, the Folk Dance League, and by the beginning of World War II established the nation's foremost international folk-dance periodical, *Viltis*, which has continued for almost a half-century.

The final establishment and symbolism of these ethnic dances as a part of American culture came in 1939 at the New York World's Fair. When officials expelled the Russians from the site and dismantled their pavilion in retaliation for Russia's invasion of Finland, a fair vice president, Robert D. Kohn, decided to use the space to honor America's ethnic pluralism. He helped design this new area—called the American Common—like a New England town square surrounded by an ethnic "Wall of Fame" with inscribed names of prominent personalities. The space within was used as an ethnic dance plaza. It was a place where Michael and Mary Ann Bodnar Herman of the Folk Festival Council regularly instructed crowds in the steps of the various groups.

This discussion of the forces that brought about international folk dance as a new element in American culture is not a full refutation of Hansen's second-generation thesis. As we have seen . . . conflict between foreigners and their American offspring did exist and was common. Yet this sense of embarrassment and shame among ethnic adolescents and young adults was not universal. Some evidence of the ethnic reassurance of dance festivals does exist. It suggests that dancing in colorful costume to the folk music of a group that the performer's family had a connection with overrode any feeling of inferiority. For example, a New York high school freshman who participated in one of the early New York Festival Council pageants in 1932 said that "I used to feel ashamed of everything 'old country,' but we have had so much fun at the festival and it was so beautiful that now I am proud of the things my mother tells me about the old country and I love my costume."

Folk dancing, then, helped to combat the superiority complex of Yankees; it may even have been a manifestation of a hostile anti-Yankee attitude. Thus, in a 1935 YWCA publication entitled *What It Means to Be a Second Generation Girl*, a Ukrainian American, Mary Ann Bodnar, told of encountering Yankee denigration of her heritage at school. Instead of blaming her parents for their foreign ways, she criticized her teachers and fellow students for their ignorance of her ancestral home. As a result she decided "to spread as much information [about her old country] as possible." She then resolved to learn Ukrainian folk dancing and found it satisfying, taking "much joy in the colorful costumes and whirling figures." She later married Michael Herman and contributed substantially to the folk-dance community. Although her expressed self-confidence may be unusual, it is not unique. Certainly, from her example one may conclude that personal security in, or dissatisfaction about, one's ethnic heritage depends not only on the response of outsiders, but also on how well immigrant parents were able to give their native-born children a sound understanding of their group culture before peer influences became effective.

Ethnic Music

My contention that some members of the second generation had sufficient ethnic awareness of their heritage to enrich our national culture in dance is pertinent to another area of popular artistic expression. At the same time that international folk dancing was emerging, a transformation was taking place in American popular music for which immigrant children were also partly responsible: the growing popularity of "old-time" music, immigrant-based tunes that broke onto the national charts by the late 1930s and early 1940s. This period, the "golden age" of polka-style old-time music, extends roughly from the "Beer Barrel Polka" of 1938 to Frankie Yankovic's 1948 hit, "Blue Skirt Waltz."

Music historians have been well aware of the various changes occurring in American popular music in the three decades before mid-century: the emergence of jazz and big-time swing, the rising appeal of musical comedy, and the shift from hillbilly to country music. Through it all, authorities tell us that music publishers and Tin Pan Alley promoters maintained their hold over popular music culture, catering especially to the American middle-class. Still, scholars have neglected one important element of popular music that also became prominent during that era: polka-style old-time.

Like international folk dancing, this musical genre was rooted in the traditions of most of America's immigrant communities. It consisted of tunes that appealed both to parents and children. With the aid of other factors such as ethnic musicians, band leaders, music store owners, arrangers, and leading American record companies and radio stations, this new musical form became an integral part of mainstream popular culture. Germans, Poles, Scandinavians, Jews, and others certainly knew and cultivated polkas, laendlers, schottisches, obereks, kolomykas, tarantellas, and the like in their colonies. Later, certain popular entertainers from those communities, individual musicians like Lawrence Welk, "Whoopee John" Wilfahrt, and Frankie Yankovic, commercialized and broadcast those pieces nationally.

Of course, traditional music was altered in the process of popularization. Folk instruments like the Norwegian Hardanger violin and the Italian stornella (bagpipe) gave way to the more widely accepted brass and reed instruments of the jazz-swing era. Peasant dance pieces became English-language songs, but the melodies and rhythms of the polka and waltz remained the same. Most important, some of the second generation not only welcomed old-time music, but they were also its practitioners.

The popularity and transformation of old-time music can be traced from within and without immigrant communities by examining examples at both the local and national level. The reference herein must be to particular localities or regions, which may appear to make such designations exceptional rather than representative. Although the illustrations are isolated in rural and urban Wisconsin, Utica, New York, and in east Texas, that geographical diversity itself suggests a certain universality in the cultivation of traditional music. In this sense American music itself consists of the sum of music from local and regional areas.

One example of the wide appeal of a particular group's traditional music across generational lines was the Norwegian house party of central Wisconsin, common in the 1920s and 1930s. This cultural practice was based on immigrant themes but was cultivated solely by members of the group's second generation. Held at a time when Norwegian immigration was declining, the house party combined both work and recreation. Norwegian-American farmers from a district—they might well include others from the area—would come together in both warm and cold weather to help a family with a major task such as quilting, building a barn, or some similar activity. They would reserve the evening for their own entertainment, clearing the barn or house for dancing. The instruments used were the fiddle and button accordion. The dances were not all the peasant variety, but rather the ones that could be danced more easily, particularly the polka, waltz, and schottische. Finally, the tunes themselves would be hybrid, somewhat altered traditional melodies.

A similar experience was that of the small community of Slovaks in Milwaukee during the same period. This group was not large, many more of them lived in Chicago, Cleveland, and Pittsburgh. But a recent publication of the Slovak Historical Society of Wisconsin expressed commonly felt sentiments of American-born members who grew up in the jazz age and took part in both the majority and minority cultures. Readers were reminded of the pleasure of learning both the fox trot at school and the czardas and polka at the Slovak dance hall. By the 1930s, the Milwaukee city directory listed sixteen Slovak bands (there well may have been more) that performed at both private and public community functions. This amazing number was only a part of the musical organizations performing; other ensembles came from Slovak communities elsewhere.

Another recorded case of the vitality of old-time music in a multi-generational ethnic community at this time was Polish polka music in Utica, New York. Like Milwaukee, this small upstate city was essentially a manufacturing center that had drawn the new immigrants of the late nineteenth and early twentieth centuries. Utica's most prominent foreigners were the Italians of East Utica and the Poles of West Utica and nearby

New York Mills. According to a folkloric field study, traditional music was very popular among several generations of Poles around 1930. Many small bands performed at private as well as the more public occasions. At least two second-generation Polish American musicians who played as teenagers in small community bands in the 1930s did so because they found they could earn some extra money. One said that he was a member of a musical family, and that both the foreign-born and some of their children comprised their enthusiastic audiences.

A final example of the popularity of old-time ethnic music was the orchestral tradition of the Baca Family Orchestra of Fayetteville, Texas. In the mid-1800s, Joseph Baca of Austria, a dulcimer player, had settled in a region of German and Bohemian farming families, the eastern Texas grasslands. He taught music to his several sons, one of whom, Frank, in 1892 established the band, which became a regional institution. The high point of the Baca Band was probably its fortieth anniversary celebration held in Fayetteville in 1932. The occasion drew four other bands and a huge audience, indicating the significance of its repertoire among central and eastern Europeans of different ages.

These examples suggest that this traditionally based music played a significant part in the lives of both immigrants and their children in the years before World War II. Sources suggest that such popular music tended to unify families rather than divide them. A similar kind of ethnic music and musical performance, with a similar impact on a group, was that of the Italian band. This ethnic musical genre however, differed from that of other immigrants because it soon achieved a distinctively high place among the general Yankee public. A number of Italian band leaders became well known in America, but one leader stands out as the most famous: Giuseppe Creatore, who rivaled John Philip Sousa in artistry and reputation.

Band music had emerged by the 1880s as a widely accepted form of entertainment for many Americans. One estimate is that by 1889 as many as ten thousand bands performed across the country. Normally, local merchants and occupational groups provided the financial support and sponsorship as part of their civic obligation as well as for more practical reasons. It was often clear that the Italian-born instrumentalists, generally the players of wind instruments, were among the more talented members of these American bands. By the turn of the century a few all-Italian bands had begun touring and establishing a wide reputation for quality performance. Their repertoire would be eclectic, to be sure, but they would include specifically Italian ethnic pieces, marches, and arias from Italian opera. Some scholars contend that the Italian band tradition originated in the Old World ritual of the *festa*, where on certain religious occasions Italian villages would honor a patron saint. Italian bands performed the same function as German, Scandinavian, and Polish bands did for their neighborhoods, and Italian bandmasters provided excellent musical entertainment. In receiving the acclaim of their Anglo-American listeners, these musicians simultaneously built individual self-esteem.

Songs such as "Beer Barrel Polka" and "Blue Skirt Waltz" were polka-style tunes that sold a million records during the thirties and forties. The reasons for this national enthusiasm for polka music are suggested by Albert Maisel, who comments on the extraordinary popularity of polkas among the younger generation. Maisel refers to the effect of the phonograph records and radio and the stylistic modifications of ethnic pieces.

> The performers who recently have exercised the greatest influence—among the juke box set at any rate—are the leaders of polka bands. For many years while such groups provided Polish language radio programs with traditional mazurkas, polkas, and obereks, they attracted only a Polish audience. Then they changed their style, added a batch of hot licks, put in a Gene Krupa beat (he too is a Pole), translated old lyrics into English, and wrote a batch of new ones. Suddenly low power radio stations found themselves capturing network audiences as millions of high school live wires began arguing the merits of Frank Wojnarowski's pressing of "Broke But Happy Polka" versus Bernie Witkowski's "Wa, He Say Mambo." In Chicago recently one disc jockey casually asked his listeners to name their favorite polka band. Within three days he had received 22,000 postcards.

Maisel was writing at the height of the enthusiasm for old-time polka music; it would soon decline in the face of the emerging rage for rock.

The reference to phonograph records and the changing forms of disseminating popular music highlight the significance of the new entertainment technology in the interwar era. Records did not neglect, but rather promoted, ethnic music. Along with radio, the new technology did much to educate its audience about old tunes. Almost from their very start, American recording companies highlighted traditional music and conveyed it beyond its original group in America. Most important, by regenerating tradition, records aided in the assimilation of ethnic members: one could even say that the new discs took some of the native-born back to their roots. A brief review of the phonograph industry and its sensitivity to ethnic music illustrates that conclusion.

Until the 1930s, record companies had no real competition in broadcasting popular songs and other musical pieces. After Edison invented the phonograph in 1877 and Berliner and Johnson perfected the disc record around the turn of the century, records became the most common and accepted form of listening to musical entertainment. The industry continued to expand; record production increased from about 325,000 in 1909 to more than 100 million by 1919, a number maintained until the depression. The medium was an integral part of the lives of Americans of all classes. Phonographs were in 250,000 homes in 1919, and in probably half of our households by 1930. Records cost a few cents; the machine on which to play them, a few dollars.

The phonograph industry, it is true, suffered serious reverses because of the depression, competition with radio, shortages of material, and strikes during World War II. Record output, for example, plummeted 90 percent with the coming of the depression. But record companies recovered by the late 1930s with the help of the jukebox. Further, radio became less a competitor and more an aid to record sales thanks to disc jockeys. Thus, by 1945, sales were again up to about $100 million, with about two hundred million records sold.

One must conclude that even with the setbacks, the impact of this musical medium was pervasive over the first half of the century. But one ought not to assume that because this was an American industry, its overall affect would be to homogenize its audience culturally, forcing majority Anglo-American influences upon particular immigrant colonies. The general impact was probably the opposite. In the early years, a majority of the pieces recorded were foreign, not domestic. The industry's philosophy from the very beginning was to meet the musical tastes of all its customers, not just the Anglo-Americans. They found a fertile market among the immigrant communities in America; by 1919, Victor was heavily promoting ethnic records, and Columbia followed. By the early 1920s, these leading record companies set up long catalog lists of the more popular ethnic pieces.

The outpouring of records designed specifically for ethnic consumption was sizable in scope and sales. For example, Victor cut 15,000 between 1923 and 1952; Columbia issued more than 1,300 Italian, almost 800 Polish, and hundreds of others for each of many smaller groups, and the other companies followed suit. Victor's "V" International Series of the 1920s and 1930s consisted of records for twenty-three different groups, including small ones like Albanians and Syrians.

A list prepared by music folklorist Richard Spottswood indicates the full extent of ethnic records in the entire industry. This discography enumerates all ethnic records made between 1893 and 1942, with about 150,000 entries. Clearly, a popular American medium through the first half of this century was recognizing the traditional although modified musical heritage of almost every one of our immigrant groups.

From a review of one type of ethnic record and the functioning of three major immigrant music firms, Sajewski and Vitak and Elsnic (both of Chicago) and Surmach of New York City, we can get a general impression of the business of making ethnic records.

Unquestionably the most popular kind of recording in the late 1920s was not the simple song, dance, or tune, but rather a skit or short playlet concerning the immigrants' most treasured life event, the wedding. It memorialized the one moment in their lives during which many traditional customs were cultivated. The piece that sold the most copies was the Okeh-Columbia recording, "Ukrainske Wesele [Ukrainian Wedding]," a twelve-inch platter led by the well-known folk fiddler Pawel Humeniak. Recorded late in 1925, it was a traditional account, with the most familiar Ukrainian songs and dances, of the relationship between marrying ethnic families. The record sold an amazing 125,000 copies, purchased by many non-Ukrainians from central and eastern Europe. In fact, Columbia realized its success and had Humeniak record another version, almost as popular, in Polish.

Of course Humeniak's success was unique only in its superior sales; many other ethnic artists did well with similar traditional pieces. The most popular Swedish accordionist, for example, was Eddie Jarl. One of his records sold close to a hundred thousand copies. Humeniak, Jarl, and a host of other ethnic musicians, artists, and singers helped to reinforce traditional values and customs, providing a bond between immigrants and their children in the interwar era.

Jane Addams, *Twenty Years at Hull-House*

FROM OUR VERY FIRST MONTHS at Hull-House we found it much easier to deal with the first generation of crowded city life than with the second or third, because it is more natural and cast in a simpler mold. The Italian and Bohemian peasants who live in Chicago, still put on their bright holiday clothes on a Sunday and go to visit their cousins. They tramp along with at least a suggestion of having once walked over plowed fields and breathed country air. The second generation of city poor too often have no holiday clothes and consider their relations a "bad lot." I have heard a drunken man in a maudlin stage, babble of his good country mother and imagine he was driving the cows home, and I knew that his little son who laughed loud at him, would be drunk earlier in life and would have no such pastoral interlude to his ravings. Hospitality still survives among foreigners, although it is buried under false pride among the poorest Americans. One thing seemed clear in regard to entertaining immigrants; to preserve and keep whatever of value their past life contained and to bring them in contact with a better type of Americans.

An overmastering desire to reveal the humbler immigrant parents to their own children lay at the base of what has come to be called the Hull-House Labor Museum. This was first suggested to my mind one early spring day when I saw an old Italian woman, her distaff against her homesick face, patiently spinning a thread by the simple stick spindle so reminiscent of all southern Europe. I was walking down Polk Street, perturbed in spirit, because it seemed so difficult to come into genuine relations with the Italian women and because they themselves so often lost their hold upon their Americanized children. It seemed to me that Hull-House ought to be able to devise some educational enterprise, which should build a bridge between European and American experiences in such wise as to give them both more meaning and a sense of relation. I meditated that perhaps the power to see life as a whole, is more needed in the immigrant quarter of a large city than anywhere else, and that the lack of this power is the most fruitful source of misunderstanding between European immigrants and their children, as it is between them and their American neighbors; and why should that chasm between fathers and sons, yawning at the feet of each generation, be made so unnecessarily cruel and impassable to these bewildered immigrants? Suddenly I looked up and saw the old woman with her distaff [spinning wheel attachment], sitting in the sun on the steps of a tenement house. She might have served as a model for one of Michael Angelo's Fates, but her face brightened as I passed and, holding up her spindle for me to see, she called out that when she had spun a little more yarn, she would knit a pair of stockings for her goddaughter. The occupation of the old woman gave me the clew [clue] that was needed. Could we not interest the young people working in the neighboring factories, in these older forms of industry, so that, through their own parents and grandparents, they would find a dramatic representation of the inherited resources of their daily occupation. If these young people could actually see that the compli-cated machinery of the factory had been evolved from simple tools, they might at least make a beginning toward that education which Dr. Dewey defines as "a continuing reconstruction of experience." They might also lay a foundation for reverence of the past which Goethe declares to be the basis of all sound progress.

Sometimes the suppression of the instinct of workmanship is followed by more disastrous results. A Bohemian whose little girl attended classes at Hull-House, in one of his periodic drunken spells had literally almost choked her to death, and later had committed suicide when in delirium tremens. His poor wife, who stayed a week at Hull-House after the disaster until a new tenement could be arranged for her, one day showed me a gold ring which her husband had made for their betrothal. It exhibited the most exquisite workmanship, and she said that although in the old country he had been a goldsmith, in America he had for twenty years shoveled coal in a furnace room of a large manufacturing plant; that whenever she saw one of his "restless fits," which preceded his drunken periods, "coming on," if she could provide him with a bit of metal and persuade him to stay at home and work at it, he was all right and the time passed without disaster, but that "nothing else would do it." This story threw a flood of light upon the dead man's struggle and on the stupid maladjustment which had broken him down. Why had we never been told? Why had our interest in the remark-able musical ability of his child, blinded us to the hidden artistic ability of the father? We had forgotten that a long-established occupation may form the very foundations of the moral life, that the art with which a man has solaced his toil may be the salvation of his uncertain temperament.

There are many examples of touching fidelity to immigrant parents on the part of their grown children; a young man, who day after day, attends ceremonies which no longer express his religious convictions and who makes his vain effort to interest his Russian Jewish father in social problems; a daughter who might earn much more money as a stenographer could she work from Monday morning till Saturday night, but who quietly and docilely makes neckties for low wages because she can thus abstain from work Saturdays to please her father; these young people, like poor Maggie Tulliver, through many painful experiences have reached the conclusion that pity, memory, and faithfulness are natural ties with paramount claims.

This faithfulness, however, is sometimes ruthlessly imposed upon by immigrant parents who, eager for money and accustomed to the patriarchal authority of peasant households, hold their children in a stern bondage which requires a surrender of all their wages and concedes no time or money for pleasures.

There are many convincing illustrations that this parental harshness often results in juvenile delinquency. A Polish boy of seventeen came to Hull-House one day to ask a contribution of fifty cents "towards a flower piece for the funeral of an old Hull-House club boy." A few questions made it clear that the object was fictitious, whereupon the boy broke down and half defiantly stated that he wanted to buy two twenty-five cent tickets, one for his girl and one for himself, to a dance of the Benevolent Social Twos; that he hadn't a penny of his own although he had worked in a brass foundry for three years and had been advanced twice, because he always had to give his pay envelope unopened to his father; "just look at the clothes he buys me" was his concluding remark.

Perhaps the girls are held even more rigidly. In a recent investigation of two hundred working girls it was found that only five percent had the use of their own money and that sixty-two percent turned in all they earned, literally every penny, to their mothers. It was through this little investigation that we first knew Marcella, a pretty young German girl who helped her widowed mother year after year to care for a large family of younger children. She was content for the most part although her mother's old-country notions of dress gave her but an infinitesimal amount of her own wages to spend on her clothes, and she was quite sophisticated as to proper dressing because she sold silk in a neighborhood department store. Her mother approved of the young man who was showing her various attentions and agreed that Marcella should accept his invitation to a ball, but would allow her not a penny toward a new gown to replace one impossibly plain and shabby. Marcella spent a sleepless night and wept bitterly, although she well knew that the doctor's bill for the children's scarlet fever was not yet paid. The next day as she was cutting off three yards of shining pink silk, the thought came to her that it would make her a fine new waist to wear to the ball. She wistfully saw it wrapped in paper and carelessly stuffed into the muff of the purchaser, when suddenly the parcel fell upon the floor. No one was looking and quick as a flash the girl picked it up and pushed it into her blouse. The theft was discovered by the relentless department store detective who, for "the sake of the example," insisted upon taking the case into court. The poor mother wept bitter tears over this downfall of her "frommes Mädchen" [honest girl] and no one had the heart to tell her of her own blindness.

I know a Polish boy whose earnings were all given to his father who gruffly refused all requests for pocket money. One Christmas his little sisters, having been told by their mother that they were too poor to have any Christmas presents, appealed to the big brother as to one who was earning money of his own. Flattered by the implication, but at the same time quite impecunious, the night before Christmas he nonchalantly walked through a neighboring department store and stole a manicure set for one little sister and a string of beads for the other. He was caught at the door by the house detective as one of those children whom each local department store arrests in the weeks before Christmas at the daily rate of eight to twenty. The youngest of these offenders are seldom taken into court but are either sent home with a warning or turned over to the officers of the Juvenile Protective Association. Most of these premature law breakers are in search of Americanized clothing and others are only looking for playthings. They are all distracted by the profusion and variety of the display, and their moral sense is confused by the general air of open-handedness.

These disastrous efforts are not unlike those of many younger children who are constantly arrested for petty thieving because they are too eager to take home food or fuel which will relieve the distress and need they so constantly hear discussed. The coal on the wagons, the vegetables displayed in front of the grocery shops, the very wooden blocks in the loosened street paving are a challenge to their powers to help out at home. A Bohemian boy who was out on parole from the old detention home of the Juvenile Court itself, brought back five stolen chickens to the matron for Sunday dinner, saying that he knew the committee were "having a hard time to fill up so many kids and perhaps these fowl would help out." The honest immigrant parents, totally ignorant of American laws and municipal regulations, often send a child to pick up coal on the railroad tracks or to stand at three o'clock in the morning before the side door of a restaurant which gives away broken food, or to collect grain for the chickens at the base of elevators and standing cars. The latter custom accounts for the large number of boys arrested for breaking the seals on grain freight cars. It is easy for a child thus trained to accept the proposition of a junk dealer to bring him bars of iron stored in freight yards. Four boys quite recently had thus carried away and sold to one man, two tons of iron.

Four-fifths of the children brought into the Juvenile Court in Chicago are the children of foreigners. The Germans are the greatest offenders, Polish next. Do their children suffer from the excess of virtue in those parents so eager to own a house and lot? One often sees a grasping parent in the court, utterly broken down when the Americanized youth who has been brought to grief clings as piteously to his peasant father as if he were still a frightened little boy in the steerage. Certainly the bewildered parents, unable to speak English and ignorant of the city, whose children have disappeared for days or weeks, have often come to Hull-House, evincing that agony which fairly separates the marrow from the bone, as if they had discovered a new type of suffering, devoid of the healing in familiar sorrows. It is as if they did not know how to search for the children without the assistance of the children themselves. Perhaps the most pathetic aspect of such cases is their revelation of the premature dependence of the older and wiser upon the young and foolish, which is in itself often responsible for the situation because it has given the children an undue sense of their own importance and a false security that they can take care of themselves.

On the other hand, an Italian girl who has had lessons in cooking at the public school, will help her mother to connect the entire family with American food and household habits. That the mother has never baked bread in Italy—only mixed it in her own house and then taken it out to the village oven—makes all the more valuable her daughter's understanding of the complicated cooking stove. The same thing is true of the girl who learns to sew in the public school, and more than anything else, perhaps, of the girl who receives the first simple instruction in the care of little children,—that skillful care which every tenement-house baby requires if he is to be pulled through his second summer. As a result of this teaching I recall a young girl who carefully explained to her Italian mother that the reason the babies in

Italy were so healthy and the babies in Chicago were so sickly, was not, as her mother had firmly insisted, because her babies in Italy had goat's milk and her babies in America had cow's milk, but because the milk in Italy was clean and the milk in Chicago was dirty. She said that when you milked your own goat before the door, you knew that the milk was clean, but when you bought milk from the grocery store after it had been carried for many miles in the country, you couldn't tell whether or not it was fit for the baby to drink until the men from the City Hall who had watched it all the way, said that it was all right.

Thus through civic instruction in the public schools, the Italian woman slowly became urbanized in the sense in which the word was used by her own Latin ancestors, and thus the habits of her entire family were modified. The public schools in the immigrant colonies deserve all the praise as Americanizing agencies which can be bestowed upon them. . . .

Stephen Henderson, "Rakhi Dhanoa and Ranjeet Purewal"

ARRANGED marriage. The words summon notions of mail-order brides. However, if the romance of Rakhi Dhanoa and Ranjeet Purewal suggests anything, it's that the more specific one is about requirements in a spouse, the more a matchmaker makes sense.

"Each wanted a love marriage," said Erica Loomba, a friend, "yet neither would dream of marrying someone who wasn't a Sikh."

Ms. Dhanoa, 27, is an immigration lawyer at the New York law firm of Winston & Strawn and a first-generation American. She said that she felt oppressed when she was young by the social conservatism of her parents, who emigrated from Punjab, India. "They were extremely strict about school, manners and culture," she said. "They wanted to keep us from being seduced by America."

At New York University, Ms. Dhanoa dated little, and entered what she called a "femi-Nazi" phase, when she read Naomi Wolf and Camille Paglia. That was followed by her "manhating" phrase, when the laconic T-shirt-wearing Marlon Brando was the only man she could endure. She built a shrine to him in her bedroom. After graduating from New York Law School, however, she came full circle and decided to wed a Sikh. "I began to appreciate that my religion is based on complete equality of the sexes," she said. But by then she was focused on her career and didn't have time to date.

Unbeknown to Ms. Dhanoa, Jasbir Hayre of Livingston, N.J., a Sikh matchmaker, was focused on her. "Ranjeet's mother had approached me several times to keep a lookout for a girl," Mrs. Hayre said.

"It makes my job a lot easier when the men are good-looking, which Ranjeet is."

Mr. Purewal, 26, grew up in Eltingville, Staten Island, the eldest son of Punjabi immigrants. "I was very bookish as a kid," he said. "My parents really stressed that." He discovered wrestling, however, and bulked up from 120 to 190 pounds. At Rutgers, his room also had a movie star altar: for Arnold Schwarzenegger. "Ranjeet acts more Italian than Indian," Chris Pak, a college friend, said. "He's always wearing muscle T-shirts."

"I was adamant that I'd marry whoever I wanted," said Mr. Pureval, now a recruiter for Leafstone Staffing in New York. "But seeing how different cultures treated their families, I realized the importance of making the right match."

When Mrs. Hayre gave a graduation party in Livingston for her daughter, she was sure to invite Mr. Purewal and Ms. Dhanoa. " 'I think *he's* the one,' my mother whispered to me," Ms. Dhanoa said, recalling that night. "I said, 'Stop it, I'm not a cow for sale!' " Of their emotionally fraught introduction, she said, "I just started laughing, and he did, too."

For two months they dated secretly, to avoid meddling by overanxious parents. But when their cover was blown, on a double date, the matchmaker was quickly summoned to negotiate marital arrangements.

On the humid morning of August 10, outside a Sikh temple in Glen Cove, N.Y., several hundred guests, including a beaming Mrs. Hayre, watched the bride's father feed Mr. Purewal a mixture of dates, coconut and almonds in a family-melding ceremony. Meanwhile, Ms. Dhanoa, who wore a blood-red dress (the Sikh color for happiness), stared at her elaborately hennaed hands, where the name Ranjeet was written among the stenciled curlicues. On her forehead was a teardrop-shape jewel called a bindi. "I hate them," she said, glancing upward. "This is the first and last time you'll ever see me wearing one."

One might have guessed that Ms. Dhanoa was chafing against the Old World pageantry swirling about her wedding. Yet by all reports, it was she who had insisted on the most traditional Sikh ceremony possible. "I was raised with a lot of stability," the bride said. "And much of that came from religion and family. When you are growing up as the first generation in America, it's important to have that identity."

Ms. Loomba, whose background is also Punjabi, offered a slightly different take: "You can't escape your ethnicity, so you just have to deal."

CHAPTER SIX

Nativism, an American Perennial

Introduction

From the very founding of the republic, there were those who feared immigration. In *Notes on the State of Virginia* (1781–1787), Thomas Jefferson expressed concern that most immigrants would necessarily come from countries with despotic governments and would either retain undemocratic principles of government (especially monarchy) or they would pass to the other extreme and be ungovernable. Though Jefferson and other Americans applauded the French Revolution in 1789 and avidly followed other revolutionary movements, especially in Latin America, it was feared that political refugees seeking sanctuary in the United States might be either too conservative or too radical to nourish the gains of the American Revolution. In 1820, John Quincy Adams made clear in his correspondence with a Dutch colleague how the United States regarded immigrants, "To one thing they must make up their minds, or they will be disappointed in every expectation of happiness as Americans. They must cast off the European skin, never to resume it. They must look forward to their posterity rather than backward to their ancestors; they must be sure that whatever their own feelings may be, those of their children will cling to the prejudices of this country, and will partake of that proud spirit . . ." As historian John Higham and other scholars have observed, by the late nineteenth century, such antiradical nativism, present from the earliest days of the nation, had become a significant dimension of American culture.

By the 1830s, the United States was beginning to receive a large flow of migration from northern and western Europe, much of it from the

George J. Sánchez, "Face the Nation: Race, Immigration, and the Rise of Nativism in Late Twentieth Century America" in *International Migration Review* 31 (Winter, 1977): 1009–1030.

Order Detail ID: 13266910. International Migration Review by George Sánchez. Copyright © 1997 by CTR For Migration Studies of New York. Reproduced by permission of CTR For Migration Studies of New York in the format Textbook via Copyright Clearance Center.

Edward Alsworth Ross, *The Old World in the New: The Significance of Past and Present Immigration to the American People* (New York: The Century Co., 1914). Public Domain.

Peter Brimelow, "Time to Rethink Immigration?" in *The National Review* (June 22, 1992). Copyright © 1992 by Peter Brimelow, reprinted with the permission of the Wylie Agency.

southern provinces of Ireland. Many American Protestants feared that there would be an American version of Europe's Counter-Reformation, with the Roman Catholic Church seeking to reassert dominance over all of Christendom and crush American Protestantism. Others saw the Church as a power-hungry, antidemocratic institution grounded in rigid hierarchy. A wave of anti-Catholicism swept across the country. Convents were burned and nuns chased away. A widely circulated pulp literature depicted Roman Catholic clergy as conspiring to undermine American values of freedom and individualism. In some states, candidates for office ran on an avowedly anti-Catholic ticket. Some expressed the fear that Catholics hoped to bring the pope to the United States to rule.

Anti-Catholicism peaked in the nineteenth century, but hardly vanished. Much of the opposition to Democrat Al Smith's presidential candidacy in 1928 was grounded in doubts that a Roman Catholic could swear allegiance to the constitution, having a conflict of interest between his country and the pope of Rome. As late as the 1960s, newspaper editorials asked without irony whether if elected, John F. Kennedy thought that he could be true to his church and his country at the same time. Reporters inquired if Kennedy would find himself in a conflict of interest if he opposed federal aid to parochial schools.

If Americans saw radical political ideas and some religious preferences as the basis for nativist apprehensions, an equally grave concern was racial differences between newcomers and the white Anglo Saxon native-born population. In addition to the racism that underlay antebellum slavery, there was an ever-present anti-Latino and anti-Asian bias. The entire Southwest had once belonged to Mexico. However, white migrants to those territories did not hesitate to regard the inhabitants as their racial inferiors. Chinese immigrants and Japanese immigrants were also the victims of nativist prejudices. In 1882, Congress passed a Chinese Exclusion Act intended to reduce the flow of this particular group to the United States. A Gentleman's Agreement between President Theodore Roosevelt and the Emperor of Japan in 1907 was negotiated to much the same end with respect to Japanese migration. Anti-Asian prejudice, especially on the West Coast, was marked. Asian children were segregated from white children in San Francisco's public schools until President Theodore Roosevelt intervened. Later, during World War II, West Coast Japanese were regarded as a threat to national security and interned in detention camps for the duration of the war.

Darker complexioned Italian and Eastern European Jewish immigrants were also often defined as the racial "other." Some scholars have contended that anti-Semitism has been a separate strain of nativism. While less dramatic than opposition to black immigrants and Asian immigrants, opposition to Jewish immigration, especially from eastern Europe, inspired the push to broader immigration restriction in the 1920s and the creation of a national origins quota system in the Johnson–Reed Immigration Act of 1924. Not until 1965 was that system abandoned. Jews and Italians also once faced quotas at universities and exclusion from a variety of businesses and voluntary associations, which certainly made them feel unwelcome in the United States.

At times, nativists have turned to medicine and science to justify the exclusion of some groups that they have defined racially. Some nativists argued that the physiques of newcomers were such that they would be too weak to support themselves after arrival and would constitute a burden to the communities where they lived, requiring charity to survive. Eugenicists believed that the human race was improvable by controlled breeding and that individuals of demonstrably inferior stock should be excluded from the American gene pool. Immigration restriction was actively advocated by Madison Grant, E. A. Ross, and other prominent early twentieth century nativists fearful that immigration could lead to what Ross called "race suicide."

Even as some contemporary Americans celebrate diversity and the many contributions with which newcomers have enriched America's culture and economy, nativism has remained a trope of American life. As historian George Sánchez observes, groups that have arrived in increasing numbers during the late twentieth century, especially Latinos and Asians, have been the most recent targets of nativists. Much of this new nativism fits an older pattern of belittling the new groups as racially inferior and inherently incapable of succeeding in American society. There is also a cultural dimension that finds these newcomers so alien to modern Western culture that successful incorporation is deemed unlikely. He deplores the writings of journalist Peter Brimelow, to whom he compares the nativists of earlier eras.

Sánchez also observes that those who express anti-immigrant feelings are not exclusively whites of European heritage. Native-born African Americans also have joined the nativists' ranks. Blacks in the United States, themselves the frequent objects of hatred and discrimination, often deeply resent immigrant competition for the private aid and public assistance that African Americans need to finish the task begun in the 1960s of tackling poverty in their community. Moreover, the assumption that upward mobility in immigrant communities is confirmation that the American system is working, contradicts the experience of many African Americans. They angrily observe that America's pervasive racism has raised obstacles to the upward mobility of African Americans and immigrants of color. These barriers are for more difficult to transcend than the barriers faced by immigrants with fair skins.

Finding the nativism of the late twentieth century a racialized nativism, Sánchez sees three different manifestations that appear aimed at Latinos and Asians. One is the extreme antipathy to multilingualism and advocacy of English-only policies in schools and public signage. A second is the belief by some Americans that racial preferences and entitlements consistently tilt the social scales against whites. Other contemporary nativists argue that the increasing number of newcomers, whether legal or undocumented, drain educational, health, and other resources to the detriment of native-born Americans. Sánchez's essay was published in 1997. The events of September 11, 2001, might well add the fear of many Americans that darker peoples of foreign birth might be threats to national security.

The next two selections are examples of nativist expressions from different eras. The second selection is from *The Old World in the New* published in 1914 by E. A. Ross, a sociology professor and outspoken Progressive reformer who taught at the University of Wisconsin. Ross was hardly alone among Progressives in believing that industrialization, urbanization, and immigration were the tripartite threat to the nation's welfare at the dawn of the twentieth century. Ross especially objected to immigrants from southern and eastern Europe who were flooding American ports. In the passage here, Ross discusses his concern about the physical inferiority of the newcomers to America's "pioneering breed." Using "eyeball analysis" as his instrument, Ross fears that "the blood now being injected into the veins of our people is 'sub-common.' " He finds them not only unattractive in appearance, but also fears that despite some who have taken advantage of American opportunity, most lack "the fundamental worth which does not depend on opportunity, and which may be transmitted to one's descendants." Contemporary immigration critic Peter Brimelow, a senior editor at *Forbes* and *National Review*, does not make Ross's racial argument. However, he does believe that immigrants' benefit to the economy has been greatly exaggerated by their advocates. He finds that a greater percentage of immigrants are on welfare than are natives, and that in 1990, the nation spent $16 billion more in welfare payments to immigrants than they paid back in taxes. Most importantly, though, he does not think the current wave of newcomers as assimilable as those who arrived in an earlier era. He characterizes "Hispanics" as a "strange anti-nation in the U.S.," who seem less anxious to assimilate than earlier groups. As George Sánchez observes in his essay, critics such as Brimelow are frightened by what the journalist calls "an unmistakable tendency to deconstruct the American nation," because of their demands for "official bilingualism and multiculturalism." Specifically, Brimelow bristles at the thought of multilingual ballots, the abandonment of English as a prerequisite for naturalization, and defining citizenship so that all children born in the United States, even the children of undocumented newcomers, are included as citizens.

Suggestions for Further Reading

Andrew Gyory, *Closing the Gate: Race, Politics and the Chinese Exclusion Act* (Chapel Hill: University of North Carolina Press, 1998).

David H. Bennett, *The Party of Fear, from Nativist Movements to the New Right in American History* (Chapel Hill: University of North Carolina Press, 1988).

Erika Lee, at *America's Gates, Chinese Immigration During the Exclusion Era, 1882–1943* (Chapel Hill: University of North Carolina Press, 2005).

John Higham, *Strangers in the Land: Patterns of American Nativism, 1860–1925* (New Brunswick, NJ: Rutgers University Press, 1955).

Lucy Salyer, *Laws Harsh as Tigers, Chinese Immigration and the Shaping of Modern Immigration Law* (Chapel Hill: University of North Carolina Press, 1995).

Matthew Frye Jacobson, *Barbarian Virtues, The United States Encounters Foreign Peoples at Home and Abroad, 1876–1917* (New York: Hill & Wang, 2000).

Ray Allen Billington, *The Protestant Crusade, 1800–1860: A Study of the Origins of American Nativism* (New York: Macmillan Company, 1938).

Roger Daniels, *Asian America: Chinese and Japanese in the United States Since 1850* (Seattle: University of Washington Press, 1988).

———, *Guarding the Golden Door, American Immigration Policy and Immigrants Since 1882* (New York: Hill & Wang, 2004).

George J. Sánchez, "Face the Nation: Race, Immigration, and the Rise of Nativism in Late-Twentieth-Century-America"

On April 30, 1992, Americans across the nation sat transfixed by a television event that grew to symbolize the sorry state of race relations in late-twentieth-century urban America. The image of Reginald Denny, a white truck driver, being pulled from his cab at the corner of Florence and Normandie Avenues in South Central Los Angeles, beaten and spat upon by a group of young African-American males, quickly became a counterimage of the inhumane beating of black motorist Rodney King a year earlier. These two events of racial conflict, both captured on videotape, dominated representations of the Los Angeles riots in a city haunted by poverty, racism and police brutality. So focused have all Americans become of a bipolar racial dynamic in this country, usually framed in white/black terms, that we lost an opportunity to dissect one of the most important and complex events of our time. As the perceptive playwright and artist Anna Deveare Smith has observed, "We tend to think of race as us and them—us or them being black or white depending on one's own color." Indeed, the Los Angeles riots provide stark, critical evidence of the rise of a racialized nativism directed at recent immigrants and the American born who racially represent those newcomers, one of the most important social movements of our era.

A closer look at the victims of violence at the corner of Florence and Normandie reveals the way in which the Los Angeles riots were fundamentally an anti-immigrant spectacle at its very beginning. Most people outside of Los Angeles are surprised to hear that Reginald Denny was not the only person injured on that corner. Mesmerized by video images of a single beating of one white man, it is difficult to imagine that at least 30 other individuals were beaten at that same spot, most pulled from their cars, some requiring extensive hospitalization. Most importantly for my purposes, only one other victim of the violence at that corner besides Denny was white—and he was, like Denny, a truckdriver passing through the region. All others were people of color, including a Mexican couple and their one-year-old child, hit with rocks and bottles; a Japanese-American man, stripped, beaten and kicked after being mistaken for Korean; a Vietnamese manicurist, left stunned and bloodied after being robbed; and a Latino family with five-year-old twin girls, who each suffered shattered glass wounds in the face and upper body. All of these acts of violence occurred before Reginald Denny appeared.

Indeed, the first victims at Florence and Normandie were Latino residents who lived in the neighborhood. Marisa Bejar was driving her car through the intersection at 5:45 PM when a metal-covered phone book sailed through her car window, opening up a wound that took thirteen stitches to close. Her husband, Francisco Aragon, was hit on the forehead with a piece of wood, while their seven-month-old infant suffered minor scratches when a large metal sign was hurled through the rear window. Minutes later, when Manuel Vaca drove his 1973 Buick into the intersection, Antonine Miller and Damian Williams threw rocks through the windshield, causing Vaca to stop the car. Six men pulled Vaca, his wife and his brother from their car, then beat and robbed them. As Anthony Brown remembered, he kicked at Vaca "because he was Mexican and everybody else was doin' it." Sylvia Castro, a fourth-generation Mexican American and prominent activist in South Central, was shocked when bricks and bottles shattered her car window. Having worked closely with gang members in the area, she was able to escape with only a bloodied nose by speeding way.

Later, after Denny's assault was recorded and broadcast worldwide, several shocked black residents of the area risked their lives to save other victims. James Henry left his porch to pull Raul Aguilar, an immigrant from Belize, to safety after he had been beaten into a coma and a car had run over his legs. Donald Jones, an off-duty fireman, protected Sai-Choi Choi after several men beat and robbed him. Gregory Alan-Williams pulled a badly wounded Takao Hirata from the bloody intersection. Another savior at that corner was 59-year-old Reverend Bennie Newton, pastor of the Light of Love Church. He rescued the life of Fidel Lopez, a twenty-year resident of Los Angeles from Guatemala. Lopez, driving to his home one block from the intersection, was pulled from his car and later required 29 stitches in his forehead for a wound received by a blow with an auto stereo, 17 stitches to his ear, which someone had tried to slice off, and 12 stitches under his chin. Laying unconscious in the street from the beating, Lopez had motor oil poured down his throat and his face and genitals spraypainted blue. His life was saved when Newton began praying over his prostrate body with a bible in the air.

Over the four days of the Los Angeles riots, the dynamics of racial and class tensions, rage against the police, and antiforeign sentiment came together in violent, unpredictable fashion. From that corner of Florence and Normandie, the mayhem spread to engulf the city, creating the worst modern race riot in American history. Fifty-two lives were lost and 2,383 people were injured. About $1 billion of damage was done to residences and businesses, and over 14,000 arrests were made. In the first three days of rioting, over 4,000 fires were set and 1,800 people were treated for gunshot wounds. The destruction occurred throughout the Los Angeles basin, and the participants and victims were indeed multiethnic. But at its core, the Los Angeles riots provide stark evidence of the way in which immigrants provided the perfect scapegoat for American populations frustrated with developments in their society.

The decisions made by angry, young African Americans at that corner as they chose whom to hurt speak volumes to anyone interested in the intertwining of issues of race and immigration in late-twentieth-century America. For some, the decision was not about who was white, but about who was not black. For others it centered around how Latinos and Asians had "invaded the territory" of South Central, one which they claimed as their own turf, despite the fact that South Central Los Angeles had a majority Latino population in 1992. Others shouted (as heard on various videotapes) to "let the Mexicans go," but "show the Koreans who rules." Although the violence began as a response to a verdict passed by an almost all-white jury against an almost all-white set of police officers, quickly other people of color—those deemed foreign or foreign looking—were engaged in the deadly exchange. The meaning of racial and national identities was consistently at issue at the corner of Florence and Normandie, with serious and sometimes bloody outcomes for all participants.

Since May 1992, more clearly visible evidence has appeared which allows most social commentators to identify our current historical moment as one experiencing a particularly sharp rise in American nativism. Two years after the Los Angeles riots, California voters would resurrect their longstanding history as leaders in anti-immigrant efforts since the days of Chinese Exclusion by passing Proposition 187, a state initiative intended to punish illegal immigrants by restricting their access to schools, medical care, and other social services. This would be accomplished by deputizing social service providers as immigration inspectors, including teachers, social workers and doctors, and forcing them to identify to local law enforcement officials students and clients who had entered the country illegally. Here was legislation that tied issues of crime and immigration into a tidy package and allowed voters to voice nativist fears in the anonymous sanctity of the voting booth, a populist solution long well known in California. Polls showed that this piece of legislation won wide-spread approval across a range of ethnic groups, including 67 percent of whites (who formed 80% of the total electorate) and 50 percent of both Asian Americans and African Americans, with only 23 percent of Latinos voting in favor.

One feature of the campaign in favor of Proposition 187 was the prominent role played by California Governor Pete Wilson, a "moderate" Republican who had lost favor with the California electorate when his term coincided with the worst economic performance in the state since the Great Depression. His support of anti-immigrant positions was a centerpiece of his political comeback in California, where he won reelection from rival Kathleen Brown in November 1994 after coming from as much as 20 percentage points behind. This was not, of course, the first time politicians had found nonvoting immigrants to be the perfect scapegoat for an attempt at political resurrection. Indeed, at the height of the Great Depression in 1930, Herbert Hoover's Labor Secretary, William Doak, had promised to rid the country of "four hundred thousand illegal aliens" who he believed were taking jobs away from American citizens, thereby causing the great economic calamity of the period.

Indeed, Pete Wilson and Herbert Hoover have more in common than their tortured political paths through economic downturns. Both had previously been ardent supporters of the easing of immigration restrictions before the convenience of immigrant scapegoating in the political process became evident. During World War I, when Hoover had been Food Administrator for the U.S. government, he had personally encouraged President Woodrow Wilson to exempt Mexican immigrants from the provisions of the 1917 Immigration Act in order to allow them to engage in much needed agricultural labor and wartime production. In 1985, during the height of the congressional debates over the Immigration Reform and Control Act, then-Senator Pete Wilson was the key player in securing an exemption for California agricultural growers, enabling them to continue using undocumented workers long after more stringent enforcement was already in place in urban areas. Pete Wilson's ill-fated presidential campaign in 1995–96 cannot obscure the fact that his career remains the epitome of opportunistic politics, taking full advantage of America's long-standing fears of immigrants and foreigners when such a strategy can bring success at the polls.

During the past year, we also have witnessed the publication and media hype of a book which can easily be characterized as our era's equivalent to *The Passing of a Great Race*, the 1916 classic by [nativist writer] Madison Grant. Grant's contemporary counterpart is Peter Brimelow, senior editor at *Forbes* and *National Review*. His *Alien Nation: Common Sense About America's Immigration Disaster* (1995) unabashedly claims that recent immigration is likely "to transform—and ultimately, perhaps, even to destroy . . . the American nation". Within the first ten pages of the book, recent immigrants are blamed for rising crime rates, the health care crisis, lowering overall educational standards, and causing Americans to feel alienated from each other. Unlike other nativists, Brimelow wants to be clear to offer an overtly racial argument: "Race and ethnicity are destiny in American politics" declares Brimelow repeatedly, so all Americans should be concerned about restricting immigration of people who are colored differently than they.

Signs, therefore, point to a resurgence of a nativism unparalleled in this country since the 1920s. From attacks on immigrants in urban unrest to legislative action attacking immigration policies to academic and media discussions resonating the familiar intellectualized examinations of racialized dissonance of the past, today's nativism is as virulent as any that has gone before. Yet this era's nativism, like this era's immigration, has unique characteristics which differentiate it from that which appeared in the early twentieth century at the height of European immigration to the United States. Traditional hostility towards new immigrants has taken on a new meaning when those immigrants are racially identifiable and fit established racial categories in the American psyche. With the increase of immigration from Asia and Latin America, a new American racism has emerged which has no political boundaries or ethnic categorizations. From the left and right of the political spectrum, and from both white and black individuals, this new racism continually threatens to explode in contemporary American society.

One point worth making is that while nativist discourse is often decidedly linked to racial discourse, they are not one and the same, and they often lead in different directions. Part of the problem in separating racism from nativism is the fact that our collective understanding of what constitutes racism has become murkier since the 1960s. Having long abandoned biological categories of race and definitions of racism which rely fundamentally on individual prejudice, most academic discourse on racism in the social sciences remains unclear and undeveloped.

One shining exception to the academic murkiness I have been describing is the work of sociologists Michael Omi and Howard Winant, who define racism as a historically situated project which "creates or reproduces structures of domination based on essentialist categories of race." Not only would this definition allow us to convincingly label Brimelow's project racist but, for the purposes of this exploration, it would allow us to differentiate and complicate our present notions of nativism. To be able to do this is critical because historically there have always been proponents of open immigration who can be characterized as racist. For example, many of the employers of Mexican migrant labor during the 1920s voraciously fought against immigration restriction on the basis that Mexicans were biologically suited for stoop labor. W. H. Knox of the Arizona Cotton Growers' Association belittled nativists' fears of a Mexican takeover of the United States in 1926 by invoking racist constructions of Mexicans to the House of Representatives.

> Have you ever heard, in the history of the United States, or in the history of the human race, of the white race being overrun by a class of people of the mentality of the Mexicans? I never have. We took this country from Mexico. Mexico did not take it from us. To assume that there is any danger of any likelihood of the Mexican coming in here and colonizing this country and taking it away from us, to my mind, is absurd.

It is not difficult to find other instances, including in the contemporary period, of antirestrictionists espousing racist views of those immigrants they want to entice to come into the country.

Moreover, it should be clearly stated that not all restrictionist positions are fundamentally based on racial assumptions. The late Barbara Jordan, Chair of the United States Commission on Immigration Reform and former Congresswoman from Texas, while presiding over two reports which emphatically favor reduced entry of legal immigrants and the toughening of measures to curb illegal immigration, nevertheless offers a picture of immigration restriction which simultaneously evokes a renewed faith in American diversity. Jordan wrote:

> Legitimate concern about weaknesses in our immigration policy should not, however, obfuscate what remains the essential point: the United States has been and should continue to be a nation of immigrants. . . . The United States has united immigrants and their descendants around a commitment to democratic ideals and constitutional principles. People from an extraordinary range of ethnic and religious backgrounds have embraced these ideals. . . . We are more than a melting pot; we are a kaleidoscope, where every turn of history refracts new light on the old promise.

Indeed, the active role of black public figures in contemporary discussions of immigration policy suggest that African Americans will play an increased role in contributing to a more exclusionary definition of American citizenship than has hitherto prevailed. Barbara Jordan was chosen by President Clinton as head of a federal advisory commission charged with proposing new measures to curtail illegal immigration, not just because of her expertise as a former member of the House, but also because of her race. Jordan's very presence on such a commission allowed her blackness to deflect potential charges of racism directed at the stringent provisions of the policy recommendations. In this new climate, it is obvious that all Americans can get caught in the white–black paradigm of race relations, a model that relies on opposites, opposites which too often substitute for the complexity and diversity of social and ethnic relations in the late-twentieth-century United States.

To understand the vexing dilemma of these issues, we must remember that two seemingly contradictory directions mark recent scholarship on race in the United States. On one hand, social scientists throughout the twentieth century have worked hard to challenge the biologistic paradigm which explained racial inferiority as part of a natural order. Despite recent exceptions like *The Bell Curve*, most scientific studies reject the notion that race should be equated with particular hereditary characteristics. Instead, social scientists have increasingly explored how race is a social construction, shaped by particular social conditions and historical moments to reflect notions of difference among human groups. Many academics have subsumed race under other categories deemed more critical to understanding social stratification, such as class or ethnicity. Yet racial theorists increasingly point out that race has its own particular role in modern society that cannot simply be buried as a byproduct of other social phenomena. Omi and Winant offer a definition of race which takes into account the instability of a social construction, yet does not see race as merely an illusion: "race is a concept which signifies and symbolizes social conflicts and interests by referring to different types of human bodies."

Indeed, the other major development in academic discussions is that "race matters" in understanding all forms of social conflicts in the modern world including those which do not, on the surface appear to be racially inspired. [The] eruption of ethnic tensions in the wake of the collapse of the Soviet Union has forced non-American scholars to reassess their previous dismissal of these conflicts as holdovers from a premodern age, likely to disappear in our new postmodern world. In the United States, while this work has shaped a critical reconsideration of the drift toward discounting racial tension as simply a byproduct of class antagonism or cultural conflict, it also has largely remained limited to a discussion of the problematic relationship between African Americans and the majority white population. Even when other racial minorities are discussed, a binary relationship with the Anglo majority remains the central focus of these academic studies. The academic discussions of multiculturalism, in other words, have yet to produce a wide array of scholarship which effectively theorizes the fundamental multiracial character of either contemporary or historical U.S. society.

Although many philosophers and theorists have stressed that "race matters" in understanding American society, race in the national imagination has usually been reserved to describe boundaries between whites and blacks. Indeed, the 1990s has produced many important works by noted social commentators that continue to utilize a strict white/black racial dichotomy. Andrew Hacker (1992), author of *Two Nations: Black and White, Separate, Hostile, Unequal,* justifies his title and emphasis by claiming that Asians and Hispanics "find themselves sitting as spectators, while the two prominent players (Blacks and Whites) try to work out how or whether they can coexist with one another." While including voices of Asian Americans and Latinos in his collection of oral histories about "race," Studs Terkel subtitles his 1992 book, *How Blacks and Whites Think and Feel about the American Obsession.*

Asian Americans and Latinos, despite their active presence in American society in the mid-nineteenth century, are depicted as only the latest of immigrant groups to America, and they are described as engaging in patterns which more clearly represent early-twentieth-century European immigrant groups than separate racial populations. [Andrew] Hacker, for example, rather than using the actual history of Asian groups or Latinos in the United States, argues that "second and subsequent generations of Hispanics and Asians are merging into the "white" category, partly through intermarriage and also by personal achievement and adaptation. No more important figure than Nobel Prize winner Toni Morrison has made this claim recently in the newsmagazine, *Time.* In a special issue dedicated to immigration [published in 1993], Morrison writes:

> All immigrants fight for jobs and space, and who is there to fight but those who have both? As in the fishing ground struggle between Texas and Vietnamese shrimpers, they displace what and whom they can. Although U.S. history is awash in labor battles, political fights and property wars among all religious and ethnic groups, their struggles are persistently framed as struggles between recent arrivals and blacks. In race talk the move into mainstream America always means buying into the notion of American blacks as the real aliens. Whatever the ethnicity or nationality of the immigrant, his nemesis is understood to be African American.

This perspective, for all its insight into the crucial place of African Americans in American history, ignores the long history of racial discrimination aimed specifically at Asian Americans and Latinos in the United States. National scholars have a responsibility to study the whole nation and its history, but too often East Coast social commentators present a very thin knowledge of U.S. history more than a few miles away from the eastern seaboard. Both "Asians" and "Latinos" have been decidedly constructed as races in American history, long before the decade of the 1960s, and today both these subgroups have become lighting rods for discussions of race, equality, and the meaning of citizenship in contemporary America.

Even more importantly, a new perspective is needed in order to encourage us to rethink the meaning of multiracial communities in American history. Rather than simply being "communities in transition" to neighborhoods of racial exclusivity, these areas of cultural exchange and conflict can come to represent the norm in American racial and ethnic life, at least in the western half of the nation, not the exception. Indeed, refocusing on the persistence of these mixed communities allow urban scholars to compare the diversity of ethnic communities in the late twentieth century to the seemingly transitional ethnic communities of the early twentieth century. For Los Angeles and other large metropolitan areas, this perspective is crucial. Watts, for example, in the heart of South Central Los Angeles, had a majority Mexican population until the late 1920s, when African Americans from the American south began to migrate in large numbers to the city. Likewise, Boyle Heights in east Los Angeles was the center of the L.A. Jewish community in the 1920s, as well as home to a large Japanese American population stretching east from Little Tokyo and a sizable Mexican American group.

More recently, post–World War II racially restrictive policies of segregation have been replaced by a return to class-based zoning. This change, coupled with extensive post–1965 immigration, has created new communities of racial interaction in most urban centers in the United States. Most of these, however, include few white Americans. Yet, multiracial communities as diverse as Uptown and Edgewater in Chicago, Mt. Pleasant in Washington, DC, and Sunset Park and Jackson Heights in New York City have begun to focus attention on this seemingly new phenomenon. This interesting constellation of multicultural enclaves has produced some rather noteworthy, but not altogether new, racial dynamics. Much residential community interaction between blacks, Latinos and Asian Americans has occurred in urban centers in the American West over the past one hundred years, but never before in such a visible—that is, national—fashion. The histories of these past multiracial communities in the West, therefore, is as important a model for ethnic community as the homogeneous *barrio* depicted in so many works of Chicano history, or the standard portrait of a completely African American ghetto.

One result of homogeneous depictions of ethnic communities can be seen in the immediate media coverage of "communities" involved in the L.A. uprising. The erasure of Latino participation in the Los Angeles riots as both full-fledged victims and victimizers is troubling to those concerned about contemporary discussions of race in American life. In the 1980s, Los Angeles County added 1.4 million residents, and nearly 1.3 million—or 93 percent—were Latino. Even though Latinos made up the majority of residents in South Central Los Angeles and 45 percent of the residential population of Koreatown by 1990, both communities were defined in such a way that Latinos were considered "outsiders" in community politics and media formulations. Latinos were the single largest ethnic group arrested during the period of the riots, not only for curfew violations and undocumented status, but also as looters of their local Korean merchants. Estimates also indicate that between 30 to 40 percent of stores that were lost were

Chicano or Latino owned. Moreover, during the three days of rioting, the Immigration and Naturalization Service took advantage of those arrested for curfew violations to deport over 2,000 Latino aliens. Yet the wider media and most academic accounts of the events of 1992 in Los Angeles have largely ignored the Latino role because it disturbs strongly held beliefs in notions of community, belonging, and race in this country. It is the constant depiction of Latinos as "newcomers" and "foreigners" that provides insight into the particular form of racialization which surrounds this group in American society.

It is time to consider what factors are at work during our current age which inform and promote our own brand of American nativism. Let me suggest three different antiforeign sentiments which mark the racialized nativism of the end of the twentieth century. The first is an extreme antipathy towards non-English languages and a fear that linguistic difference will undermine the American nation. Despite the fact that English has become the premier international language of commerce and communication, fueled by forces as widespread as multinational corporations, the Internet, popular culture and returning migrants, Americans themselves consistently worry that immigrants refuse to learn English and intend to undermine the preeminence of that language within American borders. Captured by statewide "English Only" proposals, which began in California but spread quickly across the nation, this fear seems to emanate from Americans' own linguistic shortcomings and their feeling of alienation from the discourse— be it personal, on the job, or on the radio—that monolingualism creates.

A second fear is one directly tied into issues of multiculturalism and affirmative action. Like papist conspiracy theories, this fear involves the uneasy belief that racialized immigrants take advantage of, in the words of [journalist] Michael Lind, "a country in which racial preference entitlements and multicultural ideology encourage them to retain their distinct racial and ethnic identities." Going beyond the denial of white privilege in contemporary U.S. society, this sentiment directly believes that contrived, misguided, and sometimes secretive government policies have tilted against white people in the 1990s. Though tied to a general antipathy towards people of color, the place of immigrants and those perceived as racially connected to Latino and Asian immigrants heighten the nature of some of these fears. Even some pro-affirmative action activists bemoan the extension of programs to nonblacks, having equated the history of U.S. racism as that directed against only one racial group incorrectly defined as wholly nonimmigrant. These programs, then, are deemed to be un-American, not only because they contradict America's supposed commitment to equality of opportunity, but also because they are literally favoring "non-Americans" in their results. While invoking the name of the CORE national director in the early 1960s, Lind writes:

> One wonders what James Farmer, the patron saint of quotas, would have said, if he had been told, in 1960, that by boycotting Northern corporations until they hired fixed numbers of black Americans, he

was inspiring a system whose major beneficiaries would ultimately be, not only well-to-do white women, but immigrants and the descendants of immigrants who, at the time of his struggles, were living in Mexico, Cuba, Salvador, Honduras, and Guatemala.

A third antiforeign sentiment has emerged in the 1990s, embodied in California's Proposition 187, which is quite unique and has not been seen since the Great Depression. Current anti-immigrant rhetoric focuses on the drain of public resources by immigrants, both legal and illegal, particularly their utilization of welfare, education and health care services. Unlike nativist calls which center around immigrants taking jobs from citizens, this sentiment feeds into stereotypes of nonworking loafers, particularly targeting women who supposedly come to the United States to give birth and sustain their families from the "generous" welfare state. Even when presented with evidence that immigrants are less likely to seek out government assistance than citizens, today's nativists scoff at the data and the researchers, like 187 proponent Harold Ezell who retorted to one study showing immigrant underutilization of government-sponsored medical programs by saying, "He's obviously never been to any of the emergency rooms in Orange County to see who's using them—it's non-English speaking young people with babies." The notion that immigrants are now coming to the United States to take advantage of welfare, health and education benefits has led directly to federal legislation which allows states to ban such assistance to even legal immigrants, and this has enabled Governor Wilson to mandate such cut-offs in California.

Although cultural antipathies are often at work in producing fear of newcomers, more often than not economic fears of competition have also played a critical role. Nativism has always cut across political lines, finding adherents on both the right and left. In the 1920s, the American Federation of Labor played a critical role in encouraging immigration restriction by raising the spectre of newcomers' threat to the economic security of the American workingman. Samuel Gompers, president of the AFL, who supported voluntary and relatively unencumbered immigration as late as 1892, became a virulent nativist by the 1920s. Today's nativists similarly stretch across the political spectrum, from right-wingers like Pat Buchanan, to political "moderates" like Pete Wilson, to self-proclaimed liberals like Michael Lind.

What binds these individuals together is a profound sense of the decline of the American nation. With the rise of nativism since 1965, we are once again witnessing a defensive nationalism in the wake of profound economic restructuring. In place of a period of modernization which pushed the U.S. agricultural economy towards widespread industrial production, we are now witnessing rapid deindustrialization, the rise of a service and high tech economy, and the worldwide movement of capital which undercuts the ability of American unions to protect U.S. jobs. This economic transformation, coupled with antagonistic government policies, has certainly undermined central cities in the United States and made for fertile ground for nativist sentiments.

Indeed, underlying much of the frustration of the Los Angeles riot participants was the collapse of the inner-city economy, the negative flipside of the new "Pacific Rim" global economy. Los Angeles had lost 150,000 manufacturing jobs in the previous three years, and each of these jobs were estimated to take another three associated jobs with them. The new jobs which were created were disproportionately low-wage and dead-end forms of employment; in fact, 40 percent of all jobs created in Los Angeles from 1979 to 1989 paid less than $15,000 a year. Most of these jobs were taken by recent immigrants to the area, leaving African Americans few viable options for secure employment. The average earnings of employed black men fell 24 percent from 1973 to 1989, and unemployment swelled to record levels in the innercity. Middle-income Los Angeles was rapidly disappearing, leaving little opportunity for anyone to move up the economic ladder. This inequality was also highly racialized; the median household net worth for Anglos in the city in 1991 was $31,904, while only $1,353 for non-Anglos.

Clearly, one obvious target for the frustration in the [rioters] were the Korean merchants in South Central, who had replaced the Jews who left in large numbers after the 1965 Watts Riots. In 1990, 145,000 Koreans lived in Los Angeles County, a 142 percent increase over the previous decade and a phenomenal growth from only 9,000 in 1970. Unable to transfer their education and skills to the U.S. labor market, many Korean immigrants had pooled their funds to start small businesses in ethnic communities throughout the city. Koreans now saw their businesses burn to the ground and suffer widespread looting. These small merchants had filled a vacuum created by discrimination against African-American entrepreneurs and the abandonment of the by large retail businesses.

Yet much of the damage to Korean businesses occurred in Koreatown itself, where one third of that community's businesses were located. This community was unique in that it did not represent an area of ethnic succession, well known in the East, where one identifiable ethnic group was slowly being replaced by another, with the resulting tensions that succession produces. Here two recent immigrant populations met in unequal fashion, both reflecting cultures which had long been part of the L.A. racial makeup, but neither with particular historical roots to this area before 1965. Unlike other Asian enclaves in southern California, the residential population of Koreatown was overwhelming Latino, and it was this ethnic group which was primarily engaged in the looting of these stores. In fact, 43 percent of those arrested during the riots were Latino, while only 34 percent were African Americans, contradicting the notion that the Los Angeles Riots was a simple black-Korean conflict. Economic frustrations fueled this looting and mayhem of the Los Angeles Riots, even though a different racialized nativism set the events of late April 1992 in motion.

It is clear that we are in a period of economic transformation which can and should be compared to the period of industrialization that occurred a century ago and that has provided the social context for the rise of nativism in the United States that occurred in both periods. Yet today's economic transformation is intimately tied to an economic globalization propelled by multinational corporations and an age where capital and information flows relatively freely across national borders. From 1890 to the 1920s, the industrial transformation which changed the American economy and fueled international migration led to a breaking down of local community control towards a national interdependency which propelled Americans to "search for order" in new and varied ways. Not only did bureaucracy and science rise to provide this national order, but so did immigration restriction and scientific racism emerge to provide ideological comfort to Americans in search of a glue to keep together a nation undergoing fundamental social and economic change.

Many Americans have been shielded since World War II from the convulsions of the international economic order by the enormous strength of the U.S. economy, and liberal policies of inclusion have been crafted which assume the continuation of this extraordinary growth. Most important in coming to terms with the complexities of race, immigration and nativism in the late twentieth century is a perspective which can deal with the multiple meanings of race and equality in American society in an age of liberal political retrenchment and widespread economic restructuring. During the Reagan/Bush administrations and the current era of Republican ascendancy in Congress, hard-fought victories in racial and economic policy were and are continually threatened with extinction. In addition, supposedly "race-neutral" policies, such as tax reform and subsidies to the private sector, have disproportionally and adversely affected racial minorities.

Yet increasingly we must account for the fact that at least the Reagan/ Bush era did not see a reversal of government spending despite all the rhetoric, but instead witnessed its redirection towards wealthy and corporate interests and away from long-term investment in education, infrastructure and safety nets for the poor. This "trickle-down" theory of social advancement has become the biggest failure of the 1980s, and it has left in its wake a sizable, disgruntled white electorate, one disaffected with politics that clamors for "change" at every turn. This group helped give the White House to the Democrats in 1992, handed large numbers of votes to Ross Perot, and offered the Republican Party a majority in both houses of Congress for the first time in thirty years in 1994. In this setting, one in which expectations of newfound prosperity grow with every change of political power, a scapegoat must be found amidst the citizenry that can be blamed for delaying the promised economic security. For many Americans in our era, the poor, especially the black poor, have served this role of scapegoat; increasingly, however, that role is being transferred to or combined with the blaming of the immigrant.

While the industrial economy was being sent through convulsions over the past thirty years, Americans produced largely cultural explanations for structural social problems. The demonization of black families, for example, served for white Americans as a plausible justification for the economic backwardness of African Americans, despite affirmative action and civil rights. Instead of focusing on the ravages of deindustrialization in both black and white communities, white Americans increasingly revived traditional stereotypes of black laziness. While these racialized beliefs were no longer acceptable public discourse in the post–civil rights era, researchers who take anonymous polls can still ferret out extensive negative race stereotyping rampant in the white community.

Indeed, it seems to me that cultural beliefs in innate difference have worked together with structural forces of inequality to frame (and hide) discussions of white privilege. Literary scholar Eric Lott has argued that attitudes towards blackness are shaped by white self-examination and insecurity, rather than by the realities of African-American life. Indeed, contemporary white perceptions of blacks probably tell us more about the dangers of being "white" in this era than about strongly held beliefs regarding black inferiority. In fact, it is the language of liberal individualism that keeps many whites from seeking structural explanations for racial inequality. However, liberalism has always been a two-edged sword. When economic conditions become tenuous for whites, meritocratic rhetoric about the rewards of hard work and self-reliance also generates individual anxiety and a fear of personal victimization. Whites who are faced with economic failure or insecurity in spite of their racial privilege become a sure breeding ground for the scapegoating of racial others. This classic projection further obscures the need to acknowledge or understand the structural and economic sources of one's own oppression.

Closer analysis of the workings of liberal language deepens our understanding of the relationship between liberal racial attitudes and the structural causes of inequality. For example, liberal individualism, as a dominant value in American society, has an impact on the actions of individuals of all races. Indeed, a look at liberalism's impact on blacks and other racial minorities, including recent immigrants to the United States, would reveal that routine, systematic and unyielding discrimination does not necessarily lead to collective protest. More often than not, it produces a sense of individual victimization and anger. The Los Angeles riots demonstrated that injustice can provoke African-American rage, not only against white authority, but against "racialized others," most notably Asians and Latinos living among blacks in newly "reintegrated" communities.

Today, the United States finds itself increasingly having to compete economically with nations from all over the world, including Third World nations trying to gain a stronger foothold in the international exchange of goods and services. At the same time, American corporations seem to have themselves become internationalized, more interested in gaining profit than in maintaining an economic nationalism rooted in American hegemony. It is not difficult to understand how immigrants from these developing nations can be seen as both drains on our national economy and symbols of countries who threaten American economic hegemony and the dream of a multicultural future in the post–Cold War era. These conditions have produced increasing calls for a "liberal nationalism" in the United States from the left side of the political spectrum, which often has gone hand-in-hand with calls for severe restrictions on immigration to the United States. In an analysis intended to aid working-class Americans, particularly American blacks, Michael Lind writes, "The most promising way to quickly raise wages at the bottom of the income ladder in the United States is to restrict immigration." Though always claiming that these efforts should not be characterized as nativist, the defensiveness of these renewed calls for nationalism and protectionism on the backs of recent and future immigrants point towards the eruption of a "liberal nativism" in American political discourse.

[In] the United States, the history of white on black racism blinds Americans from recognizing any other forms of interracial tensions. Racism against Asians and Latin Americans is dismissed as either "natural byproducts" of immigrant assimilation or as extensions of the white–black dichotomy. Moreover, when African Americans perform acts of racism, they are quickly ignored or recast except as a threat to a white-dominated society.

As the participants in the violence at Florence and Normandie indicate, interracial understanding and an inclusive sense of "community" is not simply formed by living in close proximity to those from other racial/ethnic groups. Rather, what is disturbing about the Los Angeles riots is the insistence that "community" reflects a single racial group. The irony of black protesters stopping construction projects in South Central Los Angeles on the basis that no one from the "community" was employed, even when Latino workers were their neighbors, seemed to be lost on everyone concerned. Moreover, these strategies of protest usually encouraged African American entrepreneurs who had left the residential neighborhood to return to invest and to hire (but not to live), with the untested assumption that they would be more likely to hire other blacks.

Indeed, to equate "community" with a particular racialized "identity" seems more to naturalize a recent geography of local communities which can easily forget the multiracial histories of the past. In Los Angeles, commentators rarely discuss the longstanding Asian and Latino communities which have been part of the region's history since the city's founding, relying instead on depictions of these racial groups as almost wholly recent immigrants. Ironically, African Americans become the perfect choice to project this historical amnesia and defend the sanctity of national boundaries, since their presence alone deflects any charge that anti-immigrant policies are racist. Since race in this nation has been constructed as a white/black affair, the continuation of this bipolar approach becomes critical to the ideology of an ordered American nation. In the United States, no less than in Germany or Japan, the power embedded in certain notions of territory must be critiqued and analyzed for the grounds upon which certain peoples and histories are privileged. Indeed, racialized immigrants have become the stepping stools for claims of American citizenship in the late twentieth century.

How have the immigrants themselves responded to these recent attacks? One response has been a marked increase in political involvement among all immigrants in U.S. politics, on the local and national levels. Within communities of immigrants from various nations in Asia, political involvement has usually emerged within racialized organizations, increasingly "pan-ethnic" in orientation. Although immigrants from Latin America have seemed to lag in their commitment to a pan-Latino consciousness, recent anti-immigrant efforts in California seem to have produced a decided turn towards political strategies and identities which go beyond national origins. Immigrant citizens and American-born ethnics in these communities have also heightened their own political involvement to fight for the rights of immigrants with the acknowledgement that their own racial construction often hangs in the balance. Surprisingly, this acknowledgement of common ties has even stretched beyond party affiliation. In California, Republican Bill Davila, the high-profile spokesperson and former CEO of Vons super-markets, took out a full-page advertisement in 1994 asking voters to reject Proposition 187, even though he supported Pete Wilson's reelection campaign, calling the measure a "divisive, unproductive, intiative . . . turning neighbor against neighbor."

Ironically, one of the most concrete expressions of this new political consciousness is the upsurge in the rates of naturalization among legal immigrants across the nation. The INS office in Los Angeles began receiving as many as 2,000 applications a day for naturalization after passage of Proposition 187, and offices around the country experienced similar increases. An all-time high was reached in 1995, with over 1 million immigrants becoming new American citizens. With the legalization of previously undocumented immigrants by the 1986 IRCA law, more long-term immigrant residents of the United States see the protection of citizenship in this time of immigrant-bashing and reduced benefits as a way to protect themselves and their families.

While on the surface these developments of political incorporation seem to reflect patterns of Americanization among earlier European immigrant groups to the United States, this is a decidedly ambivalent Americanism borne of racial tension and antiforeign sentiment. One 1994 statewide poll in California found that 25 percent of immigrants in the state personally feared discrimination and violence directed at them by virtue of looking foreign. As sociologist Rubén Rumbaut has put it, "the moral of the story is we reap what we sow. When you welcome people to a community, you encourage them to feel they matter and that they have a stake here. But if you sow hate, you'll reap the products of hate."

Edward Alworth Ross, "American Blood and Immigrant Blood"

[The] conditions of settlement of this country caused those of uncommon energy and venturesomeness to outmultiply the rest of the population. Thus came into existence the pioneering breed; and this breed increased until it is safe to estimate that fully half of white Americans with native grandparents have one or more pioneers among their ancestors. Whatever valuable race traits distinguish the American people from the parent European stocks are due to the efflorescence of this breed. Without it there would have been little in the performance of our people to arrest the attention of the world. Now we confront the melancholy spectacle of this pioneer breed being swamped and submerged by an overwhelming tide of latecomers from the old-world hive. In Atlanta still seven out of eight white men had American parents; in Nashville and Richmond, four out of five; in Kansas City, two out of three; and in Los Angeles, one out of two; but in Detroit, Cleveland, and Paterson one man out of five had American parents; in Chicago and New York, one out of six; in Milwaukee, one out of seven; and in Fall River, one out of nine. *Certainly never since the colonial era have the foreign-born and their children formed so large a proportion of the American people as at the present moment.* I scanned 368 persons as they passed me in Union Square, New York, at a time when the garment-workers of the Fifth Avenue lofts were returning to their homes. Only thirty-eight of these passers-by had the type of face one would find at a county fair in the West or South.

In the six or seven hundred thousand strangers that yearly join themselves to us for good and all, there are to be found, of course, every talent and every beauty. Out of the steerage come persons as fine and noble as any who have trodden American soil. Any adverse characterization of an immigrant stream implies, then, only that the trait is relatively frequent, not that it is universal.

In this sense it is fair to say that the blood now being injected into the veins of our people is "sub-common." Observe immigrants not as they come travel-wan up the gang-plank, nor as they issue toil-begrimed from pit's mouth or mill gate, but in their gatherings, washed, combed, and in their Sunday best. You are struck by the fact that from ten to twenty per cent are hirsute, low-browed, big-faced persons of obviously low mentality. Not that they suggest evil. They simply look out of place in black clothes and stiff collar, since clearly they belong in skins, in wattled huts at the close of the Great Ice Age.

To the practised eye, the physiognomy of certain groups unmistakably proclaims inferiority of type. I have seen gatherings of the foreign-born in which narrow and sloping foreheads were the rule. The shortness and smallness of the crania were very noticeable. There was much facial asymmetry. Among the women, beauty, aside from the fleeting, epidermal bloom of girlhood, was quite lacking. In every face there was something wrong—lips thick, mouth coarse, upper lip too long, cheek-bones too high, chin poorly formed, the bridge of the nose hollowed, the base of the nose tilted, or else the whole face prognathous. There were so many sugar-loaf heads, moon-faces, slit mouths, lantern-jaws, and goose-bill noses that one might imagine a malicious jinn had amused himself by casting human beings in a set of skew-molds discarded by the Creator.

Our captains of industry give a crowbar to the immigrant, make a dividend out of him, and imagine that is the end of the matter. They over-look that this man will beget children in his image—two or three times as many as the American—and that these children will in turn beget children. They chuckle at having opened an inexhaustible store of cheap tools and, lo! the American people is being altered for all time by these tools. Once before, captains of industry took a hand in making this people. Colonial planters imported Africans to hoe in the sun, to "develop" the tobacco, indigo, and rice plantations. Then, as now, business-minded men met with contempt the protests of a few idealists against their way of "building up the country."

Those promoters of prosperity are dust, but they bequeathed a situation which in four years [the Civil war, 1861–65] wiped out more wealth than two hundred years of slavery had built up, and which presents today the one unsolvable problem in this country. Without likening immigrants to negroes, one may point out how the latter-day employer resembles the old-time planter in his blindness to the effects of his labor policy upon the blood of the nation.

Immigration and Good Looks

It is reasonable to expect an early falling off in the frequency of good looks in the American people. It is unthinkable that so many persons with crooked faces, coarse mouths, bad noses, heavy jaws, and low foreheads can mingle their heredity with ours without making personal beauty yet more rare among us than it actually is. So much ugliness is at last bound to work to the surface. One ought to see the horror on the face of a fine-looking Italian or Hungarian consul when one asks him innocently, "Is the physiognomy of these immigrants typical of your people?" That the new immigrants are inferior in looks to the old immigrants may be seen by comparing, in a Labor Day parade, the faces of the cigar-makers and the garment-workers with those of the teamsters, piano-movers, and steam-fitters.

Even aside from the pouring in of the ill-favored, the crossing of the het-erogeneous is bound to lessen good looks among us. It is noteworthy that the beauty which has often excited the admiration of European visitors has shown itself most in communities of comparative purity of blood. New England, Virginia, and Kentucky have been renowned for their beautiful women, but not the commonwealths with a mixed population. It is in the less-heterogeneous parts of the Middle West, such as Indiana and Kansas, that one is struck by the number of comely women.

Twenty-four years ago the greatest living philosopher advised inquiring Japanese statesmen to interdict marriages of Japanese with foreigners, on the ground that the crossings of the too-unlike produce human beings with a "chaotic constitution." Herbert Spencer went on to say, "When the varieties mingled diverge beyond a certain slight degree, the result is inevitably a bad one." The greatest students of hybridism today confirm Spencer's surmise. The fusing of American with German and Scandinavian immigrants was only a reblending of kindred stocks, for Angles, Jutes, Danes, and Normans were wrought of yore into the fiber of the English breed. But the human varieties being collected in this country by the naked action of economic forces are too dissimilar to blend without producing a good many faces of a "chaotic constitution." Just as there is a wide difference in looks between Bretons and Normans, Dutch and Hanoverians, the Chinese of Hu-peh and the Chinese of Fukien, so broad contrasts in good looks may in time appear between the pure-blood parts of our country and those which have absorbed a motley assortment of immigrants.

Stature and Physique

Although the Slavs stand up well, our South Europeans run to low stature. A gang of Italian navvies filing along the street present, by their dwarfishness, a curious contrast to other people. The Portuguese, the Greeks, and the Syrians are, from our point of view, undersized. The Hebrew immigrants are very poor in physique. The average of Hebrew women in New York is just over five feet, and the young women in the garment factories, although well developed, appear to be no taller than native girls of thirteen.

On the physical side the Hebrews are the polar opposite of our pioneer breed. Not only are they undersized and weak-muscled, but they shun bodily activity and are exceedingly sensitive to pain. Says a settlement worker: "You can't make boy scouts out of the Jews. There's not a troop of them in all New York." Another remarks: "They are absolute babies about pain. Their young fellows will scream with a hard lick." Students observe that husky young Hebrews on the football team lack grit, and will "take on" if they are bumped into hard.

Natural selection, frontier life, and the example of the red man produced in America a type of great physical self-control, gritty, uncomplaining, merciless to the body through fear of becoming "soft." To this roaming, hunting, exploring, adventurous breed what greater contrast is there than the denizens of the Ghetto? The second generation, to be sure, overtop their parents and are going in for athletics. Hebrews under Irish names abound in the prize-ring, and not long ago a sporting editor printed the item, "Jack Sullivan received a letter in Yiddish yesterday from his sister." Still, it will be long before they produce the stoical type who blithely fares forth into the wilderness, portaging his canoe, poling it against the current, wading in the torrents, living on bacon and beans, and sleeping on the ground, all for "fun" or "to keep hard."

Vitality

"The Slavs," remarks a physician, "are immune to certain kinds of dirt. They can stand what would kill a white man." The women do not have puerperal fever, as our women would under their conditions. The men violate every sanitary law, yet survive. The Slavs come from a part of the world in which never more than a third of the children have grown up. In every generation, dirt, ignorance, superstition, and lack of medical attention have winnowed out all but the sturdiest. Among Americans, two-thirds of the children grow up, which means that we keep alive many of the tenderer, who would certainly have perished in the Slavic world. There is, however, no illusion more grotesque than to suppose that our people is to be rejuvenated by absorbing these millions of hardy peasantry, that, to quote a champion of free immigration, "The new-comers in America will bring fresh, vigorous blood to a rather sterile and inbred stock." The fact is that the immigrant stock quickly loses here its distinctive ruggedness. The physicians practising among rural Poles notice a great saving of infant life under American conditions. Says one: "I see immigrant women and their grown daughters having infants at the same time, and the children of the former will die of the things that the children of the latter get well of. The same holds when the second generation and the third bear at the same time. The latter save their children better than the former." The result is a marked softening of fiber between the immigrant women and the granddaughters.

There is, then, no lasting revitalization from this tide of life. If our people has become weak, no transfusion of peasants will set it on its feet again; for their blood too, soon thins. The trouble, if you call it that, is not with the American people, but with the wide diffusion among us of a civilized manner of life. Where the struggle for existence is mitigated not merely for the upper quarter of society, as formerly in the Old World, but for the upper three-quarters, as in this and other democratic countries, the effects of keeping alive the less hardy are bound to show. The remedy for the alleged degeneration of our stock is simple, but drastic. If we want only constitutions that can stand hardship and abuse, let us treat the young as they are treated in certain poverty-stricken parts of Russia. Since the mother is obliged to pass the day at work in distant fields, the nursling of a few months is left alone, crawling about on the dirt floor of the hut and comforting itself, when it cries from hunger, by sucking poultices of chewed bread tied to its hands and feet.

Morality

That the Mediterranean peoples are morally below the races of northern Europe is as certain as any social fact. Even when they were dirty, ferocious barbarians, these blonds were truth-tellers. Be it pride or awkwardness or lack of imagination or fair-play sense, something has held them back from the nimble lying of the southern races. Immigration officials find that the different peoples are as day and night in point of veracity, and report vast trouble in extracting the truth from certain brunet nationalities.

Some champions of immigration have become broad-minded enough to think small of the cardinal virtues. The Syrians, on Boston testimony, took "great pains to cheat the charitable societies" and are "extremely untrust-worthy and unreliable." Their defender, however, after admitting their untruthfulness, explains that their lying is altruistic. If, at the fork of a road, you ask a Syrian your way, he will in sheer transport of sympathy, study you to discover what answer will most please you. "The Anglo-Saxon variety of truthfulness," she adds, "is not a Syrian characteristic"; but, "if truthfulness includes loyalty, ready self-denial to promote a cause that seems right, the Syrian is to that extent truthful." Quoting a Syrian's admission that his fellowmerchants pay their debts for their credit's sake, but will cheat the cus-tomer, she comments, "This, however, does not seem to be exclusively a Syrian vice." To such miserable paltering does a sickly sentimentality lead.

In southern Europe, team-work along all lines is limited by selfishness and bad faith. Professor Fairchild notes "the inveterate factionalism and commercial dishonesty so characteristic of the [Greek] race," "the old dis-honesty and inability to work together." "One of the maxims of Greek business life, translated into the American vernacular, is 'Put out the other fellow's eye.' "

Nothing less than verminous is the readiness of the southern Europeans to prey upon their fellows. Among our South Italians this spirit shines out only when it is a question of shielding from American justice some cut-throat of their own race. The Greek is full of tricks to skin the greenhorn. A grocer will warn fellow-countrymen who have just established them-selves in his town that he will have the police on them for violating munic-ipal ordinances unless they buy groceries from him. The Greek mill-hand sells the greenhorn a job, and takes his chances on the foreman giving the man work. A Greek who knows a little English will get a Greek peddler arrested in order that he may get the interpreter's fee.

The northerners seem to surpass the southern Europeans in innate ethical endowment. Comparison of their behavior in marine disasters shows that discipline, sense of duty, presence of mind, and consideration for the weak are much more characteristic of northern Europeans. The south-ern Europeans, on the other hand, are apt, in their terror, to forget disci-pline, duty, women, children, everything but the saving of their own lives. In shipwreck it is the exceptional northerner who forgets his duty, and the exceptional southerner who is bound by it.

Natural Ability

The performance of the foreign-born and their children after they have had access to American opportunities justifies the democrat's faith that latent capacity exists all through the humbler strata of society. On the other hand, it also confirms the aristocrat's insistence that social ranks correspond somewhat with the grades of natural ability existing within a people. The descendants of Europe's lowly are to be met in all the upper levels of American society, *but not so frequently* as the descendents of those who were high or rising in the land they left.

In respect to the value it contains, a stream of immigrants may be *representative, superrepresentative*, or *sub-representative* of the home people. When it is a fair sample, it is *representative*; when it is richer in wheat and poorer in chaff, it is *superrepresentative*; when the reverse is the case, it is *sub-representative*. What counts here, of course, is not the value the immigrants may have acquired by education or experience, but that fundamental worth which does not depend on opportunity, and which may be transmitted to one's descendants. Now, in the present state of our knowledge, it is perhaps risky to make a comparison in ability between the races which contributed the old immigration and those which are supplying the new immigration. Though backward, the latter may contain as good stuff. But it is fair to assume that a *super-representative* immigration from one stock is worth more to us than a *sub-representative* immigration from another stock, and that an influx which sub-represents a European people will thin the blood of the American people.

Only economic motives set in motion the sub-common people, but even in an economic emigration the early stage brings more people of initiative than the later. The deeper, straighter, and smoother the channels of migration, the lower the stratum they can tap.

It is not easy to value the early elements that were wrought into the American people. Often a stream of immigration that started with the best drained from the lower levels after it had worn itself a bed. It is therefore only in a broad way that I venture to classify the principal colonial migrations as follows:

Super-representative: English Pilgrims, Puritans, Quakers, Catholics, Seotch Covenanters, French Huguenots, German sectaries.
Representative: English of Virginia, Maryland, and the Carolinas, Scotch-Irish, Scotch Highlanders, Dutch, and Swedes.
Sub-representative: English of early Georgia, transported English, eighteenth-century Germans.

In our national period the Germans of 1848 stand out as a *super-representative* flow. The Irish stream has been *representative*, as was also the early German migration. The German inflow since 1870 has brought us very few of the élite of their people, and I have already given reasons for believing that the Scandinavian stream is not altogether *representative*. Our immigration from Great Britain has distinctly fallen off in grade since the chances in America came to be less attractive than those in the British Empire. However, no less an authority than Sir Richard Cartwright thinks that "between 1866 and 1896 one-third at least of the whole male population of Canada between the ages of twenty and forty found their way to the United States," and this "included an immense percentage of the most intelligent and adventurous."

The children of success are not migrating, which means that we get few scions from families of proved capacity. Europe retains most of her brains, but sends multitudes of the common and the sub-common. There is little sign of an intellectual element among the Magyars, Russians, South Slavs, Italians, Greeks, or Portuguese. This does not hold, however, for currents created by race discrimination or oppression. The Armenian, Syrian, Finnish, and Russo-Hebrew streams seem *representative*, and the first wave of Hebrews out of Russia in the eighties was superior. The Slovaks, German Poles, Lithuanians, Esthonians, and other restive subject groups probably send us a fair sample of their quality.

Race Suicide

The fewer brains they have to contribute, the lower the place immigrants take among us, and the lower the place they take, the faster they multiply. In 1890, in our cities, a thousand foreign-born women could show 565 children under five years of age to 309 children shown by a thousand native women. By 1900 the contribution of the foreign women had risen to 612, and that of the American women had declined to 296. From such figures some argue that the "sterile" Americans need the immigrants in order to supply population. It would be nearer the truth to argue that the competition of low-standard immigrants is the root cause of the mysterious "sterility" of Americans. Certainly their record down to 1830 proved the Americans to be as fertile a race as ever lived, and the decline in their fertility coincides in time and in locality with the advent of the immigrant flood. In the words of General Francis A. Walker, "Not only did the decline in the native element, as a whole, take place in singular correspondence with the excess of foreign arrivals, but it occurred chiefly in just those regions"—"in those States and in the very counties," he says elsewhere—"to which those new-comers most frequently resorted."

Peter Brimelow, "Time to Rethink Immigration?"

America is a nation of immigrants, yes—but so are all nations. The question is whether we have given up on turning our immigrants into Americans.

Asking the Right Questions

Is immigration really necessary to the economy?

"We need immigrants to meet the looming labor shortage/do the dirty work Americans won't do." This item from the pro-immigration catechism seems to be particularly resonant for the American conservative movement, deeply influenced by libertarian ideas and open, somewhat, to the concerns of business.

But it has always seemed incongruous, given persistent high levels of unemployment among some American-born groups. Since these groups obviously eat, it would appear that public policy is subsidizing their choosiness about work thus artificially stimulating the demand for immigrants.

And if there is a looming labor shortage (hotly disputed), it could presumably be countered by natalist policies—encouraging Americans to step up their below-replacement birthrate. Even the current high immigration inflow is exceeded by the 1.6 million abortions in the U.S. each year.

For example, the federal income-tax code could be adjusted to increase the child allowance. In 1950, this provision exempted the equivalent (in 1992 dollars) of $7,800 for each child now, after inflation, it exempts only $2,100. Or the "marriage penalty"—by which a couple pay more in taxes if they marry than if they live together out of wedlock—could be abolished. Or the public-school cartel could be broken up, reducing the crushing costs of educating a child.

Missing from the current immigration debate is the fact that this effect operates in the other direction too. On the margin, the economy is probably just as capable of getting along with less labor. Within quite wide boundaries, *any* change in the labor supply can be swamped by the much larger influence of innovation and technological change.

The historical importance of immigration to the U.S. can be exaggerated. Surprising as it may seem, demographers agree that the American population would be about half its present size—that is, much bigger than Germany's and about as big as Japan's—even if there had been no immigration after 1790. Even more significantly, the *Harvard Encyclopedia of American Ethnic Groups* estimates that immigration did not increase U.S. per-capita output at all. Indeed, both France and Germany outstripped the U.S. in growth of per-capita output in the hundred years after the mid-nineteenth century.

As it happens, the U.S. contains one particular group that is clearly vulnerable to competition from immigration; blacks. This question has attracted attention for years. Immigration from Europe after the Civil War is

sometimes said to have fatally retarded the economic integration of the
freed slaves. Conversely, no less an authority than economist Simon Kuznets
felt that the Great Immigration Lull after the 1920s enabled Southern blacks
to begin their historic migration to the cities and the economic opportunities of the North.

Blacks themselves take a dim view of immigration, according to opinion
polls. Eighty-three percent of blacks thought Congress should curb immigration. But economist George Borjas found that blacks living in areas of
immigrant concentration did not appear to have suffered significantly
reduced incomes compared with those elsewhere. The reason, he theorizes,
is that during the years in question—the 1970s—the effect of immigration
was overwhelmed by the effects of baby-boomers and women entering the
labor market. Now, of course, these factors no longer apply. Additionally,
studies of high-immigrant areas may fail to capture a tendency for native-
born workers to relocate because of the increased competition. Across the
entire country, the wages of native high-school dropouts fell by 10 percent
in the 1980s relative to the wages of more educated workers. Borjas calcu-
lates that about a third of that decline is attributable to immigration.

Borjas, moreover, was perturbed by the tendency of low-skilled recent
immigrants, not necessarily to displace American blacks, but to join them in
swelling the ranks of the underclass: "Few issues facing the U.S. are as
important, and as difficult to resolve, as the persistent problem of poverty in
our midst . . . The empirical evidence presented here suggests that immigration is exacerbating this problem."

Since [1960], a significant part of the black community has succumbed to
social pathology. There is at least a possibility that this is related to the simultaneous opening of the immigration floodgates. In which case, it is perhaps
to current policy, and not to critics of immigration, that the over-used
epithet "racist" might best be applied.

Another important Simon qualification, unnoticed by his acolytes, is his
concept of "negative human-capital externalities." Most recent immigrants
have lower skill levels than natives, he notes. If enough of them were to
arrive, they could overwhelm and render less effective the higher skills of
the natives. "In other words, if there is a huge flood of immigrants
from Backwardia to Richonia. Richonia will become economically similar
to Backwardia, with loss to Richonians and little gain to immigrants from
Backwardia . . . So even if *some* immigrants are beneficial, a *very large* number coming from poorer countries . . . may have the opposite effect."

This is a crucial theoretical concession. Coupled with the fact that the
numbers and type of potential immigrants are unknown, it is the reason
Simon quietly declines to follow the logic of his other arguments and
endorse completely open borders (as, for example, the *Wall Street Journal*
editorial page has done). Of course, he insists that immigration levels could
be *much* higher than at present. But Richonians in California, Florida, and
New York City might not agree.

"*You have to accept the free movement of people if you believe in free trade/free
markets.*" You do? It's a more radical proposition than appears at first sight.

Third World populations are very large and their wage levels very low—
Mexican wages are a tenth of those north of the border, and Mexico is relatively advanced. So calculations of the market-clearing wage in a U.S. with
open borders necessarily imply that it must be some fraction of its present
level. This arrangement might optimize global economic utility. But it can
hardly improve American social harmony.

However, a calculation of this sort requires impossible assumptions. The
fact is that a belief in free markets does not commit you to free immigration. The two are quite distinct. Even [economist] Julian Simon, although
he favors immigration, says explicitly that immigration's benefits are not
from "trade-like effects":

> Contrary to intuition, the theory of the international trade of goods is
> quite inapplicable to the international movement of persons. There is
> no immediate large consumer benefit from the movement of persons
> that is analogous to the international exchange of goods, because the
> structure of supply is not changed in the two countries as a whole, as
> it is when trade induces specialization in production . . . the shifts due
> to international migration benefit only the migrant.

On a practical level, free trade actually tends to operate as a substitute
for immigration. Hence the Japanese have factories in the Philippines
rather than Filipinos in Japan. And Victorian Britain, with its grand strategy
of "splendid isolation" from the quarrels of Europe, combined total free
trade with almost no immigration, a policy that satisfied Liberal "Little
Englanders" and Tory Imperialists alike.

In theory, free trade with Mexico should help reduce the current
immigrant flood by providing work south of the border. In practice, however, "free-trade negotiations" (a paradox: what's to negotiate?) often get
captured by political elites seeking to favor client constituencies. Rumors
that the current talks with Mexico might lead, absurdly, to an *increase* in
immigration suggest this insidious process is well under way.

Put it another way for the U.S., immigration is not an economic necessity. It is a luxury. Like all luxuries, it can help—or it can hurt.

Is immigration really beneficial to society?

Forty-four years ago, Richard Weaver published a book the title of which, at
least convinced the conservative movement: *Ideas Have Consequences*. It is
now time to recognize a further truth: *Immigration Has Consequences*.

The crudest consequences relate to political power. Because many liber-
tarians and economic-growth conservatives are so reluctant to admit this
logical possibility, it is worth emphasizing that there are plenty of examples
of immigrants and their descendants threatening the political balance of a
state (polity), from the *Uitlanders* in the nineteenth-century Boer Republics
to the Indian politicians recently elected to govern Fiji and promptly

deposed by the ethnically Fijian army. And how about this chilling comment from the *Harvard Encyclopedia?*

> In obtaining land grants in Texas, Anglo immigrants agreed to become Mexican citizens, obey Mexican laws, accept the official Catholic faith, learn Spanish, and take other steps to become fully assimilated as law-abiding citizens. However, over the years, it became clear that these settlers, now Anglo-Mexicans, were not becoming integrated into the nation and that Anglo immigration had become a problem . . . The strains and disagreements ultimately led to the Texas Revolution in 1835.

Er, quite.

These political consequences need not threaten the integrity of the state (polity)—just its foreign policy. Thus domestic ethnic-group pressure clearly plays a role in Washington's essentially contradictory attitudes to the white settler communities of southern Africa and the Middle East.

But probably the most important consequences are cultural. "The most obvious fact about the history of racial and ethnic groups," writes Thomas Sowell in *The Economics and Politics of Race*, "is how different they have been—and still are." Sowell's work, carried on in *Ethnic America: A History*, conclusively demonstrates that cultural patterns are pervasive, powerful, and remarkably persistent, even after generations of living under common institutions, as in the United States. (Similarly, David Hackett Fischer's monumental *Albion's Seed* recently traced America's dominant folkways all the way back to four distinct waves of colonial immigration from different regions of Britain.)

"But aren't these consequences good?" Naturally, there isn't anything in the pro-immigration script about cultural consequences. However, this is the usual reaction if you insist on raising the point. It's embarrassing, of course. In the current climate, it is impossible to discuss the failings of any ethnic group.

But look at it this way: Thomas Sowell's work shows that cultural traits, such as attitudes to work and education, are intrinsically related to economic success. Germans, Japanese, and Jews are successful wherever they are in the world. Conversely, the work of George Borjas and others shows that national origin, a proxy for culture, is an excellent predictor of economic failure, as measured by propensity to go on welfare. In a recent paper, Borjas has demonstrated that disparities among the 1880-to-1920 immigrant groups have persisted for as much as four generations. Thus there can be absolutely no question that the cultural characteristics of current immigrant groups will have consequences for the U.S.—in this case, economic consequences—far into the future.

The same argument applies to crime. Random street crime, the great scandal of American cities since the 1960s, is clearly related to impulsiveness and present-orientation, a key cultural variable. More significant, however, is organized crime. This has typically been ethnically based, partly because it reduces the criminals' transaction costs and because such groups are difficult to penetrate.

In recent years the Mafia or *Cosa Nostra* has been in decline, not least because of the acculturation of Italian-Americans. But this is "dirty work" that some of the post–1965 immigrant groups are positively anxious to do—more violently, particularly in the burgeoning drug business, than the Mafia ever was. There are several such new "mafias," staffed by Russian Jews, Hong Kong Chinese, Colombians, and even less well-known communities like the Chaldeans—Iraqi Christians whose convenience stores in the Detroit ghetto are centers of criminal activity.

Today such news would be judged unfit to print regardless of its accuracy. Researchers find that official figures on immigrant and ethnic crime patterns are rarely collected. That certain ethnic cultures are more crime-prone than others, however, must be considered a real possibility.

Curiously, Congress appears to have shaken off its general paralysis to recognize that immigration can have cultural consequences—for Pacific Islanders. Five U.S. territories, American Samoa, Micronesia, the Marshall Islands, the Northern Marianas, and Palau, have been given control over immigration to protect their ethnic majorities. In American Samoa and the Northern Marianas, U.S. citizens cannot even own land unless they are Samoan, Chamorro, or Carolinian.

This double standard has incensed an extremely erudite and energetic professional writer in Rye, New York, Joseph E. Fallon. Fallon argues that controlling immigration is simply a question of American self-determination. And he is attempting to organize a class-action law suit challenging current policy on the grounds of the 1948 Genocide Convention, which banned "deliberately, inflicting upon a [national] group conditions of life calculated to bring about its physical destruction in whole or in part."

Is immigration really good for the environment?

American liberalism has survived the loss of its traditional issue, economic management, by improvising new ones. And environmentalism is one of the most important, both because it particularly appeals to the vocal upper middle class and because it appears to necessitate an interventionist government. Yet the single biggest problem for the environment is the fact that the U.S. population, quite unusually in the developed world, is still growing quickly. Immigration is currently an unusually large factor in U.S. population growth.

Like the impact of immigration on native workers, the relationship between population and pollution is subtler than it looks. A primitive band of slash-and-burn agriculturalists can cause more devastation than a much larger community of modern ex-urbanites with sealed sewage systems and manicured horse farms.

But only within limits. Something has clearly got to give if the population of California grows from 20 million in 1970 to 60 million by 2020, which is [demographer] Leon Bouvier's upper-limit projection. (His lower-limit projection: a mere 44 million. Phooey!) The fragile desert ecologies of the southwest may not be utterly destroyed. But they must be transformed. California will cease to be the Golden State and become the Golden Subdivision.

This prospect is presumably anathema to true environmentalists, who value wilderness in itself. But although a few were active in founding FAIR, most of the professional environmentalist community in Washington avoid the issue. Which is a measure of the extent to which they have been co-opted by the liberal establishment—just like the civil-rights lobby, which never voices the anti-immigration sentiments widespread among the black masses.

No reason, however, why conservatives should not use the immigration issue to wrong-foot them all.

Is the U.S. still culturally capable of absorbing immigrants?

Let's be clear about this: The American experience with immigration has been a triumphant success. It has so far transcended anything seen in Europe as to make the application of European lessons an exercise to be performed with care.

But in the late twentieth century, the economic and political culture of the U.S. has changed significantly—from classical liberalism to an interventionist welfare statism. In the previous two hundred years of U.S. history, a number of tried-and-true, but undeniably tough techniques of assimilation had been perfected. Today, they have been substantially abandoned. Earlier waves of immigrants were basically free to succeed or fail. And many failed: as much as a third of the 1880-to-1920 immigrants returned to their native lands. But with the current wave, public policy interposes itself, with the usual debatable results.

"*You can't blame the immigrants for our bad policies.*" Of course you can't. But if there's a shower when you've got pneumonia, you don't blame the rain. You just stay indoors.

Some of public subsidies to immigrants are direct, like welfare. Others are indirect, such as the wholly new idea that immigrant children should be taught in their own language, thus transferring part of the costs of immigration from the immigrant to the American taxpayer. New York's public-school system now offers courses in more than a hundred languages—and is hunting for teachers of Albanian who will probably themselves be immigrants.

Pro-immigration advocates are fighting furiously to defend the proposition that subsidies to immigrants are not a net cost to native-born Americans because of the taxes immigrants pay. But they are clearly losing.

George Borjas's most recent estimate is that immigrants' cash welfare benefits alone cost about $1 billion more than is paid in taxes each year. (Tellingly, immigrants prone to welfare dependency seem to get more addicted as they assimilate.) And he points out that there is no guarantee that any increase in total economic output from immigration will compensate those specific Americans paying taxes in high-immigrant areas.

Whatever the academic argument, Wall Street in its unideological, money-grubbing way is already pulling back its snout. As the investment firm Sanford C. Bernstein commented tersely in downgrading California's bond rating last year. "The primary reasons for the State's credit decline are above-average population growth and shifting demographics . . . the degree of public assistance required by two of the fastest growing groups, Latinos and political/ethnic refugees, is substantially higher than that of the general population." Governor Pete Wilson has been trying to control welfare and get more remedial federal aid. But he has only himself to blame. As a U.S. senator, he worked hard for the 1986 amnesty for illegal immigrants favored by agricultural interests.

Ultimately, however, any overall break-even calculation is irrelevant. The nature of averages dictates that many immigrants must get more than they give. And any public subsidies must affect whatever demand/supply balance exists for immigrants. A year for one student in the New York City public-school system, for example, involves an average taxpayer expenditure greater than the per-capita national income of Haiti. National health care, if enacted, could be an even greater magnet.

And it's not just the American economic culture that has changed. So has the political culture. Ethnically fueled "multiculturalism" taught in the public schools, as described by [journalist] Lawrence Auster and by the eminently establishmentarian [historian] Arthur Schlesinger in his current best-seller *The Disuniting of America*, raises the question of whether there is still an "American Idea"—and if so, what is it?

Actually, the outlines of what might be described as the new American Anti-Idea are already appallingly clear. It's a sort of neosocialism, derived from what Thomas Sowell calls "the Civil Rights Vision" and amounting to a sort of racial spoils system. Government power is used not to achieve economic efficiency, which traditional socialism can no longer promise, but ethnic equity—most importantly, the extirpation of "discrimination."

That's private discrimination, of course. Government-sponsored discrimination is not merely acceptable but mandatory, in the form of "affirmative action" quotas. "Quotas were originally supposed to be remedial," says Professor Frederick R. Lynch of Claremont College, author of *Invisible Victims: White Males and the Crisis of Affirmative Action*. "Now they are being justified by affirmative-action professionals as a way of 'managing diversity.' " That "diversity," needless to say, is being substantially introduced into the U.S. by current immigration policy.

Indeed, absurd as it may appear, all brand-new immigrants from the right "protected class"—black, Hispanic, Asian—count toward government quota requirements that were allegedly imposed to help native-born Americans. Hence a number of the African PhDs teaching at American colleges. The 1986 Immigration Act prohibited discrimination against legalized "undocu-mented" aliens and set up an office in the Justice Department to enforce this new law.

Symptomatic of the American Anti-Idea is the emergence of a strange anti-nation inside the U.S.—the so-called "Hispanics." The various groups of Spanish-speaking immigrants are now much less encouraged to assimilate to American culture. Instead, as a result of ethnic lobbying in Washington, they are treated by U.S. government agencies as a homogeneous "protected class," even though many of them have little in common with one another. (Indeed, some are Indian-language speakers from Latin America.) And they have been supplied with "leaders" financed to a significant extent by the Ford Foundation.

In effect, Spanish-speakers are still being encouraged to assimilate. But not to America.

Many current public policies have an unmistakable tendency to deconstruct the American nation. Apart from official bilingualism and multiculturalism, these policies include: multilingual ballots; defining citizenship so as to include all children born here—even the children of illegals; the abandonment of English as a prerequisite for citizenship; the erosion of citizenship as the sole qualification for voting; the extension of welfare and education benefits as a right to illegals and their children; congressional and state legislative apportionment based on legal and illegal populations.

End of an Era

NEXT YEAR will see the hundredth anniversary of Frederick Jackson Turner's famous lecture on "The Significance of the Frontier in American History." The Superintendent of the Census had just announced that there was no longer a continuous line of free, unsettled land visible on the American map. Closing with the frontier, said Turner, was "the first period of American history." A century later, it may be time to close the second period of American history with the announcement that the U.S. is no longer an "immigrant country."

Because just as the American nation was made with unusual speed, so it is perfectly possible that it could be unmade. On speeded-up film, the great cloud formations boil up so that they dominate the sky. But they also unravel and melt away.

And why do I, an immigrant, care? For one reason, I am the father of a nine-month-old-American, Alexander James Frank. He seems to like it here. A second reason: just as Voltaire said in the eighteenth century that every man has two countries, his own and France, so in this century no civilized person can be indifferent to the fate of America.

CHAPTER SEVEN

Becoming White: Irish Immigrants in the Nineteenth Century

Introduction

The rise of ethnic groups out of successive waves of immigration in the nineteenth and twentieth centuries has not been the only or even the major source of social differentiation and at times fragmentation in American history. An even older source is race, which has been a most significant and abiding force in the structuring of society, politics, and economics and in the forming of American self-understanding since the beginnings of European settlement in North America. In sharp contrast to the voluntary immigrations that brought millions of Europeans to these shores, Africans, Native Americans, and Mexicans were incorporated into the population by force, through enslavement and conquest. Race has also been a factor in immigration itself. In a variety of ways specific to different groups, until well into the twentieth century, American law has restricted the entrance of Africans, Asians, and other non-European peoples into the United States and has limited opportunities for citizenship among those non-white immigrants.

Yet for much of American history, race was never as clear-cut as the stark dichotomy of white versus non-white. As a number of analysts have pointed out in recent years, understandings of *race* as a concept applied to categorize and thus give privilege to or penalize individuals and groups have hardly been stable. Until well into the twentieth century, the word "race" was often

David. R. Roediger, "Irish-American Workers and White Racial Formation in the Antebellum United States" in *The Wages of Whiteness: Race and the Making of the American Working Class* (New York: Verso, 1991), pp. 133–144. Copyright © by David R. Roediger, 1991. Reprinted by permission of Verso.

"A Riot in Philadelphia. Conflicts between whites and blacks" in *Niles National Register*, August 6, 1842. Public Domain.

Frederick Douglass, "Colored Americans and Aliens—T.F. Meagher" in Frederick Douglass' Paper, September 14, 1855. Public domain.

Stephen A. Douglas [Speech at Jonesboro, Illinois], *Political Debates between Abraham Lincoln and Stephen A. Douglas in the Celebrated Campaign of 1858 in Illinois, including the Preceding Speeches of each at Chicago, Springfield, etc.* (Cleveland: Burrows Brothers Company, 1894), pp. 140–141. Public domain.

used to conceptualize what we might call *ethnicity*, so that immigrant peoples, such as the Irish or Jews or Italians and others, were often spoken of as races. When newly arrived and unacculturated, of course, such peoples looked and acted differently than native-stock white Americans, and these differences were often attributed to inner dispositions that were ultimately biological—in other words, racial—in nature. The status of these peoples, who have become completely and unquestioningly "white" by contemporary standards, was never as marginalized as that of African Americans or Asian Americans, and they were not subject to persistent, harsh discrimination. They were, in the formulation of Matthew Frye Jacobson in his influential book, *Whiteness of A Different Color: European Immigrants and the Alchemy of Race* (1998), considered, at best, "provisional" white people. Many Americans, including the descendants of previous waves of European immigrants, doubted whether they could ever be fully assimilated into American life.

One implication of this perhaps surprising history is that we have to recover the history of the process by which such racially marginalized European immigrant peoples actually became white. The wide variety of selections in this chapter develop mid-nineteenth century Irish immigrants as a case study of this process of what has been called *racialization*, which is the categorization of a group in racial terms. In this instance, though the process is certainly uneven, the Irish were first categorized as a sort of racial *other*, neither white nor black. They were often considered similar to African Americans in possessing traits that made them obnoxious to Americans, and which appeared to limit the likelihood that they might be incorporated into American society. Impoverished, possessing few skills that they could use to rapidly improve their position in society, and subject to harsh prejudices and social and economic discrimination, Irish immigrants in northern cities, such as New York and Philadelphia, often lived among free African Americans, whose social situation was similar. The relations between the two peoples were sometimes characterized by recognition of their common humanity and dreadful circumstances and by cooperation, but those relations were also, and more frequently, characterized by competition, and intense and even violent conflict. Gradually, however, through a distribution of political power and economic opportunity that greatly favored the Irish, the interests of the two peoples were separated. The Irish had begun to be admitted into the ranks of American white people, with the psychological and practical privileges that came with being white.

In the first selection, historian David R. Roediger surveys the conceptualization of mid-nineteenth century Irish immigrants as non-whites, the relations between Irish immigrants and African Americans, and the ways in which politics—and principally competition for the votes of those Irish who became citizens and voters—functioned to speed the process by which the Irish came to be regarded as white people.

The other selections are documents of various types from the mid-nineteenth century. A group of political cartoons from the nineteenth century illustrates the racialization of the Irish and the cultural stereotypes about

Figure 7.1 "An Irish Jig," by the cartoonist James A. Wales shows a wild and violent Irishman, who has grown fat on the generosity of Great Britain and the United States. John Bull and Uncle Sam, personifications of Great Britain and of the United States, seem to be discussing how they might tame this Irishman. In rolling up his sleeves, John Bull suggests he is getting ready to begin this task. (*Puck*, volume 8, number 191, November 3, 1880, 150.)

them that prevailed at the time (figure 7.1). The Irish were widely portrayed as possessing nonhuman, apelike facial features, which made them, in effect, lighter complexioned versions of the apelike African Americans who appeared in similar cartoons during the same years. The Irish were also portrayed as violent, drunken, and content to live under filthy and disorderly

Figure 7.2   "The King of A-Shantee" by Frederick B. Opper shows an Irish couple in their homeland habitat, a tumbledown shanty. The poorest of the Irish immigrants were called "shanty Irish." But the title is revealing also of the connection often made between the Irish and African Americans. "Ashanti" is an ancient West African kingdom. Here, we see the Irish portrayed with apelike features that make them seem primitive, and not unlike Africans, who were often portrayed in cartoons in similar ways. (*Puck*, volume 10, number 258, February 15, 1882, 378.)

circumstances (figure 7.2). Next we have an article from a prominent nineteenth-century newspaper that narrates the circumstances of a very destructive and bloody riot that took place in Philadelphia in 1842, in which large numbers of white working-class men attacked African Americans and destroyed African American homes and institutions.

The Irish were not the only members of the white mob, and indeed there is only a vague reference to their presence in the violent white mobs. But, as was also the case in a similar riot in Philadelphia in 1834, according to historians who have investigated these two riots and other, similar race riots in northern cities, the Irish were very prominent among the participants (figure 7.3). The 1842 riot took place toward the end of a severe economic depression, which had brought significant unemployment to skilled crafts-men and unskilled laborers. Deepening the lack of employment was the fact that immigration had continued during hard times, so there was an even greater surplus of labor desperate for work. African American dock-workers, however, continued to be employed. The mob actions along the wharf that were apparently led by Irishmen the morning after the riots began were intended to drive the employed black dockworkers out of employment and off the shipping docks. In fact, the mob was bent, as the end of the article makes clear, on driving the blacks out of Philadelphia completely, which was one way of taking over what few opportunities for employment that the blacks enjoyed. It has been noted in a number of stud-ies that northern urban African Americans were being cut out of many working-class opportunities at the time, whether through violent intimida-tion or the racial prejudice of employers and workers. These opportunities

Figure 7.3   "The Day We Celebrate" by Thomas Nast, the most eminent on nineteenth century polit-ical cartoonists, depicts a riot that took place along the route of the St. Patrick's Day Parade in New York City in 1867. The riot began when the driver of a wagon mistakenly got in the way of the marchers, and was attacked. The police then intervened, and attacked the marchers, who, in turn, fought back. Young and old alike, the Irish depicted here are truly horrifying. Apelike, drunk and armed with clubs and pikes, they let loose murderous violence on the police, whom they greatly outnumber. (*Harper's Weekly*, April 6, 1867, 1.)

Figure 7.4 "The Ignorant Vote: Honors Are Easy," by Thomas Nast, a cartoon out of the era of Reconstruction after the Civil War, when the millions of emancipated slaves in the South were being accorded political rights for the first time. Many higher status Americans believed that voting was a privilege which should be available only to people like themselves—educated, conventionally respectable, and prosperous. Under the circumstances, they were deeply troubled by the prospect of masses of both southern blacks and northern Irish immigrants obtaining significant political power. On the other hand, the cartoon suggests that the two large voting groups might cancel one another out, since the Irish were almost as solidly Democrats as African Americans were Republicans. There should be no doubt about the identity of the "white" voter. His apelike features mark him as Irish, as does the peasant hat, which was also a marker of Irishness for nineteenth century cartoonists. (*Harper's Weekly*, December 9, 1876, 1.)

were then given to whites, and especially low-wage immigrant, and very largely Irish, workers. In this way, the Irish came to share in the privileges of being white. It was an especially bitter irony that their participation in anti-black mob actions alongside white American workingmen helped mark their acceptance, at their social class level, into American life. Hating African Americans was in that sense one way of asserting one's (white) *American* identity.

The next two selections also provide evidence of the increasing separation of the interests of Irish immigrants and African Americans. The first is the bitter reflection in 1855 of Frederick Douglass, the renowned African American abolitionist and social reform advocate, on the extent to which Irish immigrants were able to obtain political power and an equal civil status to that enjoyed by native-born white Americans. Indeed, the Irish possessed enough political power in New York State to be significant in the ranks of those who voted continually to deny blacks the right to vote, when the question of equal suffrage for blacks was presented to the voters for approval (figure 7.4). With the bitter irony that often characterized his writing, Douglass observes that anti-immigrant American nativists, who were known as "Know Nothings," were at the time working to limit the political rights of the Irish, whom they especially loathed, while the Irish themselves were working to curb the rights of blacks. The final selection, taken from the famed debates between Abraham Lincoln, a Republican, and Stephen Douglas, a Democrat, when both men were candidates for a U.S. Senate seat in Illinois in 1858, presents us with an extended version of remarks by Douglas quoted by Roediger. To an audience at Jonesboro, Illinois, Douglas makes clear his belief that the privileges of American citizenship were never intended for anyone but "white men, men of European birth and European ancestry," which would have to include recent European immigrants, such as the often despised Irish. Doubtless, Douglas believed this, but it is also true that it pleased recent immigrants, most of whom voted Democratic—and no group was more Democrat than the Irish. For his part, Lincoln did not completely disagree. Several days later, in another debate with Douglas at Charlestown, he merely held out the possibility that blacks might attain a political status which, while not equal to that of whites, would allow them certain rights with which to protect what liberties they were able to enjoy. He, too, accepted the idea that even the lowliest recent immigrant, reviled in some quarters as bestial, violent, and inferior by an inborn disposition, was entitled to political rights that native-born American black should be denied.

Suggestions for Further Reading

David R. Roediger, *Working Toward Whiteness: How America's Immigrants Become White, The Strange Journey from Ellis Island to the Suburbs* (New York: Basic Books, 2005).

Ian Haney Lopez, *White by Law: The Legal Construction of Race* (New York: New York University Press, 1996).

Jennifer Guglielmo and Salvatore Salerno, *Are Italians White?: How Race Is Made in America* (New York: Routledge, 2003).

Karen Brodkin, *How the Jews Became White People and What That Says about Race in America* (New York: Routledge, 1998).

Matthew Jacobson, *Whiteness of A Different Color: European Immigrants and the Alchemy of Race* (Cambridge: Harvard University Press, 1998).

Noel Ignatiev, *How the Irish Became White* (New York: Routledge, 1995).

David R. Roediger, "Irish-American Workers and White Racial Formation in the Antebellum United States"

Low-browed and *savage, grovelling* and *bestial, lazy* and *wild, simian* and *sensual*—such were the adjectives used by many native-born Americans to describe the Catholic Irish "race" in the years before the Civil War. The striking similarity of this litany of insults to the list of traits ascribed to Blacks hardly requires comment. Sometimes Black/Irish connections were made explicitly. In antebellum Philadelphia, according to one account, "to be called an 'Irishman' had come to be nearly as great an insult as to be called a 'nigger.' " George Templeton Strong, a patrician diarist living in New York City, considered Irish workmen at his home to have had "pre-hensile paws" rather than hands. He denounced the "Celtic beast," while maintaining that "Southern Cuffee seems of a higher social grade than Northern Paddy." Nativist folk wisdom held that an Irishman was a "nigger," inside out. But by no means did nativists, who more typically developed a "moral" rather than a "racial" critique of the Irish, corner the market on calling the whiteness of the Irish into question. A variety of writers, particularly ethnologists, praised Anglo-Saxon virtues as the bedrock of liberty and derided the "Celtic race." Some suggested that the Irish were part of a separate caste or a "dark" race, possibly originally African. Racial comparisons of Irish and Blacks were not infrequently flattering to the latter group. The Census Bureau regularly collected statistics on the nation's "native" and "foreign" populations, but kept the Irish distinct from even the latter group. Political cartoonists played on the racial ambiguity of the Irish by making their stock "Paddy" character resemble nothing so much as an ape. In short, it was by no means clear that the Irish were white.

There were good reasons—environmental and historical, not biological—for comparing African Americans and the Irish. The two groups often lived side by side in the teeming slums of American cities of the 1830s. They both did America's hard work, especially in domestic service and the transportation industry. Both groups were poor and often vilified. Both had experienced oppression and been wrenched from a homeland. Many Northern free Blacks who lived alongside Irish-Americans not only knew that their families had been torn from Africa by the slave trade but had also themselves experienced the profound loneliness, mixed with joy, that Frederick Douglass described as the result of escaping North from slavery, leaving loved ones behind. Longing thus characterized both the Northern Black and Irish-American populations, and members of neither group were likely to return home again. When Douglass toured Ireland during the famine of 1845–46 he heard in the "wailing notes" of Irish songs echoes of the "wild notes" of the sorrowful songs he had heard in slavery and was "much affected." In 1829, Blacks and Irish were the co-victims of a Boston "race" riot.

Shared oppression need not generate solidarity but neither must it necessarily breed contempt of one oppressed group for the other. For some time there were strong signs that the Irish might not fully embrace white supremacy. In cities like Worcester and Philadelphia, Blacks and Irish lived near each other without significant friction into the early 1830s. They often celebrated and socialized together, swapping musical traditions and dance steps. Even as late as the immediate post–Civil War years Lafcadio Hearn described Black and Irish levee workers in Cincinnati as sharing a store-house of jokes and tales, of jigs and reels and even of dialect words and phrases. Love and sex between Black men and Irish women were not uncommon. In the 1834 anti-Black, antiabolitionist New York City riots, Irish militiamen helped to restore order. Indeed, the antiabolition riots of the 1830s generally drew little Irish participation.

Most promisingly, abolitionists noted little popular racism, and much sympathy for the plight of the slave, in Ireland. In 1842, 70,000 Irish in Ireland signed an antislavery address and petition, which called on Irish-Americans to "*cling by the abolitionists*" in seeking not just the end of slavery but of racial discrimination as well. The address advised: "Irishmen and Irishwomen! treat the colored people as your equals, as brethren." Though much abolition agitation in Ireland was initiated by the Dublin Quakers, the most celebrated Irish abolitionist was Daniel O'Connell, who also led the massive Repeal campaign for Irish freedom through an end to union with Britain. Called "The Liberator," O'Connell sponsored the 1842 petition knowing that his words would alienate some Irish-Americans and cut financial contributions to the Repeal struggle. Nonetheless, the very firmness of the politically sophisticated O'Connell's stance on Irish America and abolition suggests that he was optimistic that many in the US would ultimately stand with him. Another of Ireland's greatest mass leaders, the temperance organizer Father Theobald Mathew, joined O'Connell in sponsoring the petition drive. Men who knew a great deal about how to move large numbers of Irish people believed it quite possible that Irish-Americans, whom O'Connell saw as having much in common with all colonized people, might become critics of white supremacy.

The radical abolitionist followers of William Lloyd Garrison—including two of the Garrisonians most concerned with the white working class, Wendell Phillips and John A. Collins—busily organized for unity between the supporters of the "repeal" of British colonialism and the "repeal" of American slavery. The Garrisonians could claim a strong record of supporting Irish nationalism and rebuking American nativism, and their campaign began auspiciously when an overflow crowd of more than five thousand packed Boston's Faneuil Hall to receive the petition and to pass resolutions for Black and Irish freedom.

But it quickly became apparent that the Irish "peasants" who heartily applauded at Faneuil Hall were atypical of Irish-American opinion on slavery and race. The meeting had hardly occurred when a mob of Philadelphia Irish attacked Blacks gathering to celebrate West Indian emancipation—a cause dear to O'Connell—near the hall from which Blacks promoted temperance, Father Mathew's passion. By 1843, the British Owenite traveller John Finch would report to London readers the "curious fact" that "the democratic party and particularly the poorer class of Irish emigrants, are greater enemies to the negro population . . . than any portion of the population in the free states."

O'Connell's pleas and threats achieved nothing. Irish-American and Catholic newspapers, some of which had originally argued that the petition and address were fakes, soon began to attack O'Connell. They portrayed him as at best misinformed and at worst a meddler who associated with religious skeptics who threatened the unity of the United States. Irish-American contributions to the Repeal campaign were jeopardized, but O'Connell refused to move from his outspoken abolitionism, though he did distance himself somewhat from the religious unorthodoxy of some of the Garrisonians. Even O'Connell's pointed threat to read proslavery Irish-Americans out of the nationalist struggle failed to rally his erstwhile followers to the banner of abolition. "Dare countenance the system of slavery," he warned, and "we will recognize you as Irishmen no more."

But Irish-Americans had already made their reply: they had refused to recognize O'Connell. An important and typical Irish-American answer to O'Connell, written by miners in New York, answered his call with a sharp denial that Blacks were "brethren" of Irish-Americans and an unequivocal statement of their loyalty as Americans who were full "CITIZENS of this great and glorious republic." The statement condemned O'Connell's address as the interference of an outsider, and declared that no cooperation with abolitionists would be forthcoming. From 1843 until 1854, Garrisonians and O'Connell's followers separately pushed unsuccessfully against the "proslavery" position of Irish-Americans. They failed, succeeding only in weakening Repeal forces in both Ireland and the United States. When Father Mathew toured America in 1849, he rejected any cooperation with abolitionists, contenting himself with fighting "slavery" to alcohol.

Nor did the tremendous influx of desperate Irish emigrants fleeing the results of famine after 1845 produce significant amelioration in Irish-American attitudes toward Blacks. If the emigrants had antislavery and antiracist convictions in Ireland—and even there abolition fell on hard times after O'Connell's death in 1847—they did not express those convictions in the New World. Irish-Americans instead treasured their whiteness, as entitling them to both political rights and to jobs. They solidly voted for proslavery Democrats and opposed abolition as "niggerology." Astonishingly, for a group that easily furnished more immigrants to the United States than any other between 1828 and 1854, the Irish in New York City reportedly went to the polls in 1850 shouting not only "Down with the Nagurs!" but also "Let them go back to Africa, where they belong." Similarly, Irish immigrants became leaders of anti-Chinese forces in California. Even before taking a leading role in the unprecedentedly murderous attacks on Blacks during the 1863 Draft Riot in New York City, Irishmen had developed a terrible record of mobbing free Blacks on and off the job—so much so that Blacks called the brickbats often hurled at them "Irish confetti." In 1865 the British worker James D. Burn observed, "As a general rule, the people in the North have a lively feeling of dislike to men of colour, but it is in the Irish residents that they have, and will continue to have, their most formidable enemies: between these two races there can exist no bond of union except such as exists between the hind [deer] and the panther."

Having refused to take the path that O'Connell had charted, Irish-Americans went far in the other direction. Instead of seeing their struggles as bound up with those of colonized and colored people around the world, they came to see their struggles as against such people. Frederick Douglass, the Black abolitionist whose own quest for freedom had been substantially aided by the advice of a "good Irishman" on Baltimore's wharves in the 1830s, could only wonder "why a people who so nobly loved and cherished the thought of liberty at home in Ireland could become, willingly, the oppressors of another race here." Or again he asked how a people "so relentlessly persecuted and oppressed on account of race and religion" could take the lead among Americans in carrying "prejudice against color to a point . . . extreme and dangerous."

The making of the Irish worker into a white worker was thus a two-sided process. On the one hand, much to the chagrin of George Templeton Strong, Irish immigrants won acceptance as whites among the larger American population. On the other hand, the Irish themselves came to insist on their own whiteness and on white supremacy. The success of the Irish in being recognized as white resulted largely from the political power of Irish and other immigrant voters. The imperative to define themselves as white came from the particular "public and psychological wages" whiteness offered to a desperate rural and often preindustrial Irish population coming to labor in industrializing American cities.

Irish Votes, Democratic Votes and White Votes

Coming into American society at or near the bottom, the Catholic Irish sorely needed allies, even protectors. They quickly found them in two institutions that did not question their whiteness: the Catholic Church and the Democratic party. Although the former proved more open to promoting Irishmen to positions of power—most bishops in the United States were Irish by the 1850s—the Democratic party was far more powerful as a national institution and more consistently proslavery and white supremacist in its outlook. The church did reflect the racial attitudes of its members, with Kentucky Catholic newspapers carrying advertisements for the return of runaway slaves. New York church publications hinted at, and then spelled out, the view that the "negro is what the creator made him—not a rudimentary Caucasian, not a human in the process of development but a negro." The official Catholic paper in New York City meanwhile advised that emancipated slaves moving North be "driven out, imprisoned or exterminated." However, these strong and unpalatable Catholic stances, which existed alongside softer calls for amelioration of the slave's plight, at most reproduced existing white supremacist attitudes without challenging them. The Democratic party did more.

Jean Baker, a leading historian of the Democrats between the Age of Jackson and the Civil War, has acutely observed that the Democratic party reinvented whiteness in a manner that "refurbished their party's traditional links to the People and offered political democracy and an inclusive patriotism to white male Americans." This sense of white unity and white entitlement—of white "blood"—served to bind together the Democratic slaveholders and the masses of nonslaveholding whites in the South. It further connected the Southern and Northern wings of the Democracy. But less noticed by scholars has been the way in which an emphasis on a common whiteness smoothed over divisions in the Democratic ranks within mainly Northern cities by emphasizing that immigrants from Europe, and particularly from Ireland, were white and thus unequivocally entitled to equal rights. In areas with virtually no Black voters, the Democrats created a "white vote."

From the earliest days of the American republic, Irish immigration to the United States had caused political division. The "wild Irish," a term that invoked images of both "semi-savage" Catholics and political rebels who were sometimes Protestants, excited particular concern among conservative Federalist politicians. Defense of immigration by the Jeffersonian Democrats helped to create a lasting preference for the Democracy among newcomers, though party lines blurred considerably. In any case, how immigrants voted was of small importance nationally through 1830, when only one ballot in thirty could come from the foreign-born. By 1845, that figure was to rise to one in seven, with the Great Famine exodus still to produce, between 1845 and 1854, by far the greatest decade of immigration in antebellum American history. Immigration largely meant Irish immigration, with between 43 percent and 47 percent of migrants each year between 1820 and 1855 coming from Ireland.

By the early 1830s, the pattern of a strong Catholic Irish identification with the Democratic party, and with Andrew Jackson specifically, had strongly taken hold in urban centers like New York City. Although the existing urban Democratic political machines took time to inch away from the suspicion of immigrants felt by many of their artisan followers, Irish Catholics were welcomed as voters, party members and political muscle, though not typically as officeholders, by Democrats before the Civil War. The Catholic Irish, the immigrant group most exposed to nativist opposition, accepted protection from Democrats. Lacking a nationalist tradition of agitation for land redistribution in Ireland, too poor to move West and perhaps soured on farm life after the famine, the Catholic Irish were particularly immune to late antebellum Free Soil criticisms of Democratic opposition to homestead laws. Democrats and Irish-American Catholics entered into a lasting marriage that gave birth to new ideologies stressing the importance of whiteness.

From the 1830s, Democrats appreciated the ways in which the idea that all Blacks were unfit for civic participation could be transmuted into the notion that all whites were so fit. Pennsylvania Democrats, for example, solidified white unity by initiating the movement to codify the disfranchisement of the state's Blacks via constitutional amendment. Conflict with Mexico, and to some extent the rise of Chinese immigration, made it possible in the 1840s and 1850s for leading Democrats to develop racial schemes unequivocally gathering all European settlers together as whites against the "colored" races. At a time when most Democratic theorists were coming to accept polygeniticist ideas regarding the separate creations of the "black" and "white" races, they were also defining "white" in such a way as to include more surely the Irish and other immigrants. Thus, James Buchanan contemptuously branded the Mexicans as a "mongrel" race unfit for freedom but was glad that "Americans" were a "mixed" population of English, Scotch-Irish, French, Welsh, German and Irish ancestry. Missouri's Thomas Hart Benton wrote of a "Celtic-Anglo-Saxon race," superior to, in descending order, the yellow, brown, and red "races." Caleb Cushing aroused the Massachusetts legislature by announcing late in the 1850s that he admitted "to an equality with me, sir, the white man,—my blood and race, whether he be a Saxon of England or a Celt of Ireland." He added, "but I do not admit as my equals either the red man of America, or the yellow man of Asia, or the black man of Africa."

The most celebrated racial exchanges of the nineteenth century remain Democratic leader Stephen A. Douglas's stalkings of Abraham Lincoln as a race-mixer during the 1858 Lincoln–Douglas debates. The debates came hard on the heels of the 1856 elections—the first in which the great mass of famine immigrants were voters—when national candidates had vied to best articulate the interests of the "white man" by preventing "white slavery." In those elections Know–Nothings threatened the Democracy by running, in Millard Fillmore, a trained artisan commanding substantial loyalty from native-born workingmen who feared immigrant culture and immigrant debasement of the crafts. Douglas sought to make points among Illinois voters but also to speak to the needs of the Democracy as a national, and particularly Northern, party. He decided, in the words of a recent biographer, that "Negro inequality made up the platform on which he would stand in the ensuing years." Mixing sex and politics, Douglas spoke for "preserving not only the purity of [white] blood but the purity of the government from any . . . amalgamation with inferior races." He added, drawing lessons from the Mexican conflict, that the results of "this amalgamation of white men, and Indians and negroes, we have seen in Mexico, in Central America, in South America and in all the Spanish-American states." Douglas promised that Mexican War veterans could back his claims regarding the effects of racial "impurity." He further protested that Lincoln's belief that the Declaration of Independence applied to people of color would make the debate's listeners, who sometimes chanted "White men, White men" during his speeches, the equals of Fiji Islanders. Significantly, he meanwhile also argued that Americans' ancestors were "not all of English origin" but were also of Scotch, Irish, German, French, and Norman descent, indeed "from every branch of the Caucasian race."

Douglas spoke in the highly racialized political language increasingly common among Democrats, and to some extent among their opponents. Since Blacks wielded virtually no political power, to mobilize the white vote it was useful to declare white opponents and their ideas to be Black. Discussing Republican support in Illinois, Douglas found that "the creed is pretty black in the north end of the State; about the center it is pretty good mulatto and it is almost white when you get down to Egypt [Southern Illinois]." The Republicans became, in Democratic propaganda and especially in appeals from or directed at Catholic Irish Democrats, the "Black Republicans." Irish Democrats often scored the perfidy of the German "Black Dutch" or of "red" Germans in league with "Black" Republicans.

Lincoln's studied replies to Douglas's race-baiting stressed that a belief in natural rights applied to Blacks did not imply a desire to intermarry, that Republicans better protected the "white man's" interests than Democrats did, and that slaveholders, not Republicans, practiced racial amalgamation. Other Republican propaganda was much uglier, branding the Democracy a "nigger party" by virtue of its association with slavery and connecting its proslavery and pro-Irish policies. German opponents of Irish Democrats similarly cast doubts on the race of their adversaries.

Reginald Horsman's careful study of American "racial Anglo-Saxonism" shows that "politicians of Irish or Scotch-Irish ancestry" were especially prominent in challenging ideas of Anglo-Saxon superiority and in arguing for the existence of a new and improved "American race" of white men. Catholic Irish immigrants were also the best consumers of Democratic appeals that equated "white men" and "workingmen." As Dale T. Knobel observes in *Paddy and the Republic*, "Irish-Americans were sure to be enthusiastic about any treatment of American nationality that stressed the relevance of 'race' while putting the Irish safely within the Anglo-Celtic racial majority." The aptly named Democratic New York City *Caucasian* particularly won Irish-born readers to its view that defense of the "white working class" during the Civil War was best carried forward by attacking abolition.

Democratic paeans to whiteness must have seemed a godsend to Irish Catholics, especially amid hardening anti-Irish attitudes after 1845. By the time of the famine, it could be argued—and was argued by Irish-Americans themselves—that longstanding British oppression had kept the Irish in political "slavery" and brought utter economic dependency. Irish-Americans were deeply offended in the 1856 campaign when a remark by Buchanan implied that England had *not* made "slaves" of the Irish. But to make this argument, and to compare Irish and African oppression, forfeited any claim of Irish-Americans to be qualified for freedom by republican criteria. Past and present, their history seemed to be one of degradation.

Nativists were somewhat constrained by the historic American acceptance of Irish immigrants, by the cultural proximity of Irish Catholics with clearly assimilable Celtic Protestants from Ireland, Scotland, and Wales, and by the ease with which Irish Catholics could pass as mainstream "white" Americans. Anti-immigrant politicians therefore generally did not dwell on the popular ethnological theories that identified the Celts as genetically inferior. They instead concentrated on Irish subservience to religious authority and Irish degradation, loosely arguing at times that the famine itself had helped produce an Irish "race" incapable of freedom. Some unfavorably compared the Irish with free Blacks, not so much as racial types as in terms of their alleged records of fitness to function as republican citizens. Black leaders like Frederick Douglass generally avoided anti-Catholicism but charged that the ignorance and intemperance of the Irish and their roles as "flunkeys to our gentry" made it certain that Irish Catholics were not more desirable than Blacks as citizens of a republic.

The Democratic emphasis on natural rights within a government "made by the white men, for the benefit of the white man" appealed to Irish Catholics in large part because it cut off questions about their qualifications for citizenship. Under other circumstances, Irish-American Catholics might not have accepted so keenly the "association of nationality with blood—but not with ethnicity," which racially conflated them with the otherwise hated English. They might not have so readily embraced a view of "American nationality that stressed the relevance of 'race' while putting the Irish safely within an Anglo-Celtic racial majority." But within the constrained choices and high risks of antebellum American politics such a choice was quite logical. The ways in which the Irish competed for work and adjusted to industrial morality in America made it all but certain that they would adopt and extend the politics of white unity offered by the Democratic party.

Niles National Register—August 6, 1842—State of the Union, "Riot in Philadelphia: Conflicts between Whites and Blacks"

The well-known inveterate hostility existing between the laboring whites and colored population of the southern section of the city broke the bounds of law on Monday last, and a fearful riot ensued.

It appears that the colored people had determined to make a formal display in celebration of the emancipation of their brethren in the British West Indies . . . When the procession reached Fourth and Plumb streets in the district of Southwick, it was attacked by a volley of stones thrown by the whites, and a mischievous boy provoked a fight with one of those in the procession, a lad of about equal size, which was the origin of the whole series of results that followed. The black boy was considerable beaten by the white one, at which a black man struck the white boy over the head, and then a general fight ensued—and continued during the whole of the day. The blacks were seriously beaten at the onset, but rallied and thrashed the whites. From Fourth and Plumb streets, the crowd of both colors ran to Fifth and Shippen, then up to Sixth and South, fighting with clubs, sticks, stones, brickbats, and whatever missiles they could obtain, until they reached the corner of Sixth and Lombard streets. Some of the blacks took refuge in their own meeting houses in that neighborhood, and their procession having been dispersed, the whites went to work and destroyed houses and property indiscriminately [if] they belonged to or were occupied by blacks.

During the fight many were seriously hurt. One white man had his arm broken from a blow inflicted by a huge club in the hands of a black; another white man was stabbed with a knife or dirk in the eye; a black man named Metcalf had his right eye laid open by a blow for a weapon by a white, and some fifteen or twenty others more or less seriously injured. The most desperate of the blacks was a deaf and dumb man who did much mischief, and seriously injured several whites ere he was arrested by the police.

Persons and property were now assailed—many, both blacks and whites were dreadfully injured, before the latter finally gave way and sought safety in flight or concealment. Their domiciles were then attacked and much damage sustained. The police arrived and attempted to restore order. Some twenty of the rioters were taken into custody, and desperate and sometimes successful efforts were made by the mob to rescue them. Toward the close of the day the mob was infuriated by the discharge of a musket from a house on Bradford's alley, occupied by colored people, and wounding three young men; the police now found it necessary to protect the negroes by taking them into custody. One, however, was dragged away and dreadfully beaten; and another was battered with sticks and staves; the officers themselves being crushed to the earth by the rush of the mob. . . .

Throughout the evening, the tumult was continued, and arrests were occasionally made where the storm of the riot was most violent. Six black persons badly wounded were brought to the police office, where their wounds were temporarily dressed, and the worst of them taken to the hospital for further attention, where three or four remained during the night for safety.

At about nine o'clock suddenly, and without an intimation that the building had been entered a large four story edifice in Lombard Street near Seventh, known as Smith's Hall, newly erected by a wealthy colored man named Smith, was discovered to be on fire. The firemen hurried to the spot, but their efforts were confined to saving of buildings surrounding it, and in less than a half hour the walls fell, crushing a small two story brick house next door to the east, and knocking out its walls. This hall, it was understood, was a substitute for Pennsylvania Hall, destroyed several years ago, and supposed to be devoted to the same purpose—the discussion of abolition questions. It was entirely destroyed in less than an hour—thousands of persons standing looking at the destruction.

Before this fire had been subdued, another was discovered issuing from the colored Presbyterian church, in St. Mary street, which had been quietly entered and fired. This building was also destroyed.

After midnight, the police were left in quiet possession of the field.

Next morning the excitement burst out answer anew and extended to the Schuylkill [River]; colliers, laborers, idlers, and boys crowded every corner, most of them Irishmen armed with shilelahs[1] and clubs. Two black men exhibited themselves, which was the signal for an attack. Both were set upon by the mob in the most furious manner, and barely escaped with their lives. They were horribly beaten and cut, and but for the interference of Mr. Dewey, at the foot of Walnut Street, who got them into his storehouse and locked them up, would doubtless have been killed.

A messenger was sent to the sheriff for aid. The deputation of that officer under the charge of officer Saunders, to the number of about sixty persons, showed themselves upon the ground, each distinguished by a green ribbon tied to the breast of a coat. They passed along Walnut Street to the wharf, down the wharf to Pine, the belligerent party all the while increasing in numbers. At Pine, they turned from the wharf, and by the time they had passed half of the second square toward the heart of the city, the crowd pressed on so close, that it was necessary to quicken their pace, which was soon heightened to a full run, the mob in hot pursuit, loud in threats and imprecations. The posse of the sheriff ran across the commons to Spruce Street, but was headed off . . . ran down Third to Pine, along which they made their way . . . The crowd pursued them to Sixth and Pine, where a black man was seen, to attack whom called them off from their pursuit of the sheriff's posse.

The mob . . . returned to the southwestern section of the city, attacking every black man that came in their way, and committing many outrages. About noon they raced a poor negro at the corner of Thirteen and Shippen streets, caught him, and beat and frightened him almost to death. The police officers suffered in many cases very severely.

To add to the difficulty the authority of the mayor is limited to the city bounds. But it being ascertained that the county commissioners had refused to pay the sheriff's posse, his honor immediately called out the first brigade of city volunteers, pledging himself personally to the amount of $1000 to pay expenses. The military were under arms by three o'clock. At one o'clock the council convened and placed $500 at the mayor's disposal. The decision, energy, and humanity with which this officer seems to have acquitted himself entitles him to the thanks of the community. He was, however, knocked down during the evening by some rioters, whom he was endeavoring to disperse. A great number, whites and blacks, of those arrested were examined and committed by the police during the day.

About a thousand bayonets, under the command of determined officers, remained upon post during the night, and kept the mob down.

Toward evening and after nightfall on Monday the colored population fled in the utmost terror in every possible direction—some escaping into Jersey, some over the Market and Callowhill street bridges into the country, and others making their way with all the haste in their power to the Upper Liberties and districts of Philadelphia. Numbers sought refuge in the watch houses—in the South East watch house alone seventy females were confined all night. Many hid themselves in alleys or contrived to get into yards and concealed themselves in sheds and other outhouses. The negro residents up town barricaded their doors inside. Large bodies of men, women, and children of color, were collected on the meadows below the point house.

Note

1. *Shilelah* (also spelled, *shillelagh*), a thick wooden stick used in Ireland, especially as a weapon.

Frederick Douglass, "Colored Americans, and Aliens—T. F. Meagher"

If native born colored Americans experienced the same treatment at the hands of the National and State governments, as aliens do, we should not have so much about which to murmur and complain. We are, some of us, descendants of those, who, fought for our country, who bled for it, and died for it. Let us be treated as well as the sons of those who fought against it. We are victims, even here in the "free North," of a relentless hate. Everything is done to crush out our vitality. In the Southern States we are placed in the same category with horses, sheep, and other cattle, to be sold to the highest purchaser. Here in New York, we are looked upon as half-sheep, and half-horses, and of course, denied the rights of *men*. These Rights we demand; these Rights we intend to have.

We say unto our white fellow-citizens; treat us as well as you treat the foreigners swarming in your midst, those who *fill* your jails, and alm-houses *as well as build them.*

We see that Mr. Thomas F. Meagher, one of the Irish repealers who emigrated to this country from Van Diemen's Island,[1] has been admitted to practise as an attorney and counsellor in all the Courts of this State, by a special order of the Supreme Court. Mr. Meagher is not a citizen of the United States, and was not eligible to a regular examination. But the Judge, taking into consideration the fact of his being an Irishman . . . admits him by *courtesy.*

Now, we have not one word to utter about the admission of Mr. Meagher, on the account of his being an Irishman. We call attention to the fact; and ask those who voted against us on the equal suffrage question, to consider it, and contrast it with the fact of our treatment. The colored man, the native-born American, receives nothing by "courtesy." He lives and breathes in one continual storm, and walks through a wilderness of sorrow and of toil.—We receive nothing by "courtesy," gentlemen. Now, why should we be treated *so much worse* than aliens, and the sons of aliens? We ask the question. Who, among our ostracizers, will answer it? Are we not as virtuous, as honest, as useful, and as intelligent as they?—Let the jails and the poor houses answer the question.

We hope that when the question of Equal Suffrage shall again be presented to the consideration of the citizens of this State, they will ponder well upon the impracticability (to use no stronger term) of extending to aliens, rights and privileges, denied to their own fellow-citizens. At the polls, we were defeated on this very question, by the Irish, who rushed, as it were, *en masse* to the ballot-box, and impudently declared that *we should not have equal rights* with them. Look to it, fellow-citizens, that they triumph not again. Probably, they will have something else to attend to *now*, as *they*, too, are to come in for a share of proscription, if Know Nothingism succeeds in its cruel exactions. A fellow feeling should make us wondrous kind. We throw this remark to those "*foreigners*" who proscribed *us* at the polls.

But we are told that we are not citizens!—Well; all we have to say in reply to this absurd declaration, is, if we are not, we ought to be. *We have been in the country long enough to entitle* us to all the rights and immunities of citizenship, having been born on the soil. The colored man cannot be an alien for aliens, we believe, are not born in the country. He cannot be naturalized as foreigners only are naturalized. Not a citizen, not an alien! In the name of the Constitution, what is he?

We hope our Irish fellow-citizens who despise this proscriptive spirit, will take no exception to these remarks, but let them exert their influence in bringing their brethren to a proper apprehension of the reciprocal duties and obligations, existing between man and his fellow.

Frederick Douglass' Paper, September 14, 1855

Note

1. Thomas F. Meagher was exiled to Van Diemen's Island (now the Australian State of Tasmania) for his part in the failed Irish uprising of 1848. He escaped from there, along with a number of other Irish nationalists, and came to the United States.

Stephan A. Douglas (Speech at Jonesboro, Illinois)

I hold that a negro is not and never ought to be a citizen of the United States. I hold that this government was made on the white basis, by white men, for the benefit of white men and their posterity forever, and should be administered by white men and none others. I do not believe that the Almighty made the negro capable of self-government. I am aware that all the Abolition lecturers that you find travelling about through the country are in the habit of reading the Declaration of Independence to prove that all men were created equal, and endowed by their Creator with certain inalienable rights, among which are life, liberty, and the pursuit of happiness. Mr. Lincoln is very much in the habit of reading that part of the Declaration of Independence to prove that the negro was endowed by the Almighty with the inalienable right of equality with white men. Now, I say to you, my fellow-citizens, that in my opinion the signers of the Declaration had no reference to the negro whatever when they declared all men to be created equal. They desired to express by that phrase white men, men of European birth and European descent, and had no reference either to the negro, the savage Indians, the Fejee, the Malay, or any other inferior and degraded race, when they spoke of the equality of men. One great evidence that such was their understanding is to be found in the fact that at that time every one of the thirteen colonies was a slaveholding colony, every signer of the Declaration represented a slaveholding constituency, and we know that no one of them emancipated his slaves, much less offered citizenship to them, when they signed the Declaration; and yet, if they intended to declare that the negro was the equal of the white man, and entitled by divine right to an equality with him, they were bound, as honest men, that day and hour to have put their negroes on an equality with themselves. Instead of doing so, with uplifted eyes to Heaven they implored the divine blessing upon them, during the seven years' bloody war they had to fight to maintain that Declaration, never dreaming that they were violating divine law by still holding the negroes in bondage and depriving them of equality.

CHAPTER EIGHT

Becoming Black: Contemporary Jamaicans and West Indians in the 1990s

Introduction

Just as nineteenth-century Irish immigrants came gradually to be included in the ranks of white people, so, too, are some contemporary immigrants coming to be considered *black*. Here again, of course, we are speaking about something other than skin color. The issue is instead racialization—a social categorization that assigns people to a position on the basis of physical features, which are assumed to be of significance for understanding the behavior and thought of individuals. In understanding the process by which some contemporary immigrants become black, in this chapter we will develop the example of English-speaking immigrants from the islands of the Caribbean that once constituted the British West Indies, and pay special attention to Jamaicans, one of the largest in number of these peoples from the Caribbean who have settled in New York City. Jamaican immigration to New York City is not a new phenomenon. Jamaicans have resettled there throughout the twentieth century, but the wave of immigration after 1965 was significantly larger than any previous immigration from the island to the metropolis.

There were approximately 138,000 Jamaican-born individuals living in New York City in 1990. This large population was characterized by internal diversity, containing people at a variety of socioeconomic levels, from affluent to poor. Nonetheless, the Jamaican population as a group was known to be hard-working and achievement-oriented. In 1990, Jamaicans had relatively high educational attainment and average earnings, and relatively low unemployment compared to other immigrant groups and to some native-born American groups. Moreover, Jamaicans were characterized by high degrees of ethnic solidarity. They chose to live in distinct neighborhoods. They shared a common history and memories of their homeland as well as some distinct cultural traits, which are evident in sports, food, and music. Their ethnicity was reinforced by transnational ties facilitated by close proximity to their homeland, which is only some 500 miles from the continental United States.

Founded originally as a highly profitable colony of Great Britain with an economy based on raising sugarcane, today's Jamaicans are descendants of the African slaves brought to work in the cane fields. Over the centuries, there was much interracial sexual mixing between the British colonizers and African, slave and free. Jamaicans are a multicolored people. But color is not an especially significant issue in Jamaica, where almost everyone has African ancestry and many have a genealogy rooted in both races. In the United States, however, race is the most significant source of social differentiation, and Jamaicans find themselves considered "black" by those around them who know nothing about them, but are accustomed in daily life to read a good deal of meaning into skin color. A consequence of this racialization, Jamaicans and other West Indians believe, has been the occasionally poor treatment they receive at the hands of the New York City police, who, along with other urban police departments elsewhere in the United States, tend to associate black people with crime and criminal intent. Jamaicans acknowledge the presence of crime in their communities and want good law enforcement, but not at the expense of racial profiling, which singles them out as a particularly suspect group requiring special police surveillance.

The three selections in this chapter provide us with insight into the Jamaicans' experience of ethnicity and racialization in New York City in recent decades. The first selection profiles Jamaican community life in one neighborhood, which decades ago the Jamaican immigrant parents of retired General Colin L. Powell, once President George W. Bush's Secretary of State, settled. Though the socioeconomic differences among them are not great, this neighborhood is the most affluent—in terms of home ownership and median income—of the three principal Jamaican neighborhoods in New York City. It is also a tightly knit community, with a high degree of Jamaican ethnic identification. One commentator compares it to the aspiring middle-class neighborhoods that European immigrant groups formed earlier in the twentieth century. The community is largely captured here through the eyes of those who live in it. One soon becomes aware that the consciousness of race does not seem to play a large role in its daily self-understanding. What concerns these immigrants is home ownership, family solidarity, work, and neighborhood.

In the second selection, however, we see another view of the concerns of Jamaicans. While at times reluctant to acknowledge that race is a problem for them, they become aware, as they settle into their new lives, that race is a pervasive fact of life in the United States. They learn that not only the native-born African Americans, but new immigrants, too, have to endure prejudice and discrimination. In an analysis of Jamaican attitudes based on interviews with 100 immigrants in New York City, sociologist Milton Vickerman finds that Jamaicans adopt a variety of strategies for dealing with racialization, from public protest to denial of the problem. Central to these strategies is working out a relationship to African Americans. American racism preceded the arrival of Jamaican immigrants and both its principal target and opponent have been African Americans. To be linked to African Americans is to be linked to the older history of American racism and to engagement in the struggle against racism. In a sense, to acknowledge that linkage is to opt for a more complex identity and an expanded set of concerns, such as public confrontations with those who discriminate on racial grounds, that potentially pose many difficulties. Racism leads some Jamaicans to identify with and to make common cause with African Americans. But it leads others to seek to distance themselves and to accentuate differences from African Americans, largely through assertions of Jamaican ethnicity. It is to say, in effect, that racism is someone else's concern.

The third selection takes up the issue of the relations between New York City police and West Indian immigrants. Jamaican and other West Indian immigrants have charged that the police target them for special surveillance on the basis of color in ways in which whites are not targeted. In the dispute in 1997, to which this selection refers, it was discovered that an internal Police Department memo appeared to call for compiling arrest data only on Jamaicans and other West Indians. The precise point of this selective record-keeper is unclear, but it was considered offensive and a bad precedent for the future, because it suggested an assumption that West Indians constituted a special crime problem, much like the way in which urban police forces have long regarded African Americans. The issue of police relations with immigrants of color from the Caribbean basin would receive an even more profound shock shortly thereafter that same year, when Abner Louima, a thirty-year-old immigrant from Haiti, was brutally assaulted by Justin Volpe, a white policeman, at a precinct police station. Volpe was enraged by treatment he had received that same evening, when he and other police were called to break up a fight at a nightclub. Investigation revealed that Louima, who sustained serious injuries as a result of the assault, was innocent of any crime, and charges initially filed against him, were dropped. After an emotional trial, Volpe was sentenced to 30 years in prison. The Louima case greatly strained the relations between police and New York City minorities, and led to massive demonstrations by a coalition of immigrant groups, African Americans, and others against police brutality and racial profiling.

Suggestions for Further Reading

Irma Watkins-Owens, *Blood Relations: Caribbean Immigrants and the Harlem Community, 1900–1930* (Bloomington: Indiana University Press, 1996).

Mary C. Waters, *Black Identities: West Indian Immigrant Dreams and American Realities* (Cambridge: Harvard University Press and Russell Sage Foundation, 1999).

Philip Kasinitz, *Caribbean New York: Black Immigrants and the Politics of Race* (Ithaca: Cornell University Press, 1992).

Roger Waldinger, *Still the Promised City?: African-Americans and New Immigrants in Postindustrial New York* (Cambridge: Harvard University Press, 1996).

Tekle Woldemikael, *Becoming Black American: Haitians and American Institutions in Evanston, Illinois* (New York: AMS, 1989).

Nossiter, "A Jamaican Way Station in the Bronx: Community of Striving Immigrants Fosters Middle-Class Values"

Adam Nossiter, "A Jamaican Way Station in the Bronx: Community of Striving Immigrants Fosters Middle-Class Values"

There is the odd hole-in-the-wall serving up fiery jerk chicken, or a greengrocer with 10 kinds of exotic yams on his shelves. Cricket matches can be glimpsed in Van Cortlandt Park on summer afternoons. But it is difficult to identify overt signs of West Indian culture among the neatly kept, modest brick houses of Williamsbridge and Wakefield.

Yet these northeastern Bronx neighborhoods are home to one of the largest concentrations of Jamaicans in the city. And they are the literal descendants of the close-knit, sociable and striving community of Jamaican immigrants in the Bronx that nurtured Colin L. Powell, the retired Army general, and started him on his career.

Forty years after the Powells hit the numbers and left for Queens, as General Powell describes in his book, "My American Journey," the Bronx's role in the ascent of Jamaican immigrants is strikingly similar to what it was when the general was a child. For while Brooklyn—especially Crown Heights and East Flatbush—remains the great magnet for the bulk of Jamaican immigrants, the Bronx is the more distinct way station on their road to middle-class solidity.

Around the City

Comparing Three Jamaican Neighborhoods

Here are the three neighborhoods with the highest concentrations of foreign-born Jamaicans in 1990.

Of these, the neighborhood where Gen. Colin Powell grew up, the Williamsbridge-Wakefield area in the Bronx, is the most prosperous and the most solidly Jamaican.

Neighborhoods are identified below by their community board district numbers

	Williamsbridge-Wakefield, Bronx	Crown Heights, Brooklyn	East Flatbush, Brooklyn
Number and percent of **total**	14,074	6,488	14,655
population that is foreign-born Jamaican	11.6%	8.6%	10.4%
Unemployment rate among Jamaicans	5.7%	7.4%	8.0%
Jamaican households with **income** above $35,000	50.6%	37.9%	47.2%
Percent of Jamaicans owning their own **homes**	37.0%	13.6%	30.7%

Source: Dr. Andrew Beveridge Queens College, from analysis of 1990 census data.

In Williamsbridge and Wakefield, more than 70 percent of all immigrants are from the island, more than 14,000 Jamaicans in all, according to an analysis of census data for The *New York Times* by Dr. Andrew Beveridge, a sociologist at Queens College. And Jamaicans there are wealthier, better educated, more likely to own homes, and have more stable families than those in Brooklyn.

The reason is unclear, but several experts pointed to the housing pattern in the neighborhoods at the northern edge of the city: street after street of plain but solid single-family brick houses, attractive to strivers looking to own rather than rent.

"The Bronx plays the same role for Jamaicans as it once did for Jews," said Philip Kasinitz, an expert on Caribbean immigration at Hunter College. "It's basically stable, middle-class neighborhoods."

The Bronx Jamaican community today is a recognizable echo of the world fondly evoked in Mr. Powell's autobiography—a world of curried goat, calypso music and strong families. Ethnic pride is distinct but discrete, flourishing in tight family circles, behind the closed doors of these blocks of well-kept dwellings.

Before Arnold Anderson, a 71-year-old former mathematics teacher, left Jamaica 30 years ago, "we were poor," he said simply. Today, all seven of his children have college degrees, and all are homeowners. Several sat around their parents' cluttered living room recently, discussing why they had made good.

Karlene Anderson, 39, an X-ray technician with a degree in sociology from Lehman College, pointed to her mother, Kathleen, a retired nurse. "Mother was the doorkeep, the gatekeeper," she said. "We weren't free to go out and date other kids." Her parents made sacrifices.

"Everything we earned went into their education," Mrs. Anderson said.

The children discussed a less palpable reason for their success: their sense of Jamaicanness.

"You're Jamaican," Karlene Anderson said. "You're not going to take stuff sitting down."

Her sister, Christine Anderson Lewis, 33, said, "The longer I'm here, the more I realize how important it is to hang to who I am."

Joyce James, a Jamaican who directs the Susan E. Wagner Child Care Center in the Bronx, said of the neighborhood: "It's very cohesive. They've been here for a while. They've not necessarily comfortable flaunting the fact that they're Jamaicans."

It is a working community: in the Bronx, employment rates are higher for Jamaicans than for Dominicans, Koreans and white people born in the United States. Posses, the feared Jamaican drug gangs that made headlines in the 1980's, were a Brooklyn phenomenon.

To be sure, this is a different Bronx than the one of General Powell's youth: Jamaicans, like others, fled up the borough as the South Bronx crumbled in the late 1950's, a precipitate exodus during which, General Powell wrote, he remembers hearing people ask each other, "When you getting out?"

Shifting neighborhoods in the borough was a way of holding on to the achievements of the two initial waves of migration from Jamaica, in the first decades of the century, and from the late 1930's to 1965: houses, solid jobs, mostly in service industries, and strong family ties.

Mr. Kasinitz noted that while, in Mr. Powell's era and before, immigrants from the island tended not to be from the poorest classes, in the third great wave of Jamaican migration, which began in 1965 and continues today, "everybody now leaves Jamaica." And yet today, Jamaicans within the Bronx itself show the same unmistakable signs of upward mobility as did many in Mr. Powell's youth.

They have lower poverty rates than Asians, Dominicans, and Puerto Ricans in the borough, far greater concentrations of households in upper-income categories, and a higher percentage of people reporting a 40- to 45-hour work week than any other group, including American-born whites, according to an analysis of Bronx census data by Prof. William Bosworth of Lehman College.

"The Bronx became the first suburb for West Indians," said Karl Rodney, publisher of *The New York Carib News*, speaking from personal experience. Mr. Rodney, himself of Jamaican origin, bought his first house in the United States in Williamsbridge, before moving to Westchester in 1969, a common migration of the last several decades.

Mr. Powell wrote in his autobiography of a "degree of clannishness among West Indians, Jamaicans included." This remains a distinctive feature of the quiet Jamaican presence in the Bronx today. Typical is the Wembley Athletic Club, described by many as one of the few expressions of Jamaican associational life in the borough.

The explanation for this paucity is characteristic: "There is some, but because they work so hard, they don't want to sacrifice the time to do these things," said Jackie Nkrumah, who owns Jackie's West Indian Bakery on East 233d Street, and works the evening shift herself to ensure the freshness of the coconut gizzardas, or sweet cakes.

On a Friday night, the Wembley A.C., as members call it, rocks with nothing louder than a lively game of dominoes.

Many of the members have been in America for decades—the club president is a retired I.B.M. account manager, and friends gathered around included a skilled electrician, an insurance agent, a manager in the city's Health and Hospitals Corporation, and a retired Transit Authority supervisor.

Yet this plain, two-story brick building, tucked away on a quiet corner in Wakefield, remains their chosen spot: the members are all West Indian, and mostly Jamaican.

The sense of ethnic identification is strong. Equally strong is the conviction that ethnicity played a vital role in what the men regarded as lives of reasonable success. General Powell's upward trajectory is no mystery to them.

"We're all proud of him as Jamaicans," said John Lyn, the president of the Wembley Club, who came to the Bronx in the days when Mr. Powell's family still lived on Kelly Street in Mott Haven. "That pride, that unwillingness to back down, is probably what got him where he is. If his parents were parents like the ones we had, they would not forgive him if he denied his manhood. In Jamaica, if you allow yourself to lose your dignity—"

"You'll be thrashed," cut in Leslie Stephenson, an insurance broker who immigrated 28 years ago. "We, as best as we could, kept our Jamaican ways," Mr. Stephenson said.

Milton Vickerman, *Crosscurrents: West Indian Immigrants and Race*

Although West Indians employ several strategies to cope with racial discrimination, it could be argued that these are only short-term remedies for an entrenched problem. With respect to race, perhaps the greatest difficulty faced by West Indians is that they are socialized to deemphasize its importance. Because of this, they are constantly surprised by the blatancy with which race is played out in the United States. Much debate currently exists as to whether America is becoming a more "color-blind" society; but an often overlooked fact is that West Indians, coming from societies with lower levels of racial tension, almost inevitably perceive the United States as being very race conscious. If there was one theme that came through consistently and clearly in my interviews with the Jamaicans, it is that they experience great difficulty adjusting to the notion that in routine, everyday situations, they must take race into account. Over time, continued exposure to racial discrimination causes many West Indians to shift their paradigm from a nonracial one to one that is more explicitly racial. By this, one means that West Indians: (1) come to understand that race permeates all facets of American life; (2) expect to have unpleasant encounters because of race; and (3) often become pessimistic that the United States will become "color-blind" any time soon. In other words, the understanding that they may have had about race prior to migrating goes from being fairly abstract to being experiential and more consciously life-shaping.

To make this point, though, is only to scratch the tip of a complex situation. Saying that, over time, West Indian immigrants become more conscious of race is not to say that this process is either easy or, necessarily, desired. Many West Indians would prefer to ignore the whole issue of race. The problem is that the society will not allow them to forget. Moreover, the development of greater consciousness of race among West Indians does not negate their overriding goal of achieving upward mobility. One of the central paradoxes of the West Indian experience in the United States is that they believe that racial discrimination is widespread but that this discrimination coexists with the possibility for upward mobility. In practical terms—as the Jamaicans explained it—this coexistence means that West Indians try to maximize their opportunities—educational, financial, material, and occupational—within whatever barriers exist. They view racial barriers as long-term and try, as much as is possible, to take control of their own lives by preparing themselves in ways that will enable them to prosper in a capitalist economy.

The Jamaicans whom I interviewed ran the gamut from the minority who absolutely resisted viewing issues in racial terms to the majority who argued that though it *should* not be the case, race certainly *is* a factor in their everyday lives. A good example of strong resistance to thinking about issues in racial terms comes from my interview with Bogle, a fifty-eight-year-old small business man. He had migrated from Jamaica in 1962 and through hard work had managed to thrive. Residing, at first, in Flatbush, he eventually moved to a predominantly white suburban neighborhood after concluding that rising crime rates had made Flatbush unliveable. Initially—as he explained it—the whites in the neighborhood into which he moved expressed hostility at the idea of a black family moving in. However, all this changed when they discovered that the family was West Indian. Previous hostility melted away and was replaced by a very welcoming attitude.

Although this account sounds idealistic, Bogle expressed a strong conviction that whites are more accepting of West Indians because they have a reputation for being law abiding, hard working, and so on. He related the story of his move to the white neighborhood as a way of explaining why, in his opinion, race thinking is bad. Had he adopted that perspective, he argued, he would have limited his vistas and not moved into a pleasant neighborhood out of fear of discrimination. But, as it turned out, the whites accepted his family because of the positive stereotypes associated with West Indians. Merit, diligence, politeness, and respect rather than race thinking were, in his view, the keys to attaining upward mobility in America. Because of this view, Bogle expressed great anger at those blacks who, in his opinion, insisted on seeing everything through the lens of race.

Religion and/or ideology can also douse racial feelings. For instance, there was the case of the deeply religious, activist conservative family which severely criticized any sort of race thinking. Holding up as models for blacks to follow, Jerry Falwell, George Bush, and capitalism, they argued that liberalism, allied with a focus on race, was hindering rather than helping American blacks. While not denying the existence of racial discrimination in America, they held that a focus on hard work within the context of a free market and biblical principles would ultimately be most beneficial to blacks. The former, in their view, would assure the prosperity and independence (from hostile racial forces) of blacks, while the latter would assure God's blessing.

Although these Jamaicans expressed their antiracialist sentiments very forcefully, they were unusual in their insistence on the absolute meaninglessness of race. More typically, the Jamaicans pragmatically distinguished between the *ought* and the *is*. This differentiation produced in them an internal conflict as they realized that, to make sense of their American experiences, they would have to embrace a more consciously racial point of view. They seemed to admit this necessity reluctantly, sadly, and with more than a little pessimism. Mitchell, a thirty-two-year-old financial consultant, illustrates this:

> I still can't fathom why, because of the color of your skin, certain privileges are not available to you. I still can't understand it; I just can't understand it. . . . When you come here it's almost like after a while you learn to accept your fate. . . . So for instance, if you know you are not going to be welcome in certain places, you just don't go there . . . because you alone cannot fight this war. . . . And this situation has been here long before we came here and it will be here . . . for

as long as I can see into the future. So it's just a matter of working within the system to extract the benefits that you will need for yourself. That's how I see it.

The development of heightened consciousness of race is also associated with a great deal of anger. Neil, [a] social worker explained how he coped with persistent anger at racism by sublimating that anger:

The first experience you have of someone reacting to you vis-à-vis skin color . . . makes you angry. But that was when you were 24. I am now 45. I can't get angry every time a racist incident comes up in front of me. I [would] go crazy. . . . It all depends on the extent to which you decide that you are going to understand a situation and develop a set of controls. In other words, racism doesn't anger me less now, and I am not a whit less concerned now at 45 than I was at 24. What I have deliberately gone through is a series of experiences and also [a] looking into myself to basically temper my reaction and deal with it.

Some of the strategies for tempering reactions to racial discrimination—notably avoidance and adoption of religious/ideological viewpoints—have already been noted. Another possibility is to view racism as part of a historical trend. In this way, the individual depersonalizes racial discrimination and views himself or herself as only one of millions who have suffered such a fate. Thus, as some of the Jamaicans explained it, all blacks in white dominated societies share similar experiences; and the only difference between West Indians and African Americans is that the former disembarked from the slave ships a little sooner.

Still, the continuous experience of discrimination can be offset only so much and it tends to leave lasting scars on West Indians. Several of my interviews illustrated how these scars developed over a period of time. A good example of this was Jerry, a young minister. He had arrived in the United States at age twenty, after having attended college in the West Indies. The immediate cause for his coming was his receipt of a scholarship with which he planned to further his education. Intending, at first, to specialize in one of the "hard" sciences, he eventually shifted to the study of religion and psychology. This took him, first, to a small prestigious liberal arts college, and later to an Ivy League university where he received an advanced degree.

Jerry indicated that while in Jamaica, his outlook had been "socialistic," having been drawn to the People's National Party's attempts to empower the poor. At this stage of his life, social inequality as manifested in class differentials was the issue which engaged him. Coming to America put an entirely new spin on that issue as he started to recognize the relationship between inequality and race. He became much more race conscious than he had been in Jamaica. At first, the factors that led to this mentality were not necessarily dramatic. He indicated, for instance, that the simple act of filling out forms made him realize the premium Americans place on race. In Jamaica, this routine act had held no racial significance, but in America he was regularly required on forms to state his race. This forced him to start thinking in racial terms, a tendency that was accelerated by the fact that the society seemed to be saturated with a consciousness of race. He cited the media as being particularly significant in this regard. Attending a succession of prestigious private schools really drove home the point that race matters, because he found himself part of a distinct minority. Many of the whites with whom he interacted focused first on his skin color and, only secondarily, on his other characteristics. This behavior ranged from outright discriminatory treatment to well-meaning professors informing him that, as a foreigner, he could not really appreciate the difficulties that faced African Americans. Reacting with suspicion to what he saw as attempts to co-opt foreign blacks by ostensibly evaluating them more positively than African Americans, he threw himself into campus politics, espousing various pro-black causes.

The end result of his experiences since migrating was a mentality which saw far more similarities than differences between West Indians and African Americans. This was not a negation of his "West Indianness," since, surprisingly, he argued in favor of dating but not marrying African American women. His rationale was that marriage is a chancy proposition and the likelihood of it succeeding is greatly enhanced when the individuals involved share commonalties. West Indians and African American matches would encounter severe culture clashes that would doom the marriages. Moreover, he argued that since American society, in general, is permissive, he would raise his child to embrace West Indian values, because he viewed these as placing greater emphasis on discipline. Nevertheless, he argued that it would not trouble him if people identified him with African Americans. As he stated:

> If the term black was in there it wouldn't bother me at all. . . . I was black before I was Jamaican. Black is just who I am, and prior to any other knowledge I had of myself, I was black.

Hence, he concluded:

> There are areas in which our different histories meet. Whether it was a "classist" exploitation or it was racial exploitation—it was exploitation. . . . People were dehumanized and are still being dehumanized. I think there is more common ground between us than there are differences. . . . We tend to overemphasize the differences rather than looking for the common ground which we can build on.

Consistent with his emphasis on his racial identity, upon leaving graduate school, he deliberately chose to pastor a church in an inner-city area, viewing this choice as a means of asserting control over his life in a society that constantly sought to belittle blacks, regardless of their achievements or ethnicity. Pastoring in the inner city was a way of establishing a "comfort zone" in which he did not have to constantly justify his presence to suspicious whites. He stated that over the years he had changed from a position of relative racial innocence to a point where he felt little desire to interact with whites on an ongoing basis. Far more important to him was the fact that many blacks had acute spiritual, social, and economic needs that were going unmet. Among his inner-city congregants were people who accepted him implicitly and he, in turn, felt a greater fulfillment in his life knowing that he was helping to meet their needs.

While this minister had arrived at a position of relative contentment with the issue of race, other Jamaicans continued to feel lingering bitterness. As was true in several cases, this stemmed from unfortunate racial experiences on the job. A case in point was Stanley, the forty-year-old technician, who worked for a very large multinational corporation and, before that, for its even larger corporate parent. Like many other Jamaicans, prior to migrating to America he had grown very comfortable with being a member of a majority group in a society which lay great stress on upward mobility through merit. These facts are important because they left him quite unprepared for dealing with the racial conflict which he encountered in the United States.

In 1970, a year after he migrated, he obtained the job as technician in one of the first cohorts of blacks to be brought into the company under affirmative action. As he explained it, the company had long been dominated by the stereotypical "old boy's network" of white males and run in a militaristic fashion (for instance, employees who missed their assigned duties were referred to as being "AWOL"). Blacks were not welcomed. The first inkling Stanley had of this was when a piece of equipment which he had approved as usable was sabotaged and he was blamed for putting defective equipment into operation. He claimed that this was one example of incidents of harassment to which black workers were subjected and which were designed to get them fired. To the obvious question of how he knew that his white coworkers had deliberately sabotaged the equipment after he had approved it, he replied that thirteen years after the fact, a white colleague apologized to him for doing it but insisted that he had only been following orders from management. However, since he never found out which manager had ordered the sabotage, the apology only increased his feelings of discomfort.

Instead of firing him over the incident, Stanley's superiors transferred him to another building. His new coworkers, being primarily younger whites—and ones influenced by 1960s popular culture at that—exhibited a decidedly more laid-back culture than his previous coworkers.

The technicians that I worked with in the new area were better educated and they had higher social class, so they were less afraid of me, per se. But . . . the office where I was leaving from, they were definitely threatened by me because I guess for their own self-worth they needed to believe that blacks were lower, less intelligent. . . . But for these [new coworkers] to have an intelligent black working for them: It wasn't a problem. They would boast about me. . . . I felt confident to go in and work on anything without having to know that anybody was going to go behind my back. They were . . . all young . . . into the peace movement . . . crazy about black music and into getting high: They were . . . hippies.

Despite his more pleasant environment, over the years Stanley had several other unpleasant encounters with his superiors. These stemmed from their refusal to promote him. Indeed, as he described it, his was only one example of a corporate culture that was openly hostile to blacks. One expression of this hostility was that minority workers' attempts to redress their grievances usually resulted in them being transferred or fired. He stated:

I have considered going to the Human Rights Commission and taking the case against them about being passed over; over and over and over again. Then usually what happens to people who do that is that you get transferred to some [other] area. It's like you win the battle but lose the war. It has happened before where the black guys got together and said: "We've got to do something about this; they're doing this too far." And they actually presented their case . . . and the next week they were gone!

As a result of events such as these, many of the blacks at his company had become very disillusioned. Stanley, himself, had become extremely conscious of race and, in fact, had become known to his supervisors as one who tended to see everything through the visor of race. For instance, he stated that early in his career at the company, when he first started to realize how important race was compared to Jamaica, he tried to cope by doing as much reading as he could to educate himself about the history of blacks and race in America. During this period, he would often bring in articles to show his coworkers to educate them as to the difficulties blacks have faced in America. If anything, however, this tended to work against him, as his supervisors wanted to avoid, as much as possible, open discussion of racial issues. This lack of response has only served to embitter him further, and, when I interviewed him, he reported that he had become quite cynical, regarding himself as an "old soldier" whose singular efforts could not make much difference against the culture of a multibillion dollar corporation. He described what was required to achieve promotion in his company, indicating that he was not interested in conforming and that, in any case, such conformity would hardly benefit blacks:

Basically, you have to become white; you have to play by the white rules. . . . You can't be a radical; you can't be, "This country is unfair to blacks." You have to close your eyes to all that and just try to become a gear in the machine. . . . All the black people who have been with the company twenty, thirty years: none of them are really happy or self-fulfilled. . . . There are whites who have been with the company the same length of time and they come in in the morning. They are smiling; they are happy; they are fulfilled. They've gotten their expectations. . . .

> Most of the blacks . . . have become so bitter [that] they only do what they have to do to keep their jobs. . . . They feel that they have been used or abused in some way and the only option of getting back is not to do anything.

Because of all this, Stanley perceived America, in general, and whites, specifically, very negatively. Contrasting West Indians and African Americans, he blamed systemic racial discrimination against the latter, in the context of minority status, for the differences in attitudes between the two groups; and argued that even second and later generation West Indians were more likely than the foreign-born to succumb to what he perceived as societal pressures promoting notions of black inferiority:

> If you were educated in Jamaica; you became an adult in Jamaica, you . . . have gotten to a certain point where nobody can negate you [because you]. . . already . . . know your capabilities. . . . It's . . . your second generation, your third generation [West Indians who]. . . are being given the same indoctrination [as] the American blacks who we can't understand. We as Jamaicans come here—as Africans, as Trinidadians, as Barbadians, or whatever. We can't understand: How come they don't have any pride? How come they can allow this to happen? You know, they have all this opportunity around them and they haven't done anything. . . . We are all the same, so the only thing that's different is that they came to a country where there was a white majority and we went to a country where we [were] a black majority and the things that they did to them here, they could not get away with doing with us there because . . . we would only take so much. You can only push the majority so far before they rise up and tear you limb from limb. But when you are a minority, no matter what they do to you, you have to sit quietly and take it. . . . The system is meant to keep them there.

In fact, he was even more pessimistic than this, arguing that whites, perceiving blacks to be the source of much of their everyday troubles—preeminently crime—would, if they could, happily get rid of all of them.

> I think America is a white country and I see Jamaica as a . . . black country, and if I am a black man then I don't really have a choice . . . : This is never going to be my country. I would like it to be but . . . I perceive it on my job among the . . . middle class whites who come in from Long Island or New Jersey or Pennsylvania, or whatever, that the only reason New York City is not what it used to be is because blacks are taking over. That's the reason why there is so much crime; that's the reason why you can't park your car; that's the reason why you can't have a radio in your car: It's because the blacks are here: . . . There is that danger [as]. . . more of them come to believe that . . . the only reason there are problems is because of these foreigners, these blacks

who are not supposed to be here; and if somehow you could find a way to get rid of them, then everything is going to be great—America is going to be perfect; America is going to be the Garden of Eden.

Attitudes Toward African Americans

The tight integration of the West Indies into the communication networks emanating from North America ensures that little which transpires in this country will go unnoticed in the former region. This means, among other things, that many West Indians certainly possess a knowledge of racial conditions in the United States prior to migrating here. Perhaps more important, their relatives have quite likely communicated to them a more intimate knowledge of these conditions. Still, a large gap separates knowledge from experience. Being forced to deal with discrimination regularly raises, for West Indians, issues for which abstract knowledge does not prepare them. Among the most important of these issues is the problem of identity in a heterogeneous society. Where, before, they had been Trinidadians, Barbadians, or Jamaicans, in the United States it is not immediately obvious what they will be. The strong nationalism present in many West Indian societies reduces the salience of the identity issue in those societies. In the United States, however, West Indians' national identity prior to migrating becomes much less important than their racial identity.

From a theoretical point of view, identity becomes a problem because, rather than being a given, it is negotiated in specific social contexts. Some individuals find themselves with several valid identity options, while others may have only a few. Some may enjoy great freedom to tailor their identity according to specific preferences; while other individuals find that outsiders impose particular identities and minimize personal choice. Research in this area has shown that Americans who trace their ancestry to Europe tend to enjoy the greatest freedom to determine their identity and to shift between a number of different identities. Americans of European origin—especially those tracing their ancestry back to eastern and southern Europe—are now quite assimilated. Under such conditions, ethnicity becomes "symbolic" in the sense that identifying with a particular ancestry entails little cost and is less an integral aspect of the self than it once was. Instead, ethnicity begins to revolve around social phenomena—e.g., festivals and cuisine—that, while important, are transient. Mary Waters's research among Americans of European descent has shown how the lessened salience of having particular European ancestries enables these Americans to opt for ethnic identities to which they may have some legitimate claim; or to eschew that and regard themselves as unhyphenated Americans. For instance, a child with ancestors from, say, Germany and Ireland could claim German ancestry, Irish ancestry, or downplay both and emphasize his or her "Americanness." Stanley Lieberson has argued that the haziness surrounding issues of ethnic identity for Americans of European ancestry derives in no small part from the inevitable gaps in knowledge, regarding ancestry, that develop over time.

The further back in time an individual goes, the less certain is that individual of his or her ancestry. Over time, these gaps in knowledge make it easier for the individual to lose—without effort to maintain it—a sense of special attachment to particular identities. Thus, Lieberson found, for instance, that white southerners, because of the earlier migration of their ancestors to the United States, demonstrate the greatest tendency to view themselves as unhyphenated "Americans."

Individuals of African ancestry differ markedly from all this. Rather than enjoying freedom to define themselves to reflect the full range of their ancestries, they have imposed on them by society the label "black." The operative principle has been the rule of *hypodescent*—the so-called one-drop rule—whereby all individuals, with even remote African ancestry, become defined by society as "black." This rule has sought to subsume West Indians as well, but they have traditionally viewed it as problematic. Their societies never developed racial lines quite as rigid as those in this country. Moreover, a larger number of variables—notably social class—have been included in definitions of race. Consequently, they have enjoyed greater freedom to self-define their identities. More important, the negative stereotypes imputed, by Western culture, to African ancestry have not become as entrenched in the West Indies as they have in America. Therefore, for West Indians, assimilating into American society implies giving up greater freedom for less and embracing negative stereotypes. Because of this concession, West Indians' attitudes toward African Americans is a particularly important aspect of their encounter with race in America.

Basically, West Indians' relationship with African Americans revolves around the process of distancing and identification, sometimes leading to a synthesis of the two. Because of the restrictions and stereotypes associated with American notions of "blackness," West Indians wish to establish themselves as being different from the society's perception of African Americans. They want to be viewed by the society as "West Indians," an identity which encompasses pride in African ancestry, a focus on achievement, and somewhat conservative values. On a negative note, this attempt at identity construction sometimes involves the holding of negative stereotypes of African Americans. The irony of West Indians holding such stereotypes is that, since the society promulgates them against blacks, in general, West Indians also find themselves being stereotyped. Over time, their experiences with racial discrimination convince many that attempts to distance from African Americans are both futile and morally wrong. West Indians and African Americans, it turns out, must daily face common problems resulting from race. Thus, though some West Indians would distance themselves from African Americans, they find that racial issues which affect both groups singularly, pull them together. Or, put another way, where race becomes *the* issue, West Indians often conclude that the relevant identity to hold is "black," rather than "West Indian"—a position, it must be noted, which results from a combination of imposition of identity by powerful outsiders and choice. Taken together, these facts mean that West Indians find themselves caught between powerful cross-pressures of ethnic separatism and racial identification.

Virginia Turner, "Jamaicans Outraged: New York Police Targeting West Indians"

Jamaican and Caribbean nationals in New York are expressing outrage at an internal police memo giving directives to patrol units to compile a list of Jamaican and West Indian nationals who are arrested or booked.

Dated January 9, 1997, the memo said, "In an effort to identify individuals arrested of West Indian or Jamaican descent, effective immediately, all Patrol Boroughs are directed to have precinct personnel fax a copy of all on-line booking sheets with arrest number to: Street Crime Unit, Attention Sergeant Burke and Detective Callan . . . "

The Mayor, Rudolph Giuliani, and Police Chief Howard Safir, are distancing themselves from the memo which was signed by Louis R. Attemune, Chief of Department, and addressed to the Chief of Patrol.

Police Commissioner Howard Safir said he has never seen the memo and did not approve any such directive. And the Mayor has said that no such policy exists.

But their denials are being met with scepticism by Jamaicans.

"There is no way that a memo like this could have been drafted and written without the top officials knowing. They must have discussed it amongst the top brass such as the head of Crime Unit, Chief of Patrol, before it was drafted," said an enraged City Councilwoman Una Clarke, in an interview with *The Weekly Gleaner*.

The Jamaica-born City Council-woman has contacted the Mayor and the Police Commissioner to meet with community leaders as early as possible to discuss and resolve the matter.

Noting that in every ethnic group there are "the good, the bad and the indifferent," Clarke said she is upset by this attempt to criminalise the entire community. "I hate stereotyping and I think this is what this is all about, but we will not sit back and allow the community to be mistreated," she declared.

The Caribbean American Legal Defence and Education Fund (CALDEF) has also issued a statement expressing its concern. Noted criminal attorney and a spokesperson for CALDEF, Oliver Smith, said that he would like to know the extent to which the memo was responded to by the rank and file before it was withdrawn as this could be grounds for a class action suit. However he, like most West Indians within the community, are interested in finding out, now, what was the rationale for such a memo.

"We need to know what is the basis and we need to be given a satisfactory explanation, the mere fact that the Commissioner said he did not see it is not sufficient," Smith said.

Attorney Richard Watz, of the law firm McMickens, Curtis, Ellis and Moore, is concerned that the memo is merely articulating an unwritten policy by the Police Department.

And, this is what worries Irvine Clare of the Caribbean Immigrant Services.

"We have heard in recent months reports of people being accosted and their 'green cards' taken away from them, is this then the sentiments on the street? If so, then the top brass within the police force must meet with the community. We cannot sit and let them stigmatize the entire community," she declared.

Clare pointed out that this "unfortunate memo," came a day after the Mayor announced plans to work with the immigrant community. A community which listed Jamaicans as the fourth largest group, (over 32,000) to move into New York in the last four years, according to a Department of Planning report released last week.

The van drivers association, through the president of the Queens Van Drivers Association, Hector Rickets, would hate to think that the Caribbean community is the target of the police.

While he has no problem with the police going about their duty and reviewing arrest records, it is the selective nature of the memo which concerns him most.

"We are vulnerable. We are on the road everyday. We are very exposed," said Ricketts, who added that the association has had a much better working relationship with this administration compared to the previous one of Mayor David Dinkins.

He feels that the issue should be addressed with an apology and attorney Smith said that it is important that this apology must be race and ethnic neutral. "We are waiting to see what kind of damage control will be put in place and how effective it will be," Ricketts added, musing, "I am hoping they are not seeing us as a Caribbean mafia as that is far from the truth. We have come here to work and most of us do."

From community leaders to the man in the street such as a gas station worker, who did not want to give his name, the memo was the topic of discussion. "Some Jamaicans make it bad for the rest of us but it is wrong for them to be picking on Jamaicans."

When contacted, the Jamaican Consulate, through Deputy Counsel General, Effie Stewart, said that it had "no comment" to make but that they are pursuing the matter at "a diplomatic level."

CHAPTER NINE

What the Immigrants Make, America Takes: Work in Immigrant Communities

Introduction

Throughout the nation's history, one of the main reasons that Americans have been receptive to immigration has been the need for labor. During the colonial era, indentured servants and black slaves from Africa, involuntary migrants, supplemented the labor that European settlers poured into farms and plantations they hoped would yield sustenance for families and, eventually, commodities for commerce. In the early decades of the nineteenth century, many northern states abolished slavery as a labor system. Northern farmers found slave labor too costly and impractical for the small plot agriculture common in that region. The need for labor in the growing commercial and industrial sectors was satisfied by migrants from northern and western Europe and some free blacks. Much of the South continued to rely on black slave labor on its farms and plantations where large gangs of laborers made cotton production increasingly profitable. There, slavery persisted until the slaves were emancipated by the thirteenth amendment to the Constitution after the Civil War.

During the mid-nineteenth century, Scandinavian and German immigrants arrived in increasing numbers, farming and contributing their skills as artisans to the economies of eastern and midwestern states. Chinese migrants to the West Coast were agricultural laborers, miners, and unskilled workers building the nation's fledgling railroad system. Mexicans who migrated northward across our shifting and porous borders bent their backs and strained their muscles to plant and harvest crops. Irish males could be found

Mark Wyman, *Round Trip to America: The Immigrants Return to Europe, 1880–1930.* (Ithaca: Cornell University, 1993), pp. 45–66, 70–73. Copyright © 1993 Cornell University. Used by permission of the publisher, Cornell University Press.

Louise Odencrantz, *Italian Women in Industry: A Study of Conditions in New York City.* (New York: Russell Sage Foundation, 1919). Public Domain.

Laura Parker, "USA Just Wouldn't Work Without Immigrant Labor" in *USA Today,* July 23, 2001. Copyright © 2001 USA Today. Reprinted with permission.

in mills, laying rails, and everywhere heavy labor was required. Immigrant women were an important addition to the American economy. Some worked in textile mills, where their manual dexterity was advantageous. Others, such as Irish women, found that the ladder to upward mobility led through the kitchen or laundry room in the homes of a growing urban upper middle class. Domestic labor offered clean, safe, well-paid work opportunities. Irish women, who eventually arrived in greater numbers than Irish males, often found their domestic labor in greater demand than the manual labor of their brothers, husbands, and sons.

Post–Civil War industrialization created an unprecedented demand for semi-skilled and unskilled labor. In the bustling factories and mines, as well as in the fields, the foreign-born labored. The declining availability of low-cost land on which to settle made ownership of one's own farm less possible and industrial skills even more desirable for new arrivals. Different groups brought a variety of skills. According to data gathered by immigration officials, 66 percent of Jews arriving from the cities and towns of eastern Europe listed themselves as skilled laborers. Many were tailors in the men's and women's clothing trades or highly talented makers of jewelry. Still others worked as cigar-makers, cobblers, tanners, or furriers. However, many of the southern Italians, Poles, and Slavs who had farmed in their homelands had few skills, but their robust health and strength made them ideal for factory labor and the heavy work required in construction and mining. Although the initial arrivals were often young men, millions of women also migrated, some as part of families, but others came alone. They, too, found places in the industrial economy. Some, who found jobs in the garment industry, bent their backs over sewing machines in small cramped factories, sweatshops. Others worked in their homes. Home work often consisted of the repetitive performance of a single task, such as the sewing of the same seam on garments of the same kind piled in a stack next to the worker.

Today, new arrivals, legal and undocumented alike, find ample opportunities for employment in the United States. Migrant workers cross the Mexican border to plant and harvest. Their low-cost labor keeps the prices of fruits and vegetables inexpensive for American consumers. They often take jobs in the service sector that are either so low-paying or undesirable that native-born workers refuse them. However, at the other end of the scale, well-educated newcomers from China, India, and Pakistan are transforming America's high-tech industries, especially in areas of computer technology. The computer has rejuvenated home work. Men and women can support their families, working in a variety of industries that require online labor.

Immigrant labor has for the most part benefited the American economy, although some critics of immigration such as Peter Brimelow argue that the use of immigrant labor slowed the economic integration of African Americans into the American economy after the Civil War. He also suggests that the high wages paid to unskilled laborers in the United States as compared with other countries has drawn a disproportionate number of the unskilled to this country to compete with American workers for jobs.

American jobs and salaries have contributed to newcomers' upward mobility. Some immigrant workers have come to stay, but others have moved back and forth hoping eventually to earn enough money in the United States to live comfortably in their home country. From the perspective of arriving immigrants, the economic opportunities offered by the United States has long made it a magnet. In the late eighteenth and nineteenth centuries, inexpensive land offered the opportunity to turn hard work into security and a legacy for future generations. Highly skilled German artisans hoping to escape the factory system in Germany found that in America's small towns and cities they could continue their lives as independent artisans and craftsmen. No factory whistle summoned them to work. Quitting time came when they felt the job done, not upon the order of a foreman. Those with entrepreneurial inclinations found the pushcart or small shop the way to increase both income and control of their own lives.

When America industrialized, foreign-born workers scrambled to take advantage of higher wages in the United States compared to those in other immigrant destinations such as Canada, Argentina, Brazil, Australia, and South Africa. Later, labor unions allowed collective bargaining so workers at various levels of skills could use their numbers as leverage in negotiations for higher wages and better working conditions. Unions such as the United Mine Workers and International Ladies Garment Workers drew strength from foreign-born workers. Today, workers from all over the globe continue to migrate to the United States for higher wages and materially better lifestyles.

The first selection is a chapter from Mark Wyman's volume, *Round-Trip to America, The Immigrants Return to Europe, 1880–1930.* Wyman describes how vulnerable immigrant workers could be, often leading to injuries on industrial machinery they had not mastered. The industrial workplace was a dangerous place and immigrant workers had few protections. Nevertheless, millions of men and women moved back and forth across the Atlantic as members of an industrial workforce that was crucial to the evolution of industrial capitalism in the United States. Some intended their move to be permanent and brought families. Permanent migrations were common among groups such as Eastern European Jews and other minorities who were fleeing persecution or religious discrimination as well as economic depravation. Wyman explains that many labor migrants never intended their move to the United States to be permanent. Their initial goal was to earn money in the United States, but to spend it improving their lifestyles in their countries of origin. Immigrant workers at the turn of the last century often lived a transnational existence, migrating back and forth across oceans for higher salaries.

Labor brokers, such as the *padrones* who helped Italians find jobs, acted as go-betweens, making their own profits from pairing workers in search of high salaries with employers who needed reliable workers in quantity and often with particular skills. The increasing speed of transportation, railroads and steamships, facilitated the labor migrations. So, too, did speedier forms of communication, including extended telegraph lines and telephone lines

Figure 9.1   The artificial flower trade was popular among foreign-born workers, especially those who wished to work at home, such as the Maletestra family from Italy shown here in 1908. Flower makers avraged from ten to twelve gross per day, at six cents per gross. Courtesy of the U.S. National Archives.

into rural communities, which helped spread the news of job availability and wage scale fluctuations in different countries and different locations within countries.

American reformers were increasingly concerned about the influence of industrial life upon society's most vulnerable members, especially women and children. Louise C. Odencrantz was an investigator for the Committee on Women's Work for the Russell Sage Foundation. In 1919, she published the results of an extensive study, *Italian Women in Industry, A Study of Conditions in New York City*. Its purpose was to understand precisely how industrial life was affecting the Italian women immigrants who had entered the industrial workforce after arrival (figure 9.1). Hours, working conditions, salaries, as well as patterns of family life were all carefully documented. In this selection, Odencrantz discusses the increasingly large role of Italian women in New York's garment trades. Her explanation for this popular choice is grounded in her perception of Italian social patterns and cultural perceptions, ". . . the needle trades appeal especially to Italians. Their idea of the woman is primarily as a home maker. Just as in every home you find a sewing machine in order that the mother can make her children's clothes, so the daughter, when she is ready to go out to work, wants to choose dress-making." Such comments suggest that while the data Odencrantz has gathered are illuminating, her own analysis is grounded in her perceptions of a culture to which she is decidedly an outsider. Odencrantz also discusses how

Italian women not in the garment industry sometimes found employment in box-making, the tobacco industry, and candy-making.

The final selection suggests that the age of the immigrant worker is hardly over. Although the flow of immigration is now more frequently from Latin America and Asia rather than from southern and eastern Europe, immigrant labor is still in demand. Almost 18 million immigrant workers were working in the United States in summer 2001, when the article appeared in the newspaper, a number that has likely increased. The proposed immigration reform mentioned was stalled by the events of September 11, 2001, but the debate continues. Just as New York once drew Italian women to its garment trades, this selection explains that communities such as Memphis, Tennessee, welcome immigrants to its construction trades because, as in the past, America needs manual laborers, immigrants are looking for work, and newcomers want a role in building the United States.

Suggestions for Further Reading

David Emmons, *The Butte Irish: Class and Ethnicity in an American Mining Town, 1875–1925* (Urbana IL: University of Illinois Press, 1989).

John Bodnar, *The Transplanted, A History of Immigrants in Urban America* (Bloomington, IN: Indiana University Press, 1985).

Lizabeth Cohen, *Making a New Deal, Industrial Workers in Chicago, 1919–1939* (New York: Cambridge University Press, 1990).

Miriam Cohen, *Workshop to Office, Two Generations of Italian Women in New York City, 1900–1950* (Ithaca, NY: Cornell University Press, 1992).

Sucheng Chan, *The Bitter-Sweet Soil, The Chinese in California Agriculture, 1860–1910* (Berkeley, CA: University of California Press, 1986).

Susan Glenn, *Daughters of the Shtetl, Life and Labor in the Immigrant Generation* (Ithaca, NY: Cornell University Press, 1990).

Vicki Ruiz, *Cannery Women, Cannery Lives: Mexican Women, Unionization and the California Food Processing Industry* (Albuquerque, NM: University of New Mexico Press, 1987).

Mark Wyman, "Immigrants in an Industrializing Economy"

The "picker" machine in the Massachusetts textile mill beat the cotton to clean it as it came out of bales—beat it with knives circling in 1,500 unending revolutions a minute inside the "beater box." Like all machines it was ultimately tended by a human, in this case a recently arrived Pole named Frank Chmiel, age thirty-five. He did not speak English and had no previous mechanical experience.

Much of the success of American industry in the years following the Civil War was based on the fact that men like Frank Chmiel could be taught to operate such a complex, fast-moving device. For this was a major part of the "revolution" that made possible the industrial revolution, under which minute subdivisions were created in each work process, usually through extensive use of machinery. Laborers soon began replacing skilled workers, becoming tenders of machines rather than merely shovelers or loaders. This transformation also meant that the unskilled—immigrants and Americans, farmboys and children—could be brought to the factory and taught specific tasks without a lengthy apprenticeship. A "melter" had always been a highly skilled job in a steel mill, but by 1901 Charles Schwab of Carnegie Steel was arguing that he could take a green hand and make a melter of him in six or eight weeks. Henry Ford's foundry had 95 percent unskilled laborers by 1914, trained to do just one operation, which Ford said "the most stupid man can learn in two days." That was what the machine age amounted to for many workers in American industry.

In mining, the changes were equally spectacular and led to large-scale displacement of skilled Americans as well as veteran English, Welsh, and Scots coal miners who had come into the coalfields after the Civil War. With new undercutting machines, the pick miner was largely done away with, the Dillingham Commission reported, thereby increasing the proportion of unskilled workmen who loaded coal after machines had cut it down. Only a few days' apprenticeship was needed to teach this to inexperienced workers. Noting similar changes in metal mining, a Finnish historian summed up: "Thus the Finn, who had never been a miner, became one in the United States."

It was this transformation that brought immigrant Frank Chmiel to the Thorndike Company's picker machine in Massachusetts in 1902. Chmiel's entry into American industry was fairly typical; unfortunately, his problems with the cotton picker were not at all unusual either. He had been instructed for two weeks before working on his own, but the day after Chmiel was put on the picker the rolls feeding cotton began to clog. Failing to free them by pulling cotton away from the emerging rolls, he removed the protective cover on the beater box—as he had seen his instructor do—and reached in to pull the cotton through the feed rolls, even as the knives jabbed into them at 1,500 revolutions a minute. His arm was cut off.

Chmiel may have occupied a crucial spot in America's industrial transformation, but that held little importance for the U.S. judicial system. Though the common law of liability was changing by 1902, it still effectively decreed that few employers were forced to pay compensation to employees injured on the job, especially when the worker had removed a machine guard and thereby contributed to his own injury. The weight of legal precedent did not take account of greenhorns: rather, court traditions envisioned a perfect, English-speaking employee who never grew tired after long hours amid smoke and din, was never distracted, was not made nervous or desperate by fears of being fired, and always understood perfectly his instructions as well as each rattle and hum of the machine.

But reality was different. This case dealt with an immigrant Pole, not speaking English, having no previous mechanical experience; probably he was a peasant farmhand before coming to America. His instructor at the machine observed before the court, "As to whether Mr. Chmiel learned slowly or rapidly, I say he didn't have a good head to learn; . . . . Frank showed that he wasn't good to learn, and didn't learn well, because I showed him how to oil, and then told him how to oil there, and the third time asking him to do it he didn't do it."

Despite such testimony and the employee's peasant background, the court stated that the Thorndike Company could not be expected to have had "any reason to suppose that [Chmiel] was so dull as to require a caution not to put his arm where it would come in contact with the beater knives making 1,500 revolutions a minute." He received no compensation.

It was part of the new order of things that the industrial system booming across Europe and North America would rely for much of its thrust on inexperienced, vulnerable greenhorns like Frank Chmiel. As British labor historian E. J. Hobsbawm has observed, "the bulk of industrial workers in all countries began, like America's, as first-generation immigrants from preindustrial societies. . . . And like all first-generation immigrants, they looked backwards as much as forwards."

Immigrant Laborers

New and untried as the immigrants from European villages were, industry nevertheless depended on them, and the America fever brought an unending flow of workers willing to labor long hours for low wages. Even these conditions were often improvements over their earlier peasant drudgery outside the money economy or at the subsistence-level wages of day labor. One study of such new laborers around the world found several common features, regardless of country or period of history: originating in backward areas and lacking prior contact with industrial processes, these usually unskilled and illiterate laborers were attracted to industrial centers to take specific jobs—jobs often held in disdain by native workers. But they saw themselves initially as only short-term workers for their new employer, and only temporary residents of their new homes.

These characteristics were present in abundance in the United States among the workers brought by the millions into the industrial boom developing by the 1880s. A government study found that, by 1900, 73.2 percent of the Italian, Slavic, and Hungarian immigrants resided in the seven major industrial states that produced 61 percent of the nation's manufactured and mining products. To Americans these were seekers after a new life, the "wretched refuse" of distant shores. But as one authority has defined the issue, "from the point of view of the Atlantic Economy, all those Jews, Italians, Poles or Armenians who traveled to America were essentially migrant-laborers searching for work, people displaced by a changing, industrializing society." The contrasting views of who the newcomers were became important, she notes, because these "often accounted for divergencies in action and behavior."

They came into an America caught up in an economic explosion. Railways grew from only 35,000 miles of track at the end of the Civil War to 242,000 miles by 1900, including five transcontinental railroads. Only 1.6 thousand tons of steel had been produced by American mills in 1867, but output rose to 7.2 million tons in 1897. By 1900 steel was being sold to England, heretofore considered the world's industrial leader; American pig iron production had doubled Britain's by then. In fact, the United States had more than 30 percent of world manufacturing output as the century ended. Chicago's stockyards handled 1.5 million head of livestock during their first year of operation in 1866, but this rose to 14.6 million by 1900 and hit 18.6 million by 1924; employment reached 60,000 during World War I.

Considerable credit for this growth must go to the immigrant laborers. One economist has estimated that Europe lost one-quarter of its labor force to the New World from 1850 to 1914, and within the United States one-third of the increase in the labor force from 1870 to 1910 was accounted for by immigration. The immigrants' presence was crucial.

They flocked to industry, which meant they largely flocked into cities. Although by 1900 only 38.8 percent of America's foreign-born lived in cities of more than 100,000, these same cities were home to 73.4 percent of the Russians, 61.2 percent of the Italians, 60 percent of the Poles.

Immigrants predominated in many occupations, such as the readymade clothing industry, in which they outnumbered native-born workers two to one by 1910; they were dominant by 1.5 to one in blast furnaces, rolling mills, public works construction, and maintenance-of-way labor. But specific areas and firms frequently showed much higher proportions of the foreign-born: the Carnegie Steel works of Allegheny County, Pennsylvania, employed 14,359 common laborers in 1907, and 11,694 were East Europeans. One of Henry Ford's plants counted 12,880 employees in 1914, and 9,109 of these were foreign-born, a majority of them Poles, Russians, Romanians, Italians, Sicilians, and Austro-Hungarians. John Fitch's 1910 study of the steelworkers observed that in blast furnaces, "aside from the Irish foreman, there are seldom any but Slavs or Hungarians employed," called "Hunkies" or "Ginnies." A survey of Michigan copper miners and smelter workers found that 80 percent were foreign-born, the largest group Finns, who constituted more than one-fourth of the total.

According to the Dillingham Commission,[1] whose investigation ran through the 1907–11 period, 57.7 percent of all iron and steel manufacturing employees east of the Mississippi were foreign-born, and 64.4 percent of them had been farmers or farm laborers abroad. The same study reported that, in Pennsylvania's bituminous coal mines, 76 percent of the miners were foreign-born and less than 8 percent of these came from the British Isles or Germany. "The term 'American miner', so far as the western Pennsylvania field is concerned, is largely a misnomer," the principal investigator concluded.

The Italian became the road builder in America, the track layer, the shovel man; lacking mechanical skills, "he could contribute nothing more, and *nothing more was asked of him,* than the strength of his arms," Francesco Cerase has written. By 1890 some 90 percent of Italian wage earners in New York were engaged in public works construction; soon they consti-tuted a monopoly of the sanitation department crews in San Francisco and did 99 percent of Chicago's roadwork. The great majority of railroad builders in the mid-seaboard, New England, and the central states were Italians during the period.

These immigrants did not often turn to agriculture, despite their back-grounds. Taking up the digging of sewer lines in America proved easier than becoming an American farmer. Another reason farming did not attract these Italians, or many others drawn from the New Immigration, was that it did not suit their goals. These workers sought money, now.

Many were attracted to the United States precisely because they could plan a short-term visit: help from the shipping company agent, speedy ships, low fares, the knowledge of routes and jobs and wages—all these made it easier to plan a reduced stay abroad. "The absence was to be temporary," Julianna Puskás has written of Hungary's emigrants; "they would soon return with the money made overseas to make a better life for themselves in the environment they were attached to, the place where they *wanted* to live." Poles entering Pittsburgh's industries were said to consider their sojourn there a temporary necessity that would enable them to achieve their larger goal of increasing land holdings at home. A Ukrainian woman recalled that when she came in 1912 she planned to stay "just two or three years. Everybody had the same idea—make a little money and go back home."

Several basic points followed the decision for a temporary stay. A wife's presence was unneeded in America and could even be a detriment if she did not add to the savings but depleted them. Women continued to arrive, but in smaller numbers than males and usually as unwed single females; as such, they found ready work as household servants as well as in the sweatshops of the rising ready-made clothing industry. From 1870 to 1920 the yearly per-centage of males entering the United States fell below 60 percent only fourteen times and was never under half; it exceeded 70 percent five times in the 1900–10 decade. The peak immigration year of 1907 also produced the highest male percentage: 72.4 percent.

Some European observers of this process questioned why large numbers planned only a temporary stay, "with a mentality that was not favorable to the exhausting process of adapting to the new society" (in the words of Italian scholar Livi Bacci). They could not but wonder at the living conditions adopted by their compatriots overseas. A Croatian writer in 1910 worried that, "if our people would emigrate permanently, without the intention of returning, they could cultivate the soil in America and their life abroad would not be so difficult."

But generally it was Americans, not Europeans, who wondered at the temporary nature of their residence. The matter began to draw attention as early as 1888, when the head of Pittsburgh's Department of Charities was asked whether the New Immigrants planned to become U.S. citizens: "Well, I will give you an instance of what I have heard them say when I questioned them in regard to whether or not they came to remain here. They come here in order to get a certain sum of money, but not to remain here. I have interrogated them. They have come in[to] my place for relief." This idea became attached to the New Immigration.

A New World for Workers

With dreams of dollars in their heads, and their womenfolk safely back in the Old Country, the immigrants moved into American industry. More than 60 percent of the Poles in Philadelphia in 1915 were in unskilled occupations, with only 24 percent in skilled and semiskilled industrial work. The unskilled Poles labored in a variety of enterprises in the city—as ironworkers, steelworkers, and leatherworkers, and as general laborers in chemical factories, petroleum and sugar refineries, slaughterhouses, and tanneries as well as on the docks and in the railroad yards. One immigrant Pole's job record showed initial employment in a New York sugar factory, then to the brickyards, on to a railroad job in Boston, then a lumberyard, and finally home after the 1907 economic crisis hit. The drive to accumulate savings fueled such mobility, and another Pole responded to his wife's request that he return by vowing that he would work "as long as we have not a thousand roubles." It would not pay to stay just a year in America: "I came in order to earn something."

The mines and forests of the Lake states and Pacific Northwest attracted Scandinavians in large numbers, although Italians, Magyars, Croatians, and Slovenes also found jobs there. Italians were urged on by their government in this job quest, even receiving advice to "remember that you are in a great and free country that is like your country of labor." Although their backgrounds included many occupations in addition to farming, Italian laborers were concentrated in excavation work such as on the Bronx Aqueduct, on construction projects such as building Grand Central Station in New York, and railroad track work. ("It would be difficult at the present time to build a railroad of any considerable length without Italian labor," a Maine Bureau of Labor report stated.) As historian Rudolph Vecoli asserted, "it was the uncommon immigrant from Italy who did not do his stint working in a *ghenga* (gang) on the *tracca* (track)."

No one expected such work to be easy. "Everyone works like hell," a Finn wrote home from Michigan, and the experiences gave rise to a Polish saying: "America for the oxen, Europe for the peasant." A YMCA leader examining the immigrants' situation in Pittsburgh found that as a rule they earned the lowest wages and worked the "full stint" of hours, including twelve hours daily on a seven-day week at the blast furnaces. Long hours were common for immigrant workers; so was energy-sapping labor. An Irishman recalled a story he was told by a returned "Yank":

> At a place called Watertown near Boston, there was a man who owned sandpits and who employed a lot of men. He used to meet the boats coming into Boston and engage the immigrants. A lot of Irishmen were engaged by him and he used to tell them this was the way to work—here informant made the motion of shovelling very rapidly with a spade he held in his hands—if they wished to get on well in America. Very few were able to endure the work for very long, but he was always able to obtain fresh relays from the incoming boats. In this way he managed to keep the sand pits going at full pressure.

They agreed: you worked hard in America. One had to "sweat more during a day than during a whole week in Poland," a peasant immigrant wrote home. Returnees to Ireland said that they had worked like slaves, and some argued that "if people worked hard at home they would make as much money at home as any one in America." Interviewers with Norwegian immigrants found general agreement that they had to work harder in America than in Norway. Similar comments appeared across the continent as remigrants recounted their experiences.

Immigrant women also worked hard. A study of Chicago's Polonia in 1900 found that 38.7 percent of all employed Polish women were in the equivalent under other names—sometimes simply "boss" or "contractor." He frequently arranged for the immigrants' travel to America through contacts with confederates back home; or he was among the swarms of "vampires" on the docks and hired them on arrival. More commonly he operated through an employment agency. Chicago had 289 licensed employment bureaus in 1908, and 110 of them specialized in supplying immigrant workers; from June 1908 through June 1909 the agencies sent some 40,000 men and women to jobs. That year the Chicago agencies sent Italians, Greeks, and Serbians to railroad section work; Bulgarians, Austrians, and Scandinavians (and most native-born Americans) into construction; and Poles to the logging camps in the northwoods.

An Italian Socialist newspaper described the employment agency's operations: the shop's windows featured posters advertising jobs for 1,000 shovelers, 300 carpenters, 200 hod carriers. Contact had been made with companies building railroad lines, bridges, tunnels, and similar projects, all needing laborers. The immigrants—out of work, desperate, unable to speak

English and fend for themselves—gathered eagerly at the counter and were talked to "in the friendliest, most fatherly manner" by the padrone: "He makes them believe that he had rejected two or three hundred Slavs or Greeks in order to reserve the good jobs for the Italians. And what fine jobs! Two dollars a day, nine hours of light, easy work, the purest air, distilled water, free board, Italian boss, low cost of living—an Eldorado! They must decide quickly for few vacancies are left." The men then paid costs of $8 to $12 for the trip to the work site, plus $5 as the *bossatura*, the padrone's fee. From a gang of twelve, the padrone made $108: $60 from his $5-per-man fee plus $2 discount on the railroad ticket paid by each, plus $2 paid him for each laborer delivered to the hiring company.

At the worksite the padrone could sometimes make money in other ways, buying $100 worth of lumber to construct sleeping shacks, billing workers $1 a month each to sleep in them, charging for food if he supplied that. Often workers' wages went first through his hands. Added to this were cases of the padrone fleeing with wages or setting up his own bank allegedly to send money home but then absconding with the funds. For all these reasons, the padrone was a frequent target of immigrant complaints and governmental investigations.

Irregular employment, in addition to dismal job conditions and the search for better pay, kept the immigrants mobile. A Pennsylvania investigator admitted that he could make no estimate of the number of Johnstown's Hungarians since they were always moving; only about 60 percent of the city's foreign-born were "permanently located," in fact. The Dillingham Commission found in a survey of almost 4,000 coal miners' households that only 16.6 percent of the immigrants had worked a full twelve months the preceding year, and less than half had worked as long as nine months. This was a life known well by a Finn who described his job forays among the logging camps of northern Wisconsin and Michigan's Upper Peninsula:

> The Flambo camp stopped running in the middle of November. I spent one week going from camp to camp but could not find work. All the camps were full of men. There were not enough beds and I had to sleep on the floor. I went to one camp on Saturday evening and I was planning to stay there over the weekend. But next morning I had to start walking to another camp again to get there before dark. And when I could not find work, I drove to Bessemer. So now I lie here at Lehtonen's. I am not sure whether I can find work before Christmas.

Quitting became one of the most common responses by greenhorns to heavy exertion and degrading conditions, and they trooped out of American industry as fast as they trooped in. Turnover in Philadelphia's Polish areas often ran from 75 to 80 percent; in Pittsburgh a large machine works hired 21,000 men and women through the course of 1906 to maintain a work force of 10,000. The claim of one mining superintendent to have hired 5,000 men in a year to keep 1,000 working was challenged by the operator of the district's largest property; he admitted, however, that hiring 2,000 to keep a crew of 1,000 would not be an exaggeration. Ford reported 416 percent turnover at a plant in 1913, and the following year metal manufacturing industries had turnover rates ranging from 88 to 157 percent.

It was in some ways a symbiotic relationship, despite the unequal bargaining power between the two sides. In the "land of opportunity," the immigrants used their freedom to travel to seek the best-paying jobs where they could save the most money. Loyalty to a company did not enter into the picture. But it was a land of opportunity for employers, too, and they counted on a flexible, unending labor supply. Chicago meatpackers rebutted a union wage demand in 1904 by pointing out that up to 5,000 transient laborers gathered each morning at 7 AM to seek work outside the plant gates, but less than 10 percent of these could be hired. No special inducements were needed in such cases.

Labor economist John R. Commons encountered these realities one day when he entered the hiring office in a large factory:

> Scattered about were a number of sturdy immigrants fresh from the old country. On that day the manager was hiring Swedes. He said that the week before he had been hiring Poles, and before that he had taken on Italians. It was a good idea, he said, to get them mixed up. He told me of other large firms in that city with similar employment managers and a similar policy. They had an informal club that met usually once a week.

Commons found that managers were proud of being able to forecast the condition, even the mood, of the labor market. If raising wages 10 percent would keep workers calm, they would raise them, then lower them later. They even claimed to have contacts with union leaders who would let them know in advance where they planned to organize. At another establishment Commons observed the hiring officer walking among a hundred men waiting on the sidewalk. He "looked at their feet, sized up their nationality and fitness," and then "picked out ten or fifteen and sent them in." The rest, Commons added, "stood around with serious faces and then drifted away." These conditions—employers adjusting wages, to maintain a quiescent and adequate crew, hiring and firing immigrants at will, with an abundance of immigrants desperate for work—were said by Commons to represent "the commodity theory of labor. Demand and supply determine wages. . . . The ebb and flow of the labor market is like the ebb and flow of the commodity market."

Note

1. Forty-one volume report on immigration by a Joint Senate-House Committee Chaired by Sen. William Paul Dillingham (R-VT).

Louise C. Odencrantz, *Italian Women in Industry: A Study of Conditions in New York City*

Occupations of Italian Women at Work

Surrounding the Italian district on the lower west side is an industrial boundary of busy streets lined with high loft buildings and remodeled dwellings where the noisy work of manufacturing is going on. If you approach the district from the south, by way of Canal or Broome streets, you will notice the odor of chocolate from some candy factory, or the strong smell of glue from a paper-box plant. On the west side, along Hudson and Greenwich streets, alluring signs advertise the homes of famous salad dressings, spices, groceries, or pickles. Approach from Broadway and you pass crowded workrooms where men's clothing is made by the wholesale, hats turned out by the gross, and flowers and feathers pasted, branched, and packed for shipment to the farthest corners of the country. You pick your way through the narrow, crowded streets of Mercer, Greene, or West Broadway, where heavily loaded trucks are delivering huge rolls of cloth or carrying away the finished products in the form of underwear, neckwear, shirtwaists, or mattresses and burial supplies. To the north of the neighborhood lies the center of the industry of women's and children's clothing, not only for New York City but for the whole United States as well. Here cloaks and suits are stitched and finished for wearers from Maine to Oregon, dresses of silk, wool, or cotton for the women of Dakota or Texas, and clothing for the children of San Francisco or Atlanta. Gray buildings of 15 or 20 stories tower high to the heavens, each floor vibrating with the motion of heavy-power sewing machines. In the height of the season every nook of each loft is filled with men and women straining every nerve to satisfy the frantic demands of jobber and retailer.

The location of this Italian colony within these industrial boundaries is typical of the bond between its members and the life of the city. When the woman leaves her home, however Italian in its customs, it is in these streets seething with American industry that she seeks her day's work. Her work place is the means by which she may come to look upon herself not alone as an Italian, but as a part of the big American labor force.

Manufacturing is the leading pursuit of Italian women in New York City. Although no general statistics are available about the occupational distribution of the various nationalities since 1900, it is worth while noting the figures showing conditions at that time. In 1900, 77 percent of the women workers of Italian parentage were engaged in manufacturing, as compared with 36 percent of those of all nationalities. The Italian woman does not turn to domestic or personal service. While 40 per cent of all the women at work in 1900 in New York City were in domestic and personal service, only 13 per cent of the Italian women were found in this field. In table 9.1, the occupations of the groups of women investigated are compared with those in which all Italian women in New York City were found at work in 1900.

Table 9.1　Main groups of occupations for Italian women workers investigated, for all Italian women and for all women workers in New York City, 1900[a]

Main occupational groups	Italian women included in investigation		All Italian women		All women	
	Number	Percent	Number	Percent	Number	Percent
Manufacturing	1,027	93.9	9,391	77.1	132,535	36.1
Trade and transportation	55	5.0	984	8.1	65,318	17.8
Professional service	7	0.6	150	1.2	22,422	6.1
Domestic and personal service	6	0.5	1,602	13.2	146,722	39.9
Agriculture	—	—	45	0.4	440	0.1
Total	1,095	100.0	12,172	100.0	367,437	100.0

Note:　[a]　Twelfth United States Census, 1900. Occupations, p. 638 et ff.

Manufacturing

For this reason the investigation soon resolved itself into a study of Italian women in manufacturing. Most of them worked in factories within walking distance of their homes. Some had ventured to dressmaking shops on Fifth Avenue, to department stores or offices as far north as Thirty-fourth Street, or to factories uptown or even in Brooklyn or New Jersey, often in these latter cases to continue work in a shop or factory that had originally been located in this downtown district. But usually, the fact that a firm had moved was sufficient excuse for leaving a position. Statements like "I don't want to spend 10 cents a day to ride up there," or "It was too far to walk to Thirty-third Street," or "I didn't want a job where I had to ride," showed why the majority were still to be found in the factories in nearby streets.

Of the total group of 1,095 women who were investigated, 1,027, or 94 percent, were employed in manufacturing. Only seven had entered work that could be called at all professional in nature. These were a model, a singer, a teacher, an assistant in a laboratory, and three social workers. Six were in domestic or personal service as waitresses, maids, or cooks. Seventeen were in stores, 38 in offices, 11 of whom were stenographers, and four bookkeepers. The other 23 clerical workers did such unskilled work as addressing envelopes, opening mail, or simple filing. Only occasionally did girls express the opinion that office work, however unskilled, was superior to that in a factory. The latter was generally accepted as offering perfectly respectable employment for any girl, with the possibility of better earnings than office work. A woman of twenty-four, who had been opening mail in a large publishing house for ten years, explained that few Italian girls were willing to do clerical work as the pay was too poor. "Their mothers wouldn't stand for it. Most Italian girls are operators because they can make more money."

The group of Italian women investigated probably included a larger proportion of factory workers than would be found among wage-earning Italian women in the city. The limitation of the investigation chiefly to an Italian district where few would be engaged in domestic service has affected the proportion in this occupation. A tabulation, however, of the occupations of a group of 608 Italian immigrant women who had arrived alone in this country, visited by the International Institute in 1912–13, showed that factory work predominated among them also. The list of their occupations showed 77 per cent engaged in manufacturing, while only 16 per cent were in domestic and personal service, and a little more than 1 per cent in sales work. Thus, whether the women were recent arrivals, came over as children, or were born here, they found employment chiefly in the factory trades. Table 9.2 gives the occupations of the 1,095 women by age at coming to the United States.

Table 9.2   Occupations of Italian women workers, by age at time of Coming to the United States

	Women who were		
Kind of work	Foreign born 14 years old or more at time of coming	Native born and foreign born less than 14 years old at time of coming	All women
Manufacturing	364	663	1,027
Flowers and feathers	33	123	156
Men's and boys' clothing	64	31	95
Women's tailored garments	38	12	50
Custom dressmaking	6	18	24
Wholesale dressmaking	59	54	113
Shirtwaists	18	33	51
Muslin underwear	6	34	40
Corsets	7	15	22
Hand embroidery	21	21	42
All other women's and children's clothing	15	55	70
Paper boxes	5	24	29
Other paper goods	8	31	39
Tobacco	22	5	27
Candy	22	46	68
Other foodstuffs	11	16	27
Headwear	3	34	37
Textiles and miscellaneous sewed materials	11	65	76
Rubber, fur, and leather goods	9	14	23
Miscellaneous manufactured goods	1	23	24
Laundry, dyeing, and cleaning	5	9	14
Store work	—	17	17
Office work	1	37	38
Professional service	3	4	7
Domestic service	5	1	6
Total	373	722	1,095

Among the 1,027 women employed in factories, 75 industries were represented, the number in each of these industries varying from 156 employed in artificial flowers and feathers and 113 in making women's and misses' dresses for the wholesale trade, to the one or two employed in the manufacture of paper bags, burial supplies, or raincoats. The variety of the list, even for this small group, shows that Italian women have invaded almost every woman-employing industry in the city.

The clothing trades led in the employment of both native and foreign born. About half, or 507 of those in manufacturing, were making men's, women's, and children's clothing. In the two industries of men's clothing and women's cloaks and suits, where the work for women consisted chiefly of hand sewing, the foreign-born women who had come over as adults, predominated. Many had not yet learned English. Few had entered such trades as muslin underwear and corsets, where the work was chiefly power operating.

Again, of the women engaged in the manufacturing of clothing, nearly half were twenty-one years of age or over. For the entire group, however, the young workers predominated, two-thirds being under twenty-one. Only 16 per cent of the group were twenty-five years or over, though it included many women who had emigrated to this country as adults. The unskilled trades, such as flowers, feathers, candy, and paper boxes, employed the majority of the young girls.

The Needle Trades: That the needle industries should lead in employing Italian women is not surprising when we consider that in 1909 the two leading industries in New York City measured by value of products were women's and men's clothing. In this city was manufactured 69.3 per cent of all women's clothing in the United States, and 38.4 per cent of all men's clothing. Here alone were employed 55,601 women on women's clothing, or more than half of those so employed throughout the United States, and 23,228 women on men's clothing. These two industries combined employed 40 per cent of the total women counted in manufacturing establishments in New York City in 1909.

Moreover, the needle trades appeal especially to Italians. Their idea of the woman is primarily as a home maker. Just as in every home you find a sewing machine in order that the mother can make her children's clothes, so the daughter, when she is ready to go out to work, wants to choose dressmaking. In this way she believes that she will some day be able to sew her own clothes. Unfortunately they have no realization of the fine subdivisions that exist in this trade today, when such tasks as sewing on buttons on shirtwaists, cutting threads off petticoats, operating a ruffling or buttonhole machine, or setting in sleeves may be the one process that a girl will work at year after year. Even when she has secured a chance to work in a custom dressmaking place she rarely learns how to make a whole garment, but spends the day as a finisher, sleeve draper, waist finisher, repair or alteration hand, or even as a presser or stock girl. Though the work is still done for individual customers, the increasing size of such shops tends to greater subdivision of labor for the workers, and there is as little chance for a woman to learn how to make a whole garment as in the shops where dresses are made by the wholesale.

Lucy, an interesting, ambitious girl of twenty-one, who was busily cutting out a dress on the floor while talking to the visitor, said that most Italian girls went into dressmaking and the sewing trades because they believed they would be useful to them after marriage. "We have to think of the future and not always of the present." Her sister, however, disputed the fact that the trade would teach her much about making her own clothes. "In a shirtwaist factory," she said, "you may have to do only one part of the waist, sleeves, closing-in, or hemming, and you will have to work fast at that one thing." Another girl of seventeen, who during her three years' work in a flower factory had been the principal support of her old mother and father, still regretted that she had never been able to "learn a trade—something like dressmaking, so I could make my own clothes."

Many of the women had learned fine hand sewing in the public or convent schools in Italy; others had worked as apprentices and finishers with the village dressmaker, or had themselves been the dressmaker for the village. Over four-fifths of the group of 65 who had worked at some form of sewing in Italy were in needle trades in New York City. One girl, who began to learn dressmaking as soon as she left school, said that nearly all girls in Italy do this so that they will know how to sew. Lola became an apprentice in a shop in Turin at the age of twelve. After she had worked three years without pay, she received *buona paga* (good pay), $5.20 a month. She said that girls trained in Italy as dressmakers were much in demand here, as they knew all the processes and did better work than those who had learned the trade in this country. Another young girl, who had been here only six months, earned up to $9.00 a week as an operator on dresses. At twelve she had gone to work for a dressmaker in her native village. After a year or two she went into a regular dressmaking establishment in a larger town; later to Milan to learn the fashionable work. She explained that big shops are called "schools," but that they are in reality like the factories here.

Some of these women had been able to advance quickly. For instance, in a year and a half, Lena, who was only twenty, had worked up to sample making at $12 a week. She had begun at the age of twelve in a large shop in Turin, earning 60 cents a month. After learning the trade she earned $15 a month. Not satisfied, she had gone to France and worked for six months in a shop in Dijon where she made $10 a month besides room and board. She found factory work hard in America, as she was not accustomed to working fast. She liked to make the whole dress and to work carefully and thoroughly. "But if a girl worked that way in a wholesale house here, she could not make anything and would soon get laid off."

"Your work is all right provided it is done quickly enough" was a criticism frequently made. "They do only cheap work in this country. Everything must be done in a hurry. In Italy it would take six months to do a pillow and here it must be done in three or four hours. Cheap work!" said Linda Baia, an expert embroiderer. A finisher on dresses complained that she had to learn the trade all over again when she came here because in Italy there was more hand sewing and no subdivision of processes. If one worked fast there, people would say that the work must be badly done, and everyone was taught to do as beautiful sewing as possible. There it would take months to make a dress.

Perhaps these criticisms are not always fully merited, as the women have not realized that they are no longer making garments for individual customers but for wholesale. In the group of 65 who had worked at sewing or dressmaking in Italy, seven had gone to work in the specialized line of men's clothing, nine on women's cloaks and suits, three on shirtwaists, 29 at wholesale dressmaking, two on muslin underwear; only four were in custom dressmaking, where they might have some prospect of doing the careful and all-round work to which they had been accustomed. The others were struggling with the piece-work system, extreme specialization of processes, the operation of the power machine, with the emphasis on speed and output rather than on quality.

Hand embroidery had likewise presented an opportunity of employment to some of these immigrants, especially to some of the better type who had learned the work in the convents or schools of Italy as a personal accomplishment. Here, when embroidered fancy waists and dresses were in fashion, they found an unexpected commercial value in their skill. For instance, one woman who could speak only a few words of broken English was making $14 a week at embroidery and beadwork. Another was earning $13 a week embroidering beads on chiffon. She was doing the finest work in her shop and her sisters, all embroiderers, estimated that the "boss" was making about $20 a day on her work. Three sisters earned their living by embroidering waists and chiffon dresses. They agreed that Rose, the youngest, was the poorest worker as she had learned the trade in this country and not in Italy.

Other immigrant women were found in the needle trades besides those who had learned to sew in Italy. Many, especially the older ones, who had been farm hands or housewives in Italy and were often illiterate, had turned to the simple work of finishing on both men's and women's tailored garments. Little training is required for this work. Moreover, the organization of the work in the shop requires so little supervision by the employer that ignorance of English forms no bar to these women. As piece workers they may be trusted to work at top speed to earn the small wage of $6.00 or $7.00 a week. Through neighbors or relatives who did home work, some newly arrived immigrants had heard of jobs in these shops and, according to the law of least resistance, there they went to work. Often, too, the friendly home worker would show the woman the rudiments of the trade, so that she did not feel as "strange" as if she had been plunged into the midst of work in a noisy candy or paper-box factory. This appealed especially to the older women, who were timid in seeking work. That men's clothing is an industry employing many new arrivals is shown by the fact that 111 of the 362 women who had gone to work immediately after landing had first worked on tailored garments.

The extensive advertising in Italian papers by New York firms—American, German, and Russian—especially for workers in the clothing trades shows that to them, at least, Italian women are desirable employees. Often advertisements in Italian to attract those who cannot speak English offer special inducements of *"buona paga, lunga stagione*, union shop" (good pay, long season, union shop). Advertisements appear for *"operatrici per vesti di sciffon $15 a $25 per settimana"* (operators on chiffon dresses to earn $15 to $25 a week). *"20 ricamatrici cercansi, lavoro a pazzi o a settimana. Si da lavoro a casa"* (20 hand embroiderers wanted, piece or week work. Work given home). Or *"operatrici, guarnitrioi e* body makers *si cercano per camicette di lawn. Buona paga. Lavora fisso tutti l'anno. Non si da lavoro a gente dell' unione"* (operators, trimmers, and body makers wanted on lawn waists. Good pay. Steady work all year. No work given to members of the union).

The Italianizing of such English words as "bushelers" into *bucellatrici*, "operators" into *operatrici*, "drapers" into *drappergiatrici*, and "pressers" into *pressatori* or *pressatrici*, "dressmakers" into *dressatrici*, suggests that no equivalent terms for these specialized occupations exist in Italy. The name of her industry and her particular job are usually the first English words that the immigrant learns. A woman will shrug her shoulders helplessly when you ask her where she lives or how long she has been in this country. Her attempt to answer you with "feenisher," "press," "west [rest]," "dress," or "cloding," suggests that her work forms the strongest link with her new world.

The Flower and Feather Trade: The flower and feather industry, which has come to be looked upon as the Italian women's trade, especially attracted the young English-speaking girls of American birth or women who had been here since childhood. The few older women who were found in this trade were mainly employed at the heavy but unskilled work of pressing petals or leaves. Angelina Delibro, a woman of fifty, had been handling a pressing machine for five years, but made only $5.00 a week. She was glad of a chance to make 10 cents extra by working half an hour overtime on Saturdays. Although the work was unskilled, she claimed that she earned so little because she was too old and her fingers were too stiff for her to learn to do good work.

For the young girl as she left school it was often the first choice. Perhaps she had been making flowers at home after school ever since she could remember. When the time came for her to find work outside her home, even this slight experience or the offer of a job from the boss who had supplied her mother or a neighbor with home work, easily accounted for her entering this trade. Of the 156 who were in flower and feathers, 65 had done such work at home before leaving school. Antoinette Baretti wanted to be a nurse when she left the public school, as her teacher had told her about the work. But when she learned that in a hospital a nurse may have to scrub floors, she decided she would rather be a shop girl. Dressmaking would have been her choice if her eyes had not been so weak. Finally she went to work in a flower and feather factory where her aunt was a forewoman. An attractive, up-to-date American-born girl of nineteen was found sewing ostrich plumes at piece work. She also had planned to go into dressmaking, but a friend offered to take her into a position in a feather factory, "and so my mother thought I might as well go there," she explained. "It was right after my father died." Her sister, Celestine, had remarked to a visitor two years before, while still in school, that she was going into dressmaking and not flower making, although she had made flowers at home for years, because "that is no trade." But she became a flower maker. "I couldn't do anything else, so I had to," she exclaimed hopelessly. A woman of twenty-nine had been working at branching and flower making since she was twelve. Three other women had been sewing ostrich plumes for over twenty-five years. None of these had ever ventured into any other work and were proud of their trades.

Few in this industry or in any other, however, showed as much enthusiasm for their work as did a charming light-haired American-born girl, thoroughly absorbed in sewing ostrich feathers. Warned by an older sister not to go into candy making because "that is no kind of a trade and a woman can't work at it after she is married," Milly took up feather making. She had grown to love her occupation, and it was a rare pleasure for the visitor to hear her describe the different processes, and to watch her deft fingers as she scraped, pared, tinted, and sewed a plume.

This very requirement of deftness of touch and pliability of the fingers suggests why few of the adult immigrants were feather or flower makers. Farm work or heavy housework had hardened their hands, and even in the heavier work in this trade they are handicapped.

Paper-Box Making: Paper-box making was another trade employing principally the American born. They were young girls of seventeen, eighteen, or nineteen, and eight out of 29 in this trade had been in it for less than a year. The girls agreed that the work was monotonous and sometimes heavy, that very little skill was required, and experience counted for little. It had attracted only the less ambitious, and often girls sought to impress the visitor with the fact that they were in the trade only because they could get no other work. Raphaela, nineteen years old, had been standing for two years at her table pasting paper on the bottoms of boxes. "You get used to it, but in the summer your feet get sore." She was ashamed to tell anyone her trade. "I always imagine that people think it is a dirty trade, and they ask me if I can't get anything better to do." Ida had worked up from turner-in and stripper to setter-up. With four years' experience she was earning a fairly steady piece wage of $9.00 or $10, although the danger of having a finger crushed in the machine limited her speed. Angelina Bellini was the oldest of eight children in a family where the father had unsteady work as a day laborer. Leaving public school at eleven, she had been working for nine years in the paper-box trade. As a paster she usually earned $10 a week, but with overtime and Sunday work for as much as seventy-six hours in one week, she had earned up to $15.50 in a week. She thought it the hardest trade there was, but since she had learned it she was not willing to go back and begin over again at a low wage in something else.

Mrs. Bardi, a widow of thirty-two with three children to support, finished paper boxes. She usually earned $5.00, but sometimes added $2.00 a week by putting rings on strings at home. A young girl of seventeen was a stripper, but had never made over $5.00, although she was born in this country and had gone to a New York public school. The shiftlessness and low standards of her home were reflected in her work and lack of ambition. She first began work on paper boxes, then for three months worked in a steam laundry, nine months in a hair goods place, and then at paper boxes again, although she thought it "an awfully bad trade."

The Tobacco Trade: The tobacco industry had the largest proportion of foreign born, only one out of the 27 so employed claiming the United States as her birthplace. It is also the industry having the largest proportion of women who could not speak English. Two-thirds had not yet learned it, although only five of the group had been here for as short a period as two years. Among these were several older women who had been accustomed to farm work in Italy and who had not objected to the smell or the stain or the rough wear on the hands to which the Americanized girl or woman would object.

Candy Making: Although there was a general verdict against candy making as a desirable trade, yet 68, or over 6 per cent of the group investigated, were employed in it at the time of the interview, while 136 had tried it at some time in their work careers. In this trade were found both the older immigrant women and younger American-born girls. Immigrant women who could speak no English were employed at the less desirable and dirty work of peeling cocoanuts or almonds, or sorting peanuts. Biagia, who had come four months before from Sicily, was peeling almonds in a large west side candy factory for $4.50 a week. As she could speak no English, she could not get anything better than this work which she had secured through the aunt with whom she lived. The girls of American birth, or those who could speak English, worked as packers, wrappers, or at the better paid work of dipping by hand or machine.

Whether they had been in the trade for a few months or many years, they cared little for it. Mrs. Sartori, who worked at the trade before her marriage and had returned to chocolate dipping, said the candy trade was about the worst there was, especially on account of the long hours. She hoped that her daughters would never go into it, "unless they are forced to," and she was struggling to send the oldest to a trade school so that she might escape. Josephine, only fourteen, had had no other choice than a position as a plat carrier. As she had to be on her feet all day and carry quite heavy loads in the ice-room, her mother was afraid her health would suffer, but she did not know how to find anything else for her. Carmela Lenaro, however, was one of the few who seemed satisfied. She had been a packer for two years. "I was walking along the street and the forelady was standing outside. She said to me, 'Little girl, are you working? If you want, you can come in here and learn packing.' So I went in and now I am used to the trade and wouldn't like to work at anything else."

Processes of Work

We can understand better the demands made upon the skill and experience of these girls and women by considering the processes at which they work instead of the industry. The name of the industry gives little clue to the nature of the tasks that the workers are called upon to do. Table 9.3 classifies the women according to the specific process at which those in manufacturing were engaged.

The mere fact that it is possible to make such a classification as the table shows is in itself significant and is proof of the present minute subdivision of labor. More than a fifth of the women were operators of power-run sewing machines. They were at work on dresses, shirtwaists, underwear, corsets, petticoats, veils, curtains, straw hats, dress shields, and mattresses. As operators they guided strip after strip or article after article into the machine, with no opportunity even to hold a needle in their hands. Whatever basting was required was done by others. Nor did their machine work mean that they made a complete garment. In making the simplest muslin underwear, operators described themselves still further as tuckers, rufflers, double hemmers, lace runners, fly makers, buttonhole makers, or button sewers. One girl, who thought there was no trade so good as that of underwear, had

Table 9.3 Processes of work performed by Italian women workers in manufacturing industries

Process of work	Women
Operating sewing machines	222
Feeding and tending machines	64
Fine hand sewing	61
Medium-grade hand sewing	185
Coarse hand sewing	36
Hand and machine processes combined	27
Pasting	90
Branching (flowers and feathers)	45
Cutting	19
Hand stamping	7
Measuring and weighing	9
Sorting	15
Examining	12
Folding	7
Packing	48
Wrapping and tying	8
Ribboning	6
Pressing and cleaning	21
Processes peculiar to certain industries	76
Work incidental to manufacturing, such as supervising and stockkeeping	38
Work not stated further than as "general," or learning	31
Total	1,027[a]

Note: [a] Of the 1,095 women investigated, 68 were not employed in manufacturing industries.

managed to learn how to make a whole muslin nightgown, but her day's work consisted merely in sewing in yokes. A few sample makers only, perhaps made a garment throughout.

This fine subdivision of work was also found in hand sewing and other hand processes. In making shirtwaists or dresses, for example, women were employed at processes so unskilled as distributing work to the operators, sewing on buttons by hand, marking for buttons. Other girls were examiners, pressers, or packers. Rarely did a girl combine even two of these simple processes, and even more rarely hand and machine work. Only 27 women were combining a hand and machine process in their work. Yet as has been said it was the opportunity to learn to make a garment throughout that had attracted many of these women into the needle trades. Hand sewing was the work of 282 women. One group did fine hand sewing, such as embroidery or the making of buttonholes, occupations requiring neat, careful stitches. Another group of 185 women did hand sewing of a medium grade, finishing clothing, sewing on braids and passementerie, preparing and trimming hats, making neckwear, or finishing and lining furs. A third group were coarse sewers, whose task was to make things hold together. They sewed on buttons, tacked covers on umbrellas, or sewed ostrich feathers, lampshades or teddy bears.

The functions of the workers, in processes of the same name, vary widely in different industries. Because a girl knows how to branch flowers it does not follow that she knows how to branch feathers. Packing flowers, which requires an artistic sense, is far different from packing candy. The pasting of samples on cards, requiring a neat, deft touch and a sense of color, is quite unlike the mechanical pasting of labels on wine bottles. Nor does the wrapping of a chocolate in silver foil bear much resemblance to the wrapping of pamphlets in a paper cover.

A description of occupations for even one nationality gives a cross-section of the complex makeup of the work force in an industry. We have seen one trade attracting large numbers of young girls, another a majority of the older women; one industry where the new immigrant ignorant of English predominated, another where the American-born girl was found in every kind of job. On the other hand still others employed Italian women of every age and degree of skill and education. Such variations should give pause to any desire to generalize and put into one pigeonhole the skilled, and into another the unskilled industries.

Laura Parker, "USA Just Wouldn't Work Without Immigrant Labor; Demand Will Continue to Grow for High- and Low-skilled"

Memphis—Carlos Nieto holds a degree in engineering from a university in Mexico but earns far more here, laying bricks in "McMansions," than he would at home. He made his way to this Southern river port in the mid-1980s, arriving in time to cash in on a construction boom that created a surplus of jobs and drew legions of his countrymen here.

Nieto has been part of the great economic expansion of the 1990s, the longest in U.S. history—and one that has made the United States dependent on immigrant labor, especially to fill low-income jobs scorned by American citizens.

Immigrant labor has become a hot political issue, too. Early this month, the Bush administration floated a plan to grant legal status to the 3 million Mexicans in the country illegally. Then Senate Majority Leader Tom Daschle, D-S.D., and House Minority Leader Richard Gephardt, D-Mo., raised the ante. They called for granting legal status to all illegal immigrants working and paying taxes here, regardless of nationality. There are 8.5 million illegal immigrants here.

Immigrants—legal and illegal—now make up 13% of the nation's workers, the highest percentage since the 1930s. They dominate job categories at both ends of the economic spectrum. Immigrants hold 35% of the unskilled jobs, according to the Center for Immigration Studies, a think tank in Washington, D.C. They also command a significant share of highly skilled technology jobs. At the height of the dot-com boom, as many as a third of the techies working in California's Silicon Valley were from Asia.

Most of the nation's 17.7 million immigrant workers toil, like those who preceded them, in jobs that native-born Americans refuse to do. They work as meatpackers, hotel maids, hamburger flippers, waiters, gardeners, seamstresses, fruit and vegetable pickers, and construction hands.

Who will do the hard jobs?

"There are places in this country where we wouldn't survive without immigrants," says John Gay, a lobbyist for the American Hotel & Lodging Association, which is pressing Congress to allow more "essential workers" into the United States. "The trend is to push our own children into college to be rocket scientists or computer programmers. But who is going to do these hard jobs that we have? Who is going to change bedpans in a nursing home? Or change beds in hotels?"

Their presence has changed the nation in ways that are only now becoming clear. Immigrants have kept wages low in low-skill jobs, yet also have provided organized labor new members to fuel a revitalized union movement. American companies' need for immigrant labor has silenced much of the anti-immigrant rhetoric of a decade ago.

And, lured by employers who have recruited them aggressively, immigrants have moved from the coasts and border states and settled in the heartland. That has prompted dramatic cultural changes in places such as Loudon, Tenn., and Garden City, Kan., that had little experience with foreigners when the 1990s began.

Jobs in poultry plants across the South, once held almost exclusively by American blacks, are now dominated by Mexican immigrants. Textile plants run largely on the labors of Hispanic workers. In the Kentucky coal fields, mining companies are considering recruiting miners from the Ukraine.

So many nurses from the Philippines have been recruited to fill a nursing shortage of historic proportions that their very recruitment has become an industry unto itself. Likewise, public school administrators are increasingly venturing abroad to fill teaching jobs that would otherwise stand vacant. This year, the Chicago school system signed 110 teachers from 31 counties, including Nepal, Hungary, and France.

America's reliance on immigrant labor is as old as the country. European immigrants built, under perilous and often fatal conditions, the Brooklyn Bridge and other New York landmarks. Chinese labor gangs, paid what were pejoratively called "coolie wages," built the railroads that connected the Atlantic with the Pacific.

Despite the current round of layoffs by U.S. businesses, government officials project a continuing need for immigrant labor. The Bureau of Labor Statistics predicts that the country will have 5 million more jobs than it has workers before the end of the decade.

8.5 million illegals

The current wave of immigration brings about 700,000 legal immigrants into the United States every year. That pace, which Congress sets through an elaborate system of quotas, is expected to continue. An additional 300,000 immigrants arrive illegally or overstay their visas every year.

In total, there are an estimated 30 million immigrants in the country, of which about 8.5 million are here illegally.

"If the anti-immigrant folks ever got what they wanted, and if all these illegal immigrants disappeared from this country, the economy would collapse," says Greg Siskind, an immigration lawyer in Memphis.

In Washington, the debate over immigration is framed this way: Employers and businesses demand that even more immigrants be admitted to the country on temporary work visas. Labor unions and immigrant rights activists counter that the government first should grant amnesty to illegal workers who are already here.

Last December, after pressure from the high-tech industry that included a personal plea from Microsoft founder Bill Gates, Congress doubled the annual quota on temporary work visas granted to high-skilled workers to 195,000.

Now the Essential Worker Immigration Coalition, which includes restaurateurs, hoteliers, nursing home operators, landscapers and construction executives, wants foreigners working in those fields to be granted visas allowing them to remain in the United States on a long-term basis.

"There is no (visa) category available to these folks," says Margaret Catillaz, past president of the American Immigration Lawyers Association. "We've got more jobs than we've got capable people to do them, even with the bust that's going on."

But labor unions say they won't support an expanded guest worker program without first winning legal rights for the illegal workers already here.

The Bush administration changed the tenor of the debate when it floated the proposal to grant legal status to the 3 million illegal Mexican immigrants. It was immediately denounced by opponents of amnesty, some of whom suggested that Bush was merely trying to buy Hispanic votes.

"As far as trial balloons go, this one won't get off the ground," Rep. Lamar Smith, R-Texas, said.

Congressional Democratic leaders, meanwhile, said the proposal should be expanded to include other nationalities.

Although no details of a plan have emerged, White House spokesman Ari Fleischer explained it is one of a series of options under consideration as part of a broader guest worker program that would ensure "a more orderly, humane, legal and safe migration."

The administration has been engaged in talks with Mexico since February over border-safety and immigration issues. President Bush wants to work out an agreement before Mexican President Vicente Fox's state visit to the United States in September.[1]

Secretary of State Colin Powell, who is heading the talks along with Attorney General John Ashcroft, clarified the administration's position in an interview with USA TODAY. He said that there would be no blanket amnesty, but that the administration is considering "steps that would provide paths to residency for those who do not have an entitlement."

Changes sweep Memphis

Here in Memphis, the sweep of the changes wrought in the last decade can be glimpsed in full. When Nieto arrived in 1986, the population was evenly divided between blacks and whites, and the city was defined largely by a long history of conflict between them.

To Nieto, 38, who migrated here as an undocumented worker after a short stint in the Houston oil fields, Memphis seemed an unlikely destination. But Memphis promised better wages than Texas and cheaper rents than California.

When the economy turned red-hot in the '90s, Nieto was the first of a growing stream of Latinos to find their way here.

"It's a nice place to live, better than Texas," Nieto says. "When we came, there were only a few Mexicans here, maybe 100. Sometimes we'd see one guy. The next week we'd see another guy. Now everybody is coming here. You see the change in the stores. They started selling Mexican food."

From 1995 to 1999, Memphis added 54,700 jobs, according to a University of Memphis study. Many of them offered low wages in the warehouse industry that feeds Memphis' corporate crown jewel, Federal Express, and in the construction trades. Downtown Memphis went on a redevelopment binge. Just across the border in Mississippi, 10 Las Vegas-style casinos, with accompanying hotels, restaurants and shops, were erected in five years.

Soon, there were so many Hispanic workers in construction that a local contractors' association began offering Spanish classes to the bosses on top of the English classes it had begun for workers.

"We had to find a way to communicate with each other," says Mike Carpenter, director of the western Tennessee chapter of the Associated Builders and Contractors, which represents 200 commercial builders.

Tennessee's Hispanic population increased 278 to 123,838 in the past decade, according to the Census 2000. Hispanic workers moved into each of Tennessee's 95 counties. They work in cities such as Nashville, filling tourist industry jobs, and in small towns such as Bells, which is dominated by a Pictsweet vegetable-packaging plant.

As word of Memphis' job shortage spread, the number of illegal workers rose. Today, they are entrenched in the local economy. Fake documents are easily obtained on the street. A Social Security card goes for $ 50; the coveted "green card," signifying legal residency, costs $ 100. Forgers advertise their services in a Spanish-language newspaper.

Although the Census recorded 23,364 Hispanics in Shelby County, of which Memphis is the county seat, local Hispanic leaders estimate that a more realistic count is twice that number.

Community leaders are intent on assimilating and protecting their new workforce. When illegal immigrant workers, who are known to carry large amounts of cash, became the victims of violent robberies, Bartlett Bank in Memphis set up a way for them to open bank accounts without the proper documents.

In April, the Tennessee Legislature made it easier for legal and illegal immigrants to obtain Tennessee driver's licenses by dropping the requirement that drivers have a Social Security number. Within a month, 30,000 Hispanics applied for licenses or identification cards.

Meanwhile, Nieto, who has since been granted permanent residency, marvels at his good luck. He is married to another Mexican immigrant, has a small son born in this country, and owns a house.

He is somewhat puzzled by all the analysis that this latest wave of immigrants is receiving from statisticians and demographers. "The people are coming for work," he explains. "If they cannot find it here, they'll find other places to go."

Note

1. As of Summer, 2005 no such agreement has been reached by Mexico and the United States.

CHAPTER TEN

Family, Domestic Economy, and Women's and Men's Lives

Introduction

One of the contemporary aspects of immigrant life about which we may confidently say there are some profound differences from the past is that encompassed by women's lives, especially in regard to work and family. But the changes we observe in women's lives are much larger than the world of immigrants. They are general changes that pervade American society, which has witnessed in the last three decades a remarkable expansion in the public roles of women. In the article that you are about to read, anthropologist Nancy Foner points out the great differences in the lives of European immigrants of the turn-of-the-century era and contemporary immigrant women in New York City, continuously one of the most significant immigrant receiving centers throughout American history. In the past, when it was believed a woman's place was in the home caring for a husband and children and keeping house, immigrant women stayed at home and their daughters left school to work and earn money to help maintain their parents' household. If immigrant mothers and wives needed to earn money to supplement the income of their husbands and resident children, they did so working at home. They took in boarders, who paid for their meals and living space, and they did various types of industrial home work, especially sewing, for which they were paid. Today, mothers and wives work outside the home, and daughters go to school, and it is expected that men will share in the responsibility for housework and childcare. This current situation

Nancy Foner, "Immigrant Women and Work in New York City, Then and Now" in *Journal of American Ethnic History*, 18 (Spring, 1999): 95–108. Reprinted with the permission of Nancy Foner. Copyright © 1999 by Transaction Publishers. Reprinted with permission of Transaction Publishers.

Margaret Byington, *Homestead: The Households of A Milltown* (University of Pittsburgh Press). Copyright © 1910 by The Russell Sage Foundation, Copyright © 1974 by The University Center for International Studies, University of Pittsburgh, pp. 145–157. Public domain.

Sonia Shah, "Three Hot Meals and a Full Day at Work: South Asian Women's Labor in the United States," Shamita Das Dasgupta, ed. in *A Patchwork Shawl: Chronicles of South Asian Women in America* (New Brunswick: Rutgers University Press, 1998), pp. 206–221. Sonia Shah is a freelance journalist and former editor at South End Press. Reprinted with permission of Sonia Shah.

provides women with more independence and participation in a wider
world than immigrant women in the past, but it is not without its own difficulties. Immigrant women are more likely than native-born women to do
low-wage, low-status, dead end work, and husbands do not always share
equally in housework and childcare, and what they contribute is often
done grudgingly. The two selections that accompany Foner's essay provide
some substantiation of her central themes. In "Family Life of the Slavs,"
Margaret Byington, an American social worker, writes about the lives of
Slovak immigrant women and their families in turn-of-the-century
Homestead, Pennsylvania, the site of one of the nation's largest steel mills.
Since its inception in the 1870s, the Carnegie Steel Works, which became
U.S. Steel in 1901, had increasingly depended on immigrant labor to be the
core of its largely unskilled labor force. Living in the shadow of the giant
mill, these Slovak families had difficult lives. The men's work was dirty,
dangerous, and subject to periodic unemployment when the economy
contracted, and the wages earned were barely able to support a family. The
women kept house in small, crowded houses and apartments, in which they
cared for husbands and children and often, to supplement the family
income, boarders, who were unmarried, recently arrived men from
Slovakia. The women's lives, like those of the men, were lives of constant
toil, and they lived without privacy or the type of amenities that we take for
granted, such as running water, indoor plumbing, electricity, and household
appliances. The frugal existence they were forced to live was reinforced by
self-imposed saving, not only intended to prepare for times of unemployment, but also intended for use in making the down payment on a home in
a better neighborhood.

That we have the essay of Sonia Shah, who was born not long after her
parents immigrated to the United States from India in 1968 (the editors
were not able to find any personal testimony written by a turn-of-the-century
Slovak immigrant woman), suggests something about the changes in
women's lives during the twentieth century. Many of the Slovak immigrant
women were illiterate, but just as important, they had little time for self-
reflection and lived in a culture that hardly encouraged women to find their
own voices and speak their minds. Though not the intimate look at the
home lives of immigrant women that we find in Byington, Shah's essay
combines autobiographical reminiscences with analysis of employment
trends among South Asian women in the United States. In general, Indian
women and men alike in the United States actually have better jobs than do
most white Americans. But in Shah's analysis, this achievement is qualified
by the fact that they leave a country that needs their skills but cannot afford
to employ them, that they face racial discrimination in the United States
that leads many of them to take jobs below the level of their educational and
professional preparation, that they work longer and harder than white
American counterparts, that they have less control of the money they earn,
and that men do not share equally in the responsibilities of housework.
From her feminist perspective, Shah is eager to attack the "model minority"
thesis that interprets Indian success, and generally Asian success, in the

United States as resulting from the cultural values that these immigrants bring with them. This view of Asian immigrants makes them living embodiments of the rags-to-riches myths that are dear to the hearts of Americans. Shah describes Asian success in the United States as having more complicated roots and manifesting itself more unevenly among classes and between men and women than the model minority hypothesis suggests.

All three selections have in common an important point: across time and group boundaries, immigrant women's lives remain different from those of men and in some significant ways, singularly burdened by discrimination and an unequal share of family responsibilities.

Suggestions for Further Reading

Donna Gabaccia, *From the Other Side: Women, Gender, and Immigrant Life in the United States, 1820–1990* (Bloomington: Indiana University Press, 1995).

Elizabeth Ewen, *Immigrant Women in the Land of Dollars: Life and Culture on the Lower East Side, 1890–1925* (New York: Monthly Review, 1985).

Louise Lamphere, *From Working Daughters to Working Mothers: Immigrant Women in a New England Industrial Community* (Ithaca: Cornell University Press, 1987).

Mei Nakano, *Japanese American Women: Three Generations, 1890–1990* (Berkeley: University of California Press, 1990).

Sarah Deutsch, *No Separate Refuge, Class, Culture, and Gender on an Anglo Hispanic Frontier in the American Southwest, 1880–1940* (New York: Oxford University Press, 1987).

Nancy Foner, "Immigrant Women and Work in New York City, Then and Now"

Today's immigrant women enter a society that has undergone remarkable changes since the last great immigrant influx early in the century. Perhaps most dramatic, there has been a virtual revolution in women's involvement in the labor force. Whereas in 1900 only 20 percent of all the nation's women worked for wages, by 1995 the figure had reached nearly 60 percent. There is a difference also in who works. At the turn of the century, the vast majority of women workers were young and single. It was generally assumed that work outside the home was temporary for a young girl; when she married, she would move back into the domestic domain. Indeed, in 1900, only 6 percent of the nation's married women were in the labor force.

Today, working daughters have given way to working mothers. Women now enter the labor force later—and they stay. Whether they work for economic need, to maintain or raise their family's living standards, or for personal satisfaction, the fact is that by 1990, almost three quarters of married women in the United States with children under 18 worked in the paid labor force, many doing so full time and year round.

This analysis is part of a larger comparative project on immigrants in New York today and at the beginning of the century, the two peak periods in the city's immigration history. Between 1880 and 1920, over one million immigrants arrived and settled in New York City so that by 1910, fully 41 percent of all New Yorkers were foreign born. In this earlier period, the focus is on Eastern European Jews and Italians—the vast bulk of the new arrivals at the time, who defined what was then thought of as the "new immigration." Today, no two groups predominate this way, and New York's immigrants now include sizable numbers from a variety of Asian, West Indian, and Latin American nations and European countries as well. For this reason, the discussion of the present draws on material on a larger number of groups. Since the late 1960s, immigrants have been streaming into New York City at what is now a rate of over 100,000 a year. Altogether, by 1996, some 2.5 million New Yorkers were foreign born, representing a third of the city's population.

A comparison of migrant women in the two eras reveals some striking differences. Wage work has empowered immigrant wives and mothers in late-twentieth-century New York in ways that were not possible for Jewish and Italian married women of an earlier era, who rarely worked outside the home. Yet, despite this contrast, gender inequalities are still very much with us, and, despite improvements in their status as women in New York, migration has not emancipated the latest arrivals. As feminist scholars have emphasized, migration often leads to losses, as well as gains, for women. The analysis of contemporary migrant women shows that "traditional" patriarchal codes and practices may continue to have an impact, and women—immigrants as well as the native born—still experience special burdens and disabilities as members of the "second sex." Indeed, immigrant mothers' continued responsibilities for child care and domestic tasks add new complications for them today when they are more likely to work outside, as well as inside, the home.

Jewish and Italian Women Then

From the beginning, in the move itself, Jewish and Italian women typically followed men—husbands, fiancés, and fathers—who led the way. Women were a minority, too. The Italian migration was, more than anything else, a movement of single men coming to make money and go home. In most years of the peak migration between 1880 and 1910, about 80 percent of Italian immigrants to the United States were male. The Jewish movement was mainly a family affair, but even then men predominated; women made up 43 percent of the migration stream to the United States between 1899 and 1910.

What work did women do in the Old World? In Eastern Europe, Jewish women had a central role in economic life. Patriarchy ran deep in Jewish communities—women were excluded from seats of power and positions in the religious sphere—but they were expected to, and did, make important economic contributions to their households. Indeed, the hardworking scholar's wife, who supported a highly-respected man who devoted himself to full-time religious study, "acted as a legitimating symbol of the female breadwinner for the masses of east European Jews. If the scholar's wife worked, then why not the merchant's, the trader's, the watchmaker's, or the tailor's? And that was the pattern." Women's work, throughout the world of Eastern European Jews, was considered necessary and respectable.

Large numbers of Jewish wives worked in business or trade, sometimes helping in a store formally run by their husbands or keeping a store or stall on their own where they sold food, staples, or household wares. Some women were peddlers who stood in the marketplace or went from house to house selling food they had prepared at home or manufactured goods that were bought in small lots in cities. Jewish wives became tough bargainers who developed a knowledge of the marketplace and a certain worldliness about the society outside their own communities.

By the end of the nineteenth century, with the development of factory production in Russia and the movement of many Jews to cities, increasing numbers of unmarried Jewish women were drawn to artisan's shops and small factories, making matches, cigarettes, and other goods. When they married, Jewish women rarely took factory jobs that demanded long hours away from home, but many were involved in various kinds of home-based production. The sewing machine created new opportunities for doing outwork, and thousands of Jewish married and single female homeworkers made dresses or did other kinds of needlework for contractors who then distributed garments to stores.

In the Sicilian and southern Italian villages that most Italian immigrant women left behind, married women supervised household chores, organized clothes-making and food preparation, and managed the family budget. Often, they tended animals and tilled the garden, producing food for family consumption and for sale at local markets. While artisans' wives, who helped out in the shop, worked in the privacy of their homes, peasant women's work took them outside of the house as they hauled water, sat together at open streams laundering clothes, or did their chores in the street or court-yard alongside neighbors. Wives in poor families often had no choice but to help in the fields as day laborers during harvest periods, picking fruit and nuts, husking almonds, and threshing wheat.

These patterns of work underwent significant change in New York. For many Jewish and Italian women, the journey to New York led to new constraints and they were forced to lead more sheltered lives than they had in the Old World.

Hardly any Jewish or Italian wives went out to work for wages. The 1905 census recorded only 1 percent of immigrant Russian Jewish households in New York City with wives working outside the home; for Italians the figure, at 6 percent, was not much higher. Marriage, typically around the age of twenty to twenty-two, spelled the end of wage work for the vast major-ity of Italian and Jewish immigrant women. Eventually, some returned to the paid workforce for a stretch in the 1930s and 1940s when their children were grown, but immigrant women who came to New York as married adults often never worked outside the home at all.

Most Italian and Russian Jewish wives and mothers earned money by working at home. In the early years of the immigration, in the 1880s and 1890s, many Jewish women did piecework at home in the needle trades, but by the early twentieth century, the numbers had fallen sharply. By this time, taking care of boarders, virtually indistinguishable from other domestic duties, had become a more attractive alternative—and the main way Jewish wives contributed to the family income. According to the Immigration Commission's 1911 report, as many as 56 percent of New York Russian Jewish families had boarders living with them. Many immigrant wives helped their husbands in "mom and pop" stores and some ran shops of their own. Minding the store was considered an extension of a woman's proper role as her husband's helpmate; often the family lived above or in back of the store so that wives could run back and forth between shop counter and kitchen.

Although many Italian wives added to the family income by taking in boarders, this was a less frequent practice than among Jews. Homework was more common. By the first decade of the century, most industrial home-workers in New York City were Italian. Working in the kitchen or a bedroom, Italian women finished garments or made artificial flowers while raising their children and caring for the house. Women were aware that factory jobs paid better, but the demands of caring for young children and household duties as well as the widely accepted notion that women should leave the workplace after marriage usually kept them at home.

In one view, immigrant women's "retirement" to the domestic arena was a blessing. By taking in boarders and doing piecework at home they contributed much-needed money to the family income at the same time as they reared children and performed time-consuming domestic duties. Cleaning, cooking, and doing the laundry were labor-intensive chores for poor immigrant women who could not afford mechanical conveniences or hired help. The weekly laundry, for example, meant a laborious process of soaking, scrubbing, wringing, rinsing, and drying and ironing clothes. Although women did a tremendous amount of daily housework, they defined their own rhythms.

Unlike the factory, where bosses were in control, women exercised real authority and set the pace in their own households. Apart from nurturing and disciplining children, women managed the family budget. Husbands and sons usually gave them the larger part of their wages each week; most daughters handed over their entire paycheck. The role of housewife and mother, moreover, if done well, carried with it respectability and the approval of family and neighbors.

Yet women's housebound existence had a downside as well. By and large, married women's lives were more circumscribed in New York. Immigrant mothers did, of course, socialize with friends and neighbors and go out to shop. The Jewish housewife, as the family member most responsible for decisions about household purchases, presided over a process of acquisition of consumption items. Their housebound existence made it more difficult to learn the new language and customs. Their husbands picked up English in the workplace; their daughters learned American ways in factory work groups. Many Jewish mothers, however, remained fluent only in Yiddish and felt uncomfortable in new situations outside the Jewish community. They had to depend on their children to learn American customs or, as a few managed to do, attend night school to learn English.

Most household chores, as well as industrial homework, were done within the walls of their tenement apartments. Those from small towns and villages, used to doing chores like laundry in the company of other women, now faced the more lonely and difficult task of washing clothing by themselves inside cramped tenement apartments. Because they now lived a more "inside" life, the move from Sicily to Elizabeth Street, Donna Gabaccia concludes, "limited immigrant women's opportunities to interact with others," and these limitations were a source of dissatisfaction with their new environment.

Even as modern plumbing freed women from some of the more rigorous chores they had known in the Old World, more rigorous standards of cleanliness and new household acquisitions complicated housework. In small Eastern European towns and villages women went to the river once a month to wash clothes; now the laundry was a weekly task. Another example: mattresses in Eastern Europe were generally made of straw and in cold weather feather bedding was common. In America, beds came with mattresses that required sheets and blankets; these needed washing and airing on a regular basis.

For the Jewish women who had been charged with providing a major portion of the family livelihood in Eastern Europe, migration reduced their economic role. In New York, immigrant wives' income-earning activities rarely represented the major contribution to the family economy. Industrial homework or taking in boarders was not as lucrative as work outside the home, and wives were seen as helping out their husbands in family businesses. Married women's earnings in America were now eclipsed by the wages of working daughters in the industrial labor force, who emerged as the main female breadwinners in the Jewish family.

Immigrant Women Now

Much has changed for the latest arrivals. Women immigrants now outnumber men in virtually all of the major groups in New York, and more women come on their own rather than follow in men's footsteps. Today's immigrant women also include a much higher proportion with professional and middle-class backgrounds. Above all, the world they live in gives women opportunities and benefits unheard of a century ago—and this is particularly evident in the sphere of work.

Today, adult immigrant women are the main female contributors to the family income, while their teenage daughters are generally in school. With the expansion of high schools—and colleges—over the course of the century and the raising of the school-leaving age, women (and men) start working later than they used to. Today's immigrant daughters are often eighteen or older when they enter the labor market full-time compared to fourteen or fifteen a century ago. Marriage no longer spells a retreat from paid employment outside the home. Industrial homework, while not entirely a thing of the past, is much rarer than in the era of Italian and Jewish immigrants. Now it is socially accepted, even expected, throughout American society that wives and mothers will go out to work.

As of the 1990 census, 60 percent of New York City's working-age foreign-born women (compared to 66 percent of the city's working-age women generally) were in the labor force. At the high end, Filipino women, who often came to work in health-care jobs, have a labor force participation rate of over 85 percent; West Indian women are not far behind, with labor force participation rates in the 70–80 percent range. Dominican women are near the bottom, with 52 percent in the work force. Given the wide variety of groups today, and the diversity of immigrant backgrounds, immigrant women occupy an equally wide range of jobs, from nurses, secretaries, and health technicians to domestics and factory workers.

These new patterns have important consequences. Now that most immigrant women work outside the home, they are able to obtain a kind of independence and power that was beyond the reach of Jewish and Italian wives and mothers a century ago, and that was often beyond their own reach before migration. How much improvement women experience when they migrate depends to a large degree on their role in production and social status in the home country as well as their economic role in New York. What is important here is that migration, for the majority of female newcomers today, has led to gains because they earn a regular wage for the first time, earn a higher wage than in the sending country, or make a larger contribution to the family economy than previously.

In cases where women did not earn an income, or earned only a small supplementary income, prior to migration, the gains that come with a shift to regular wage work in New York are especially striking. The much-cited case of Dominican women fits this pattern. They left a society where, in 1990, only 15 percent of women were in the labor force. Now that so many Dominican immigrant women work for wages—often for the first time— and contribute a larger share of the family income, they have more authority in the household and greater self-esteem.

In New York, Dominican women begin to expect to be co-partners in "heading" the household, a clear change from more patriarchal arrangements in the Dominican Republic. Whereas men used to control the household budget, now husbands, wives, and working children usually pool their income in a common fund for shared household expenses. Indeed, Dominican women are eager to postpone or avoid returning to the Dominican Republic where social pressures and an unfavorable job market would probably mean their retirement from work and a loss of new-found gains.

Of course, many immigrant women, including some Dominicans, had regular salaries before emigration. Even these women often feel a new kind of independence in New York because jobs in this country pay more than most could ever earn at home and increase women's contribution to the family economy. This is the experience for many Jamaican women, who come from a society where almost 70 percent of women engage in paid work. Many Jamaican women I interviewed who had held white-collar jobs before emigration said they had more financial control and more say in family affairs in New York where their incomes are so much larger.

The sense of empowerment that comes from earning a wage—or a higher wage—and having greater control over what they earn comes out in studies of many different groups. Paid work for Chinese garment workers, according to one report, not only contributes to their families' economic well-being, but also has "created a sense of confidence and self-fulfillment which they may never have experienced in traditional Chinese society." "I do not have to ask my husband for money," one woman said, "I make my own." For many Salvadoran women, the ability to earn wages and decide how they should be used is something new. As one woman explained: "Here [in the U.S.] women work just like the men. I like it a lot because managing my own money I feel independent. I don't have to ask my husband for money, but in El Salvador, yes, I would have to. Over there women live dependent on their husbands. You have to walk behind him."

The female-first migration pattern involving adult married women that is common in some groups reinforces the effects of wage earning on women's independence. Many women who have lived and worked in New York without their husbands, change, as one Dominican woman put it, "after so many years of being on my own, being my own boss." One study suggests that Asian men who move to the United States as their wives'

dependents often have to subordinate their careers, at least initially, to those
of their wives since the women have already established themselves in this
country.

Work outside the home in New York brings about another change that
women appreciate. Many men now help out more *inside* the home than
before they moved to New York. Of course, this is not inevitable. Cultural
values in different groups as well as the availability of female relatives to lend
a hand influence the kind of household help men provide. Korean men,
staunch supporters of patriarchal family values and norms, generally still
expect their wives to serve them and resist performing household chores
like cooking, dishwashing, and doing the laundry. Such resistance is more
effective when the wife's mother or mother-in-law lives in the household,
a not infrequent occurrence in Korean immigrant families. Yet much to
their consternation, Korean men in New York with working wives often
find themselves helping out with household work more than they did in
Korea—and that wives make more demands on them to increase their share.

Research on Latin American and Caribbean groups shows that when
wives are involved in productive work outside the home, there is a change
of productive labor within it. We are not talking about a drastic change in
the household division of labor or the emergence of truly egalitarian
arrangements. Indeed, Latin American and Caribbean women strongly
identify as wives and mothers and they like being in charge of the domestic
domain. What they want—and what they often get—is more help from
men than they were accustomed to back home. Mainly, men oblige because
they have little choice.

West Indian men, for example, recognize that there is no alternative to
pitching in when their wives work and their children (particularly daughters)
are not old enough to lend a hand. Working women simply cannot shoulder
all of the domestic responsibilities expected of them, and they do not have
relatives available to help as they did back home. Even if close kin live nearby,
they are usually busy with work and their own household chores. Wives'
wages are a necessary addition to the family income, and West Indians cannot
afford to hire household help in New York. Indeed, West Indian couples with
young children often arrange their shifts so that the husband can look after
the children while the wife works.

While the exigencies of immigrant life—women working outside the
home, a lack of available relatives to assist, and an inability to hire help—are
mainly responsible for men's greater participation in household tasks,
American cultural beliefs and values have an influence, too. Many Dominicans
claim that they self-consciously pattern their more egalitarian relations on
what they believe to be the dominant American model. Whatever men think,
immigrant women may feel they can make more demands on their husbands
in this country where the dominant norms and values back up their claims for
men to help out.

In addition to the independence, power, and autonomy that wages bring,
there are the intrinsic satisfactions of work itself. Women in professional and
managerial positions gain prestige from their positions and often have

authority over others on the job. Those in lower-level occupations often get a sense of satisfaction from doing their job well and from the new skills they have learned in New York. And there is the sociability involved. In factories, hospitals, and offices, women make friends and build up a storehouse of experiences that enrich their lives and conversations. Indeed, when women are out of work, they often complain of boredom and isolation. "Sometimes," said a Chinese-garment worker, "I get frustrated if I am confined at home and don't see my coworkers." Dominican women who are laid off say they miss not only the income but also socializing with workmates and the bustle of the streets and subways.

There is, however, a negative side to women's increased participation in the paid labor force. Wage work brings burdens as well as benefits to immigrant women and may create new sets of demands and pressures both on the job and at home. Moreover, despite changes in women's status in New York, premigration gender role patterns and ideologies do not fade away; they continue to affect the lives of migrant women, often in ways that constrain and limit them.

Going out to work, as immigrant women commonly explain, is not an option but a necessity for their family's welfare. And it typically brings a host of difficulties. On the job, women's wages are still generally lower than men's. In addition, women are limited in their choice of work due to gender divisions in the labor market—often confined to menial, low-prestige, and poorly-paying jobs. Working in the ethnic economy does not help most women either. Recent studies of Chinese, Dominican, and Colombian women in New York who work in businesses owned by their co-ethnics show that they earn low wages and have minimal benefits and few opportunities for advancement. Some of the success of immigrant small-business owners and workers in the ethnic enclave is due to the marginal position of immigrant women. The many Korean women who work in family businesses are, essentially, unpaid family workers without an independent source of income. Although many are working outside the home for the first time, they are typically thought of as "helpers" to their husbands; the husband not only legally owns the enterprise but also usually controls the money, hires and fires employees, and represents the business in Korean business associations.

For many immigrant women, working conditions are extremely difficult. Apart from the low wages and long hours, most garment workers have to keep up a furious pace in cramped conditions in noisy, often unsafe, sweatshops; domestic workers often have to deal with humiliating and demeaning treatment from employers. Some women with fulltime jobs have more than one position to make ends meet. I know many West Indian women, for example, who care for an elderly person on the weekend to supplement what they earn from a five-day child-care job.

Added to this, of course, are the demands of childcare and the burdens of household work. Going outside to earn means that childrearing is more complicated than at the turn of the century when married women typically worked at home. Only very affluent immigrants can afford to hire maids or housekeepers, and female relatives, if present in New York, are often busy at work themselves. Occasionally, women can juggle shifts with their husbands so one parent is always around; sometimes an elderly mother or mother-in-law is on hand to help out. Many working women pay to leave their children with babysitters or, less often, in day-care centers. Childcare constraints are clearly a factor limiting women to low-paid jobs with flexible schedules; they may prevent women from working full-time—or, in some cases, at all. Sometimes, women leave their young children behind with relatives in the home country so they can manage work more easily, a common pattern among West Indian live-in household workers.

Immigrant women in all social classes have the major responsibilities for household chores as well as childrearing so that a grueling day at work is often followed or preceded by hours of cooking, cleaning, and washing. "I'm always working," is how Mrs. Darius, a Haitian nursing home aide with eight children, put it. Although her husband, a mechanic, does not help much around the house, Mrs. Darius gets assistance from her mother who lives with her. Still, there is a lot to do. "I have to work 24 hours. When I go home, I take a nap, then get up again; sometimes I get up at two in the morning, iron for the children, and go back to sleep."

Take the case of Antonia Duarte, a Dominican mother of three children, who put in a 17-hour day. At 5:00 A.M., she was up making breakfast and lunch for the family. She woke her three children at 6:00, got them dressed, fed, and ready for school, and then took them to the house of a friend, who cared for the 4-year-old and oversaw the older children's departure to and return from school. By 7:15, Antonia was on the subway heading for the lamp factory where she worked from 8:00 A.M. to 4:30 P.M. five days a week. She collected her children a little after 5:00 and began preparing the evening meal when she got home. She didn't ask her two oldest children to help—the oldest is a 12-year-old-girl—because "I'd rather they begin their homework right away, before they get too tired." Her husband demanded a traditional meal of rice, beans, plantains, and meat which could take as long as two hours to prepare. She and the children ate together at 7:00, but her husband often did not get back from socializing with his friends until later. He expected Antonia to reheat the food and serve it upon his arrival. By the time she finished her child care and other domestic responsibilities, it was 11:30 or 12:00. Like other Dominican women, she explained that if she did not manage the children and household with a high level of competence, her husband would threaten to prohibit her from working.

Women in groups where strong "traditional" patriarchal codes continue to exert an influence may experience other difficulties. In some better-off Dominican families, wives are pressured by husbands to stay out of the work force altogether as a way to symbolize their household's respectability and elevated economic status. In many groups, working women who are now the family's main wage earners may feel a special need to tread carefully in relations with their husbands so as to preserve the appearance of male dominance. Indeed, one study shows professional Korean women making conscious attempts to keep their traditional lower status and to raise the position of their husbands by reducing their incomes. A nurse explained: "My basic salary exceeds his. If I do overtime, my income will be too much—compared to his—and so, when overtime work falls on me, I just try so hard to find other nurses to cover my overtime assignments. . . . [B]y reducing my income, I think, my husband can keep his ego and male superiority."

Finally, there is the fact that women's increased financial authority and independence can lead to greater discord with their spouses. Conflicts often develop when men resent, and try to resist, women's new demands on them; in some cases, the stresses ultimately lead to marital breakups. There are special difficulties when men are unemployed or unsuccessful at work, and become dependent on women's wage-earning abilities, yet still insist on maintaining the perquisites of male privilege in the household. In extreme cases, the reversal of gender roles can lead to serious physical abuse for women at the hands of their spouses. Indeed, in some instances, increased isolation from relatives in the immigrant situation creates conditions for greater abuse by husbands, who are freer of the informal controls that operated in their home communities.

Margaret Byington, "Family Life of the Slavs"

One morning I entered a two-room tenement. The kitchen, perhaps 15 by 12 feet, was steaming with vapor from a big washtub set on a chair in the middle of the room. The mother was trying to wash and at the same time to keep the older of her two babies from tumbling into the tub full of scalding water that was standing on the floor. On one side of the room was a huge puffy bed, with one feather tick to sleep on and another for covering; near the window stood a sewing machine; in the corner, an organ,—all these, besides the inevitable cook stove upon which in the place of honor was simmering the evening's soup. Upstairs in the second room were one boarder and the man of the house asleep. Two more boarders were at work, but at night would be home to sleep in the bed from which the others would get up. Picture if you will what a week or a season means to a mother in such a home, the overwork, the brief respite from toil—to be increased afterward—when the babies come?

Yet it is even more disastrous to the children both in health and character. In the courts[1] studied, out of 102 families who took lodgers, 72 had children; of these, 25 families had two, 10 had three, and seven had four. There were 138 youngsters in all. A comparison of births and deaths of children under two, shows that among the Slavs one child under two years of age dies to every three children born; among the English-speaking Europeans, one dies to every seven born; among the native whites and colored, one to every five.

Against many of these deaths was the physician's entry "malnutrition due to poor food and overcrowding"; that is, the mother too poor, too busy, and too ignorant to prepare food properly, rooms over-tenanted, and courts too confined to give the fresh air essential for the physical development of children. A priest told me he believed that the taking of lodgers caused the appalling death rate among the babies in his parish. Neither preaching nor pointing out to women personally the folly of the economy had sufficed to check the habit.

Not only is the mother too busy to give much time to her babies, but she also suffers from overwork during pregnancy and from lack of proper care afterward. Housework must be done, boarders must be fed, and most women work until the day of confinement.[2] In accordance with their home customs, almost all of them employ midwives and call a doctor only in an emergency. I was told by a local physician that nearly half of the births in Homestead, the large proportion of them among the Slavic people, were attended by midwives. These women, who charge $5.00 or $10, include in their services the care of both woman and child for several days, and thus perform the services of trained nurse as well as doctor. While of the 21 midwives registered in Homestead, five or six have diplomas from schools of midwifery abroad, most of them are ignorant and are careless about cleanliness. In a paper before the Allegheny County Medical Society, Dr. Purman, a local physician, reported numerous instances where both mother and child had suffered serious injury from the ignorance of these women.

The necessity for mothers to be up and at work within three or four days adds to the harm. In at least 10 of the 29 Slavic families visited, special reference was made by the Slavic investigator to the ill health of the mother due to overwork and to lack of proper care during confinement. The strength to bear much doubtless comes to these women from years of work in the fields, but the change to the hot kitchens where their work is now done undoubtedly entails a strain which not only injures them but lessens the vitality of the children. This weakened condition at birth combines with the inadequate food and insufficient air and the neglect which comes through over-burdening the mother to produce the appalling infant death rate in these courts.

Yet sometimes as you watch the stunted, sickly looking children, you wonder if the real tragedy does not lie rather in the miserable future in store for the babies who live, many of them with undervitalized systems which may make them victims either of disease or of the dissipation that often fastens upon weak wills and weak bodies.

Keeping lodgers ruins the training as well as the health of the children. The overworked mother has neither time nor patience for wise discipline. As the men who work on night-turns must sleep during the day, crying babies must not be allowed to disturb this uneasy rest. All this adds to the mother's weary irritation and makes it harder to maintain any sort of uniform control. This failure of intelligent discipline was noticeable in most of the families I visited, where cuffs and sharp words were the usual form of correction. One of the Protestant missions which tried through mothers' meetings to give the women some suggestions as to child training, found them too busy to come. Fortunately, however, the children who attend the public schools receive some training. This the parents value. A teacher in the Second Ward school said that while she had a great deal of trouble in teaching the Slavic children obedience, she at least found the parents willing to uphold her in whatever action she took.

Even more serious is the injury to the moral tone of the Slavic community caused by the crowding together of single men and families. In only four instances in the courts studied were lodgers found in families where there were girls over fourteen, but even younger children learn evil quickly from the free-spoken men. With the husband at work on the night shift the situation is aggravated, and reports are current of gross immorality on the part of some women who keep lodgers; two or three actual instances came to my knowledge from unquestioned sources. Since half the families in the courts studied used the kitchen as a sleeping room, there was close mingling of lodgers and family among them. This becomes intolerable when families living in but two rooms take lodgers. Even when extreme crowding does not exist, family and lodgers often all sleep in the kitchen, the only warm room, in winter.

Certainly there is little to quicken mental and spiritual development in these crowded tenements where there is neither privacy nor even that degree of silence necessary for reading. We agree in the abstract that the individual needs room for growth, yet complain of the stunted mental stature of these people who have the meagre development of seedlings grown in a mass.

Moreover, families who live in narrow quarters have no room for festive gatherings. In the evening a group often gathers around the stove gossiping of home days, playing cards, drinking, and playing simple musical instruments. On the Saturday after pay day the household usually clubs together to buy a case of beer which it drinks at home. These ordinarily jovial gatherings are sometimes interrupted by fights and the police have to be called in. One officer who had been on the force for nine years said that these men were generally good-natured and easy-going, and in all his experience he had never arrested a sober "Hunkie" a disparaging term for a worker of Eastern European background; it was when they were drunk that the trouble began.

The women have few opportunities for relaxation. Sometimes they gossip around the pump or at the butcher's, but washing, ironing, cleaning, sewing, and cooking for the boarders leave little time for visiting. The young people perhaps suffer most from the lack of home festivities. A two-room house has no place for games or "parties," or even for courting;[3] there is not even space enough, to say nothing of privacy. So young folks are driven to the streets. Almost the only time when the house is really the scene of festivity is when those primal events, birth, and marriage, and death, bring together both the old-time friends and the new neighbors.

On most of these occasions, whether weddings, christenings or funerals, joy and grief and religious ceremony are alike forgotten in a riotous good time. The weddings are the gayest affairs in the life of the community. After the morning service at the church, all return home if the house is big enough, and if not, they go to a hall, and there the dancing begins. Each man pays what he can, usually a dollar, for the privilege of dancing with the bride, and the money—their form of a wedding present—helps furnish the home for the young couple. At one wedding during the winter $75 was thus received, but the girl by evening felt that she had earned the money. In the afternoon the drinking begins and by midnight the revel is at its height. The neighborhood considers a family under obligation to provide these festivities.

Some old-world customs, too, are maintained which seem strangely at variance with new-world conditions. All summer over the doors and windows are seen dried, smoke begrimed branches from which the faded leaves hang disconsolately. These decorations are part of a joyous religious festival in the spring time similar to those that added merriment to the village life at home. At Eastertide they keep up an old custom, said to date from pagan days. On Monday the men go about with willow branches and switch the women until they make them a present, while on the following day the women retaliate by throwing water on the men.

In other superficial habits of life they show themselves eager to adopt American customs. This tendency is clearly—sometimes humorously—exemplified in the quickness with which they adopt our style of clothing. The men on Sunday can often be differentiated from the American workmen only by the unmistakable Slavic type of face. Even in their own homes the women quickly adopt the machine-made cotton wrapper and on Sunday the streets blossom with cheap ready-made adornments. I was fairly startled by one apparition in a gay pink hat, crude blue skirt, and green silk waist, all products of a department store, which evidently gave the wearer a proud sense of being dressed like other Americans. As I stood Easter Sunday watching the kneeling women, the mass of vivid colors showed how easily they copy the less desirable habits of their native-born sisters. If opportunity offered they would doubtless be as ready to pick up our customs in other more essential matters.

Lack of intercourse, however, hinders. The Slavs must keep up their own festivities the more because they cannot join in the amusements of the rest of the community. To the better class of entertainments they are not welcomed, and to others the difference in speech is still a barrier. Thus cut off from what little normal amusement Homestead offers, they cling to the few festivities their limited opportunities make possible.

In summer there are of course more chances for recreation; trolley rides and picnics in the park make a welcome variety from the heat of the courts. The following statements, taken from the notes of the Slavic woman who assisted in making the investigation, tell the story simply:

—They do not go to amusements of any kind on account of being so poor and feel so badly after they have finished their day's work.

—Husband and wife go to the lodge dances, which they enjoy very much. Wife goes to the five cent theatres, to the parks in the summer and for trolley rides. Is fond of all kinds of amusements and goes when they can afford it.

—The family have no amusements at all outside of their own home, simply because they cannot afford it. They would like to be able to go to some places of amusement, if they could. Spend their Sundays at home in a pleasant way. The mother and children go to church every Saturday evening to say the rosary, which is one of their chief pleasures.

Starting in with such a household as that described at the opening of this chapter, how far do any of these Slavic families succeed in working out ideals they have set for themselves?

If we turn from the crowded courts with their two-room tenements to the homes of some who have attained their ambitions, we find conditions that show an inherent capacity for advancement in the race. As an illustration, note the change in type in two houses, the homes of families from the same place in the old country, the one newcomers, the other among the "oldest inhabitants" of the Slavic community. The first family live in a one-room tenement, where even though the furniture includes only absolute necessities, it is hard to keep all the crowded belongings in order. One wash-day morning the disorder is increased. Nevertheless, the home is kept as neat as the circumstances permit, and the bright pictures on the wall are proof of a desire to make it attractive. As the man earns only $9.90 a week, they must keep their rent low if bills are to be paid and anything laid by for the future. In the other picture, the "front room" with its leather-covered furniture is in a five-room house which the family owns. The sacred pictures with their vivid coloring relieve the severity of the room while they also reveal the religious note in Slavic life, for if happiness is to stay with the family, the priest must come yearly to "bless the home." This family after many years in America has, by hard work and thrift, succeeded in obtaining a real home.

Turning from this visible evidence of the way in which an individual Slavic family has prospered, we find in the mill census that the number of skilled, and therefore highly paid members of the race, are few. Of the 3,603 Slavs in the mill in 1907, 459 were ranked as semi-skilled, 80 as skilled. The Slovaks from Austro-Hungary are the most numerous of the race in Homestead, and were the first of this stock to come here. Among them we find proportionately a slightly larger number of semi-skilled workers.[4]

We have seen that of the budget Slavs still earning laborers' wages, a third had been here over ten years; it is apparent, however, that individuals are slowly making their way into skilled work—a movement which, as the older English-speaking men drop out, is probably bound to increase. In the 29 immigrant families keeping budgets all of the men who earned $12 or more a week had been here over five years. It is interesting to note that some had come here when they were very young, eleven, fifteen, sixteen, or seventeen years old; for example, a tonnage worker had been here ten years; a man at one of the furnaces earning $3.50 a day, seventeen years, and a machinist who earned about the same amount, eighteen years. Even with the higher wages, their families continue to make sacrifices to secure the desired property more rapidly. A helper at one of the open-hearth furnaces, who had been here for seven years, was earning $2.50 to $3.00 a day. The husband and wife still took in two boarders, so that with their two children there were six people in a two-room house, which was but scantily furnished. They had a bank account of at least $400. Another Slav, the head of a family of three, had been here ten years and was working on tonnage, in good times earning about $6.00 a day. They, too, lived in a two-room house, but it was neat and from their standpoint probably seemed large enough as they had no lodger. They had purchased the farm in the old country and besides had a $500 bank account. Again, take a family of six. The father, still only about thirty years old, had been here for over fifteen years. Out of his wages—about $3.50 a day at fairly skilled work in the mill—he was buying a small house with a garden. He was naturalized and the family stood as a fair type of our new citizens. They took no lodgers, but the limitations imposed by such thrift as they practiced are illustrated by the notes on this household made by my interpreter. Herself a Slav, their circumstances were a matter of no special interest, and she therefore wrote her notes with no attempt to add "local color" such as a person of another race would have put into them. To her the statement was simply one of facts:

Conditions of Work: The man works on day and night shifts alternately.

Home: They don't own their own home, on which there is a mortgage. The man gives all his earnings to his wife and when he needs any spending money, he asks for it.

Furniture: They live in two rooms comfortably furnished, one a living room and the other a bed room. They have a sewing machine on which the mother does the sewing for her family. Does her washing by hand.

Clothes: They wear plain clothing. The woman does all her own mending with care. The father buys ready-made clothing. They have a change of clothing for Sundays, of a fairly good quality.

Food: They buy their food at grocery stores; don't get all at one store. They live principally on vegetable diet, not using much fruit. The man works hard and they are obliged to have good substantial food. The family eat their evening meal together.

Woman's Work: The woman does her own work at home, but does not earn anything outside, her time all being taken up with caring for her family.

Lodges: The man belongs to St. Stephen's Lodge, and his wife belongs to St. Catherine's, both church lodges. They attend one meeting every month unless something to prevent. When not able to go, they send in their dues. The man gets $5.00 a week sick benefits, also a death benefit of $1000 to his family after his decease. His dues are $2.00 monthly and the wife's dues are $1.00 a month. In case of death of the woman the family gets $700. The wife's reason for belonging to above lodges is that their family may have benefits paid by the lodges in case of a death.

Health: This man is in good health. The woman is not in good health, having gone to work too soon after her confinement; was attended by a midwife. She did not have proper care during her confinement. The children are sickly. One of them had typhoid fever.

Education: There are four children, the oldest seven years and now attending public school. The only reading matter they have is his Lodge paper, which he gets once a week.

Accidents: The man had one accident, but no help from the Carnegie fund.[5]

Drink: The man drinks at home and sometimes at saloons. Pays for himself. He does not get intoxicated. The woman drinks a little when she has it at home.

Amusements: The man goes only when his lodge gives a dance, it being expected of every member to buy tickets. Neither he nor his wife ever attend theatres, on account of being kept at home with their family. The woman cannot remember having been to any of the parks or amusements of any kind.

It is by such thrift that some of the Slavs attain their ambition to own a home. An official in the foreign department of one bank said he knew of 25 Slavs who had purchased homes in 1907. Sometimes these families continue to live in the Second Ward. One family, for example, had bought an eight-room house on one of these busy streets. The four rear rooms they rented, but with evident regard for appearances lived themselves in the four that faced the front. With the aid of the rent from the rear tenement they had succeeded in freeing the house from the mortgage. The families more often, however, move further from the mill. One I knew bought a house on the hill with two porches and a big yard where they kept chickens. While they had only succeeded in paying $500 on the $1700 the place cost, now that a son was at work they hoped to be able to clear the debt. In the meantime they truly rejoiced in being on the hill above the smoke and away from the bustling courts.

The English-speaking families on such streets rarely extend a cordial welcome. A woman who lives next door to a Slavic family told me that some of the neighbors objected because they were rather noisy and drank a good deal, though she herself found them pleasant enough.

All the Slavs who prosper, however, do not try to buy property here. Some prefer a bank account. It is authoritatively stated that about 1,600 Slavs have savings bank accounts in Homestead ranging from $100 to $1000, and even in a few instances to $1500. Occasionally this zeal for saving gets a setback. A few years ago a Slav ran an "exchange bank" in Homestead and when he had secured a goodly sum departed. One family was so discouraged at losing the $400 it had on deposit with him, of hard earned savings, that the woman ceased to take boarders and the man to work hard.

Yet not all the extra money goes into bank accounts and houses. If we compare the budgets of the 10 Slavic families spending more than $15 a week with the average of the 42 budget families (of all races) in the same expenditure groups, we shall find that the former increase their expenditures along much the same lines as do the other peoples, though it is to be noted here, as in the general averages, that the Slav spends a slightly larger percent for food and a slightly smaller percent for rent.

If, on the other hand, we compare the Slavic families spending over $15 with those spending less than $12, we find that the expenditures which have increased less rapidly than the income are the essentials, food, rent, fuel, and clothing; that insurance increases a little more rapidly, but that the great part of the increased pay goes for more distinctly cultural expenditures.

This comparison, though fragmentary, suggests that on the whole these Slavs made a wise use of their increased earnings—that there is an actual increase of expenditure for every item, but that by far the largest gain is in that sphere which stands for the less material side of life, church, education, recreation and savings.

For most Slavic households, however, the increased income which would make such increased expenditure possible must be looked for not from the man's wages, but, at least in the first years, from other sources. We have seen how the first recourse of the young couple is to keep lodgers and the cost to health and childhood that that involves. Time goes on, brings children, and household expenses rise, and even with increased earnings, tends to keep the couple at this double work.

Notes

1. Neighborhoods of homes of working class families.
2. The time just before, during, and after childbirth when conventional medical practice of the time insisted that women stay in bed.
3. Visiting and private conversation between single men and women.
4. They formed 51.7 percent of all the Slavs in the mill in 1907, 60.1 percent of the semi-skilled Slavs, and 56.2 percent of the skilled Slavs.
5. A fund established by Andrew Carnegie at the time of the founding of the U.S. Steel Corporation for the relief of injured workers and former employees who were elderly and needy. The Carnegie Steel Company was the core operation of U.S. Steel Corporation.

Sonia Shah, "Three Hot Meals and a Full Day at Work: South Asian Women's Labor in the United States"

There's a story my mother tells about when I was around five years old or so and playing "doctor" with the little boy next door. My mother immigrated to the United States from Coimbatore, India, in 1968, having recently married my father, who hailed from Bombay. "I have to be the nurse," I apparently declared, "and you have to be the doctor." My mother likes to tell this story because she is, and was, as I was supposedly aware at the time, a practicing physician. Yet, even given this real-life example of a woman doctor, my own mother, I was convinced that women were meant to be nurses, while men were supposed to be doctors.

My earliest memory of a career ambition was to be a baby-sitter. I also remember wanting to be a secretary, as I liked to fill out the blanks on the medical forms my parents used to bring home. My father is also a physician. When I was around eleven years old or so, he used to bring me to his office in the summers, where I would "work" with the women in the secretarial office. They gave me the oversize, heavily bound appointment book, which I would date years into the future. I remember enjoying this work, and feeling it was useful to the secretaries.

At home, I did very little work, as I recall. My mother seemed to do most of the housework, including buying groceries, cooking at least three hot dishes for dinner each night, cleaning the kitchen, vacuuming, sweeping, and doing the laundry. At the time, she was working part-time as a physician while my father was working full-time. My father would often put me and my sister to bed or give us baths. I liked to draw and to write stories, and my parents encouraged me to channel those proclivities into applied crafts, such as architecture and journalism.

When I was about fifteen, I went to India to visit my extended family there. One stop on my trip was Tirupur, a small town where my aunt and cousins lived. I hated visiting Tirupur, as I found it a stultifying town. There were no restaurants or theaters in Tirupur and no running water or electricity. But it wasn't a poor town; there were several successful factories located there. My cousin's factory, for example, produced cotton clothing for export on contract. He brought me to see the factory one day.

I was surprised to find that he employed dozens of young girls, even younger than I was at the time. The vision of these disheveled little girls clambering over the mounds of bright white cotton is still vivid to me. They crawled over the cotton like mice, twisting and cutting and sewing it. Their brownish rags contrasted with the brightly colored and starched oversize cotton T-shirts that they were making to be sold to little girls in France. My cousin told me proudly that he preferred hiring the little girls, as he could pay them significantly less than the little boys.

It was disturbing to me that my cousin didn't feel it was wrong to exploit children. And the obvious misuse of their and his labor struck me. Because the little girls would work for so little money, my cousin could offer competitive contracts to foreign buyers, who could then make a healthy profit by selling the cheaply bought products abroad. It seemed so clear that the girls, my cousin, and the town could all benefit themselves much more if they were to direct their energy and labors toward meeting their own material and social needs; if the girls went to school to develop their skills while my cousin used his resources to help build the town, which the girls would one day inherit. Instead, the men exploited the girls and all worked too hard, just to make a throwaway item for some kid—a rich one, relative to the workers—across an ocean.

What were the forces that resulted in such a wasteful and unjust situation? I wondered. And how would these forces affect my own place in society? Until then, my main goal was to find work that was interesting and meaningful to me. I started asking myself a different question: Who and what do I want to work for?

U.S. feminists have long fought for expanded employment opportunities for women, for more and better jobs for women. They have been concerned with the *quality* of women's work. In terms of quality, Indian women in the United States—myself and my mother included—have been relatively successful. By and large, we are better employed than our white counterparts, as are the men in our community. If quality of work were the sole criterion on which to judge our labor, then Indian women would have much to celebrate.

And so we should. But we must also look at our labor in terms of the greater historical and economic forces that dictate its role in society. For, while it is true that Indian women have predominantly better jobs than their white counterparts, as do Indian men, it is also true that our labor has contributed to the underdevelopment of India, and to racial antagonism and exploitative capitalism in the United States. And, our resources—our education, our paid and unpaid labor, and our social relationships—have been devalued and used for others' gain.

My mother was the first physician and the first to immigrate to the United States in her family of six children. Her father worked hard all his life in a family-owned warehousing business, his long hours of paid work made possible by his wife, my grandmother, and some poorly paid servant women, who performed the unpaid labor of child rearing and housekeeping. Since my mother was the only child to pursue an advance degree, one can assume it was at the cost of the other children's not being able to do so.

But why did she, and my father, want to leave India? Then, as now, emigrating to the United States was considered a path to certain upward mobility. It was and is possible for elites to accumulate much wealth in India. But Indian immigrants to the United States consistently cite economic-related reasons for leaving: corruption, poverty, lack of opportunity. For example, when my mother graduated from medical school in the late 1960s, the postcolonial Indian economy suffered a surplus of educated labor. India's educated unemployed numbered 1.53 million in 1969, and 3.3 million in 1972.

At the same time that more and more Indians pursued higher degrees in a postcolonial economy that could not absorb them, the United States experienced a shortage of skilled professional workers, physicians in particular. The expansion of hospital-based medical care, and the institution of broad social programs, such as Medicare and Medicaid in 1965, resulted in the need for thousands of skilled professionals. The 1965 Immigration Act, which abolished national quotas in favor of those based on professional status, aimed to encourage the immigration of such professionals. Thousands of unemployed professionals from India and Pakistan flocked to the United States, my parents among them. Medical graduates especially were encouraged, with offers of free apartments and secure jobs at hospitals.

While the U.S. economy may have benefited, it was the Indian economy that bore the cost of the investment in these professionals. If one considers the colonial practice of siphoning resources from the colonized nation to be one reason for India's poverty relative to the West, the 1960s' flow of educated emigrants from India to the United States deepened the inequity. If the per-capita average education cost for these emigrants is estimated at $20,000, then skilled emigration to the United States between 1962 and 1967 represented a loss of $61,240,000 for India. While, according to some commentators, a lesser-developed country such as India does not need highly skilled workers as much as it needs semiskilled workers, the loss of highly skilled workers still means a loss of intellectual leadership, and thus "widens the technological gap" between less-developed and more-developed countries. Ironically, while Western intervention in India led to underdevelopment in the first place, postcolonial emigration to the West further deepened India's relative poverty.

Indian immigration to the United States is thus most accurately characterized as a transfer of wealth from an underdeveloped country to a developed country. The fact that Indian immigrants' relative economic success in the United States is due to the resources they brought with them from India—their work skills and education—is in direct contradiction to the second of two assumptions of the "model minority" myth. The model minority myth holds that Asian Americans have been more successful in the United States than native ethnic groups and that they have been more successful because of their cultural heritage, not the material resources they brought with them. Of "uptown" Chinese immigrants to the United States, who are as well educated as many of the 1960s Indian immigrants, Teresa Amott and Julie Matthaei write:

> Uptown Chinese, many of them women, come to the United States with excellent English, top-level educations, and often with considerable financial resources. Since these credentials allow them to find lucrative professional jobs, their presence raises the average income statistics for Chinese Americans and gives the false impression that Chinese are easily

upwardly mobile in the United States. In reality, uptown Chinese were already educationally and socially advantaged in Taiwan and China, and simply transferred these achievements and status to the United States. Indeed, their experience in the United States is one of *downward* mobility. Discrimination exists even against such "model" immigrants, who earn less than whites with equal educations and have less access to managerial promotions than equally qualified whites.

Indian government and industry encourage their emigrants to the West to invest in India. Possibly such investment could help balance the loss of these productive workers.

According to the 1990 U.S. Census, 58 percent of all Indian women in the United States are employed outside the home, 45 percent of whom work in high-paying, upwardly mobile fields, as opposed to 39 percent of white women. Over 80 percent of Indian men in the United States are employed outside the home, and over half of them, compared with a third of white men, hold high-salary, upwardly mobile, secure jobs. But these professionals have not necessarily enjoyed the full benefits of their skills and education. Once in the United States, many of them encountered a number of obstacles that prevented them from reaching the most lucrative private-sector jobs, steering them into the government-run jobs in the inner-city and rural areas where native professionals were unwilling to go. According to the U.S. Commission on Civil Rights, Asian immigrants encountered a glass ceiling that prevented them from moving up the ladder as fast as their white counterparts. They encountered racist attitudes, difficulties in networking with other professionals, a lack of mentors, and a corporate culture hostile to outsiders. Their accents were the basis for exclusion and harassment on the job. And their foreign educations have been devalued and held to higher-than-usual standards than those for U.S.-educated professionals. Some of them ended up not working in the fields for which they had trained: "College-educated, they can be found operating travel agencies, sari shops, and luncheonettes featuring pizza, souvlakia, and Indian 'fast food.' They are also news-stand operators in the subways of Manhattan. . . . Asian Indians have also found a niche in the motel business: they own fifteen thousand motels, or 28 percent of the nation's 53,629 hotels and motels."

Immigrant medical graduates "serve in disproportionate numbers in rural areas, often in solo and partnership practices, in public hospitals, in smaller not-for-profit hospitals, and in regions of the country that have experienced emigration of population because of declining industry and high unemployment. Poor populations and Medicaid recipients also are often reliant on FMGs [foreign medical graduates]." According to sociologist Paul Starr, immigrant physicians from India, Korea, and the Philippines "often took jobs that Americans did not want (for example, in state mental institutions). In effect, the peculiar slant of American health policy (expanding hospitals, but keeping down medical enrollments) was producing a new lower tier in the medical profession drawn from the Third World."

According to Cheng and Bonacich, such discriminatory treatment renders immigrant workers especially exploitable by employers, and thus well serves the needs of the capitalist economy: "Employers want to keep them as an especially exploitable sector of the working class, a position rationalized by such ideological concomitants of imperialism as racism. Local workers, however, are fearful of being undercut by the presence of an especially exploitable group of workers. These competing interests give rise to anti-immigrant movements. . . . Thus, the treatment of immigrant workers, including the prejudice and discrimination they face, must also be seen as part of the world capitalist system."

While imperialism and capitalism have shaped South Asians' work experiences in the United States, the specific work experiences of women have also been shaped by their gender. Women bear much of the direct loss of the transfer of resources from poor nation to rich nation. Such was the case with the first immigrants from South Asia, the 6,400 young Indian men who came to the United States between 1900 and 1920, the majority of whom were Sikh. U.S. industrialists were eager for the opportunity to employ workers whom the 1908 *Overland Monthly* deemed "willing to work for 'cheap' wages and able to 'subsist on incomes that would be prohibitive to the white man.'" Many came from a farming background but were mostly employed as railroad workers in the United States, and as replacements for striking workers.

Although between one-third and one-half of these immigrants were married, of the five thousand Indians in California in 1914, only twelve were women. In the beginning, the men hoped either to return to India with newfound riches or to send for their wives and children. By and large, having mortgaged their farms in India to work for low wages in a discriminatory U.S. environment, they did not make enough money to do either. By 1917, anti-Indian sentiment—sometimes violent—among the white workers who considered them competitors resulted in an immigration restriction law that barred Indians from immigrating to the United States.

Ronald Takaki recounts the story of a married Indian worker who tried to bring his wife to the United States to join him:

> Moola Singh had left his wife in the Punjab in 1911 and had saved enough money to pay for her passage to America. But by the time he had sent the money to her, the law had already been enacted. "She worry," Singh told an interviewer many years later. "She good, nice looking, healthy, but she love. You know love, person no eat, worry, then maybe die. Mother wrote one time letter, 'she sick, you gotta come home.' Then I write her letter from Arizona, to her I say, 'I'm coming, don't worry, I be there. . . .'" But she passed away in 1921 before Singh could return. "If we had our women here," said a fellow countryman, "our whole life would be different."

These workers could work for low wages in large part because their female relatives bore the cost of caring for their families in India and ensuring their long-term social security at home. These were costs that U.S. employers did not have to bear, as they did for local white workers. This is not to imply that those women who provided this unpaid labor were somehow at fault for following the cultural dictates of the sexual division of paid and unpaid labor. It does show, however, how capitalist economies were able to exploit such a gendered division of labor to their advantage in ways that these workers and families were not able to interrupt. Finally, between 1920 and 1940, half of the Indian population left the United States. Their cheap labor no longer needed in the United States, the men returned to India no richer, and those who stayed started families with Mexican and other non-Indian women.

Among the 1960s-era educated Indian immigrants, there is evidence that the relative success of some of the women has been because they have worked longer and harder than their white counterparts. Asian-American women were found to work more hours per year and more consistently through their life cycle, regardless of family circumstances, than white women. They were also found to receive lower economic returns than white women with comparable educational backgrounds. Finally, according to studies from around the world, women's income is more likely to be invested back into the household than men's. Thus, women are less likely personally to enjoy the benefits that accrue to them from their employment. The many Indian motel-owning families are an example of this. According to Suvarna Thaker's study of Indian motel-owning wives in Los Angeles:

> Women do most of the work involved in running motels. . . . Though she does hard work in the motel, she has no help in the kitchen or [with] other household work which is traditionally considered "women's tasks." When asked if her husband ever helps her with the dishes, etc., Mrs. C's quick reply is "No, never, I cannot think of him doing that!" For many, what they do in the motels is in a way an extension of their household work. The type of work involved in running a motel does not require any special skill. It is like an extension of domestic work so some women do not get the feeling that what they do is really one kind of employment, and they derive little job satisfaction from it."

In addition to their paid work, South Asian women in the United States, like women everywhere, perform the lion's share, if not all, of the labor in the home. According to the United Nations, women perform almost two-thirds of the world's labor, but receive only one-tenth of the world's income and own less than one-hundredth of the world's property. Also according to the United Nations, $16 trillion worth of women's work in the home, family businesses, and in child care is unpaid and undervalued in economic statistics.

"Most women have to work . . . a 'double day': they work for wages in the labor market and work without pay in the home." This is true for women everywhere. In addition, South Asian women in the United States are less likely than other similarly well-employed women to rely on restaurants, laundries, hired help, paid child care, fast foods, and other bought conveniences that cut down on home labor. Further, the cheap household help and the help of extended family members that were available in South Asia are by and large not available in the United States. Yet given all these differences between the South Asian and U.S. environments, South Asians in the United States have not significantly altered their standards of cleanliness, cooking, and child rearing. Evidence shows that South Asian communities in the United States have "retained their taste for traditional food, along with their values concerning home, family, children, religion, and marriage," and have "transplanted old-world gender ideologies and clearly dichotomized sex roles in their adopted country of residence." Religious, cultural, and linguistic traditions thus prevent such South Asian families in the United States from using McDonald's, European nannies, or microwave ovens as comfortably or as easily as a white family, even if they can afford to.

Among South Asian women in the United States, the men are more and better employed outside the home than the women. Over 80 percent of Indian men in the United States are employed outside the home, and over half of them, compared with a third of white men, hold high-salary, upwardly mobile, secure jobs. While it is true that South Asian women are better employed than white women, it is also true that, like all women, they are employed in worse jobs than men. According to the 1990 U.S. Census, over half of working Indian women work in low-wage, low-mobility, unstable positions such as clerical, service, and certain low-ranking sales fields. This discrepancy between Indian men and Indian women, in fact, is even larger than that between white men and white women.

About 55 percent of working Indian women work in the secondary labor market; 42 percent in the "upper tier" and 13 percent in the "lower tier." While both tiers of the secondary labor market comprise low-paying, unstable positions with little or no possibility of upward mobility, jobs in the lower tier also entail poor working conditions. These positions include private household occupations, some service occupations, farming, forestry and fishing, and handlers, equipment cleaners, helpers, and laborers. In contrast, just over 30 percent of Indian men are in the secondary labor market; of these, the majority are in jobs with the better working conditions of the upper tier secondary market.

These census statistics probably do not reveal the whole picture either. South Asian women who make *chapatis* and *samosas*[1] for South Asian grocery stores and cater South Asian food may not be considered "working" by the census. As well, the many women, including motel owners' wives, who work for free in their family's convenience stores and newspaper stands may not be counted.

Since 1976, Indian immigrant professionals have been sponsoring their less-educated relatives for immigration to the United States. Between 1980 and 1990, the Indian population in the United States more than doubled, growing from 247,801 to 786,694. While the 1960s immigrants were primarily professionals ready to be incorporated into the middle- and upper-middle classes, the 1980s and 1990s immigrants are more likely to be semiskilled and working class.

Given capitalism's tendency to use race and gender differences among paid and unpaid workers to exploit labor and maximize profits, it seems likely that the growing class disparity in the South Asian community may well be fodder for such manipulation as well. Racial differences among native and immigrant workers have ended up weakening worker solidarity against employers. The sexist division of labor between men and women in immigrant communities has been instrumental to keeping immigrant labor cheap and expendable for employers.

For South Asians and other Asians in the United States, the myth of the "model minority" is key to providing the rationale for racial and class divisions—and for their manipulation—between South Asian and other communities. By promoting this myth, mass media outlets serve the interests of capitalist employers and the government and other elites that support them. For example, the model minority myth obscures the role of South Asian investment in its emigrants and in their subsequent relative success as immigrants and, with it, the continued transfer of wealth from poor Third World countries to the West. It deceptively offers as evidence that culture rather than resources creates economic success, thus strengthening arguments against material benefits for poor workers and communities. It creates the false impression that South Asian communities are monolithically successful, obscuring the class and gender divisions within the community. Obscuring those divisions makes cross-cultural women's and workers' solidarity less likely, and the divisions themselves, with the competing interests they create, fragment South Asian community organizing.

Note

1. Indian "fast food": chapatis/fried flat bread; samosa/fried, stuffed vegetable pastry like a pita pocket.

CHAPTER ELEVEN

Language: Social and Political Perspectives

Introduction

An abiding issue in the experience of immigrants and of the societies that receive them is language difference, which probably more than any other marker sets off the immigrant from the native-born residents of the host society. At the present time, English is proliferating around the world as the principal global language of business, popular culture, and electronic journalism, and more and more people outside the United States aspire to learn English. As a result, it is probably the case that many more contemporary immigrants have some familiarity with at least some English than did immigrants in the past. Yet the vast majority of immigrants still arrive in the United States facing the need to obtain mastery of a language with which they are largely unfamiliar.

Language difference has asserted itself as a problem in two distinct but related ways throughout American immigration history. First, there has been the problem for the individual of attaining mastery of English, which has proven both necessary to negotiating ordinary, daily encounters with others on the streets, or while shopping, or in government offices, and useful to achieving success in school and at work. Immigration has always been, for most migrants, a matter of seeking opportunity for a more secure and full life. Access to opportunity has decidedly and increasingly correlated with proficiency in English, especially in the urban environment, in which salaried or wage-earning employees have come to work in large organizations where English is the unquestioned language of corporate culture. Lower-paying work that doesn't offer much chance for improvement, and work in smaller businesses, often owned by members of the same ethnic

Stanley Lieberson and Timothy J. Curry, "Language Shift in the United States: Some Demographic Clues" in *International Migration Review*, 5 (Summer, 1971): 125–137. Reprinted with the permission of the authors and the Center for Migration Studies of NY, Inc.; www.cmsny.org

Richard Rodriguez, *Hunger for Memory: The Education of Richard Rodriguez. An Autobiography* (New York: David Godine, Publisher, 1981), pp. 19–26. Reprinted by permission of David R. Godine, Publisher, Inc. Copyright © 1982 by Richard Rodriguez.

Guillermo X. Garcia, "Border Battle Centers on Spanish-only Town" in *USA Today*, December 17, 1999. Copyright © 1999 USA TODAY. Reprinted with permission.

group, have not required English-language skills. On the other hand, even in an industrial setting, employers have often believed that production efficiency and safety are directly correlated with their ability to communicate with workers in English. Not all immigrants, however, have availed themselves of the opportunity to learn and to become proficient in English, so one question that arises in understanding immigrant language change is which settings have lent themselves to learning, or to inhibiting the learning of, English. Relatedly, there is the question of generations in the process of language shift, for throughout much of American immigration history, the children of immigrants have been more likely to acquire proficiency in English than their foreign-born parents. While the use of English presented the second generation with the promise of greater opportunity, it also had the potential to open a rift between generations.

Second, language has asserted itself continuously as a question for social and political policy. Whatever the period of time in which mass immigrations have been experienced, immigrants have raised the specter of a loss of cultural coherence and political unity. They are seen as a threat to those institutions and habits of daily life that bring people together and hold them together. A common public language has been seen as perhaps the most important element in the effort to combat the potential for disunity that immigration appears to constitute. Immigrants may speak whatever language they prefer in private settings, such as while socializing with friends or in their family circles. However, certain public endeavors, especially education in public schools and contacts with government—becoming a citizen, voting, jury service, and owning property—ought for necessitate English in the view of many Americans. They believe that use of a common language in such instances, promotes the ideal of unity and encourages immigrants and their children to shift to the use of English. The goal of a common public language is certainly a plausible one, but the success of the quest for a monolingual America has always depended on the sensitivity and intelligence with which the goal has been pursued. Resentment is caused by policies that seem coercive, especially when they are insensitive to the pride people take in their native tongue. Or, efforts on behalf of monolingualism may also be insensitive to the potential of language shift and cause alienation between the immigrants and their children, or confusion that inhibits learning among young children, who must speak one language at home and another in school. At the very least, they may simply be insensitive to the fact that a habit as profound as speaking one's language cannot be expected to be changed quickly. Moreover, in places, whether rural or urban, in which immigrants of one group have settled in large numbers in relatively self-enclosed ethnic worlds, it has been tempting for them to believe that English, even in public contexts, was not necessary at all. Whatever the particular circumstances, it is easy to see how language may become a matter for intense and emotional debate in times of mass immigration. It is also easy to understand how the question of the language of instruction in schools has repeatedly been a matter of controversy, because ultimately the question involved has been the relations of children to their parents and to their parents' culture and community.

The selections in this chapter take up a number of these themes. Looking at the years between 1840 and 1924, the peak years of European immigration, Stanley Lieberson and Timothy Curry are impressed with how rapid and complete was the triumph of English over its competition. Their analysis of how this massive shift of languages came about concentrates not on public policies, such as the insistence on the use of English in public school instruction, but rather on how daily life lent itself in a variety of circumstances to the use or non-use of English. They are interested in the ways in which, for example, concentrations of immigrants sharing the same native tongue in various settings, such as neighborhoods and workplaces, inhibited acquisition of English, or in which certain types of employment correlate with the ability to speak English. They also concern themselves with the role of immigrant parents in both language maintenance and language shift among children born and raised in the United States.

The second selection takes up some of the themes about the influence of generational factors within the family and of group and neighborhood on language in immigrant families. It is from the much-discussed and controversial autobiography of writer Richard Rodriquez, who was raised in middle-class American neighborhoods in Los Angeles by Mexican immigrant, working-class parents, who spoke English haltingly and used only Spanish at home. Rodriquez's memoir is controversial, because exponents of bilingual education—the view that the children of immigrants can be taught most effectively in school using their parents' language rather than, or in the company of, English—find his arguments hostile to their views. Also controversial is his view of the immigrant's mother tongue, which he regards exclusively as a private language of home and family. For him, it is most important for children to learn English because it opens the door not only to opportunity, but also to the larger public world of American society. Advocates of bilingualism do not see why Spanish, too, cannot be conceived of as public language. But Rodriquez's testimony to the problems he faced making the transition to speaking English, which was insisted upon by the Catholic nuns who were his teachers, is powerful and credible. His initial reluctance to speak English was conquered with the help of his teachers and his parents, but ultimately only at the expense of the warmth of a family circle sustained by sharing its relationship through Spanish, their ancestral language. He recognizes that he both lost and gained simultaneously by becoming fluent in English.

Not everyone agrees with Rodriquez that English has, or should have, exclusive control of the public sphere in the United States. The third selection concerns this issue, and demonstrates how controversial the issue of the dominance of English in the public sphere may become. In August of 1999, El Cenizo, a small town on the Texas-Mexico border with an overwhelmingly Spanish-speaking population, which was composed of many legal and illegal immigrants, captured the news all over the United States and indeed around the world, when its city council voted to make Spanish the official language of local government. The council took this unusual step, it was explained, in order to make government accessible to the town's

Spanish-speaking majority, which could not make sense of laws, regulations, and instructions written in English. This certainly seems a plausible step in the direction of effective democratic government. It is not unlikely that in the past, on an *unofficial* level, American local governments have often made exceptions to the usual English-only policy to accommodate large linguistic groups, such as nineteenth century Germans, Swedes, or Norwegians in the rural Midwest, in their jurisdictions. The contemporary federal government routinely publishes instructions for the decennial census and for personal tax forms in languages others than English. Local governments today often make voting instructions available in languages other than English. But for many the El Cenizo council's actions, giving Spanish *official* dominant status in all governmental matters, carried heavily symbolic and dangerous meanings. For those who feared that the contemporary massive migrations of Spanish-speaking people to the United States put English and other aspects of traditional European-American culture in jeopardy, or for those who feared that consequences for national unity of dozens of ethnic groups insisting on their own language rights, it seemed an ominous sign of emerging social divisions and cultural chaos. In addition, the council's decision mobilized the racists of the Ku Klux Klan, who oppose immigration, especially of people who are not white, and see the threat of non-white domination everywhere. As of this time, there has hardly been a rush to copy the example of El Cenizo and further topple English from its position of prominence, so the fear that the council's actions were the first step in the unraveling of the United States seems greatly exaggerated. But the controversy suggests the particular power that language, which can both unite and divide people, has in a society as culturally diverse as the contemporary United States.

Suggestions for Further Reading

Nancy Faires Conklin and Margaret *A. Lourie, A Host of Tongues: Language Communities in the United States* (New York: The Free Press, 1983).

James Crawford, *Hold Your Tongue: Bilingualism and the Politics of English Only* (Reading: Addison-Wesley, 1992).

James Crawford, editor, *Language Loyalties: A Source Book on the Official English Controversy* (Chicago: University of Chicago Press, 1992).

Joshua Fishman, *Language Loyalty in the United States* (New York: Arno Press, 1978).

Joshua Fishman et al., *The Rise and Fall of the Ethnic Revival: Perspectives on Language and Ethnicity* (New York: Mouton, 1985).

Calvin J. Veltman, *Language Shift in the United States* (New York: Mouton, 1983).

Stanley Lieberson and Timothy J. Curry, "Language Shift in the United States: Some Demographic Clues"

Compared with the situation in many nations, a staggering number of immigrants and their descendents in the United States have given up their ancestral languages and shifted to a new mother-tongue. Nearly two-thirds of the 35 million immigrants between 1840 and 1924 were native speakers of some other tongue. Except for such groups as the Spanish-speaking residents of the Southwest, the Pennsylvania Dutch, the French-speaking residents of New England, and the Creoles in the Louisiana Bayous, the shift to an English mother-tongue was both rapid and with relatively little inter-group conflict. The conflict that did exist was confined more to battles between generations within each group rather than with the English-speaking residents. Despite efforts on the part of all immigrant groups to maintain their ancestral languages, their descendents soon contributed to the growing number of English monoglots in the United States. The shift was rapid, involving but a few generations in most cases, and it was final.

Using the data available in earlier censuses of the United States, this study provides some demographic clues to the causes of this remarkable change. A complete understanding is perhaps no longer possible, but every effort should be made to determine the forces operating during the heyday of language contact in the United States. Not only does this provide us with an opportunity to understand one of the most distinctive features of American history, but it also offers valuable material for comparison with language contact in other nations.

To be sure, there are some obvious macro-societal forces operating to encourage the acquisition of English as at least a second language. Knowledge of this tongue was advantageous for economic, spatial, and social mobility. Moreover, widespread universal education insured that many youngsters would learn English at a very early age. But we still need to learn more about the nature and speed of this shift as well as the specific mechanisms whereby these macro-societal characteristics influence language behavior.

Demographic Issues

There are two crucial demographic events necessary for mother-tongue shift. First, non-English speaking immigrants or their descendents must learn English as a second language. Second, bilingual parents must pass on English as the mother-tongue of the next generation. If only the first step occurs, but the bilingual parents maintain their mother-tongue in socializing the offspring, then a stable multilingual situation will exist in which bilingualism does not generate mother-tongue shift. With the data available in the censuses, it is possible to offer some clues to both the factors influencing the acquisition of English by non-English-speaking immigrants as well as the forces affecting mother-tongue shift by bilingual parents.

Although the language outcome in the United States is known, an examination of the magnitude of these shifts is still instructive. In 1910, 31 percent of the foreign born whites were unable to speak English. This was a substantial increase from the 19 percent reported in 1900, but not much higher than the 27 percent in 1890. Why the drop off between 1890 and 1900? Very likely it was due to the slower increment in the foreign born during that decade than in both the decade immediately before and immediately after. An analysis of inter-city variation suggests that immigrants had a strong propensity to learn English after they stayed in the United States for a few years. As a consequence, a fairly high percentage of immigrants unable to speak English could be maintained only with sizable numbers of newcomers. With the decline in new immigrants because of World War I and later restrictions, relatively few of the immigrants were recent arrivals. As one might expect, the percentage of the foreign born in the United States unable to speak English consequently fell sharply, reaching 15 in 1920 and then 8.5 in 1930.

Not only was there a strong thrust towards the acquisition of English among the immigrants, but virtually no hold-outs are found among the children of immigrants. Less than one per cent of the second generation whites in the United States were unable to speak English in either 1890 or 1900. Granted that a larger percentage of the second generation may have been descendents of immigrants from English-speaking nations, the very low percentage obviously means that the acquisition of English, at the very least as a second language, was a real issue only for the immigrant generation.

The causes of bilingualism in the second generation were not merely a duplication of those operating on the immigrants. There is considerable variance between cities in the frequency of English-language learning among the foreign born, but the percentage of the second generation whites unable to speak English shows very little association with immigrant rates in the same cities.

Likewise, there is not much of an association between the percentages unable to speak English among the two generations when classified by their industries. Although the industries vary rather widely in the percentage of immigrant employees unable to speak English, there is relatively little difference between second generation employees in these industries.

Causes of Bilingualism

Inter-city Variations

Several features of city composition operate to influence the variation between cities in the proportion of immigrants unable to speak English. First, there is an inverse association with the percentage of the city population who are native whites of native parentage. Cities where third or later generation whites are numerically important are also cities where few immigrants fail to acquire English. Moreover, there is some evidence to suggest that the absolute number of immigrants from a given group influences their propensity to acquire English. Examination of inter-city variation in the number of Italians unable to speak English suggests a non-linear relationship such that cities with larger numbers of Italians tend to have greater percentages unable to speak English.

The magnitude of mother-tongue diversity within the immigrant segment of a city's population is another compositional feature that influences the acquisition of English. A strong association is found between the degree of diversity and immigrant bilingualism. Cities whose immigrant mother-tongue composition is relatively homogeneous are also cities in which the acquisition of English is relatively low. This relationship holds even after the native white of native parentage compositional factors is taken into account. Relatively homogeneous immigrant populations are less likely to acquire English since the possibility of communication through their old-world mother-tongue is much greater than in a city where the immigrant groups are from diverse sources and hence do not share a common language alternative to English.

This last finding suggests an important way in which language contact in the United States differs from many other nations. Although the nation received relatively heavy influxes of non-English-speaking immigrants, the groups came from diverse parts of the world and did not possess a single common mother-tongue. Consequently, as the correlation with diversity indicates, resistance to the acquisition of English was reduced. Aside from the obvious economic and social pressures that generated an acquisition of English, one should not overlook its function as a *lingua franca*.[1] In a city that is linguistically diverse because of the migration of groups with a variety of mother-tongues, there is the added need to acquire some language to overcome this diversity. The strength of English as a second language among the immigrants is thus derived not only from the institutional pressures supporting English within the host society, but also the pressures to develop some medium of communication between immigrant groups with different mother-tongues.

Occupations

Immigrants in various jobs differ considerably in the proportion unable to speak English. In most of the professional occupations, where education is obviously a prerequisite, virtually all of the foreign born are able to speak English. By contrast, very sizable proportions of the immigrants in other occupations are unable to speak English. Table 11.1 provides some illustrative percentages for selected occupations in 1890.

Obviously, there are a wide variety of factors influencing these variations. The educational prerequisites are crucial for some occupations. In other cases, the magnitude of interaction with others is virtually nil or else requires minimal linguistic skills. Undoubtedly, some of the immigrants held

Table 11.1 Foreign born white males unable to speak English, by occupation, 1890

Occupation	Percent unable to speak English
All	23
Agricultural Laborers	28
Miners (coal)	55
Stock Raisers, Herders	52
Professional Service	8
Dentists	4
Lawyers	2
Bartenders	6
Launderers	30
Auctioneers	4
Clerks and Copyists	6
Salesmen	5
Artificial Flower Makers	30
Brick and Tile Makers	46
Harness and Saddle Makers	10
Iron and Steel Workers	33
Printers, Lithographers	8
Tailors	29
Tobacco and Cigar Factory Operatives	44

Note: Persons born in England, Ireland, Scotland, and Canada (English) are excluded since it is assumed that virtually all could speak English prior to migration.

occupations that required extensive communication, but could get along without English since their co-workers or customers shared the same non-English tongue. But at the very least, one can say that an ability to speak English offered the immigrant certain advantages since it meant a wider range of potential occupational opportunities.

An important issue is whether those unable to speak English were merely confined to certain work settings or whether they were also handicapped in the quality of their employment. Because of the linguistic demands in the more desirable jobs or the greater competition for them, were those unable to speak English confined to the less desirable occupations? Using two different indicators of occupational desirability, unemployment among the native whites in each occupation, and income, the results indicate that the immigrants unable to speak English are handicapped. Those unable to speak English are more likely to be found in occupations with low incomes or relatively high unemployment rates.

An unresolved issue is the extent these occupational differences are a function of factors other than selectivity along a language dimension. Do the occupational percentages reflect either different learning experiences after employment or differences between immigrant groups in the occupations that they select? There is some evidence to indicate that post–employment factors were not that influential. For some occupations, data are available on the language skills of apprentices as well as those who are presumably more experienced. Comparing apprentice with seasoned-worker, there is little evidence of a sharp change in the proportion unable to speak English in these occupations. Subject to better data, this suggests that employment experience had only a moderate influence on bilingualism. Perhaps jobs requiring a knowledge of English were not opened to those unable to speak the language.

Overall, this occupational analysis suggests that important economic advantages existed for immigrants who could learn to speak English. The foreign born in the better paying occupations, as well as in those with lower levels of unemployment, tend to have very low percentages unable to speak English. Thus occupational pressures undoubtedly increased the proportion of immigrants who learned English. However, it is easy to overestimate the dominant role of this factor in generating language shift. For one reason, there is no association by occupation between linguistic ability in the first and second generations. This means that the advantages or disadvantages that knowledge of English offered were a superfluous cause of English language learning in the *second* generation. Occupational pressures, to be sure, influence the possibility of mother-tongue shift between the generations. Nevertheless, there is some basis for speculating that the occupational pressures were not necessary for the fairly complete acquisition of English among the second generation. Very likely widespread universal education was a sufficient cause.

Other Factors

Census data can not provide information about all of the factors influencing the learning of English among those with some other mother-tongue. There are a few additional clues available, however, from these data. Comparing a number of different immigrant groups within each of ten different United States cities, those more highly segregated also tend to have larger proportions unable to speak English. This relationship appears to hold even after immigrant differences in their length of residence in the United States are taken into account.

Another factor that can only be touched on here is the relationship between the language skills of parents and the performance of their children in school. Within each immigrant group, school performance is compared between the children of fathers who do not speak English and those who do. Retardation is uniformly greater among the first group of children. By "retardation" is meant children in a lower level class than would normally be expected for the child's age. Variations between immigrant groups in the percentage of their children who are retarded can be explained in good part by the different ethnic patterns in the use of English at home. Among those fathers able to speak English, there is considerable variation in the proportion who use it at home. In turn, the proportion of their children who are retarded is related to the propensity of their English-speaking immigrant fathers to use English at home.

What these results suggest is that the acquisition and use of English by the immigrant had an effect on the performance of their children in school. Such a relationship is hardly surprising. But it does mean an additional impetus for immigrants to learn and use English.

Mother–Tongue Shift

As noted at the outset, the causes of mother-tongue shift need not be the same as the causes of bilingualism. Or to put it another way, the acquisition of English by the immigrants and their children does not necessarily mean that English must be passed on as the mother-tongue of their offspring. In some settings, for example Montreal, bilingualism does not lead to mother-tongue shift.

There is evidence that the magnitude of mother-tongue shift from the first to the second generation is influenced by the degree of mother-tongue diversity within the foreign born population. The proportion of the second generation with English mother-tongue is relatively high in cities where the mother-tongue composition of the immigrants is rather diverse. By contrast, in cities with low mother-tongue diversity among the immigrants, English is the mother-tongue of a relatively small segment of the second generation.

These results are extremely suggestive when contrasting the linguistic pattern in the United States with other nations. Additional evidence indicates that diversity within the immigrant population of the United States helped to generate mother-tongue shift. In nations whose language contact involves only two major groups, one might expect considerably greater resistance to shift. Certainly there are extremely diverse nations such as India that have not experienced much in the way of mother-tongue shift. But it should be kept in mind that the local contact settings in India are much more homogeneous than one might expect from just the national figures. This is due to the intense territorial segregation of language groups in India. Nevertheless, the reader must keep in mind that immigrant diversity is clearly not the only factor accounting for the distinctive quality of language contact in the United States.

The frequency of mother-tongue shift among the second generation tends also to be linked to bilingualism among the foreign born. In other words, immigrant groups that are specially prone to learn English are also the groups with English as the mother-tongue of sizable proportions of the second generation.

Although the data are not reported here, this type of association between the frequency of bilingualism among the foreign born and mother-tongue shift in the second generation is also found when examining the rates for different groups within cities as well as for the nation as a whole. But all of this may appear painfully obvious at first glance, since there are both methodological and substantive reasons for expecting to find such a linkage between bilingualism and shift. If the proportion of children whose shift to

English remains constant for the bilinguals of different immigrant groups, then those immigrant populations with specially high frequencies of bilingualism will also appear as the groups with high levels of inter-generational shift.

In effect, the likelihood of inter-generational shift is greater among those bilinguals in groups with the greatest frequency of second-language learning. When a sizable segment of the immigrant generation is unable to speak English, then the bilingual parents in the group are less likely to raise their children in English.

If a sizable segment of an immigrant group is unable to speak English, it means a relatively greater communication loss with ethnic compatriots if the child is raised in English. By contrast, a child raised in the old-world language also learns English later on and is therefore able to speak to all members of the ethnic community. On the other hand, if the proportion of the first generation able to speak English is rather high, then offspring raised as native speakers of English can communicate with nearly all ethnic compatriots and there is less reason to resist mother-tongue shift.

This analysis seems to suggest that mother-tongue shift is caused not simply by the factors influencing bilingualism. Rather, the frequency of bilingualism within the immigrant group is, itself, an important influence on the likelihood of shift. Bilingual immigrants in a group with a sizable percentage unable to speak English are themselves less likely to raise their children in English than are bilingual parents who belong to an immigrant group with a high level of bilingualism. Given the fact that the acquisition of English is almost universal among the children of immigrants, at least as a second language, it follows that the shift of mother-tongues in the United States will take place rather rapidly from that generation on if other factors remain constant. The earlier analysis of communication advantages with ethnic compatriots also suggests that any decline in the numbers of new immigrants settling in the United States would tend to raise the rate of mother-tongue shift among the earlier settlers. In effect, newcomers unable to speak English provided an incentive for resisting mother-tongue shift among immigrant compatriots who were bilingual.

Note

1. A common, unifying language shared by all groups that enables them to communicate with one another.

Richard Rodriguez, *Hunger for Memory:*
The Education of Richard Rodriguez—
An Autobiography

Supporters of bilingual education today imply that students like me miss a great deal by not being taught in their family's language. What they seem not to recognize is that, as a socially disadvantaged child, I considered Spanish to be a private language. What I needed to learn in school was that I had the right—and the obligation—to speak the public language of *los gringos.* The odd truth is that my first-grade classmates could have become bilingual, in the conventional sense of that word, more easily than I. Had they been taught (as upper-middle-class children are often taught early) a second language like Spanish or French, they could have regarded it simply as that: another public language. In my case such bilingualism could not have been so quickly achieved. What I did not believe was that I could speak a single public language.

Without question, it would have pleased me to hear my teachers address me in Spanish when I entered the classroom. I would have felt much less afraid. I would have trusted them and responded with ease. But I would have delayed—for how long postponed?—having to learn the language of public society. I would have evaded—and for how long could I have afforded to delay?—learning the great lesson of school, that I had a public identity.

Fortunately, my teachers were unsentimental about their responsibility. What they understood was that I needed to speak a public language. So their voices would search me out, asking me questions. Each time I'd hear them, I'd look up in surprise to see a nun's face frowning at me. I'd mumble, not really meaning to answer. The nun would persist, "Richard, stand up. Don't look at the floor. Speak up. Speak to the entire class, not just to me!" But I couldn't believe that the English language was mine to use. (In part, I did not want to believe it.) I continued to mumble. I resisted the teacher's demands. (Did I somehow suspect that once I learned public language my pleasing family life would be changed?) Silent, waiting for the bell to sound, I remained dazed, diffident, afraid.

Because I wrongly imagined that English was intrinsically a public language and Spanish an intrinsically private one, I easily noted the difference between classroom language and the language of home. At school, words were directed to a general audience of listeners. ("Boys and girls.") Words were meaningfully ordered. And the point was not self-expression alone but to make oneself understood by many others.

Three months. Five. Half a year passed. Unsmiling, ever watchful, my teachers noted my silence. They began to connect my behavior with the difficult progress my older sister and brother were making. Until one Saturday morning three nuns arrived at the house to talk to our parents. Stiffly, they sat on the blue living room sofa. From the doorway of another room, spying the visitors, I noted the incongruity—the clash of two worlds, the faces and voices of school intruding upon the familiar setting of home. I overheard one voice gently wondering, "Do your children speak only Spanish at home, Mrs. Rodriguez?" While another voice added, "That Richard especially seems so timid and shy."

With great tact the visitors continued, "Is it possible for you and your husband to encourage your children to practice their English when they are home?" Of course, my parents complied. What would they not do for their children's well-being? And how could they have questioned the Church's authority which those women represented? In an instant, they agreed to give up the language that had revealed and accentuated our family's closeness. The moment after the visitors left, the change was observed. "*Ahora*, speak to us *en inglés*,"[1] my father and mother united to tell us.

At first, it seemed a kind of game. After dinner each night, the family gathered to practice "our" English. Laughing, we would try to define words we could not pronounce. We played with strange English sounds, often overanglicizing our pronunciations. And we filled the smiling gaps of our sentences with familiar Spanish sounds. But that was cheating, somebody shouted. Everyone laughed. In school, meanwhile, like my brother and sister, I was required to attend a daily tutoring session. I needed a full year of special attention. I also needed my teachers to keep my attention from straying in class by calling out, *Rich-heard*—their English voices slowly prying loose my ties to my other name, its three notes, *Ri-car-do*. Most of all I needed to hear my mother and father speak to me in a moment of serious-ness in broken—suddenly heartbreaking—English. The scene was inevitable: One Saturday morning I entered the kitchen where my parents were talk-ing in Spanish. I did not realize that they were talking in Spanish however until, at the moment they saw me, I heard their voices change to speak English. Those *gringo* sounds they uttered startled me. Pushed me away. In that moment of trivial misunderstanding and profound insight, I felt my throat twisted by unsounded grief. I turned quickly and left the room. But I had no place to escape to with Spanish. My brother and sisters were speaking English in another part of the house.

Again and again in the days following, increasingly angry, I was obliged to hear my mother and father: "Speak to us *en inglés*." (*Speak.*) Only then did I determine to learn classroom English. Weeks after, it happened: One day in school I raised my hand to volunteer an answer. I spoke out in a loud voice. And I did not think it remarkable when the entire class understood. That day, I moved very far from the disadvantaged child I had been only days earlier. The belief, the calming assurance that I belonged in public, had at last taken hold.

Shortly after, I stopped hearing the high and loud sounds of *los gringos*. A more and more confident speaker of English, I didn't trouble to listen to *how* strangers sounded, speaking to me. And there simply were too many English-speaking people in my day for me to hear American accents anymore. Conversations quickened. Listening to persons who sounded eccentrically pitched voices, I usually noted their sounds for an initial few seconds before

I concentrated on *what* they were saying. Conversations became content-full. Hearing someone's *tone* of voice—angry or questioning or sarcastic or happy or sad—I didn't distinguish it from the words it expressed. Sound and word were thus tightly wedded. At the end of a day, I was often bemused, always relieved, to realize how "silent," though crowded with words, my day in public had been.

At last, seven years old, I came to believe what had been technically true since my birth: I was an American citizen.

But the special feeling of closeness at home was diminished by then. Gone was the desperate, urgent, intense feeling of being at home; rare was the experience of feeling myself individualized by family intimates. We remained a loving family, but one greatly changed. No longer so close; no longer bound tight by the pleasing and troubling knowledge of our public separateness. Neither my older brother nor sister rushed home after school anymore. Nor did I. When I arrived home there would often be neighborhood kids in the house. Or the house would be empty of sounds.

Following the dramatic Americanization of their children, even my parents grew more publicly confident. Especially my mother. She learned the names of all the people on our block. And she decided we needed to have a telephone installed in the house. My father continued to use the word *gringo*. But it was no longer charged with the old bitterness or distrust. Hearing him, sometimes, I wasn't sure if he was pronouncing the Spanish word *gringo* or saying gringo in English.

Matching the silence I started hearing in public was a new quiet at home. The family's quiet was partly due to the fact that, as we children learned more and more English, we shared fewer and fewer words with our parents. Sentences needed to be spoken slowly when a child addressed his mother or father. (Often the parent wouldn't understand.) The child would need to repeat himself. (Still the parent misunderstood.) The young voice, frustrated, would end up saying, "Never mind"—the subject was closed. Dinners would be noisy with the clinking of knives and forks against dishes. My mother would smile softly between her remarks; my father at the other end of the table would chew and chew at his food, while he stared over the heads of his children.

My *mother!* My *father!* After English became my primary language, I no longer knew what words to use in addressing my parents. The old Spanish words I had used earlier—*mamá* and *papá*—I couldn't use anymore. They would have been too painful reminders of how much had changed in my life. On the other hand, the words I heard neighborhood kids call *their* parents seemed equally unsatisfactory. *Mother* and *Father; Ma, Papa, Pa, Dad, Pop*—all these terms I felt were unsuitable, not really terms of address for *my* parents. As a result, I never used them at home. Whenever I'd speak to my parents, I would try to get their attention with eye contact alone. In public conversations, I'd refer to "my parents" or "my mother and father."

My mother and father, for their part, responded differently, as their children spoke to them less. She grew restless, seemed troubled and anxious at the scarcity of words exchanged in the house. It was she who would question me about my day when I came home from school. She smiled at small talk. She pried at the edges of my sentences to get me to say something more. She'd join conversations she overheard, but her intrusions often stopped her children's talking. By contrast, my father seemed reconciled to the new quiet. Though his English improved somewhat, he retired into silence. At dinner he spoke very little. One night his children and even his wife helplessly giggled at his garbled English pronunciation of the Catholic Grace before Meals. Thereafter he made his wife recite the prayer at the start of each meal, even on formal occasions, when there were guests in the house. Hers became the public voice of the family. On official business, it was she, not my father, one would usually hear on the phone or in stores, talking to strangers. His children grew so accustomed to his silence that, years later, they would speak routinely of his shyness. (My mother would often try to explain: Both his parents died when he was eight. He was raised by an uncle who treated him like little more than a menial servant. He was never encouraged to speak. He grew up alone. A man of few words.) But my father was not shy, I realized, when I'd watch him speaking Spanish with relatives. Using Spanish, he was quickly effusive. Especially when talking with other men, his voice would spark, flicker, flare alive with sounds. In Spanish, he expressed ideas and feelings he rarely revealed in English. With firm Spanish sounds, he conveyed confidence and authority English would never allow him.

The silence at home, however, was finally more than a literal silence. Fewer words passed between parent and child, but more profound was the silence that resulted from my inattention to sounds. At about the time I no longer bothered to listen with care to the sounds of English in public, I grew careless about listening to the sounds family members made when they spoke. Most of the time I heard someone speaking at home and didn't distinguish his sounds from the words people uttered in public. I didn't even pay much attention to my parents' accented and ungrammatical speech. At least not at home. Only when I was with them in public would I grow alert to their accents. Though, even then, their sounds caused me less and less concern. For I was increasingly confident of my own public identity.

I would have been happier about my public success had I not sometimes recalled what it had been like earlier, when my family had conveyed its intimacy through a set of conveniently private sounds. Sometimes in public, hearing a stranger, I'd hark back to my past. A Mexican farmworker approached me downtown to ask directions to somewhere. "¿Hijito . . . ?"[2] he said. And his voice summoned deep longing. Another time, standing beside my mother in the visiting room of a Carmelite convent, before the dense screen which rendered the nuns shadowy figures, I heard several Spanish-speaking nuns—their busy, singsong overlapping voices—assure us that yes, yes, we were remembered, all our family was remembered in their prayers. Another day, a dark-faced old woman—her hand light on my shoulder—steadied herself against me as she boarded a bus. She murmured something I couldn't quite comprehend. Her Spanish voice came near, like the face of a never-before-seen relative in the instant before I was kissed. Her voice, like so many of the Spanish voices I'd hear in public, recalled the golden age of my youth. Hearing Spanish then, I continued to be a careful, if sad, listener to sounds. Hearing a Spanish-speaking family walking behind me, I turned to look. I smiled for an instant, before my glance found the Hispanic-looking faces of strangers in the crowd going by.

Notes

1. "Now speak to us in English."
2. "Little boy . . . ?"

Guillermo X. Garcia, "Border Battle Centers on 'Spanish-only' Town"

El Cenizo, Texas, adopts the language of 80% of its residents. Officials say it's easiest; critics say it's wrong

El Cenizo, Texas. Last summer, officials in this dirt-poor border town hit upon a way to get more residents, most of whom speak only Spanish, involved in local government. They adopted Spanish as the official language.

The three-person city commission succeeded. Attendance at monthly City Council meetings has doubled to 20.

The adoption in August of the ordinance made sense, city officials argued, because 80% of the town's 7,800 residents speak and understand only Spanish.

But in becoming the first U.S. city to conduct all official business in a language other than English, El Cenizo attracted what its residents never could have imagined: national headlines, a U.S. Border Patrol crackdown and threats from white supremacists to burn the of own down.

All official meetings are in Spanish. Ordinances written in Spanish can be translated into English, should anyone request one. "We did this for one reason and one reason only: to make it convenient for the majority of residents to know how we are trying to serve them. Anyone who attaches any other motive, nationalism, politics, is just wrong," Commissioner Gloria Romo says.

But the new policy that thrust this community of modest bungalows and aging mobile homes 15 miles south of Laredo into the national spotlight is viewed by some as an affront and an effort to reject the United States.

"This is nothing more than the beginning of the linguistic ghettoization of the United States. If they don't want to learn English and they officially adopt a foreign language, are we seeing the Balkanization of America?" asks Tim Schultze of U.S. English, The Washington, D.C.-based organization seeks to make English the nation's official language.

Schultze predicts that if large pockets of immigrants in other parts of the country don't feel the need to learn English, the United States will become "a Tower of Babel, which will only lead to ethnic division, not ethnic diversity."

Just about everyone in this town of working poor either emigrated from Mexico, is married to an immigrant or has parents who are immigrants.

The city's mayor, Rafael Rodriguez, was a citizen of Mexico before he became a U.S. citizen 20 years ago. At the time the city adopted the ordinance, Rodriguez said more than half the residents were undocumented citizens of Mexico. That drew the immediate attention of the U.S. Immigration and Naturalization Service.

At the same time it adopted the language regulation, the city also adopted a resolution that, in effect, says the U.S. Border Patrol is not welcome. Any city employee—there is only one, apart from the three-person, elected commission—would be subject to firing if the employee helped Border Patrol agents catch an undocumented immigrant, or informed border agents of any suspected undocumented people living in town. All of El Cenizo's city services are provided by surrounding Webb County.

Major cities such as Austin, Los Angeles, Chicago and New York have adopted immigrant-friendly ordinances stating that city employees will not assist immigration agents. But El Cenizo is the first town to threaten to fire a worker who assists border agents.

Meanwhile, the Ku Klux Klan has threatened to burn the town down and drive the residents back to Mexico, where it says they belong. City officials keep on file a thick stack of letters containing crude epithets and conspiracy-filled language about the town's perceived goal to secede from the United States.

Since the ordinance was passed last summer, U.S. Border Patrol four-wheel-drive vehicles make frequent runs through here. Border law enforcement agents also set up checkpoints on the one street leading out of town to stop and interrogate passengers on public buses.

Patrol officials deny that they target El Cenizo residents. They say the buildup of agents is part of a year-long, border-wide enforcement effort that only recently reached into south Texas.

Yet "when the mayor gets up and says on TV that (the majority) of the residents are illegals, you bet that got our attention," says Mike Herrera, a Border Patrol spokesman.

"We don't really know how many are legal here, and frankly, we don't care. Why should we? Our job is to provide service to the people of the community, illegal or not," says Romo, who disputes the Border Patrol's assertion.

"Because we look like we do, speak Spanish and don't carry around our (U.S.) birth certificates or naturalization card, and because of (the ordinances), the Patrol has targeted us," Romo says. "You don't see the Patrol stopping city buses in Laredo, only here."

She maintains that the city is not trying to defy the federal government but is simply carrying out the wishes of the residents. She also says all of the residents unanimously back the city.

But that is not the case.

Berta Torres, a single mother raising two children, one of whom is learning-impaired, says she is proud of her Spanish heritage but feels that English is the language to learn to get ahead.

"I came here from Mexico not to expand the Mexican empire, but so that my children can have a better life," she says, proudly displaying her cinderblock, two-bedroom, one-bath home. She paid $700 for the lot six years ago and estimates that she has spent another $4,500 to build the still-unfinished residence. "I don't understand English, so I can't help my kids with their schoolwork," she says. "What I pray for is that my kids learn English, not so that they will forget their 'Mexican-ness' but so they can succeed. Opportunity may have passed me by. I don't want that to happen to my children."

CHAPTER TWELVE

The Physical Health and Mental Well-Being of Immigrants

Introduction

Throughout human history, communities have feared the stranger. One of the principal concerns has been that when newcomers arrive in a community, they sometimes bring with them dangerous baggage—diseases that weaken and, at times, kill their hosts. Beginning in the Middle Ages, communities protected the health of their inhabitants by quarantining new arrivals and travelers who had ventured abroad before allowing them to enter the community. American colonial communities had quarantine laws that became state laws after the United States became an independent nation. Still, foreigners were often stigmatized as disease carriers, especially when their arrival was coincident with an epidemic of a particular disease. In 1832, New Yorkers blamed a deadly cholera epidemic on the Irish Catholic population that comprised an underclass in antebellum New York and many other cities. As recently as the 1980s, lack of understanding of HIV/AIDS resulted in the stigmatizing of Haitians immigrants in the belief they were responsible for bringing the disease to the cities of North America.

By the end of the nineteenth century, germ theory, the notion that most diseases were caused by harmful microorganisms, was generally accepted by American physicians. Quarantine seemed an insufficient defense. When millions of immigrants began to migrate to the United States between 1890 and the 1920s, the United States Marine Hospital Service (later renamed the U.S. Public Health Service) assumed responsibility for inspecting and interrogating newcomers. Federal physicians hoped to identify and exclude

Alan M. Kraut, " 'That is the American Way. And in America You Should Do as Americans Do': Italian Customs, American Standards" in Alan M. Kraut, *Silent Travelers: Germs, Genes, and the Immigrant Menace* (New York: Basic Books, 1994). Reprinted by permission of Alan M. Kraut.

John Foster Carr, *Guide for the Immigrant Italian in The United States of America*. Published under the auspices of the Connecticut Daughters of the Revolution (Garden City and New York: Doubleday, Page, & Company, 1911). Public Domain.

Sarah Kershaw, "Freud Meets Buddha: Therapy for Immigrants" in *The New York Times*, January 18, 2003. Copyright © 2003 by The New York Times Co. Reprinted with permission.

newcomers who had contagious diseases that might endanger native-born Americans or who were insufficiently robust to be able to be self-supporting and productive contributors to American economic growth, especially industrial development. At immigration depots such as New York's Ellis Island and San Francisco Bay's Angel Island, newcomers were subjected to individual inspection by federal physicians. While those migrants who traveled in first- or second-class passage on transoceanic steamships were inspected in the privacy of their cabins, all others had to stand in a line inspection at the depot. Long lines of newcomers passed before the clinical gaze of uniformed doctors. Those suspected of being ill or injured or mentally unfit were pulled from the line, subjected to closer inspection, and sometimes, denied admission to the United States. Most new arrivals were admitted. In the peak migration era, 1880–1920, under 3 percent of new arrivals were denied admission, though improved diagnostic techniques allowed an increasing percentage of those excluded to be barred for reasons of ill health.

Just as newcomers brought with them other aspects of their culture, including their religious beliefs, political ideologies, and preferences in music and cuisine, new arrivals have always brought with them their definitions of health and disease as well as therapies that they believe to be effective. At times, these beliefs, often steeped in religious and spiritual notions, have differed dramatically from those shared by physicians who accept the empirical tradition of scientific medicine. Immigrants to the United States have often had to assimilate new ideas about illness and therapy as part of the broader process of adjustment to life in a new society. On the other hand, American physicians, nurses, and medical institutions have had to cope with treating newcomers who questioned their medical judgments and refused their therapeutic recommendations.

The selection from Alan M. Kraut's volume, *Silent Travelers: Germs, Genes and the "Immigrant Menace,"* deals with migrants from southern Italy arriving in the late nineteenth and early twentieth centuries. These southern Italians, the largest group among the 23.5 million arrivals in this era, mostly arrived robust, healthy, and ready to work. Having grown up and worked outdoors under the warm sun of Italy's southern provinces, the *Mezzogiorno*, young men and women from these towns and villages arrived healthy, but often did not stay that way for long. Exhausting hours of work in factories and on construction sites under unhealthy conditions and living in congested, poorly ventilated tenements caused many Italian immigrants to lose their good health and return to their hometowns and villages suffering from a variety of diseases, including the great killer of the nineteenth century, tuberculosis.

When they considered matters of health and disease, many Italian townsmen, *contadini*, turned to a belief system that was a synthesis of Christianity and pre-Christian folk belief. Illness was defined as the result of the bad wishes of others, sometimes expressed with the evil eye. Therapies included wearing non-Christian symbols on chains around the neck, incantations, or visits to local folk healers. Prayers to a favorite saint or the Virgin Mary were regarded as a path to recovery, as well. It fell to Italian immigrant physicians, such as Dr. Antonio Stella, to encourage American understanding of the Italians' health problems and to foster Italian immigrant trust in physicians and modern medicine.

While some Americans advocated immigration restrictions that would slash the number of southern and eastern European immigrants admitted to the United States, others believed that education would successfully modify old world views and promote adaptation, including in matters of health. The second selection is from the *Guide for the Immigrant Italian in the United States of America* by John Foster Carr, a pamphlet published in English and translated into Italian under the auspices of the Connecticut Daughters of the American Revolution in 1911. In a section entitled "The Importance of Caring for the Health," Carr instructs his readers, presumably Italian immigrants, in the differences between the health environment of the United States and Italy. Explaining the stake that immigrants have in living healthy lives, Carr writes, "A workingman's capital is a strong, well body." Emphasizing prevention as the best cure for disease, Carr warns in bold print, "**Avoid bad air, bad food, bad water, bad habits**." Not hesitating to apply moral judgment to his health advice, Carr preaches avoidance of strong drink, observing, "Strong drinks make weak men."

In Carr's era, Americanization through conformity to American standards of health and hygiene was a duty. The most that newcomers could expect was the advice on how to conform that Carr and others provided. However, more recently there is greater acceptance of diversity in definitions of disease and therapy and standards of health and hygiene. Although the clash of cultures that often accompanies the health care of immigrants remains a matter of concern to contemporary physicians, there is considerable effort on the part of today's doctors and nurses to understand the cultural context in which their immigrant patients are experiencing illness, especially those health care providers concerned with mental health.

Mental problems may differ considerably among cultures. In a current newspaper report, "Freud meets Buddha, Therapy for Immigrants," psychologists familiar with anxiety, depression, or schizophrenia explain that their Asian immigrant patients sometimes complain of ailments not found in any psychiatric textbook. Few native-born Americans complain of *pa-feng*, a fear of wind and cold that affects some Chinese patients or *hwa-byung*, a Korean suppressed anger syndrome. American psychiatrists of Asian descent attempt to use their medical expertise and cultural sensitivity to bridge the gap between their patients and the American medical establishment. Often it requires great skill and experience to bring newcomers the kind of medical attention that will allow them to reconcile old world ways with the new so that they can lead healthy and productive lives in their new country.

Suggestions for Further Reading

Amy L. Fairchild, *Science at the Borders, Immigrant Medical Inspection and the Shaping of the Modern Labor Force* (Baltimore: The Johns Hopkins University Press, 2003).

Anne Fadiman, *The Sprit Catches you and your Fall Down, a Hmong Child, Her American Doctors, and the Collision of Two Cultures* (New York: Farrar, Strauss and Siroux, 1997).

Gerald N. Grob, *The Deadly Truth, A History of Disease in America* (Cambridge, MA: Harvard University Press, 2002).

Howard Markel, *Quarantine!, East European Jewish Immigrants and the New York City Epidemics of 1892* (Baltimore: The Johns Hopkins University Press, 1997).

Howard Markel, *When Germs Travel, Six Major Epidemics That Have Invaded America Since 1900 and the Fears They Have Unleashed* (New York: Alfred A. Knopf, 2004).

Nayan Shah, *Contagious Divides, Epidemics and Race in San Francisco's Chinatown* (Berkeley: University of California Press, 2001).

Alan M. Kraut, " 'That Is the American Way.
And in America You Should Do as Americans Do':
Italian Customs, American Standards"

By 1916, millions of Italian immigrants, most from the south of Italy, had arrived in the United States. Approximately 4.5 million came between 1880 and 1921, more than any other group. Many settled in the New York area, at least initially. In New York, the polio death rate per 1,000 estimated population of children under ten years of age was 1.63 for Italian children, well below the 3.42 for the native-born or the 3.27 for German youngsters. The reasons remain unknown, but as Health Commissioner Haven Emerson observed, "Certainly the social and economic conditions under which these people live are no more favorable than those under which the Americans, Germans and Irish live, among whom the mortality of the disease is the highest." However, while the Italian mortality rate for polio was low, the 1,348 polio cases contracted by those of Italian nativity in New York City was the highest for any immigrant group, second only to the 3,825 cases among the native-born.

By their very nature, epidemics are intense. Polio epidemics struck suddenly, in summer, when New York youngsters of modest circumstances were enjoying the freedoms of childhood, frolicking in the city streets. Because there were so many Italian immigrants, living in tightly concentrated neighborhoods, and because immigrants were viewed by many as a marginal and potentially subversive influence upon society, the incidence of Italian polio made a dramatic impact upon the imagination of a public already shaken by the virulence of the epidemic and the youth of its many victims.

Rumors spread that the epidemic had been brought by immigrants from Italy to the United States rather than contracted here by the newcomers. Although that rumor was quickly dispelled by the U.S. Public Health Service, some were still prepared to connect this particular immigrant group to the epidemic, arguing that Italians' poor hygiene and unhealthy lifestyles made them vulnerable to polio, which they then spread to natives and other newcomers alike.

The charge that Italians were especially unclean and unhealthy was not new. The Italians in New York City, mostly impoverished workers from the southern provinces, were frequently denigrated by critics. In 1890, Richmond Mayo-Smith, a Columbia University professor of political economy, described Italian immigrants in New York's tenements: "Huddled together in miserable apartments in filth and rags, without the slightest regard to decency or health, they present a picture of squalid existence degrading to any civilization and a menace to the health of the whole community." In 1914, two years before the polio epidemic, an equally uncharitable E. A. Ross wrote, "Steerage passengers from a Naples boat show a distressing frequency of low foreheads, open mouths, weak chins, poor features, skew faces, small or knobby crania, and backless heads. Such people lack the power to take rational care of themselves; hence their death-rate in New York is twice the general death-rate and thrice that of the Germans."

Ross was far better at polemics than statistics. A careful statistical analysis of mortality data by Louis Dublin of the Metropolitan Life Insurance Company using sex and age data from the 1910 census for New York State and Pennsylvania confirms that in New York the Italian death rate was generally lower, not higher, than that for the native-born of the same age and gender and considerably lower than that for the comparable age and sex category of the German group.

What, then, was the link between Italian immigrants and polio in some minds? The answer appears to be filth, especially filth resulting from the unsanitary habits and personal hygiene of newcomers in the eyes of their hosts. Even as they searched for the living organisms responsible for infantile paralysis, public health professionals could not completely wean themselves from sanitarian patterns of thought. Reports suggested that the high number of polio cases in the Italian population might have something to do with their habits, including cultural customs and traditions.

In the summer of 1916, during the height of the epidemic, New York public health officials labored mightily to curb polio where many thought it was originating—among the immigrants, but especially among the Italians, because they had the highest number of cases. Italian neighborhoods were deluged with health department pamphlets and signs in the Italian language warning immigrant mothers about polio and urging them to be hygienic in their personal habits and child-rearing practices. The Department of Social Betterment of the Brooklyn Bureau of Charities issued one hundred thousand leaflets printed in Italian, Yiddish, and English. All public gatherings of the urban poor were monitored by health officials, including block parties and public playgrounds. However, a large gathering of Italians must have seemed a particular health threat because in New York City, the three-day *festa* of Our Lady of Mount Carmel [see chapter 13] was cancelled by order of the health department. Although eastern European Jews and Polish immigrants were sometimes mentioned as carriers of polio, Italians—the immigrant group most victimized by polio—were generally held in greatest suspicion of implication in spreading the disease.

When education and bans on public assembly proved insufficient, quarantine was tried. Decisions to quarantine a household were made upon the recommendation of visiting nurses. Public health nurses who climbed tall tenement staircases to report on polio cases as part of New York City's Special Investigation of Infantile Paralysis under the Rockefeller Institute's Dr. Simon Flexner were often angry and impatient with immigrant families. Italian families more than others irritated nurses and aroused their suspicions. Italians brought with them to America a basic distrust of people in positions of authority; this encompassed nurses and doctors. Not surprisingly, because they possessed the power to recommend that a family be confined to its home, nurses were often feared and resented as intruders by Italian immigrants, especially the parents of children stricken with the

disease. Mutual distrust, then, prompted an anti-Italian sentiment in many of
the nurses' reports. After visiting one-year-old Petro Pollizzi, one nurse
wrote, "These people neither understand nor speak Eng. so I could get very
little accurate information. . . . These people are very ignorant and suspicious." Often nurses noted whether families with stricken children were
being treated by an Italian physician, with the implication that the care of
such doctors was suspect. Similar comments on the physicians treating other
groups of newcomers are absent.

Insensitivity to cultural differences between the native-born and the
Italians nurtured a disdain among the nurses for those they were treating.
Nurse Ida May Shlevin heaped scorn on the practice of kissing the dead, an
Italian custom that was part of the ritualized expression of grief and respect
for the departed. Shlevin saw, instead, disrespect for both the living and
medical science in the custom and indicted this ethnic tradition as one
cause of the epidemic ravaging the city.

Some members of the Italian community vigorously sought to sever the
link between ethnicity and polio in the public forum, pointing instead to
anti-Italian nativism as the source of the stigma suffered by the group. One
writer who refused to give his last name wrote to Mayor John P. Mitchel,
denouncing the prejudice. He fumed, "I wish to say emphatically that the
American Italian is not to be singled out and charged with anything." Their
only culpability was "nationality," he wrote. Instead, the protester urged the
mayor to consider poor sewage systems and inadequate garbage disposal
facilities as the source of the scourge.

More often, though, impoverished and fearful Italian immigrants simply
resisted what they perceived to be the intrusion of health officials, who
might even be spreading the disease themselves simply by going from house
to house. Apprehensive immigrant parents barred their doors to visiting
nurses. On at least one occasion, an irate Italian parent tried an old world
technique of intimidation. A pediatric clinic nurse, who often reported cases
of polio and violations of the sanitary code in a Brooklyn neighborhood
known as Pigtown, had her life threatened in a letter sent by the "black
hand," the traditional name of the Mafia. Whether or not the nurse was the
target of the feared criminal organization, after the threat she was escorted
to and from the clinic by a policeman.

The behavior of individual Italian families, who dealt with being
stigmatized by firing off indignant letters and slamming their doors in the face
of municipal health workers in 1916, suggests that they perceived public
health measures as unwelcome and unwarranted intrusions. They resented the
pressure to submit to institutionalized forms of social control at the price of
social ostracism. They perceived such intrusions as almost always motivated by
a lack of understanding of their ways and American ethnocentric prejudice.

Beginning in the latter part of the nineteenth century, most Italian
immigrants to the United States were townspeople, or *contadini*, from the
Mezzogiorno, the impoverished southern provinces. For *contadini*, how one
lived was determined not by the government but by *la famiglia* and *l'ordine
della famiglia* (the rules of family behavior and responsibility). Long and

bitter experience with public officials—and the large landowners they shielded—had left the *contadini* with a cynical attitude toward all forms of authority other than the family. Such cynicism, embodied in the adage *la legge va contrai cristiani* (the law works against people), was exacerbated by unification in the 1870s. The lot of the *contadini* deteriorated; reform never filtered south.

As they had been for centuries, illness and remedies were bound closely to a blend of religion and folk beliefs that varied somewhat from place to place. Christianity had come to the cities long before the countryside, where pagan deities continued to hold the attention of peasants. From Rome northward, Italian Roman Catholicism resembled that practiced in the rest of northern Europe, but south of Rome, it was blended with traditions and customs of pagan origin. Even in the south, there was great diversity. Campania and Sicily retained much from the Greco-Roman tradition. Coastal areas colonized by the Greeks became part of Magna Graecia and were influenced by the Hellenistic medical tradition through the migration of Greek physicians. Other regions in the south, such as Abruzzi-Molise, remained isolated from Greco-Roman influence; there reliance upon superstition and magic remained especially strong.

Transcending regional differences, certain patterns were generally common in the south. Preservation of health was tied closely to worship of objects, especially statues and sacred relics, and the attachment of particular powers and qualities to individual saints. "Saint Rocco protected devotees against illness, Saint Lucy guarded their eyesight, and Saint Anna helped during the pangs and dangers of childbirth." Such saints found in southern Italian worship appear in neither the Bible nor the writings of the early Christian fathers, but were folk substitutes for old Greek and Roman gods and spirits of the forests, rivers, and mountains. When peasants prayed to a local Madonna for good health or the cure for a particular affliction, they were engaged in a pre-Christian ritual. The Catholic Church had assimilated such folk customs across Europe, having found they could not be successfully excluded from popular worship.

At the annual celebration of a town's patron saint, worshippers took the saint's image from the church and carried it in a procession through the streets. Offerings, especially money and jewelry, would be cast at the saint's feet. On such festive occasions, the personal clothing of a sick person might be placed at the statue's foot. Believers contended that, when the garments were again worn, the goodness of the saint imbued the body of the worshipper and restored health.

Many southern Italian beliefs about illness are common in most peasant cultures, such as attributing illness to the influence of one who practiced *jettatura* (sorcery), through use of the *mal'occhio* (evil eye), a belief that had no basis in Roman Catholic theology and that the church never succeeded in supplanting. According to the contemporary sociologist Phyllis Williams, southern Italian peasants blamed illness or misfortune on the influence of "an ever-present menace, the power of envy." Those jealous men or women who possessed the evil eye could, with a glance, cause physical injury, sickness, or even death. Amulets could ward off the *mal'occhio*. Popular amulets whether of a precious metal, coral, or lava represented animals' horns, claws, or teeth. Fish, scissors, knives, and a male—but not a female—hunchback were common symbols for amulets. They could be placed over a doorpost, on a bedroom wall, on a chain around the neck, in pockets, or in the lining of clothing. When someone suspected of having the evil eye approached, the amulet was to be grasped and pointed unobtrusively in the offending individual's direction. In the absence of an amulet, one might protect health and well-being by extending the index and pinkie fingers from an extended fist to represent a set of horns.

Southern Italians coped with illness by applying folk remedies derived from a reservoir of folk traditions and customs, and by consulting specialists such as witches, barbers, midwives, and herbalists. There were few physicians; small towns usually had one who was paid by the state out of community coffers. His salary was fixed, though he often received free use of a house in exchange for treating the most impoverished gratis. Wealthier patients paid for special attention, which allowed the physician to supplement his income. These town physicians were not highly respected. In part, townspeople were suspicious of scientific medicine. But equally important, folk wisdom taught them "when it don't cost anything you might know it is no good." Such fear and loathing of the physician as intruder, common in rural southern towns, was not the case in larger cities such as Naples and Palermo, where a more cosmopolitan view of medicine and its practitioners prevailed.

Contadini in southern Italy found many virtues in folk medicine. It cost little because most medicine was practiced by experienced housewives or neighbors. Should an herbalist be called, he or she could make diagnoses and concoct required medicine from materials readily available in nearby fields and forests.

The ailments that both folk healers and physicians confronted in southern Italy at the end of the nineteenth century were endemic to poor rural populations. Respiratory diseases such as tuberculosis, bronchitis, and pneumonia were relatively rare. Indeed, Dr. Antonio Stella, an Italian physician in the United States, described Italy as a country that "yields less victims annually to consumption than any other nation on the continent under similar demographic conditions." Nonetheless, TB was especially feared because accurate diagnosis was rarely made until the disease was in its last stages. Sicilians called it the *male sottile* (insidious sickness) because it seemed to sneak up on its victims and then quickly overcome them. Peasants so feared the disease and its stigma as an almost certain death sentence that those infected would refuse to use a receptacle for sputum, preferring to spit on the dirt floor of the house as did healthy people.

Most common were diseases accompanied by high temperatures such as malaria, typhoid, and rheumatic fever. Always, the disease was defined by its symptoms and it became the focus of folk healers and physicians alike. Also quite prevalent were childhood diseases such as measles, chicken pox, and scarlet fever. Peasants understood that if they exposed their children to these ailments at a young age, mild cases ensued and recovery was virtually certain.

Smallpox was so common that a Sicilian proverb cautioned, "a girl cannot be termed beautiful until she has had smallpox," so it could be determined whether scarring had destroyed her beauty.

Among the very young, cholera infantum and intestinal infections were common. A lengthy period of nursing, as long as two years, made for healthy infants, free from the ravages of contaminated milk, but the quick transition to full adult fare at an early age may account for the complaints of intestinal irritation. Cures for children varied from sitting the child in ritualized body positions—right leg to left arm and vice versa—or dressing the child in a miniature copy of the black habit worn by St. Anthony for a part of each day for several weeks.

Cures varied from prayers and rituals separate from the body to efforts at restoring a chemical balance to the body. In the former category was the custom of humiliation and sacrifice. Women with chronic diseases sometimes begged for money door-to-door. The funds were then taken to a priest as a contribution for a mass to be said for her recovery. A family surrogate begged if the patient was too ill to move about. In the latter case, excesses of acid or salt in the body or the accumulation of too much blood in one location were often blamed for inflammation. Aside from allowing diseases to run their course, a first principle of folk medicine, cures were administered until one worked. As one observer noted, "It never seemed to enter anyone's mind that death might be due to the conglomeration of treatments or that recovery took place in spite of them." The therapeutic transformation away from traditional remedies was an uneven process in modernizing societies. In rural communities such as those in southern Italy, the move to modern therapeutics was especially slow. A physician, if and when he was summoned at all, frequently had to content himself with allowing his therapies to compete with those offered by family members. His medical degree did not earn him a priority in the eyes of those at the bedside of a sick relative or neighbor.

Folk medicines could be animal, vegetable, or mineral in substance. Common vegetable cures were olive oil, lemon juice, wine, vinegar, garlic, onion, lettuce, wild mallow, flour baked into bread, rue, and tobacco, known as the *erba santa* (sacred plant). As for animals, those used in whole or part were wolf, chicken, viper, lizard, frog, pig, dog, mouse, and sea horse. Of necessity, all were available to southern Italian peasants from a nearby forest or purchasable from merchants. Similarly, minerals most frequently used were those available locally, such as rock salt and sulfur, especially popular with Sicilians who could find sulfur in mines along Sicily's southern coast.

Bodily secretions, especially saliva, urine, mother's milk, blood, and ear wax, were all valued curatives. Saliva was thought to be especially valuable as "fasting spittle," sputum taken from the mouth early in the morning before the ingestion of food. Mothers used it to bathe the eyes of children suffering from conjunctivitis. When taken from a seventh male child, fasting spittle was used to treat impetigo. Spittle was a critical antidote to the evil eye, as well. In some parts of southern Italy, it was customary to spit three times behind the back of a woman suspected of being a whore who had kissed a newly born infant. Obviously, several episodes of infant death had led to a diagnosis grounded in moral values, and spittle was the purgative. Because spittle could break curses and spells, those paying sick calls on neighbors fended off contagion's threat by spitting hard at the house door in self-defense. Women in extended labor moved the process along by asking a neighbor to spit out the window of the birthing room, banishing any curse or spell that might be stalling a healthy, normal delivery.

Contadini blended various substances to produce medicines. Sulfur and lemon juice were mixed as an ointment for scabies, for example. Others were simply fastened to the body. A live frog fastened to the temple was thought to be a cure for some eye ailments. Slices of potato or lemon were bound to the wrists to reduce fever. Sometimes cures were affected through an incantation or by wearing a particular garment. Sicilians found the wearing of a red scarf a cure for erysipelas, a dermatological disease characterized by red lesions. Black silk scarves were tied around the neck to cure sore throats.

As they had since the Middle Ages, barbers cured through bleeding, cupping, and scarifying. They set fractures, cauterized wounds, and opened abscesses. External growths could be removed, but internal growths, such as cancers, were regarded as incurable. Barbers were of little help with venereal disease. Known as the "French sickness" or the "woman's sickness," gonorrhea was held to be cured only by contact with a virgin. In Sicily, young women regarded as feebleminded became the cure in some cases.

The closed world of the Mezzogiorno at the end of the nineteenth and the early years of the twentieth century and its complex patterns of folk ritual and Christianity was not shaken by the arrival of nonbelievers but by the departure of natives for other countries in search of jobs. The already crippled economy of the region was further worsened at the turn of the twentieth century by a series of natural disasters such as blights, earthquakes, and volcanic eruptions. Natural disasters such as these were rarely the root causes of emigration, but often they were the catalysts. The peak exodus year was 1907, with 285,731 departures. The scramble also altered the gender composition of Italian immigration. Prior to the turn of the century, most emigrants were young males in their teens or early adulthood, who left their parents or young wives and children behind as they pursued opportunity abroad. Immigration officials estimated that 78 percent of the Italian immigrants were men. After 1910, the character of migration changed. By 1920, 48 percent of southern Italian arrivals were female.

As did members of other immigrant groups, millions of Italians found jobs in urban areas of the United States and lived in tenement hovels and congested neighborhoods near the factories or construction sites, where they found employment and no shortage of advice on improving their health and hygiene. Some of it came from assimilated Italians such as Dr. Antonio Stella and other physicians. In an essay on "The Effects of Urban Congestion on Italian Women and Children," Stella concluded by urging policymakers to engage in social planning and institute a program of education aimed at the individual immigrant. He called "for a better distribution of the immigrants *not after* they have reached Ellis Island, but *before* they decide to leave their motherland, by informing them of the wonderful resources of this vast continent, outside and beyond the large cities; let us educate them to the principles of hygiene and life, when they are settled here, and above all, let us distribute the work in appropriate areas outside of the city limits, so that proximity of the factory should not be . . . the chief reason for their congesting the city." Stella also urged the building of model tenements at a rent low enough so that it would not absorb more than a third of a worker's salary. The physician quite explicitly asserted the relationship between improving the physical and moral condition of newcomers, because "when we shall have given the people clean, healthy homes, full of light and sunshine, we shall have accomplished the physical and moral regeneration of the masses; we shall have given them that to which every human being is entitled, health and happiness."

Perhaps no native-born reformer could have more clearly stated the need for the newcomers to change and for American society to provide the opportunity. But who should make the first move? Stella thought that society had the obligation to offer newcomers better housing, education, and a healthy environment, leaving implicit the obligation of the newcomers to avail themselves of the opportunities. More typical, though, were the native-born reformers who saw the burden falling primarily upon newcomers to educate themselves and change habits.

Southern Italian immigrants in the United States had a medical spokesman who mediated between them and the larger American community. Dr. Antonio Stella compiled data, constructed arguments, and published articles defending southern Italian immigrants against those who saw the newcomers as subpar.

Antonio Stella's roots were not humble, nor was his life an epic in overcoming obstacles. He was born in Muro, Lucania, a southern province, in 1868, but his father was a lawyer and a noted numismatist, not a peasant. Stella was educated at Naples, where he attended the Royal Lyceum. He received his MD from the Royal University in 1893. After graduation, he immigrated to the United States and was naturalized in 1909.

Stella wrote a book designed to shed the most favorable light upon the Italian contribution to the United States. The volume's subtitle, "Statistical Data and General Considerations Based Chiefly Upon the United States Census and Other Official Publications," was clearly an effort to establish the credibility of the arguments within by grounding them in data generated by Americans themselves. Among the many topics explored through the use of his data were the health and vitality of Italian arrivals.

Stella boldly asserted that whatever health problems Italians in the United States might suffer, they were acquired on this side of the Atlantic. Speaking of the Italians in their homeland, he described them as "one of the healthiest in the world on account of [their] proverbial sobriety and frugality, also perhaps on account of the fact, that natural selection has had there [in Italy] freer play than elsewhere." He vehemently denied the "wild accusations" that syphilis was arriving with the newcomers from Italy, citing inspection data from Ellis Island: "In the month of July 1921, 11,000 immigrants were given intensive examination at Ellis Island, performed with removal of clothing, and of all this number only 43 were found to be afflicted with venereal diseases." Stella appealed to empirical evidence, noting "The freedom of italian immigrants from syphilis is not only a matter of common experience, but is strikingly evinced by the sturdy and vigorous physique of these peoples and by their extraordinary fertility." He proudly boasted, "The very increase in population of this country is almost wholly due to the high nativity [fertility] of the immigrants."

In 1904, Stella published an article on tuberculosis among Italian immigrants in *Charities*, the publication of the Charity Organization Society of New York. He told readers that "exact information" was often missing because of Italians' mobility. He advised, "one must follow the Italian population as it moves in the tenement districts; study them closely in their daily struggle for air and space; see them in the daytime crowded in sweat-shops and factories; at night heaped together in dark windowless rooms; then visit the hospitals' dispensaries; and finally watch the out-going steamships, and count the wan emaciated forms, with glistening eyes and racking cough that return to their native land with a hope of recuperating health, but often times only to find a quicker death."

Contagious disease among returning immigrants was not the only health problem, however. Some appeared to be victims of homesickness or nostalgia. Others were diagnosed as mentally ill. In 1906, only one case of mental illness was recorded among the thousands traveling third class to America, but of those returning, 72 sought treatment for mental disorder, including 55 men and 15 women. There were also a greater number of suicides on the return voyage. Dr. T. Rosati observed in 1910 that there had been two suicides on a recent return voyage from America, "something to think about—that suicide is more frequent among the repatriates." Council of Emigration member Luigi Rossi recorded what he had heard about returnees in the port of Genoa. There he heard that returnees from different countries could be distinguished by the condition of their bodies and their wallets, because "those returning from the United States come with sufficient health and money, those from Argentine return with their health but no money, and those from Brazil bring neither health nor money." Bad as conditions in America might be for the "bird of passage," conditions elsewhere were worse.

American reformers, even those willing to concede the influence of unfavorable socioeconomic conditions, laid much of the blame for Italian ill health at the feet of the immigrants themselves. First-generation approaches to health and disease did not differ markedly from those in southern Italy. The home or domus, the term preferred by some social scientists to describe the collectivity of family and possessions, remained the main focus of life. Matters of health and disease were treated there, if at all possible. Obviously, remedies used in folk cures required some modification. Phyllis Williams, a sociologist whose handbook was designed for social workers, physicians, and others serving the Italian immigrant community, observed changes occurring almost immediately after arrival because of "inability to procure materials, such as wolf bones, from which to compound accustomed remedies." However, immigrants found an array of substitutes for the "medicine cupboard," including "a bewildering array of mushrooms and other foods as well as . . . plants, berries, and barks." Plants that did not grow wild, such as basil and rue, were cultivated in gardens or in window boxes that sat on the sills of tenement apartments high above city sidewalks.

Illness was still often defined as an enemy's curse, a work of human jealousy or spite administered through the gesture of the *mal'occhio*. Restored health was a divine blessing, often a sign of the Madonna's indirect intervention. Such a blessing was meant to be shared with others. In a ritual carried from villages in the Mezzogiorno to New York's East Harlem, where the Madonna of Mount Carmel presided, the clothing of recently healed children was donated by their parents to the church for distribution to the community's poor, a transaction that expressed appreciation of "the intimate connection between private grief and joy and the claims and contributions of the community." The transaction was conducted on the day of the *festa* in the saint's honor and suggested that "the Madonna's healing action created the requirement of social reciprocity and entailed a moral response."

With the exception of prominent public figures such as Antonio Stella, physicians remained unpopular objects of suspicion and distrust, often consulted only to mollify authorities. At times, Italian immigrant parents preferred the assistance of witches, *maghi*, (*iannare* to Neapolitans), to battle polio-induced paralysis. One mother claimed that a witch had cured her child of polio by rubbing her with some salve and mumbling an incantation. Although the child was also under treatment by an Italian physician, the mother gave all the credit for the cure to the *maga*, explaining, "They had only gone to the physician because the nurses at the hospital where the child had been treated at the time of the paralysis insisted upon it."

Psychiatrists, especially, had difficulty with Italian immigrant patients. To those who believed in witches and evil eyes, the probing stares and questions of a psychiatrist appeared threatening but in a way that could be diffused, much as evil spells had been combated on the other side of the ocean. In her handbook, Phyllis Williams cites a typical episode:

> A woman consented to a psychiatric interview, even though she had no faith in the physician. She did so purely because she was fond of the visiting nurse and wished to please her. She arrived at the clinic with a large handbag clutched in her arms with which she was greatly preoccupied. Nothing could persuade her to part with it. "I tell you after," she confided mysteriously and went into the psychiatrist's office. When she came out, she opened the bag and exhibited a quantity of amulets against the Evil Eye. She had added all she could borrow from her neighbors to those possessed by her family. "The doctor," she triumphantly asserted, "he no hurt me."

Williams sensitively advised psychiatrists who would be seeing Italian immigrant patients to inform themselves of the "vagaries of Italian folklore," including the influence of witches and witchcraft, as an aid to understanding their patients.

The relationship of Italian immigrants and their children to modern medicine did not remain stagnant. Customs, traditions, and beliefs altered in the pressure cooker of assimilation with each succeeding generation raised in the United States. A study of southern Italian women in the North End of Boston suggests what might be described as a one-and-half generational depth to traditional beliefs after immigration. Women of the immigrant generation, largely from the regions of Abruzzi-Molise, Campania, and Sicily, and their older American-born daughters raised prior to World War II tended to cling to traditional perceptions of illness and cures. "The older women . . . had been recipients or observers of the traditional folk cures in childhood or early adulthood more often than the younger second genera-tion women." By contrast, those younger second-generation women had begun to rear their children in the 1940s "at a time when effective therapy in the form of vitamins, immunization and antimicrobial drugs had become generally available." These women and third-generation women largely avoided the religious aspects of *festas*. Unlike the elderly, they did not "view the roles of the saints and the physician as complementary," nor did they perceive recovery from illness as "a miracle wrought by the timely inter-vention of both the saint and the doctor." Younger second-generation women tended to attach more importance than their mothers or older sisters to "the skills and technology of modern medicine," although they, too, sometimes resorted to "prayer and petition" in an extreme health crisis.

Traditional beliefs associated with the evil eye as the cause of illness still found expression at times in all generations, but the belief was hardly pervasive and appears to be importantly linked to the class position and individual personality of believers. Regional differences among southern Italians were evident, but it is difficult to determine the role that contact in the United States among the different regional groups may have exerted. Patron saint observance was among the more notable differences. Abruzzese immigrants had not organized patron saint societies as did newcomers from Campania and Sicily. However, in the streets of Boston's North End, the former often attended the *festas* of other groups.

The loudest calls for change in Italian habits of health and hygiene came from within the community itself. Often the voice was that of an Italian physician, bitter over the sickness and suffering he could not spare his patients. In 1904, Dr. Rocco Brindisi observed with some sympathy, "The Italians, like all peoples with ancient habits and traditions, cling to many prejudices and superstitions, which often hamper those who work with them." Brindisi was confident that his compatriots were on the road to "regeneration" and that he himself was an instrument of change: "It is edu-cation through the public institutions and the missionary work of the physi-cians, that will bring the principles of hygiene and their practical benefits into the Italian homes, while waiting for the more substantial fruits of the schools." For Rocco Brindisi "there was not the slightest doubt in my mind that the rising generation of our Italians will be, in regard to sanitary conditions, on the same level with the American people."

John Foster Carr, *Guide for the Immigrant Italian in the United States of America*

The Importance of Caring for the Health

The conditions of life in America are not the same as they are in Italy; and because Italians are not familiar with them, they are apt to suffer greatly in consequence—particularly on their first arrival. They meet with accidents because our civilization depends far more upon machinery than that to which they have been used. They fall victims to disease because of difference in working and living conditions.

A workingman's capital is a strong, well body. But when men live crowded together, as they do in our tenement houses and in the shanties of a camp, their vitality is lowered, and they become ready subjects to such diseases as pneumonia, and, what is far worse, consumption. A great many Italians who have been strong and well on their arrival in this country have died from tuberculosis within three years of their coming.

To avoid disease and lowered vitality you should keep very clean, eat well, sleep in well-ventilated rooms, and live much in the open air.

It is never dangerous in America to sleep with your windows open. If there are mosquitoes put nets on the windows. **Prevention is the best cure for disease. Avoid bad air, bad food, bad water, bad habits**.

Rules of Health—Clean water, clean food, clean bodies, clean clothes, clean houses, clean streets keep us healthy.

Keep your hands clean, especially for eating. Long, dirty fingernails may be the pastureland of myriads of germs.

Cleanliness, with sunlight, and plenty of fresh air protect the well and help cure the sick. They are often the best medicines.

Eat heartily of different kinds of food. Variety of food is necessary.

Avoid strong drinks. Strong drinks make weak men.

Drink a great deal of water each day. Water aids digestion and circulation. Water carries away the waste of the body. But the water that you drink should be pure. When it is impure, it causes typhoid fever and other diseases. If possible drink well water, but the well must not be near a stable or other outbuilding that might take sewerage into it. If the water does not look clear be sure to boil it before using, because boiling removes dangerous qualities that might cause disease.

Never give wine or beer to children. When children take these drinks they do not eat enough, and sometimes faint in school. Alcoholic drinks are too stimulating for them and prevent the natural development of their little bodies.

Bathing removes the dirt that stops up the pores of the body. Bathing washes away dead skin, the perspiration, and other waste of the body. Bathing makes the skin clean and soft. It gives tone and strength to the whole body. Bathing prolongs life. **Bathe the whole body once every day**.

At the Market—Buy only fresh meat and fresh fish.

Do not buy bread and cake at dirty bakeries.

Are your grocer and butcher cleanly in person? Are their clerks cleanly?

Does your grocer keep his butter and milk in clean, cold places, and are they covered? Select a milkman who has clean hands, clean clothes, clean wagon, clean cans, clean bottles. Tuberculosis kills 5,000,000 people annually. It may be carried through infected milk. Do not forget that dirty milk may kill the baby.

Canned meats must be free from mold and greenish hue when opened. If the top of the can is raised in the centre, the meat has begun to spoil and should not be eaten.

Don't buy bargain-counter food.

In the Kitchen—Keep all food covered in icebox or cupboard. Do not leave milk uncovered anywhere. Do not leave milk in a warm room or unchilled icebox. Protect it from flies.

Wash thoroughly all meat, fish, vegetables, and fruit before using.

Dishes should be clean, and food fresh cooked.

The cook's hands must be clean. Typhoid fever and other diseases have been contracted from dirty hands.

Keep flies out of your house, especially the kitchen. Grease and dirt attract them. They cause many diseases. Bugs and mice carry infection: they never stay in clean places.

Sweeping and Dusting—Dust contains germs that cause disease. When you sweep or dust make as little dust as possible. The best way to sweep is to moisten a newspaper, tear it into small pieces, and scatter these upon the floor. It will catch the dust, and hold it fast as you go over the room with the broom. The best way to dust is to use slightly moistened cloths and wash them when you have finished.

General Advice

It is the **duty of the citizen** to do everything possible for the good health of himself and his fellows. Garbage and ashes should be dumped promptly into the receptacles provided for them. Where conditions are not hygienic either in the care of water-closets, the disposal, of garbage, or the plumbing of houses, complaint should promptly and freely be made to the Board of Health. That is the American way. And in America you should do as Americans do.

The Board of Health in all American cities has great power given to it. It can oblige people to keep their houses and living rooms in a sanitary condition. It has power to force employers to keep their shops and factories in a sanitary condition. In every American city it watches to see that food is properly kept in the stores where it is sold. In the case of large cities it sends its inspectors to visit every part of the country from which the milk supply of the city is drawn. It publishes for gratuitous distribution circulars—in New York and in some other places printed in Italian—that tell about the care of babies, of their feeding, and the use of pasteurized milk, which has saved thousands of lives. Other circulars tell about the treatment of different diseases like consumption, the care and preparation of food, and general living conditions. These things may all be had freely, and are very important to those who do not understand the conditions of life in America.

The Board of Health also watches over the children in school, and by means of its doctors makes frequent examinations of the eyes, ears, teeth, throat, and so on, of the children. The sickly child is always behind in his studies. Only well children make progress.

The large cities of the United States offer **many advantages that make for health and pleasure**, all paid for by the taxes. There are large public baths. There are playgrounds for children, with open-air gymnasiums for men and boys. In New York there are recreation piers built out into the river, where mothers can take their small children during the hot weather, and where it is pleasant to promenade in the evening, and often upon these piers excellent concerts are given. Public parks with their frequent concerts give the city dweller opportunities for rest and for breathing the fresh country air.

In Sickness—Beware of the Medical Institutes that advertise in the Italian papers, which pretend to cure every kind of disease, even those that are incurable. They will take your money and often make your disease worse.

Beware of patent medicines—particularly those for children.

When you are sick, go to a hospital or to a dispensary. American hospitals are supported by the taxes and by the gifts of the wealthy. They are entirely free to the poor. They are splendidly equipped, and in them rich and poor are treated with equal skill and tenderness. Besides general hospitals, in all large cities, there are a great variety of special hospitals: Maternity hospitals and hospitals for children, as well as hospitals for special diseases; cancer, tuberculosis, contagious diseases, for disease of ear, eye, throat, and so on. In New York there are two hospitals for Italians: one, the Italian Hospital, at No. 165–167 West Houston Street, the other, Columbus Hospital, at 226 East Twentieth Street.

Consumption—In the great majority of cases consumption, once considered incurable, is not a fatal disease. It can nearly always be cured if its presence is recognized early. If you are troubled with continual coughing and catarrh [inflammation of nose and throat], you may be in danger, and should immediately consult a doctor or go to a hospital or dispensary for examination. If you then find you have tuberculosis, do not be swindled by advertised cures, specifics and "special methods"—the remedies so widely advertised in the Italian papers. The only cures are pure air and sunshine, outdoor life, and nourishing food. The Board of Health in New York, and in many other cities, publishes the rules for its care. If you have not the means to procure the attention of a skillful physician, go to the Clinica Morgagni, No. 173 West Houston Street, first floor, New York City, an Italian institution that takes special care of the tuberculous poor, and provides in case of need for sending them to sanatoria.

Contagious Diseases—It is the duty of the doctor in charge of one ill with contagious disease to report the nature of the disease to the Board of

Health. The Board of Health may isolate any person sick of a contagious disease. If a landlord rents an apartment knowing it to be contaminated, without making declaration of the fact to the one taking the lease, he is responsible for all damages incurred by reason of the infection. Persons sick with contagious disease may be carried to a hospital and held there. One sick with contagious disease is liable to be punished if **he exposes himself or another similarly** sick in any public place.

Vaccination—Vaccination is not required by law, but the man who is not vaccinated may be prevented from entering the country, and unvaccinated children are liable to be excluded from school.

Sarah Kershaw, "Freud Meets Buddha: Therapy For Immigrants"

Disorders from the East Emerge Here

The patients may suffer from classic mental ailments: depression, anxiety, schizophrenia.

But as they make their way to a sprawling mental hospital in northeast Queens, they also complain of problems that the average New York City psychologist has rarely encountered: *pa-feng*, a phobic fear of wind and cold that occurs in Chinese patients; *hwa-byung*, a suppressed anger syndrome suffered by Koreans; and *Latah*, a Malaysian and Indonesian psychosis that leads to uncontrollable mimicking of other people.

They are the kinds of illnesses that psychologists refer to as culture-bound syndromes. Experts say that while they are fairly common among New York's exploding immigrant population, they are often undiagnosed, or are confused with other conditions. But a growing number of mental health professionals are now focusing on patients' ethnicity and country of origin to treat mental illnesses.

Westerners have their own culture-bound syndromes. Anorexia nervosa, for example, most often afflicts young women exposed to movie and television images of an idealized skinny female body.

But immigrants tend to have poor access to mental health care and until recently, there were few mental health services like the new program in Queens, the Asian-American Family Clinic at Zucker Hillside Hospital. Dr. Yong Cho and Dr. Quixia Mei Lan opened the clinic four months ago, and they are already treating 40 patients who came from across Asia.

Dr. Cho, 34, an immigrant who was a chaplain in the South Korean Army, blends Zen Buddhism, Confucianism and psychotherapy in treating his patients, he said, tailoring the therapy to each patient's culture and needs. In his office, there is plenty of Korean green tea, used for meditation.

The treatment of culturally specific disorders may wind up being similar to the treatment of classic depression and other more general illnesses, with the use of psychotropic drugs or talk therapy or both. But for Asians it may mix different approaches: meditation and medication, Freud and Buddha. The main difference, cultural psychologists say, lies with the diagnosis: one person's depression is another's suppressed anger syndrome.

Dr. Cho's partner, Dr. Lan, a Chinese immigrant in her forties, is a psychiatrist who also specializes in culture-bound syndromes. Dr. Lan said that her patients were accustomed to using herbs or to thinking of their problems as purely physical ones—they often complain only of a backache or a stomachache and not of depression—so it can take several sessions to persuade even severely depressed patients to try drugs. But both doctors said that more immigrants are becoming comfortable with the use of antidepressants and other medications.

The stigma and shame attached to mental illness, which can be much fiercer in Eastern cultures than in the West, can keep immigrants from seeking treatment, according to several experts and a 2001 report by the United States surgeon general. Many of the 800,000 Asian immigrants in New York City live in close-knit communities, where word spreads fast.

"Asians are often very reluctant to seek help," Dr. Cho said. "They may go to a pastor, a fortuneteller or a friend's mother, but never talk to a shrink."

Ol Y., 46, a patient of Dr. Lan's and Dr. Cho's from Hong Kong, who spoke on the condition that only her first name and the initial of her last name be used, suffers from bipolar disorder. She waited years to seek treatment, filled with shame and with fear that the members of her church or her neighbors would find out something was wrong with her.

She was treated with drugs by a Western doctor, she said, but her "trembling," anxiety and depression still would not go away. Her husband, who was laid off from his job as a software consultant for Wall Street companies soon after September 11, 2001—only adding to Mrs. Y.'s stress—said that he felt desperate to find her some help.

He began surfing the Internet and came upon information about the new program in Queens. Two months ago, Dr. Lan adjusted Mrs. Y.'s medications. Then Mrs. Y. began talk therapy with Dr. Cho, who draws on a mixture of approaches, including Mrs. Y.'s deep belief in Christianity, to treat her for the disorder.

Besides her bipolar disorder, Mrs. Y., who immigrated here 20 years ago, suffers from stress related to culture shock and often feels isolated, Dr. Cho said. In treating her, he has focused heavily on the way her mood, her anxiety, and her fears have been affected by going to New York and her lack of support in the tiny network of immigrants she knows.

"I can stand on my own feet," Mrs. Y said. "I don't have to lie down all the time. I'm getting better and better."

Asian patients have physical differences that also make their treatment different from people of Western backgrounds. Many Asians develop side effects to medications at lower doses compared with other ethnic groups. The precise reasons are unclear, but it is believed that biology—such as how the liver absorbs and the body processes medication—plays a large role.

Depression has been shown to be a condition that can be aggravated or brought on by adjustment to life in a new country. The stress of learning English or the inability to speak it can also lead to anxiety or can intensify a mental illness, according to Dr. Cho, particularly for immigrants who were highly educated in their native countries but find themselves barely able to communicate here.

Even among immigrants who do seek treatment, many are often afraid or reluctant to spell out what is bothering them. Dr. Cho said that he often had to coax his patients into talking and that traditional approaches to therapy— like asking, "So what's going on?" and then just listening—did not work.

In fact, some languages, like Korean, have no specific word for depression, Dr. Cho said. There is a term for "a little bit irritable," and someone feeling depressed may talk about having a "down heart," while tapping a fist against the chest.

But such culture-bound syndromes, which are listed in the standard reference [book] of psychiatry, the *Diagnostic and Statistical Manual of Mental Disorders*, are not limited to Asians.

A common disorder among Hispanics, for example, is a condition called "ataque de nervios," in which so much pent-up anxiety and anger come out that a sufferer will fall on the floor and may experience uncontrollable shouting, attacks of crying, and heat in the chest, said Dr. Julia Ramos-Grenier, a psychologist and professor at the University of Hartford.

Dr. Ramos-Grenier said that although some disorders linked to different countries with different names may seem similar, many are distinct. Ultimately, she said, cultural experiences are essential to understanding mental illness.

Making it even harder to diagnose some diseases is that, in some cultures, anger and anxiety can become bottled up because talking about mental distress is not acceptable, Dr. Cho said.

The Korean suppressed anger syndrome, *hwa-byung*, is particularly common among middle-aged Korean women, who may have felt afraid to express their feelings for much of their lives, Dr. Cho said.

Dr. Cho said the syndrome is common among Korean immigrants, and knowing about it is crucial.

"Otherwise," he said, "you might not be able to understand them. You might be able to understand their symptoms, but you might not understand what's really happening behind their symptoms."

CHAPTER THIRTEEN

Traditions and Invented Traditions

Introduction

Migrants never travel from one place to another without baggage. In addition to the material belongings they pack, they bring those dimensions of their culture that are most important to them. From the very first settlers in the Americas, those migrants from somewhere in central Asia who migrated across the land bridge where the Bering Straits are now, to the most recent arrivals from Latin America and Southeast Asia, newcomers have brought traditions that they practiced in their homelands. Such traditions are a part of their identity and remind them of who they are and of their most cherished values no matter how far they may be physically removed from their place of origin. However, traditions are sometimes forgotten or lost or prove inadequate to reflect changes that occur in a group's identity. Then groups frequently engage in a process of inventing traditions. These invented traditions are inauthentic in that they are not transported from a homeland. But they are quite genuine reflections of a group's aspirations and its desire to recall its past in a particular way. Repetition is quite important in legitimizing such invented traditions. Historian Eric Hobsbawm has characterized the process of tradition invention as "formalization and ritualization, characterized by reference to the past, if only by imposing repetition."

Native American peoples were rich in traditions, especially traditions that explained natural phenomenon such as changes of seasons or that were spiritual in nature, and incantations to cure illness or banish bad fortune. The shattering of tribal life by devastating epidemics of smallpox or measles after contact with Europeans often required the remnants of tribes to merge for survival. Tribal traditions thus became diluted and, at times vanished or were observed, the reason for particular traditions becoming dimmer and dimmer over time. New ones were invented to reflect the reconstituted group's values. A similar experience was the fate of those Africans ripped from their homelands by slave-catchers and brought to the Americas in chains. Rituals reflecting tradition often comprised the only baggage slaves brought. Masters discouraged slave rituals, realizing that slaves were most easily disciplined if they could be separated from traditions that defined their identities. Some traditions were allowed, such as those involving healing the body, because they benefited masters as well as slaves when Western medicine failed to cure. Soon the slave culture of the plantation spawned its own invented traditions.

European and Asian migrants of the nineteenth and twentieth centuries brought traditions. Some traditions reflected immigrants' national origins and others their religious beliefs. The former were often sacrificed on the altar of adaptation more easily than the latter. Irish and German immigrants arriving in the middle of the nineteenth century could relinquish customs and traditions, even traditional cuisine. However, practicing Catholics did not readily relinquish attendance at mass on Sundays or the sacrament of communion. Marriage, too, was a sacrament and had to be performed by a priest. Recent emigrants from Ireland or Germany did not need to struggle to retain memory of their homelands. However, over the generations, such memories, passed from parents to children, were diminished in their potency to bind the group together and celebrate the values consistent with an Irish or German identity. Customs and traditions had to be invented to retain the ethnic identification across the generations, to remind those of Irish or German heritage where their forbears had originated. Irish St. Patrick's Day parades and German Steuben Day parades organized by fraternal organizations were annual reminders of each group's past.

A similar pattern prevailed among Asian newcomers. Chinese immigrants relinquished wearing the traditional braid of hair or queue worn out of respect for the Chinese emperor, but did not immediately relinquish religious rituals upon immigrating to the United States. Most immigrants were either Buddhist or Taoist. Transplanted Chinese communities had shrines and temples where gods such as Cai Shen, the god of wealth and Guan Gong, the protector, could be worshiped (figure 13.1). The Ching Ming Festival when ancestors were remembered and the Lunar New Year Festival were among those that continued to be celebrated after emigration. The celebrations of such festivals organized by fraternal organizations in Chinatowns kept the past alive.

At the turn of the century, Italians, Eastern European Jews, Greeks, Poles, Mexicans, and many other groups came in large numbers, all bringing customs and traditions with them. Each group negotiated its place in American society and culture. Tradition was often the currency. Eastern European Jews had little difficulty relinquishing traditions that were Russian or Polish or Rumanian, but struggled to retain their religious beliefs even in the face of life in a secular American society. In spite of economic necessity, many Jews tried to avoid jobs in factories or shops that required working on the

Figure 13.1 Transplanted Chinese communities sought to preserve their traditions, especially at rites of passage such as birth, marriage, and death as suggested by this Chinese funeral procession (ca. 1900) (Courtesy of the Library of Congress).

Sabbath. Some men retained their beards and wore skullcaps, or *yarmulkes*, consistent with orthodox custom. Married women wore wigs, *sheitels*, over their hair, in accordance with the orthodox standard of modesty that permitted women to display their natural hair only in the presence of their husbands. A myriad of rituals reflected traditional Jewish beliefs about food. Religious Jews only eat foods and engage in food preparation consistent with the laws of *kashruth*.

Italy had been a unified nation only since the 1870s and there was a strong sense of regionalism among those who came from different towns and cities. Sicilians, Neapolitans, Genoese had different traditions which they brought with them to the United States. Inadequate in numbers to sustain these unique traditions beyond a generation or two, migrants from different regions and towns relinquished some of their traditions and increasingly accepted the generic identity, "Italian." Different approaches to Catholicism in the provinces south of Rome lasted longer. Some practiced a faith that was a synthesis of Catholic belief and pre-Christian pagan ritual. Emigrants brought with them religious objects and often clergy from their village church to make them feel at home in the United States and to perpetuate the values and relationships embodied in sacred statuary or rituals.

The practice of bringing traditions and inventing traditions continues with contemporary immigrants. Hmong tribesmen from Cambodia prefer amulets and incantations to blood tests and surgery in diagnosing and curing the body's ills. Latinos practice the traditions of *Santeria* to make sick bodies healthy. However, both groups are engaged in cultural compromise, especially in the second and third generations after migration. Sunday parades and a host of invented traditions eventually substitute a created past for the ways of the homeland. Older groups travel ever further down the path to diluting traditions. Vendors at Italian festas celebrating the saint of a home village now sell Coca Colas with the ziti and Michael Jordan t-shirts a few feet from crucifixes and religious medals.

The following selections speak to the issue of tradition and invented tradition among newcomers. The selection by anthropologist Robert Orsi deals with the history of the Madonna of Mount Carmel on East 115th Street in Harlem. In 1881, Italian residents of East Harlem began to have annual celebrations of the Madonna brought from their village to the United States. The annual festa, including parading with the statue of the Madonna through the streets of East Harlem, which occurred every July, was an invented tradition and the occasion for public displays of religious devotion. However, the true importance of the Madonna was that she embodied the social as well as religious values of the community. In their highly emotional adoration of the Madonna, Italian East Harlemites prayed to her for favors—the recovery of an ill relative, a spouse for an eligible young woman—but also affirmed the ethnic lifestyle of which they believed she approved. As the years passed, the ritual surrounding the Madonna became less physically passionate, but remained central to the community's cohesiveness.

The second selection speaks to the issue of what can happen when the traditions of different religions met on American soil because of immigration. *The Forward* was the largest selling Yiddish language daily newspaper. Socialist in its politics, *The Forward* often tried to span the gap between its orthodox Jewish readers and the secular America to which they had migrated. One of the most popular early twentieth century *Forward* editors was Abraham Cahan, a Russian Jewish writer widely respected in the immigrant community. It was Cahan who began a letters to the editor column called in Yiddish a *Bintel Brief* ("Bundle of Letters"). Cahan hoped that newcomers could air their anxieties in this column and, perhaps, that he could actively assist them in their personal negotiation for acceptance among their new neighbors in America. The column became so popular that illiterate newcomers would often pay a nickel to have someone else write a letter that they dictated to the *Forward*.

One of the problems that first generation immigrants encountered was looking on as its children and grandchildren celebrated the traditions of other cultures in the permissive, cosmopolitan atmosphere of American society. Although some Jews had already begun to lose their piety prior to emigration as they entered European industrial society, many others arrived with their orthodox Jewish beliefs intact only to watch the next generation stray. Christmas was a problem because its celebration was ubiquitous and had been secularized. While many Christian Americans knelt in prayer at churches, many others simply enjoyed the color and festivity of Christmas trees. Those who did not join in the celebration could easily feel alienated. In this 1941 letter to the editor, a wife and mother describes her religious

husband's disappointment that their American-born son had erected a
Christmas tree in his living room so that his own children would not feel
any different at holiday time than their non-Jewish friends. Cahan admon-
ishes the son because while Christmas is a national holiday, it is a religious
holiday on the Christian calendar. However, Cahan sees enough blame to
go around and scolds the father for not having educated his son in Judaism
well enough to insulate him from Christmas American-style.

Invented traditions often take on a life of their own and become so
entertaining to the general public that their relationship to a particular
group's history and values is all but lost. The final selection describes the
annual St. Patrick's Day parade in Savannah, Georgia. That southern city,
boasting one of the oldest Irish communities in the United States, is today
only 1.0 percent Irish. However, the city continues to have one of the most
spirited St. Patrick's Day celebrations of any American city. What do green
grits and green beer have to do with the dramatic story of the Irish diaspora? Very little. However, for some, the Savannah parade inspires thoughts
of the Irish struggle to survive the mid-nineteenth century famine and to
carve out places in other lands. For others, the parade and festivities are just
good community fun.

Suggestions for Further Reading

Alan M. Kraut, "Ethnic Foodways: The Significance of Food in the Designation of Cultural Boundaries Between Immigrant Groups in the U.S., 1840–1921," *Journal of American Culture* 2(Fall, 1979): 409–420.

Andrew R. Heinze, *Adapting to Abundance, Jewish Immigrants, Mass Consumption, and the Search for American Identity* (New York: Columbia University, 1990).

Elizabeth H. Pleck, *Celebrating the Family, Ethnicity, Consumer Culture, and Family Rituals* (Cambridge: Harvard University Press, 2000).

Hasia R. Diner, *Lower East Side Memories: A Jewish Place in America* (Princeton: Princeton University Press, 2000).

Hasia R. Diner, *Hungering for America: Italian, Irish and Jewish Foodways in the Age of Migration* (Cambridge: Harvard University Press, 2002).

Kathleen Neils Conzen, "Ethnicity as Festive Culture: Nineteenth-Century German America on Parade," in Werner Sollors, ed. *The Invention of Ethnicity* (New York: Oxford University Press, 1989), pp. 44–76.

Victor Turner, ed. *Celebrations: Studies in Festivity and Ritual* (Washington, D.C.: Smithsonian Institution Press, 1982).

Robert Anthony Orsi, "The Origins of the Devotion to Mount Carmel in Italian Harlem"

The Madonna of 115th Street shared the history of the people of Italian Harlem. She journeyed to the new world with the immigrants and lived among them in their neighborhood. She shared the poverty and ostracism of their early days. When Italians were relegated to the basements of churches in East Harlem, so was she; like the immigrants, she was an embarrassment to the Catholic church in New York City. The Madonna left the basement of the church on 115th Street at the same time that Italians and their children were beginning to take control of political and social life in Italian Harlem: just at the time when the Italian language was accepted by the Board of Education for study in New York's public high schools, when LaGuardia took his seat in Congress and Corsi began his long career at Haarlem House, and just at the time of Italian Harlem's first successful rent strike, the Madonna took her place on the main altar of the church.

She heard the changing needs of the community. First she heard prayers for families left behind in Italy and then she began to hear prayers for families sinking roots in the new world. She was asked for help in finding jobs during the Depression. Her protection was sought for the men of Italian Harlem who went off to fight in the Second World War, and she was taken out of the church to greet them when they returned. In the years after the war, she heard younger voices pleading for assistance in school and in finding homes and success outside of Harlem; and she heard the voices of older men and women pleading with her to keep their children from forgetting them and the ways of life of Italian Harlem. Like these older men and women, she waited in her home in Harlem for those who had left to come back and visit, which they did at least once a year. Images of the Madonna were taken away by those who left and set up on bureaus in the Bronx and Westchester next to pictures of the folks still in Harlem and of themselves when they had lived there too.

The story of the devotion to la Madonna del Carmine in East Harlem begins in the summer of 1881, when immigrants from the town of Polla, in the province of Salerno, formed a mutual aid society named after the Madonna, who was the protectress of Polla. Mutual aid societies, which were quite popular in Italian American colonies, were regional organizations composed of immigrants from the same Italian town who gathered together to provide some unemployment and burial benefits and to socialize. They allowed paesani to get together and enjoy each other's company; they also encouraged and enabled the immigrants to remember and preserve traditional customs in the new world. One of Covello's informants described the meaning of mutual aid societies in these terms: "the Italian feels safer when he pays homage to the patron saint of his hometown or village who in the past was considerate to the people. . . . Our Italians, and I mean the old folks, feel that without guardianship of their former patron saint, life would be next to impossible." These interwoven themes of protection, mutual support, and faithfulness to the values and history of the paese are expressed in the most important function of the societies, according to the immigrants—the assurance of support for burial in accordance with southern Italian customs. Covello's informant emphasized this function of the mutual aid societies:

> The older Italians, even while in good health, are never overlooking the event of death. Preservation of funeral rituals is sacred to the old folks. Prospects of a "potter's field" [buried place for unknown or indigent person] fills them with terror. . . . To bury one without proper customs is hurtful to the pride of every Italian. And so the Mutual Aid Societies are fulfilling their probably most important role in assuring a member of a dignified funeral.

But the deep need for this assurance was also indicative of a profound mistrust of the effect the United States might have on Italian faithfulness and tradition: "I personally also think that the main motive of joining a society for burial reasons is the man's constant suspicion that here in America his relatives may skip on their traditional duties and be negligent towards him when he dies." So the formation of the mutual aid society by Pollese in East Harlem in 1881 expressed the immigrants' commitment to their past but also their uncertainty and unease in the present.

The members of the new society determined to organize a festa in honor of their patroness. The first celebration took place in 1882 in the courtyard of a house on 110th Street near the East River; in the following year, the festa was held on the first floor of a house on 111th Street and the East River in a rented room that measured eight by thirty feet. The other rooms in the building were let out to poor Italian workers, and in the back courtyard, right behind the altar of the little chapel to the Madonna, there was a rag-sorting yard where local rag pickers brought their daily hauls to be sorted, washed, and packed. Such celebrations were common among Italian immigrants. One Catholic observer noted in 1900 that when immigrants from the same town managed to take over an entire tenement, they would transform the building's backyard into the setting of their religious celebrations. Another Catholic commentator remarked in 1899 that Italians seemed to prefer outdoor devotions to entering a church.

During these earliest years, the festa was intimate and intense and intensely Neopolitan, and there is no indication of any ecclesiastical supervision; it was a popular, lay-organized celebration—as these feste usually were, to the consternation of both the American and Italian Catholic clergy. The first celebrations were quite simple. The immigrants knelt in someone's apartment or behind a tenement, in a courtyard—though this euphemism undoubtedly obscures the real conditions of the setting—especially decorated for the occasion, before a small printed picture of the Madonna that had been sent for from Polla. They said the rosary, prayed the Magnificat, and then sat down to a huge meal together. In 1883, for the first time, an Italian priest, Domenico Vento, was present at the festa. He said mass, joined in the procession, and delivered, as was the custom, a moving panegyric on the life of the Virgin and on the wonders she had performed for the people of Polla. Father Vento remained in the community throughout 1883, saying mass and administering the sacraments on the first floor of a house on 111th Street and the East River. Then he disappears from the story.

By 1884, the official history tells us, the devotion to the Madonna del Carmine in northern Manhattan had already become a great popular celebration. By this time, the Confraternity had sent for and received a statue of the Madonna from Polla, a transaction which, together with the acquisition of benches for the chapel and rent, put the group in serious debt. In a historical sketch on the devotion prepared for the church in the mid-1920s, it is noted that thousands gathered for the celebration in 1884, coming from far and wide, both immigrants and their children. This proved to be an important year in the history of the devotion to Mount Carmel in East Harlem for a number of reasons. It was, first of all, the year that the Pallotine fathers arrived in the community. Slowly awakening to the "problem"—as it would be called for the next thirty years—of the religious life of Italian immigrants, the New York Archdiocese, at this time under the actual direction of Bishop Michael Corrigan ruling on behalf of the dying John Cardinal McCloskey, invited the Pallotine order to New York to work with the growing Italian population. The Pallotines had been conducting a ministry among Italian immigrants in London, where Cardinal McCloskey had met them and been impressed. The first Pallotine priest, Father Emiliano Kirner, arrived in New York in May 1884 and was soon given care of the little chapel on 111th Street in East Harlem.

The ecclesiastical history of the devotion to Mount Carmel also begins in 1884 with the completion of the church on 115th Street and the formation of the official "Congregazione del Monte Carmelo della 115ma strada." The latter, which was a church society more or less under the authority of the parish clergy, replaced the regional society of Pollese as the official sponsor of the church celebration. Both the erection of the church and the formation of the society mark an official change in the public life of the devotion, which was now officially associated with a church. The members of the society were all male, as was customary with such organizations. For the entire history of the devotion, this celebration of a woman, in which women were the central participants, was presided over by a public male authority.

Soon the plans were ready for a church on 115th Street near the river, a church, in the words of the official history, "built by Italians, the first church which would be called, 'the church of the Italians in New York.'" So committed were the immigrants to this project that many of them came home after terrible and exhausting days of work and with their own hands dug the foundation of the new church and laid its bricks. Junkmen and icemen lent their carts and horses to carry building materials and people in the community prepared refreshments for the workers. When organizers from the masons' union objected to the free work being done by Italian men on the church, Italian women from the neighborhood tied back their hair and took over the job.

Feste were the most obvious declaration of what was unique and different about Italian Catholicism. They were held more frequently in the United States, where any Italian neighborhood could boast dozens of festa societies, than in Italy, and they quickly became the representative characteristic of Italian American communities. Throughout the 1890s, the upper-class residents of West Harlem would stroll over to the East Side on Sundays and holidays to observe the festivities in the "foreign village" along the East River. The Irish American church also took note of these feste, which were held by their fellow Catholics, after all, as non-Catholics were happy to remind them. An Irish policeman standing by and watching a festa in Brooklyn told Antonio Mangano, an Italian Protestant clergyman, that he thought all the money Italians spent on these frequent and violent festivals would be better spent building churches and orphanages.

Irish American Catholics could not understand Italian popular spirituality. In a bitter attack published in *The Catholic World* in 1888, the Reverend Bernard Lynch excoriated "the peculiar kind of spiritual condition" of the Italian immigrants, fed on pilgrimages, shrines, holy cards, and "devotions" but lacking any understanding of "the great truths of religion." The feste provided some American Catholics with material for ridiculing Italians. In an abusive article published in the prominent magazine *America* in 1935, H. J. Hillenbrand told his readers that an Italian workman he knew, whom he calls "Spot"— "one smelly old workhorse"—had told him that feste are really just "street carnivals" for old men and women. If the American church was going to tolerate feste it would only be if they were conducted under the control of the parish clergy and only if they functioned as a means of getting Italians into church and accessible to the authority of "their Cardinal Archbishop."

Besides being an embarrassment both to American Catholicism and to the Italian American clergy, who at times longed for their people to behave in ways more acceptable to the American church within which they had to function too, feste challenged the authority of official Catholicism over the religious lives of the immigrants. Italians make a rather clear distinction between religion and church, and they often view the latter with critical cynicism. The feste and the festa societies competed successfully with the clergy for the people's loyalty, devotion, and money. Jacob Riis saw this clearly in 1899, when he wrote of a festa on Elizabeth Street:

> Between birthdays . . . the saint was left in the loft of the saloon, lest the priest got hold of him and get a corner on him, as it were. Once he got into his possession, he would not let the people have him except upon the payment of a fee that would grow with the years. But the saint belonged to the people, not to the church. He was their home patron, and they were not going to give him up.

Italian and American clergy in Italian parishes knew that they were financially dependent on the festa societies; Italian people might not contribute to the church or toward the building of a Catholic school, but they contributed extravagantly to the festa societies. Beyond this, they also realized that they were pastorally dependent on the feste. It was a widely accepted fact in East Harlem that people who would not set foot in church on any other occasion attended with fervent devotion on the feast day of the Madonna. This religious competition could take a more direct form. An American Catholic observed in 1913 that Italians would hold their feste on the steps on the local church, crowding the streets, while inside the priest said Sunday mass before empty pews.

The process of crowning a particular statue of the Virgin and elevating a shrine to the officially recognized dignity of a sanctuary is a formal ecclesiastical procedure with specific rules and requirements. Between 1681 and 1954, fewer than three hundred statues of the Virgin had been granted this dignity, and only three of these were in the new world: Our Lady of Perpetual Help in New Orleans, Our Lady of Guadalupe in Mexico, and the Madonna of 115th Street. All three of these new world coronations had been decreed by Pope Leo XIII. This procedure held several advantages for Rome. It provided first of all an occasion for a diplomatic gesture of goodwill toward the nation that housed the shrine. It also enabled the church to assert its authority over popular devotions, which are always potentially disruptive and independent of official control.

An official vote was taken in Rome on April 19, 1903; the result was announced in New York on July 16, 1903; and the Virgin was crowned before an enormous concourse of people on July 10, 1904. This was the first communal event of Italian Harlem.

The crowning of the Madonna of 115th Street had both a local and an international context. This double meaning is symbolized by the crown placed on the Virgin's head in a ceremony held in Jefferson Park because the church could not contain the crowds. The crown was made in New York of gold donated by the immigrants in gratitude for the graces they had received, and it was set with precious stones donated by Leo XIII and his successor, Pius X, and by Archbishop Farley. The gold that the immigrants had to give was family gold—rings and brooches and the family heirlooms that southern Italians cherish; their gift to the Virgin was a most intimate one, a great sacrifice made at the center of their moral world. Of the ceremony itself, we are told by the official history that "it seemed as though all the Italians in America had poured into Jefferson Park for the privilege of witnessing such an event."

In the years that followed, the church and the devotion grew and changed with the community of Italian Harlem. When poor men and women are asked to tell the story of their lives, if they have been fortunate enough to have built a house, they make the event of this building the centerpiece of their autobiographies. This is particularly true of Italians, for whom the home is a shrine and who value so highly the construction of a house. The centerpiece of the history of East Harlem is the building and constant beautification of the church of Mount Carmel, which the immigrants identified explicitly as *la casa della nostra mamma* [our mother's house].

The next significant event in the public life of the devotion after the crowning of the Madonna was the renovation of the interior of the church.

In 1919, Gaspare Dalia became the Provincial Superior of the Pallotines. He was determined to establish la Madonna in her rightful place in the main church. On Christmas Day, 1920, he shared his dream of rebuilding the interior of the church into a proper home for la Madonna, and the people responded generously. Work was finished in 1922. On June 23, 1923, the statue of la Madonna del Carmine, the Neopolitan queen who had become the protectress of all Italian Harlem, was moved to a throne on the main altar. In 1927, after Dalia had returned to the church as pastor, the bell tower of the church was completed; the first notes were heard on Christmas Day.

The way the history of the campanile is told in the parish records illustrates how Mount Carmel reflected and symbolized—and by symbolizing helped to shape—the life of Italian Harlem. The bell tower was rich in meaning for the people of Italian Harlem. They were still very poor, and at first, we are told, the campanile, like the church and the crown before it, had seemed a distant dream. Yet the people made the necessary financial sacrifice, so great was their love and respect for the Madonna. Just as the poor insist on dignified and even costly public funerals as a demonstration of respect and loyalty, so the people of Italian Harlem wanted their divine mother's house to be beautiful. There was certainly more money in Italian Harlem by this time, and the campanile reflects this hard economic fact. But the bad times were not over, and for the people the real significance of the tower was that it revealed their continuing love and faithfulness to their protectress by their financial sacrifice.

It was also emphasized in the souvenir journal that the bell tower was built by all the Italians of East Harlem, not by immigrants from any one region of the mezzogiorno. Italian Harlem, as we have seen, eventually attained a real sense of community identification, solidarity, and loyalty transcending the campanilismo that the immigrants brought with them from Italy. The cult of Mount Carmel and events such as the construction of the bell tower and the inevitable celebration that followed it contributed to the redirection of the people's loyalties to Italian Harlem. The church and the devotion belonged to the entire community, not to any particular neighborhood or region of Italy.

The construction of the bell tower was also a celebration of the community's Italian heritage. With the campanile, the church—and the neighborhood—looked more Italian. The street in front of the church now had the feel of an Italian village square.

On July 16, 1929, just a few months before the financial crisis that was to throw the community back into hardship, East Harlem celebrated the fifteenth anniversary of the coronation of the Madonna. At 5:30 in the afternoon, the statue of la Madonna was carried out into the street, where she was greeted by a volley of fireworks, the pealing of the church's bells, and by the tears and hymns of the crowd surging up the steps of the church. The windows and fire escapes of Italian Harlem were decorated and the streets were lit by arches of colored lights. The hot night was redolent with the familiar festa smells of food and incense and gunpowder. Those who could not march in the procession leaned out their windows to see

la Madonna high above the shoulders of her massed followers. The parish
journal tells us that at sunset, particularly beautiful on this day, excitement
reached its peak as Dalia stood weeping on a raised platform in Jefferson
Park. Italian Harlem was celebrating and creating itself as it celebrated
la Madonna. Fifty-seven years after the first celebration of the festa of
Mount Carmel in a tenement on the East River, the Madonna was presiding
over a strong and real and troubled community of immigrants and their
children in northern Manhattan.

During the period of Italian Harlem's maturity, the Church of Our Lady
of Mount Carmel—the church as Italian and Italian American shrine, not as
an American Catholic parish—came to occupy an important and unique
place in the history and life of the community. Mount Carmel became the
village church of Italian Harlem and one of the centers of community
life. The front doors were kept open wide all the time, and people dropped
in throughout the day on their way to or from work and while they were
going about their daily chores. From the street, passersby could see the main
altar, glowing with the warm light of hundreds of candles, each representing a plea or the gratitude of some member of their community. The
Madonna herself stood high above the altar, watching over Italian Harlem.
Men and women in the community preferred to have their significant rites
of passage enacted at Mount Carmel even if they were members of other
parishes. These rites of passage—baptisms, weddings, requiems—which
incorporated individuals into the community or sent them on their way, did
not seem legitimate unless they were performed at the symbolic center of
that community.

The women of Italian Harlem turned to the Madonna during the difficult
years of the war, imploring her to watch over their men on distant battle-
fields. They promised their protectress special devotions and penances if she
answered their prayers, promises that were still being kept throughout the
1950s and 1960s. One woman gratefully observed after her son had
returned from the Pacific, "I know that only through the aid of Our Blessed
Mother was it possible [for him] to escape without a scratch." Another
woman brought her grandson, on the eve of his departure for the war, to the
little *Cappella dei Soldati* [Soldier's Chapel] which had been set up in the
lower church and made him promise that, if he survived the war, he would
faithfully attend the annual festa with her. Women went to the Madonna for
solace and peace of mind for themselves too, for comfort during the long
wait for the war's end. One woman expressed the tension felt by others in
the community: "Many times, in this long period of four years, I was without any news, and my heart suffered terribly. But I never gave up—instead,
I kept on praying." These fears and prayers were expressed directly to the
Madonna in letters written to her by the women of Italian Harlem and
published in the parish journal.

The voice of Mount Carmel's bell calling from the campanile announced
the end of the war in Europe to the community. Men and women gathered
in great numbers in front of the church to pray and sing and to thank their
protectress for peace. During this spontaneous celebration, the statue of the

Madonna was carried out into the street among her people. The festa drew a huge crowd in 1946, as "countless mothers, wives, sisters, brothers came back to give thanks for a safe and sound return of a loved one, or to pray for the eternal rest of a soul." In the same year, the Catholic War Veterans of Italian Harlem held a communion breakfast at the church on Mother's Day and then marched through the streets in a great procession. Several months before this happy occasion, the Cappella dei Soldati was closed and the names of the men of Italian Harlem who had been killed in action were "recorded in a special album and kept near the Miraculous Image of Our Lady of Mount Carmel." The community turned again to the tasks of peacetime.

In the years after the war, Mount Carmel increasingly became an Italian American Catholic parish eager to conform to the styles and values of American Catholicism. This represents the fulfillment of a trend that had been under way in the official life of the church since at least 1930. But in the earlier period, the power of the popular devotion to the Madonna in the community overwhelmed this official Catholicism of the parish and kept it to tentative statements in the parish journal. After the war, however, the festa itself was slowly overwhelmed by the church. In part, this reflected the changing social and economic position of Italians in the United States, in part the passing of the first generation. Its result was clear: by the 1950s, Mount Carmel had become a church with an annual festa rather than a festa housed in a church.

Italian Americans still came to the festa in great, although ever-diminishing, numbers throughout the 1950s and 1960s, but these were very different Italian Americans coming to a very different festa. They had left the neighborhood and had become more American; they returned to an Italian American Catholic parish that had an annual feast. The church was now described as the Pallotine order's most important parish rather than as *la casa della nostra mamma*. Throughout the postwar period, the parish clergy redefined the nature of the festa. A greater emphasis on order and decorum appeared, as the clergy attempted to control what they saw as the less acceptable features of the devotion; and there was at last a chance of their succeeding in this. In 1953, the pastor urged all those who were planning to attend the celebration to make sure they went to confession and communion during the festa. Then he warned: "The Mt. Carmel Feast is not a feast of games, orgies and outside pastimes. Although there will be some moderate outside signs of joy, yet the Mt. Carmel Feast, the real and true feast will be in the Church, at the feet of the Miraculous Statue of the Virgin, it will be in your HEARTS." The meaning of the festa is interior, controlled, a matter of the heart and not the street. The people have come not to march and eat and cry in the hot streets, but to go to church.

For some, of course, the festa seemed not to change: for older Italians, and especially for those still living in East Harlem, which would soon more accurately be called Spanish Harlem, and for the younger people who were essentially rooted in the perceptions and ways of their parents and grandparents, the festa held something of its old power. This is reflected in the two completely different accounts of the annual feste, in English and Italian, that began to appear after 1947. The English-language versions emphasize the importance of proper behavior and "perfect order" at the celebration. In 1954, the pastor urged the people of the neighborhood to clean their sidewalks and be courteous to visitors to the community, but above all to "give good example, refraining from vulgar noise and foul language." The Italian accounts, on the other hand, continue to be cast in the passionate language of devotion to *la Mamma celeste* [the Heavenly mother].

The difference between these two conceptions of the festa is quite sharp in the parish journal of 1947. The English discussion of that year's festa begins by noting that a "huge and hectic" crowd had attended the celebration. It observes that the festa "brought back a touch of local color to the festivities." The author hopes that the Madonna will grant her children all "necessary graces" and concludes on a hollow and perfunctory note, "July 16th, ever memorable in the annals of our parish, had passed round the corner into the realm of its many historical predecessors." Expressions of gratitude follow to all those "whose loyal and generous cooperation was largely instrumental for the smooth and efficient manner in which all arrangements were handled."

The Italian version appears to be describing another event; it speaks from another culture, another experience of the festa. Written in the familiar, impassioned prose of the earlier days of the devotion, the Italian account celebrates the fervor of the people's faith, which kept them before the throne of the Madonna all day and night. The author recounts what he saw and heard in the sanctuary: passionate expressions of joy and grief, faces bathed in tears, the sounds of sighs and sobs. Then he builds to a fervent conclusion: "The Sanctuary of the Madonna of Mt. Carmel of 115th Street is the eternal flame which lights the difficult paths of our lives, it is the safe port for those shipwrecked by society and it is the inexhaustible font of graces and blessings."

Like the old Italian women in East Harlem living in a changed world, their children off in New Jersey or the Bronx, the Madonna lost her power in the postwar world. Not completely, of course: the old folks in Harlem still commanded the respect, devotion, and attention of their children and so did the Madonna. But she no longer possessed her awesome power of the past. This is strikingly revealed in an exchange in the parish journal in January 1954. A sick man wrote in to say that at the festa of the previous summer he had prayed for Saint Vincent Pallotti to be his doctor in this illness—and the Madonna to be his nurse. The pastor of the church comments, "What a happy ideal Vincent the doctor, the Madonna the nurse." The triumph of church over cult is complete. The Madonna has been relegated to a subordinate position, the handmaid of the priest who founded the order in charge of the church on 115th Street. Is this the same figure men and women begged to heal them, to enter their lives and sufferings? Did the Madonna of 1882 and 1925 need the assistance of a male church official? Is Saint Vincent's assistant really the woman who once presided over the people of Italian Harlem? The days of power were over.

Once that power had been great. The Madonna of 115th Street did not work miracles in any spectacular sense. There are stories of children healed after tumbling out of third-floor windows, but these are rare. Instead, the Virgin's power was intimate; the graces she granted were intensely private, rooted in the daily lives of the people. Her power was in the family; it was into this setting that she was most often asked to come to help with problems that could be quite mundane. She was asked to heal the minor burns that women received while cooking, or to help someone recover quickly from a cold so she could get back to her housework. She was also asked for help in breaking painful emotional ties or for success in love. These intimate affairs of everyday life were the source and locus of the Madonna's power. So if we hope to understand her power, we must study the intimate lives of the people of Italian Harlem.

A Reader from the Bronx, "Letter to the Editor" (of the *Jewish Daily Forward*)

1941

Dear Editor,

My husband and I came from Galicia to America thirty-three years ago right after we were married. At home I had received a secular education, and my husband had been ordained as a rabbi. However, he did not want to be a rabbi here, and since we had brought along a little money from home, we bought a small business and made a good living. My husband is religious but not a fanatic. I am more liberal, but I go to *shul* with him on *Rosh Hashanah* and *Yom Kippur*.

We have five childen—two boys and three girls. The boys went to a *Talmud Torah*, and the girls, too, received a Jewish education. We always kept a Jewish home and a *kosher* kitchen.

Our eldest son is now a college teacher, tutors students privately, and earns a good deal of money. He is married, has two children, four and seven years old. They live in a fine neighborhood, and we visit them often.

It happened that on Christmas Eve we were invited to have dinner with friends who live near our son and daughter-in-law, so we decided to drop in to see them after the meal. I called up, my daughter-in-law answered the telephone and warmly invited us to come over.

When we opened the door and went into the living room we saw a large Christmas tree which my son was busy trimming with the help of his two children. When my husband saw this he turned white. The two grand-children greeted us with a "Merry Christmas" and were delighted to see us. I wanted to take off my coat, but my husband gave me a signal that we were leaving immediately.

Well, I had to leave at once. Our son's and daughter-in-law's pleading and talking didn't help, because my husband didn't want to stay there another minute. He is so angry at our son over the Christmas tree that he doesn't want to cross the threshold of their home again. My son justifies himself by saying he takes the tree in for the sake of his children, so they won't feel any different than their non-Jewish friends in the neighborhood. He assures us that it has nothing to do with religion. He doesn't consider it wrong, and he feels his father has no right to be angry over it.

My husband is a *kohen*[1] and, besides having a temper, he is stubborn, too. But I don't want him to be angry at our son. Therefore I would like to hear your opinion on this matter.

With great respect,
A Reader from the Bronx

ANSWER:

The national American holidays are celebrated here with love and joy, by Jews and Gentiles alike. But Christmas is the most religious Christian holiday and Jews have nothing to do with it. Jews, religious or not, should respect the Christmas holiday, but to celebrate it would be like dancing at a stranger's wedding. It is natural that a Jew who observes all the Jewish traditions should be opposed to seeing his son and grandchildren trimming a Christmas tree.

But he must not quarrel with his son. It is actually your husband's fault because he probably did not instill the Jewish traditions in his son. Instead of being angry with him, he should talk to his son and explain the meaning of Christmas to him.

Note

1. A *koken* is a Jewish male who is a descendant of Aaron, the first High Priest, and, as a priest, has special duties during religious services.

Bruce Frankel, "Savannah Going All-out Irish: Just 1% Irish, but City Boasts Gigantic Fest"

Savannah, GA—At noon today, Michael Ryan will ceremoniously cast green dye into the stateliest fountain in town to kick off the St. Patrick's Day celebration of the South.

Savannah bills its tribute to the Irish as the nation's second largest, after New York's, and one of the oldest at 172 years.

Visitors are often startled to learn the parade's status until they're reminded of Gone with the Wind heroine Scarlett O'Hara and the colorful history of Irish settlement in the South.

Green grits, green beer, and green-hatted crowds will swell Savannah's resident population of 150,000 to 500,000 and transform this sleepy coastal town, best known for its 18th- and 19th-century homes and moss-wreathed oak trees.

"St. Patrick's Day is as much a part of Savannah's identity as Mardi Gras is to New Orleans," says Rick Lott of the Savannah Waterfront Association.

About $ 6 million will be spent over the three-day celebration. Most of the 8,000 hotel rooms in a 60-mile radius have been booked for months. Vendors will sell tens of thousands of glasses of green beer and T-shirts with Confederate flags with cross bars of shamrocks.

Savannah, with more than 5 million visitors a year, is in the midst of a tourist boom.

Parade organizers are conscious that the St. Patrick's Day celebration has a reputation as a citywide binge. Drinking is now banned in the line of march.

"It's a day to take pride in our heritage and think about the Irish who've suffered" through potato famines and persecution, says Grand Marshal Ryan, 52.

Only 1% of Savannah's population is Irish. But, being the parade's grand marshal remains one of the city's highest honors.

On Saturday, 35 floats, 22 marching bands and 250 Irish groups will snake around squares bright with tulips, daffodils, camellias and red-bud trees to the old Cotton Exchange on the riverfront. For Janice Norbert, 63, it's a reason for her clan to gather from across the United States, "Everyone's happy and having a good time, and that's what it's all about," she says.

At Kevin Barry's Irish Pub, Vic Power, 54, expects to pour 36 kegs of Irish stout and 36 kegs of American beer.

Nancy Hillis has boosted the price of rooms at the Hamilton-Turner House from $ 150 to $ 450 a night. "This house has the best vantage point in town," she brags.

Not everyone is as delighted.

"Each year, it gets bigger and bigger. It's become . . . an excuse to get drunk and throw up," says John Duncan, 58, a bookshop owner. "We close our doors and flee."

The South was settled by immigrants from Ireland. Now, Savannah's St. Patrick's Day is uniquely inclusive.

"Everybody's Irish for the day," says Tom Coffey, 73, author of *Only In Savannah*.

Savannahians tend to lump together as "Irish" all Catholics, including Italians, Germans and Lebanese, he says.

Blacks, 52% of Savannah's population, and Jews, whose ancestors here date back to the establishment in 1733 of the first Jewish community in the South, say they're happy to share in the fun.

"I feel like I'm black Irish," says Rose Webbs, 47, an African-American Savannah native who has cooked for restaurants on St. Patrick's Day for 30 years. She'll go through 40 cases of corned beef and 200 pounds of cabbage to make a meal that originated in the South to feed Irish laborers.

"It's a whole lot of preparation," she says.

CHAPTER FOURTEEN

Ethnicity and American Popular Culture

Introduction

There has been an ongoing debate in American society over how best to characterize the culture of this nation of nations. Some have argued that migrants to the United States engage in an adherence to a slightly modified English style of behavior, an *Anglo-conformity*, after arrival because so many aspects of the American political and judicial systems are derived from the English heritage of the Founders. While not all newcomers choose to learn English immediately upon arrival, most eventually wholly or partially conform to the linguistic and cultural patterns derived from the experience of the former English colonists who fought the revolution and formulated the constitution, according to this model.

Others offer an alternative view, *ethnic pluralism*, observing that immigrant groups do not readily relinquish their separate identities even as they are incorporated into the political and economic institutions of the country. Although most eventually eschew their native languages for English, aspects of immigrant groups' identities remain. For example, Americans of Irish descent may continue to perceive themselves as Irish on St. Patrick's Day and favor corned beef and cabbage at holiday time, although at other times of the year things Irish often seem less important. Racial groups such as African Americans and Asians hardly conform in appearance to an English Caucasian model, nor do most Catholics, Jews, and Moslems conform to the Protestant faiths of the Founders. Therefore, some argue, *ethnic pluralism* may be a more accurate way to describe American society. These observers characterize the United States as a society in which groups live side by side in harmony but never thoroughly lose consciousness of their separate identities and enrich the country by their very differences.

Neither *Anglo-conformity* nor *ethnic pluralism* account for the kind of culture and identity that is derived from the presence of so many individuals of different heritages living elbow to elbow in the same place. From the earliest years of the American experience, some posited that a new kind of person, the American, emerged from a merger or melting of different cultures. Americans often speak with pride of their society as a *melting pot*, though few know the derivation of the term.

A "melting pot" is used by metallurgists to mix liquefied metals in various proportions to develop alloys. An alloy often has qualities, for instance, strength, flexibility, heat resistance, greater than any of its components. Are Americans enhanced by their varied pasts and culturally enriched by the varied origins of the American population? Is this mixing of pasts too great a price to pay for the opportunities of American life? Do all groups have equal opportunity to enter the blend? Can groups refuse to enter the melting pot, or only partially join the mix?

Differing reactions to the melting pot notion were reflected in the reviews of Israel Zangwill's play, *The Melting Pot*, when it opened before an American audience in Washington, D.C. in 1908. The play told the story of young David Quixano, a Jewish immigrant who fled Czarist Russia for the United States following his family's slaughter in a pogrom, a massacre of local Jewish populations by Russians, often with the tacit approval of government officials. As the plot unfolds, David writes a great symphony and falls in love with another immigrant, a non-Jewish Russian noblewoman. In the final scene, the symphony receives great acclaim and the young immigrant wins the lady's hand. Despite the prohibition in Jewish law forbidding intermarriage, David follows his own heart and marries the noblewoman. In the very first act, Zangwill has David observe that "America is God's Crucible, the great Melting Pot where all the races of Europe are melting and reforming!" By the last act, the melting pot is being equated with Americanism itself as David exclaims, "A fig for your feuds and vendettas! Germans and Frenchmen, Irishmen and Englishmen, Jews and Russians—into the Crucible with you all! God is making the American."

Advocates of the melting pot loved the play. President Theodore Roosevelt, seated next to Zangwill's wife on opening night, cheered loudly. Roosevelt had long believed that "The man who becomes completely Americanized—who celebrates our constitutional Centennial instead of the Queen's Jubilee, or the Fourth of July rather than St. Patrick's Day and who talks 'United States' instead of the dialect of the country which he has of his own free will abandoned—is not only doing his duty by his adopted land, but is also rendering himself a service of immeasurable value." However, not all agreed with the president.

Immigrant newspapers panned the play as offering audiences an idealized version of incorporation. The Jewish immigrant press with a large orthodox readership was offended by the endorsement of intermarriage by Zangwill, a secular Jew from England. Others who had experienced religious prejudice, acts of discrimination, or the conflict that sometimes erupted among newly arrived groups, found the melting pot an inappropriate paradigm for the process of becoming American. Most of all, it offended those who sought to reconcile their native culture with their new cultural environment. They had no desire to submerge their past and be resurrected as Americans.

While no model or metaphor of incorporation posed by scholars appears to be thoroughly satisfactory, some offer a different vessel, a *salad bowl*, as a substitute for the melting pot. A salad might be likened to American culture. It is identifiable as a separate and unique dish. But those who have ever eaten a salad know that the component vegetables do not lose their distinctiveness, but contribute their flavors to the good taste of the salad.

For every immigrant group to the United States, popular culture has been a vehicle for expressing its relationship to the United States and American life. At times, popular culture has even been a bridge between newcomers and native-born. American popular culture is hard to define or categorize because it is an amalgam of many different cultural traditions brought to the United States by the foreign-born. And yet, similar to the salad bowl, different themes and expressions of American culture can be traced to particular traditions that were part of the baggage of earlier arrivals. Styles in American art, music, theater, fashion, and food are imports. Jazz rhythms were brought from different parts of Africa by slaves ripped from their homes and cultures only making their way to the cities of the North after an incubation period in the American South. Those who have a passion for polka acknowledge its central European origins and the recent popularity of Klezmer music suggests echoes of the Eastern European Jewish experience. Theater, too, often reflects the experiences of different groups. The popularity of Irish playwrights Brendan Behan and Sean O'Casey speaks to the power of Irish culture to capture the attention of American audiences, even as Isaac Bashevis Singer's short stories and novels knit the experiences of Eastern European Jewry into the American literary mainstream.

No dimension of American popular culture has been more obviously shaped by immigration than American cuisine, from the breakfast bagel derived from the Eastern European Jewish experience to the Chinese dumplings that can be delivered to the door at dinnertime. Most newcomers prefer to continue the food ways of their homelands after arrival. Such preferences allowed immigrant entrepreneurs and fellow ethnics of later generations to carve out niche markets. New arrivals, nostalgic for their homelands, nourished their memories as well as their bodies with every bite. However, it was not long before entrepreneurs sought to widen their market to include members of other groups. Prior to the 1960s, the emphasis on "melting" discouraged the consumption of foods because of their foreignness. However, by the end of the 1960s, ethnicity was "in." And as one famous advertisement trumpeted, "You do not have to be Jewish to love Levy's Real Jewish Rye." It was fashionable to eat ethnic. Now Americans scanned the shelves for a tomato sauce that most resembled what they had enjoyed in the increasing number of Italian restaurants that were springing up in towns as well as large cities. American cuisine was multiethnic cuisine.

In the first selection, "The Big Business of Eating," historian Donna R. Gabaccia explains that the identification of particular foods with certain ethnic groups has generated business opportunities for ethnic and non-ethnic businessmen. Food is a highly marketable dimension of popular culture. Initially, entrepreneurs found in each ethnic group a market for the particular foods favored by that group, what Gabaccia terms an "enclave market." However, some ethnic businessmen uncoupled their ethnic identities from the products they sold. There is nothing especially Swedish about Carl Swanson's TV dinners, for example. Some companies such as Procter and Gamble learned how to take their widely used products and target them to an ethnic audience. The company advertised Crisco to Jews as a kosher alternative to lard. After World War II, ethnicity was attractive to a broader cross section of the American market than ever before. The result, according to Gabaccia, was large corporations in pursuit of ethnic food enterprises. When Pillsbury acquired Progresso, it did not seek to obscure the company's Italian past; quite the contrary. Pillsbury emphasized Progresso's Italian heritage because marketers understood that the broader public was seeking to embrace ethnicity and redefine it as American. If some sauces and soups were popular because they smacked of Italian authenticity, that was fine because real Italian had come to be included under the broader rubric, "real American."

The second document is the cover of some Yiddish sheet music (figure 14.1). The title of the song is printed in Yiddish and an attempt at an English version, *Menshen-Fresser*, or *Man-Eater*. The title refers to the feared killer of the nineteenth century, tuberculosis (TB). Eastern European Jewish immigrants did not confine their musical tastes to cantorial chants in synagogue. Newly arrived immigrants wrote popular songs reflecting their concerns, from homesickness to anxiety over finding a mate to the illnesses that threatened to shorten their lives. Although rates of TB among Jewish immigrants were actually lower than among non-Jews, the disease was often called the "Jewish disease" or the "tailor's disease" because so many Jews lived and worked in disease-producing, congested conditions that both young and old contracted the disease.

As Jewish immigrants fought debilitating diseases, their struggles became the stuff of popular cultural expression. This song described how the lungs of victims were invaded by *mikroben* (Microbes) that destroyed their lungs and brought death. Because tuberculosis menaced many groups, such songs had a broader exposure than just Jewish audiences. However, each group had composers who treated themes important to their group, but touched the lives of others, as well.

As the cover suggests, the composer may have been engaged in a struggle of his own. According to the sheet music, the song's words and music are the creation of Solomon Small. However, the composer's show business name, Small, is followed by his real name in parenthesis, Smulewitz. The construction

Figure 14.1 Solomon Small, "*Menchen-Fresser*" Sheet Music. Hebrew Publishing Company, 1916.

suggests that the composer does not wish his Jewish audience to think that by using the name "Small" (a stage name) he is seeking to conceal his Jewish identity.

The third selection, "World's Fare," returns to food, not its production and marketing, but instead its consumption. In America's increasingly diverse classrooms sit students who are part of the most recent wave of immigration to the United States. These young newcomers often find lunchtime a stressful period rather than an hour of relaxation. The issue is meals that are not palatable to these foreign-born youngsters who need to nourish their bodies so their minds can absorb the lessons that will allow them to succeed in their new country. In the greater Washington, D.C. area, culturally sensitive school officials are changing luncheon menus to accommodate a broad range of tastes. No longer do school officials insist that all students, regardless of what they are used to eating, learn to love tuna fish on white bread, milk, and an apple. As newspaper reporter Emily Wax observed, students in northern Virginia's Fairfax County dine on dishes as varied as beef teriyaki to African-style rice and stews to Spanish-style rice and beans. Accommodating different tastes requires that the students broaden their culinary perspectives, too. Administrators find that with a little prodding students learn to enjoy each others' cuisines. Even the applications for school lunches reflect the multiethnicity of the student body. In the Fairfax school system, applications for school lunches are printed in six languages, including Cambodian and Farsi. The ingredients of American popular culture are as varied today as they were a century ago. And once again, the definition of American culture is being revised to reflect the identity of the newest Americans.

Suggestions for Further Reading

Richard Alba & Victor Nee, *Remaking the American Mainstream, Assimilation and Contemporary Immigration* (Cambridge: Harvard University Press, 2003).

Hasia R. Diner, *Hungering for America, Italian, Irish, & Jewish Foodways in the Age of Migration* (Cambridge: Harvard University Press, 2001).

Lawrence H. Fuchs, *The American Kaleidoscope, Race, Ethnicity and the Civic Culture* (Hanover, NH: Wesleyan University Press, 1990).

Hasia R. Diner, *Hungring for America: Italian, Irish and Jewish Foodways in the Age of Migration* (Cambridge: Harvard University Press, 2001).

Milton M. Gordon, *Assimilation in American Life: The Role of Race, Religion and National Origins* (New York: Oxford University Press, 1964).

Marilyn Halter, *Shopping for Identity, The Marketing of Ethnicity* (New York: Schocken Books, 2000).

John Hingham, "The Immigrant in American History," *Send These to Me: Jews and Other Immigrants in Urban America* (New York: Autheneum, 1975), pp. 3–28.

Russell A. Kazal, "Revisiting Assimilation: The Rise, Fall, and Reappraisal of a Concept in American Ethnic History," *American Historical Review* 100 (April, 1995): 437–471.

Donna R. Gabaccia, "The Big Business of Eating"

What better symbolized corporate food and American eating in the postwar period than the TV dinner? Standardized, quick-cooking, convenient, and marketed initially in a novel cardboard box that looked like a TV, the same TV dinner sold coast to coast. It was mass produced for mass markets, and it is one of several 1950s corporate novelties that continues to sell well, although in somewhat new evolutions, down to the present.

Swanson's, the inventor of TV dinners, was founded by a Swedish immigrant, Carl Swanson, who had arrived in the United States in 1896. He moved from an early job as a grocery clerk to success first as a wholesale grocer and then as the largest processor of turkeys in the United States. With the development of freezing technologies and the spread of community freezer lockers and then home freezers after World War II, Swanson's sons began manufacturing frozen potpies, hoping to extend sales of turkey beyond the holidays. In 1954 they marketed their first frozen TV dinner of turkey with dressing, green peas, and mashed potatoes.

It is unlikely that anyone anywhere in the United States thought of Swanson's TV dinners as Swedish. Swanson's was not an enclave limited to one ethnic group business, marketing to persons of Scandinavian descent. Nor was it interested in crossover marketing of Swedish-inspired dishes to the multiethnic consumers of the Midwest. Swanson's sons made no effort to market their dinners as ethnic fare; they did not care about the ethnic ties of their customers. They took on the role of all-American businessmen, in an all-American corporation, completely devoid of ethnic labels or regional distinctiveness. Their TV dinners were quintessentially all-American food, acceptable to a wide variety of tastes: turkey or fried chicken with mashed potatoes and a tiny compartment for soft vegetables or applesauce on the side. They offered it in the mass-produced, standardized forms of the modern American food industry. And they offered it everywhere in the United States.

In the same period, Chef Boyardee spaghetti in cans became a popular item with baby boom children and with their suburban moms, who sought to add variety to kids' meals without spending long hours in the kitchen. Chef Boyardee products had originated with Hector Boiardi, a chef from Piacenza, Italy, whose brother worked in the hotel business and helped him get started in the United States. Hector Boiardi first had his own Italian restaurant in Cleveland. He decided to can and distribute his sauce, initially packaging it with dry spaghetti and a packet of grated cheese, through his own business Chef Boiardi Food Products Company. Boiardi changed the name of his company (and its product) to Boyardee in the 1930s, mainly to ease pronunciation by non-Italians, as he sought a regional, crossover market of multiethnic consumers. By the late 1930s, Boiardi was successfully selling canned spaghetti to A&P stores and reaching a national market. Boiardi even became a supplier to the U.S. army during World War II, further building a taste for Chef Boyardee among returning GIs. Its consumers assumed they were buying Italian food when they purchased this spaghetti in a can. But the boomers and their mothers who ate canned Boyardee spaghetti in the 1950s no longer bought the product from immigrant businessman Boiardi. In 1946 he had sold his company to American Home Foods, a large conglomerate. Boiardi served as an occasional consultant and adviser to American Home Foods, but he was neither a shareholder nor a manager in the corporation. American consumers recognized spaghetti's Italian origins, but its production, packaging, and marketing now rested in non-Italian hands. Its profits, furthermore, went to an all-American mix of shareholders.

In somewhat different ways, Swanson's TV dinners and Chef Boyardee spaghetti mark the final phase of the march of enclave businessmen and ethnic foods into the national marketplace and the cultural mainstream of American life. While both represent a clear departure from the past, when immigrants and racial minorities worked only in the lowest levels of food corporations, both also reveal a paradoxical relationship between the corporate and the ethnic or regional in the national food marketplace. While Swanson's sons remained in active control of the family business in the 1950s, they and their product had completely lost any ethnic or regional labels and seemed quintessentially all-American. Chef Boyardee's canned spaghetti retained its Italian label and associations, but its Italian inventor no longer controlled its mass production within a modern corporation. In both cases, though in different ways, the local or ethnic seemed somewhat out of place in mass production for mass markets. When the sons of immigrant businessmen remained in control of production, their foods no longer bore ethnic labels; when ethnic labels remained attached to mass-produced food, their producers were no longer the ethnic businessmen who developed them.

The integration of enclave businessmen into the nation's large corporations and the mass production of enclave foods for the national market were the last phases in a rather lengthy process of market consolidation, mobility, and cultural change. Before World War II, ethnic businessmen who succeeded in national markets most often did so by selling either products with no ethnic labels attached or products marked by origins in an ethnic group other than their own. By contrast, it was typically businessmen with no obvious ethnic affiliations who popularized ethnic foods for consumers nationwide. Going corporate in order to become American thus required not so much the eradication of ethnicity as the uncoupling of enclave foods from enclave businessmen.

In the nineteenth century, immigrants and other outsiders, whether African-American or Mexican-American, were central actors in the history of modern food corporations. But the role they played was that of poorly paid wage-earners, either working for vast agribusinesses as field laborers, or in the canning or baking industry, or on the meat-processing floor. Most of them produced foods that had no ties to their own enclave foodways, and very few succeeded as founders of modern food corporations. The occasional immigrants who made their fortunes in mass production or mass retailing were often outstanding innovators, but they too rarely achieved their successes by specializing in foods unique to their own culinary traditions. On the contrary, success in the national market in the nineteenth century seemed to require the production and marketing of foods with no ethnic associations or labels.

In corporate life, as in American life generally, immigrants started near the bottom of the food chain. Agribusiness on both the West and East Coasts could not have developed without foreign laborers, and even today this economic sector depends on new immigrants from the Caribbean, Central America, Mexico, and the Philippines to raise, plant, and harvest crops from large factory farms. In nineteenth-century California, a succession of immigrant groups labored in the earliest of these agricultural corporations. The Japanese replaced the Chinese, sometimes in competition with Italian, Greek, Portuguese (East) Indian, and Korean harvesters around the turn of the century. After 1920 Mexican and Filipino harvesters arrived in ever larger numbers. On Hawaiian sugar and pineapple plantations, too, Chinese and native workers eventually gave way to Japanese, Korean, and Portuguese laborers at the turn of the century. On the East Coast, migratory Italian labor in the early years of the century was replaced by African-American and then Caribbean labor in New Jersey and Florida beginning in the 1920s.

As one employer of immigrant labor explained, large farms located far from urban centers where most immigrant populations lived found it difficult to recruit enough laborers. Most turned to immigrant labor contractors, who provided large gangs of workers of a particular background. Owners maintained this segregation of harvesters by "race" when they set up camps. On one large California farm, an owner recalled building "an American camp for white people. We had a camp for Japanese. We had a camp for Mexicans. We had a camp for Filipinos." When asked why workers were segregated by ethnicity, he explained that it "had to do with the eating habits of the people . . . They each require different types of food and prefer them. And so we had to have cooks of the proper nationality in each of those camps."

In Chicago, packinghouse workers in the huge meat-packing plants, with their mass-production disassembly lines, were overwhelmingly immigrants from Central and Eastern Europe—first Germans and Irish, later Slavs, and then Mexicans and eventually African-Americans in the years just after World War I. In Pittsburgh canneries, Irish and German women gave way to Polish, Slavic, Italian, and African-American laborers. In California, the women who processed the bountiful harvests of agribusiness included Jewish, Italian, Portuguese, Japanese, and Mexican workers. Pecan-shellers in Texas were also Mexican women—and on San Antonio's west side in the 1930s they worked so cheaply that owners actually replaced mechanical shellers with women.

Not all immigrants remained at the bottom, even in the nineteenth century, however. Immigrant entrepreneurs were especially important as investors and innovators in the production and marketing of novelty foods, and many of the snack foods that we think of as characteristically American emerged from immigrant pushcarts in the late nineteenth and early twentieth centuries. For example, the German immigrant F. W. Rueckheim invented

Cracker Jacks after opening a popcorn and candy stand in Chicago in 1871. In the 1890s he combined all the treats he sold (popcorn, molasses candy, and peanuts) into one, and his new product found favor at the city's Columbian Exposition. It became even more popular when Rueckheim began marketing Cracker Jacks as a ballpark treat.

In a somewhat similar evolution from pushcart to national marketplace, the Italian immigrant Amedeo Obici, having learned the nut trade from an uncle in Wilkes-Barre, in 1896 decided to install a peanut roaster in his California fruit stand. After adding salt and chocolate to some batches, he soon found he sold more peanuts than fruit. By 1906 he and a partner, Mario Peruzzi, had formed the Planters Nut & Chocolate Company, which exists to this day. Like immigrant workers in agriculture, canning, and meat-packing, Rueckheim, Obici, and Peruzzi worked with foods that had no obvious ties to the eating habits of their homelands. Even as innovators and investors, these immigrants did not "bring ethnicity" with them into the corporation or the national marketplace. Their foods carried no ethnic labels at all.

Probably the most successful immigrant agribusinessman before World War II was Joseph Di Giorgio, who revolutionized the distribution of fresh produce throughout the nation. Joseph Di Giorgio's father, Salvatore, had been a landowner in Cefalú, where he raised lemons commercially for export to the United States. Dissatisfied with both his lemon broker (in Baltimore) and his son (who did not want to study for the priesthood), he sent the 14-year-old Joseph to New York with a cargo of lemons in 1888 or 1889. (Di Giorgio himself later claimed he ran away.) When Di Giorgio arrived in the United States, few urban Americans ate much native-grown citrus or other fruit. Until about 1870, urban Americans were as likely to see lemons and oranges from Sicily and dried fruits from the Mediterranean—as well as pineapples, coconuts, and bananas from the West Indies, Cuba, and Central America—as native varieties. With the help of co-ethnic *paesani* in Baltimore, the young Di Giorgio rented a store to sell his lemons. Since he could market these only in the summertime, he sought a winter occupation, and became interested in importing bananas from the West Indies.

Duplicating a marketing practice common in Europe, Di Giorgio set up auctions for his imported fruits in New York, Baltimore, Pittsburgh, Chicago, Cleveland, Cincinnati, and St. Louis. Eventually, fruits came also from California and Florida to these eastern cities; they traveled, furthermore, on the same refrigerated cars that delivered meat from these cities to the agricultural hinterlands. According to Di Giorgio's nephews, auction houses near railroad terminals in large cities received shipments of fruit, catalogs, and bills of lading during the night, and set up samples in different rooms in the early morning. Sales followed between 8 AM and 12 PM, with deliveries to local businesses beginning at noon. Within 24 hours after fruit arrived in New York, it was in the hands of thousands of retailers, from municipal markets to street vendors. The auction collected a commission on all sales. Some auctions like these survive today, but many more went out of business as chain stores and supermarkets began to purchase fruit independently in the 1930s.

As the oral historian Ruth Teiser noted of Di Giorgio, "His success was due to the fact that he knew first what the market was, and then worked back to supply what the market wanted." In 1910 Di Giorgio began to expand vertically, acquiring lands and canneries in California; by 1920 he had purchased the Sierra Vista Ranch, a large farm that was still desert, along with orchards in the Pacific Northwest, totaling about 24,000 acres. Later he purchased citrus groves in Florida. Linking auctions, shipping, and growing, he formed the Di Giorgio Fruit Company in 1920. Like his American counterparts, Di Giorgio depended heavily on immigrant labor to grow, transport, and can his produce. But most were not Italians. In fact, in the 1960s his company would become embroiled with Mexican laborers organized by Cesar Chavez.

According to Teiser, Di Giorgio "marched along with or a bit ahead of, much of our agricultural history." His expertise and familiarity with fruit came from his Sicilian past, and his system of auctioning fruits seemed to be borrowed from European precedents. But the products he sold carried no ethnic labels, and he sold them to Americans across the nation, regardless of their cultural food preferences.

In the history of American canning, Henry J. Heinz (born in 1844 outside of Pittsburgh to German parents) presents a comparable case of early success in the modern food industry and the national marketplace. Heinz got his start as a bottler of horseradish, celery sauce, and pickles—foods broadly popular with both English- and German-origin peoples in Pittsburgh. After some initial business reverses, he opened a Pittsburgh plant in 1876 to can tomato ketchup, and he quickly added red and green pepper sauce, which was popular in the oyster bars of the period. By the 1880s Heinz was exporting to England and had expanded his products to include vinegars, apple butters, fruit jellies, and mince meat. An early master of modern advertising gimmicks, Heinz attracted flocks of visitors to his Columbian Exposition booth by giving away miniature pickle pins; in 1896, he began to advertise his famous "57 varieties" (a meaningless number he had pulled from his hat) of canned sauces, pickles, and preserves and to develop a Heinz pleasure pier at Atlantic City to keep his brand and its "57 varieties" in the public eye.

Just as Joseph Di Giorgio did not produce or market foods deemed Italian, Henry Heinz did not produce or market German ones. These were not businessmen using their ethnic origins or enclave ties to sell products labeled as ethnically distinct. Nor did their customers share their ethnic backgrounds. Still, Heinz, in particular, was quite aware of his cultural roots, and proud of them. He took German lessons to perfect his knowledge of the language before his first return trip to Europe; he then traveled yearly to Germany to enjoy its many health spas. The Heinz family maintained ties to Germany into the twentieth century; Heinz's sister even married a paternal cousin from their father's hometown.

The businesses of Heinz and Di Giorgio resembled smaller-scale ethnic enterprises—and differed from most modern food industries—in remaining family firms and employing many family members for two generations, sixty or eighty years or more. Their business operations grew to national and even international stature under direct family ownership, well before they incorporated.

The companies founded by Di Giorgio and Heinz represent a pattern that can be seen in many twentieth-century American corporations. Though both men seem to have identified with their immigrant family roots, they found success in national markets by mass producing and marketing products with no identifiable ethnic markers. Unlike cross-over businessmen, neither man hired his laborers through ethnic networks. In the second generation, family members remained employed in managerial positions, but within businesses organized as corporations. By the third generation, family members might own stock, but outsiders managed and represented the business to the corporate world. Whatever ethnicity or ethnic associations Heinz and Di Giorgio had brought with them as individuals into their corporations disappeared with their children.

Di Giorgio and Heinz themselves created large and modern—if initially family-controlled—corporations that helped create a national market for their products. But most entrepreneurs who got their start in regional cross-over markets followed a different path to the corporate world and the national market. This path, too, uncoupled ethnicity both from the businessman and the product. Successful entrance into the national marketplace most often occurred through sale of a family firm to a corporate food conglomerate, managed and run by native-born Americans with no cultural ties to the products they produced and marketed.

The first commercial canner of soups and Italian foods, twenty years before Hector Boiardi, was a company called Franco-American. Founded by French émigré Alphonse Biardot in 1887, along with his sons Ernest and Octave, the business began as a commercial kitchen in Jersey City, near the tomato fields of the Garden State. Having worked as a major-domo in the Greek royal household, Biardot set as his goal to "market foods that would introduce Americans to French traditions of masterful cooking." His Franco-American company canned higher priced specialty goods aimed at a cultivated palate—if not robber barons, then those who at least knew of the sophisticated associations of French foods. Among Franco-American's most successful products, however, was a food widely perceived as "Italian": spaghetti á la milanaise—a tomato, cheese, and macaroni combination that became popular nationwide only after Arthur Dorrance purchased controlling interest in Franco-American. Arthur was the younger brother of the founder of Campbell's canning and processing company, nearby. In 1915 Arthur sold his Franco-American stock to brother John, and in 1921 Franco-American was merged with the Campbell Soup Company, its competitor, giving an Italian food, first canned by a French immigrant, access to Campbell's national distribution system.

National marketing of Tex-Mex food followed a similarly multi-ethnic path to corporate success and a national market. William Gebhardt, a German from Essen who arrived in Texas around 1885, began serving chili to Germans at a cafe in back of a popular saloon in the German town of

New Braunfels in 1892. Chili, at the time, was still a seasonal specialty in San Antonio, made with fresh produce. Gebhardt began importing ancho chiles from Mexico, and—using a meat grinder—pulverizing the chiles so they could be dried successfully and used year round. For several years, Gebhardt marketed his Tampico Dust—which a 1925 critic claimed had been "tamed for the timid tongue"—around San Antonio in his own wagon. A tinker and mechanic, Gebhardt subsequently developed 27 machines for the manufacture of Tampico Dust, and after opening a factory in San Antonio he began, in 1908, to can a chili concoction for wider distribution and sale. (Gebhardt was not the first: in the 1870s a Texas Anglo had marketed a canned chili with goat meat as "Montezuma Sauce.")

In 1911 Gebhardt sold his company and his Eagle Brand chili to his brothers-in-law, who expanded their product line to include beans, tamales, and other local specialties. In the 1920s they introduced to the tourist trade Gebhardt's Original Mexican Dinner Package. Priced at $1.00 and packed in a colorful box, the souvenir contained a can of chili con carne, a can of Mexican-style beans, a can of shuck-wrapped tamales, 2 cans of deviled chili meat, and a bottle of Eagle chili powder. This marketing strategy, along with a widely distributed cookbook, helped spread the taste for chili into the upper Midwest. In 1962, after being purchased by Beatrice Foods, Gebhardt's Eagle Brand products became available nationwide.

So strongly were Eagle Brand foods associated with Mexican-Americans that a journalist in 1976 described shock and surprise when he visited Gebhardt's. "I arrive hungry, ready to be filled with enchiladas and filled with nostalgia: stories of little Mama Esperanza Ramirez Lopez Gonzalez who ground corn for the first 10 million tamales by hand. The three loyal sons who took over the business from ailing (perhaps arthritic) Mama, and who still taste a bit of every refried bean to make certain it meets Mama's standards." Instead, the journalist met Gebhardt manager Lyle Van Doozer, who admitted, "I really don't know too much about Mexican food. Before Beatrice transferred me, I worked for La Choy."

As these examples suggest, ethnic foods had already found a limited place in national food markets by 1940. The creators most often succeeded in mass production and mass marketing when they either left their ethnic affiliations at home, handled products with no ethnic labels, or sold out to corporations with no enclave ties. These patterns did not change significantly as culinary cultural pluralism broadened markets for ethnic foods and as toleration of ethnic diversity increased after World War II. This new openness was inspired in part by the multi-ethnic experiences of many GIs, who had been in combat units with fellow Americans of diverse ethnic backgrounds and had been stationed in posts outside the United States for the first time in their lives. It also owed much to GIs' actual eating experiences during the war, when many of them had no choice but to eat outside their own enclaves. While stationed in the Pacific, for example, young men from the mountains of Georgia and the Carolinas found themselves eating rice and other foods to which they were unaccustomed. The "discovery" of cultural diversity during World War II, and the big business of foods associated with that diversity did, however, encourage corporate leaders to rethink their philosophies of both mass production and mass marketing and to rediscover the power of ethnicity to influence consumer decisions.

Corporate interest in ethnic groups as niche markets had actually developed slowly before World War II. Perhaps because Jewish communities had long contained significant numbers of middle-class consumers, large department stores in the early twentieth century began to construct special Passover departments, packaging dried fruits into one-pound boxes (certified kosher by a San Francisco rabbi) and offering fruit preserves, matzos, nuts, meal, noodles, soup nuts, cakes, coffee and tea, cooking oils, fats, dessert pudding powders, and gift baskets. As early as 1916, a Chicago study called *Winning a Great Market on Facts* gave potential advertisers advice on how to reach foreign-born consumers. In New York, Joseph Jacobs's advertising firm specialized in connecting corporations to Jewish consumers; Jacobs convinced Joel Cheek of Maxwell House Coffee to advertise in the Yiddish press, telling him that "the big chains and the big food companies did not know how to promote to a Yiddish-speaking population since they employed no Jews." Jacobs also convinced Procter & Gamble to advertise Crisco to Jews as the perfect solution to their longstanding search for a kosher alternative to lard. The company's slogan—"Jews have been waiting 4,000 years for Crisco"—proved wildly successful. Another advertising man, Joshua C. Epstein, convinced Heinz to make kosher vegetarian baked beans; together with Rabbi Herbert Goldstein and Heinz, Epstein then popularized the Orthodox Union's U symbol for kosher certification.

While corporations attempted to reach into ethnic niche markets, ambitious enclave businessmen attempted to expand sufficiently to compete with them. Even in the 1990s, small firms with ties to the Jewish community could often compete successfully with large conglomerates. The company founded in 1921 by Yugoslav immigrants Bella and Elias Gabay (Gabila and Son's Knishes) remains a family operation: Bella first cooked up knishes (crispy square potato pies) for Coney Island pushcarts. Elias then patented a method for producing square knishes en masse, marketing them through delis and stadium concession stands. In the 1990s the firm produced frozen knishes, in four packs, for national distribution. "While the home of the knish will always be New York," a family spokesman explained, "we're looking forward to entering new markets" like Kalamazoo, Michigan. To succeed, however, the company had to accept rabbinical supervision and certification for the first time: word of mouth could no longer assure their customers of the purity of their products.

Expansion into national markets could also generate considerable controversy within cultural enclaves, imposing pressures on small businesses that large corporations could not feel. Hebrew National hot dogs seemed to resemble Oscar Mayer wieners in many ways: its hot dogs had become firmly part of the American snacking mainstream—no longer marketed exclusively to Jewish or kosher consumers. But when Hebrew National planned to move its production from Queens to Indianapolis and to manufacture their beef hot dogs in a plant formerly used to process pork, its

Maspeth, Long Island, unionized workers as well as the three rabbis it employed to ensure kosher criteria went on strike. One of the striking rabbis insisted, "Making kosher food in Indianapolis—such a thing is impossible to think." The company—and its many consumers—respectfully disagreed.

The kosher niche itself was significantly transformed by commerce at a national level. Kosher foods now include a U on their labels—rather than a Hebrew letter—to certify that they have been prepared under rabbinical supervision. The reason for the change? Neither Heinz nor his Jewish counterparts wanted to discourage Gentile purchasers of kosher foods by appearing "too Jewish." As author Joan Nathan discovered when writing about kosher food production, "Of the 6,500,000 people who purposely buy kosher foods, only 1,500,000 are kashrut-observing Jews. The great majority are Black Muslims, vegetarians, and Seventh-Day Adventists." Such consumers were little concerned whether kosher products emerge from corporations with ties to the Jewish community, from New York, or from non-Jewish corporations with plants in Indiana. They care only about the U.

Compared with small-scale enclave producers, however, corporations that uncoupled ethnic foods from their communities of origin often found themselves without much insight into the desires of ethnic consumers in the postwar period. The case of Frito-Lay, long-time manufacturer of potato and corn chips, is illuminating. Fritos originated in San Antonio, where they were a popular Mexican-American variation on tostadas (fried tortillas) but made from fried masa meal. In 1932 the Anglo Elmer Doolin (a floundering salesman of ice cream) paid 5 cents for a bag of them in a Mexican-owned San Antonio cafe. Locating the Mexican maker of the chips, Doolin claimed to buy the recipe with one hundred dollars borrowed from his mother (who had pawned her wedding ring). Doolin called his chips fritos; local Mexican-Americans had called them friotes or tamalinas. Doolin quickly acquired nineteen store accounts for his products, and he sold the rest out of the back of his Model T, expanding sales as far east as St. Louis.

In 1945 Doolin met Herman W. Lay, the potato chip manufacturer, who agreed to distribute Fritos for him. (Typically, Frito-Lay claimed not to know the name of the Mexican from whom Doolin bought the fritos recipe; some believe he was a man who returned to Mexico to manage a national soccer team. Others claim the Mexican-American owners of a San Antonio masa grinding mill invented them.) From 1953 until 1967 Frito-Lay assumed that children were their target consumers, and Frito-Lay advertised the corn chips with the cowboy-clad but ethnicity-less Frito Kid. In 1963, with growing awareness of niche markets and how ethnicity might shape consumer tastes, the Frito-Lay Company switched to the Frito Bandito. This corporate strategy, a display of appalling ignorance about the targeted community that had invented the snack, backfired: the Mexican-American Anti-Defamation Committee accused Frito-Lay of insensitivity, stereotyping, and racism. The Frito Bandito soon disappeared. But Frito-Lay, undaunted, in 1965 introduced Doritos, a chip they believed looked and tasted more like "authentic" tostadas, and they have become tremendously popular nationwide.

Since enclave entrepreneurs still best knew ethnic tastes, some did succeed in building major postwar corporations to cater to ethnic groups scattered across the country, much as kosher industries had done somewhat earlier. An enclave economy, in other words, could still function nationwide. Typical was La Preferida; the president in 1995 was David Steinbarth, a fourth-generation member of the founding Chicago family of Mexicans. La Preferida had begun humbly, packaging foods for Mexican-Americans in glass jars; they had stocked canned refried beans, pinto beans, and the like. By the 1970s La Preferida was producing and marketing frozen foods to supermarkets. In the 1980s they introduced fat-free products to enhance their appeal to a mass market that included increasing numbers of non-Mexicans.

Even more successful was Goya Foods, the Secaucus, New Jersey, firm founded in 1933 (some sources say 1936) by the Unanue family. Selling initially to New York's Spanish, Puerto Rican, and Cuban residents, Goya expanded into an import and processing (canning, freezing) company with 600 employees and an annual business of $465 million. Family members still serve in key positions (including general manager) at Goya, and the corporation still distributes through small stores, employing a largely Spanish-speaking sales force. It dominates most of the market for the products it produces. But Goya also successfully negotiates contracts with supermarket chains, hoping to reach Hispanics who live or shop outside of their ethnic community. Thus, for example, it licensed its label to Frozen Desserts Resources, which then marketed a child's ice cream treat (with a sombrero) and the English advertising slogan "Oh Boy-A Goya."

Like Frito-Lay, however, Goya faced some real challenges in building ties to Hispanic consumers of increasing diversity, including those of Mexican and South American origin. Goya introduced frozen guacamole and new fruit juices to appeal to them. At the same time, Goya hoped to attract non-Spanish-speaking customers interested in good prices for such basic items as olives, olive oil, beans, and rice. Not surprisingly, Goya's success makes it the focus of considerable corporate attention. The Campbell Soup Company developed its own food line (Casera) to compete with Goya in New York and Miami, while other corporations sought to purchase the company to pursue their own niche marketing strategies.

In the postwar period, enclave businessmen continued to hesitate at the doors of corporate boardrooms, even those boardrooms that had every reason to want enclave entrepreneurs who could help them capture ethnic niches. When enclave businessmen made fortunes, it was still by selling foods associated with culinary traditions other than their own. Jeno Paulucci, for example, founded Chun-King, which raised the question—as one good-humored journalist put it—"Can an Italian American find success making Chinese food in a Scandinavian section of Duluth, Minnesota?" The founder of Chun-King was a fruit barker at age fourteen, known for his piercing hawker's voice. Later he became a salesman in a wholesale grocery firm and attempted without success to sell dehydrated garlic. In 1947 Paulucci borrowed $2,500 and began growing and canning bean sprouts; he eventually expanded to chop suey and chow mein. In 1967 he sold out to R. J. Reynolds for $63 million. (In an interesting twist, R. J. Reynolds sold the floundering Chun-King in 1989 to Yeo Hiap Seng, the largest food and beverage manufacturer in Singapore.) Paulucci went on to develop Jeno's frozen pizza, which he then sold to Pillsbury in 1985 for $150 million. Experiments with ethnic restaurants, real estate, frozen dinners, and a Chinese-food home delivery business called China Kwik followed—and failed.

Nothing better symbolizes the resistance of ethnic entrepreneurs to corporate employment and the persistence of uncoupling the businessman from his ethnicity than the contrasting stories of Tom Carvel and Reuben Mattus, two ice-cream innovators. Tom Carvel was born Thomas Andreas Carvelas in Athanassos, Greece; he came to the United States as a child in 1906. After living on a chicken farm in Connecticut with his family, he followed a pattern typical among Greek Americans. In 1934 he loaded an old ice cream truck with ice cream to begin peddling; his garage tinkering in the 1920s had resulted in a machine that could manufacture a soft, frozen custard, which soon found a good market. Carvel then built a small factory in Yonkers to manufacture and sell his frozen custard machines, but few understood how to use them, so in 1955 Carvel began training and licensing franchisees. Customers did not see Carvel's frozen custard as Greek; and in the business community Tom Carvel was viewed as a businessman eccentric, not as an immigrant—even though he worked in a field, ice cream, which had been a Greek niche for generations. Carvel had refused to use an advertising agency, and served as radio spokesman for his own product, earning Carvel considerable professional ridicule—to which he characteristically appended, "but who cares?"

Reuben Mattus, the American-born son of a Jewish immigrant, was the inventor of Häagen-Dazs Ice Cream. Born in 1912, Mattus had been selling family-made ice cream in the Bronx for thirty years. Like Carvel, he had started with a horse and wagon, peddling his ice cream to multiethnic New Yorkers. According to analysts of Mattus's later success with Häagen Dazs, other entrepreneurs had realized that upper-income Americans in the prosperous 1960s were increasingly willing to pay more for a product they perceived as superior. According to a *New York Times* reporter, Mattus "was the first to understand that they would do so if they thought it was foreign. So he made up a ridiculous, impossible to pronounce name, printed a map of Scandinavia on the carton and the rest is history." (Although Danes had a long tradition in the United States of working in dairy, Mattus supposedly chose a Danish-sounding name because Danes had rescued so many of their Jewish population during World War II.) In 1993 Mattus sold out to Pillsbury, but (like Paulucci and others before him) he ventured off into a new business—Mattus' Lowfat Ice Cream. Unfortunately, he died shortly thereafter.

By the late 1960s, large corporations were scrambling to buy up successful ethnic food enterprises like Stella d'Oro, Lender's, and Boston's Star Markets. They acquired regional brands and marketed their products nationally for quick profits. Kraft alone purchased Lender's, Celestial Seasonings, Tombstone Pizza, and Frusen Gladje, all in 1984–1987. Progresso sold to Ogden Food Products, which was acquired later by Pet and then in 1995 by Pillsbury. When Pillsbury acquired Progresso, it assessed its ethnic appeal and decided to play up its Italian-American heritage—"The brand has an underlying Italian personality but it's not strictly Italian food"—presumably because Americans of a wide variety of ethnic backgrounds now eat Progresso spaghetti sauces and soups.

Emily Wax, "World's Fare: Schools Offer Ethnic Dishes to Entice their Increasingly Diverse Students"

With her 15-year-old stomach rumbling, Sara Arbieto hurried into the Mexican line of the "International Food Court" inside her T. C. Williams High School cafeteria and grabbed a plate of tacos buried in beef, beans and cheese.

"Not exactly as good as my mom makes," said Sara, who is from Peru. "But I don't like too much pizza. This is a little bit like Peruvian food."

Without leaving the cafeteria, Sara has plunged her plastic utensil into everything from Indian-style chicken curry to Jamaican jerk pork and fried plantains this school year. So much for the idea that a school lunch means soggy Tater Tots and a rubbery hamburger.

In Alexandria [Virginia] and other school districts with large immigrant populations, the lunchroom menu is slowly changing to suit the taste buds of students from around the world, the latest example of how new Americans are influencing life inside public schools.

Fairfax County students have dined on beef teriyaki and African-style rice and stews. In Prince George's County [Maryland], students can sample Spanish-style beans and rice and Middle Eastern yogurt sauces. Even schools with a relatively small influx of immigrants, such as those in Loudoun County and Southern Maryland, have introduced "Latin American Food Day" within the last two years.

"It's happening all across the country in schools that are becoming more diversified and are trying to serve their customers," said Patti Montague, director of member services and marketing for the American School Food Services Association. "In Texas, in California, you also see schools serving Asian and Latin-style dishes."

Food service directors say the expansion of choices is necessary to lure young customers, especially at high schools that allow students to go off campus for lunch, as T. C. Williams does.

At the Alexandria high school, which has 2,000 students, the number of students eating a cafeteria lunch has increased from 400 to 500 a day since the international food court made its debut in September 1998. The school's students come from more than 78 countries and speak more than 52 languages.

"It's a real challenge to keep kids on campus," said Ralph Schobitz, food service director of Alexandria schools. "We wanted to create something that would allow students to say, 'This is from my country.' "

The food court has Mexican and Italian food every day and a rotating menu of American and Asian dishes, including Polynesian sweet-and-sour turkey ham and Japanese vegetables. The taco counter was even designed to look like a Mexican restaurant, with walls painted bright purple and a drawing of a huge chili pepper wearing sunglasses.

Inside the cafeteria on a recent day, the line included students from Pakistan, El Salvador, the Philippines and Sierra Leone. Some said the ethnic food is sometimes a flimsy, watered-down nod to their culture. There was the Greek theme day, for example, when steak sandwiches were served instead of the more authentic gyros.

Still, most students said they appreciated the school's effort to accommodate them, as well as the chance to sample cuisine from another culture.

At a table filled with students from Somalia, Nigeria, Mexico and the Middle East, Nesrin Alkhalil, 18, from Lebanon, sat looking at a plate of tacos.

"I've never had this before," she said, as friends poked her and told her to try it.

"When I first came here, I wouldn't try anything except what I was used to in Lebanon. I never even tried peanut butter and jelly."

She wrinkled her nose and finally gave in to the peer pressure. "Not bad," she said of the taco. "It's not hummus, but it's okay."

Ifrah Elmi, 18, from Somalia, agreed with several of her table mates that they had recently tried cafeteria dishes they had never heard of before. "I like the food," Elmi said. "To me, it's interesting. There's more than hot dogs and cheeseburgers."

Peggy McConnell, director of food and nutrition services in the Fairfax school system, not only serves food from around the world but prints applications for school lunches in six languages, including Cambodian and Farsi, so that parents who don't speak English can make sure their children are signed up for the school lunch program.

"The students also get to learn about the country the food is from, and we go into the classrooms and talk about it," McConnell said. "We want everyone to feel that we are including their cultures, and food is a great way."

Schobitz, who grew up on hearty German-style dishes such as potato dumplings and red cabbage and roast pork, said he understands the needs of newly arrived immigrants.

"We have such a wide range of people, it's hard to please everyone. But we want to try and touch some of the students," said Schobitz, who received the national Silver Rising Star award from the American School Food Services Association last month for his innovative efforts.

His focus on serving ethnic food extends to Alexandria's elementary schools, where each month there is a different food theme. This month the theme is China, and students are being served egg rolls, fried rice and fortune cookies along with American choices.

To make sure that the recipes for the food court at T. C. Williams were reasonably authentic, he consulted with an Indian custodial worker when making the curry chicken and got advice on jerk pork from a staff member who has a husband from Jamaica. But Schobitz toned down the curry a few notches, afraid that some non-Indian students would find the taste too spicy.

Despite his efforts, some T. C. Williams students cannot be wooed. Standing outside the cafeteria last week, some rolled their eyes and laughed at even the thought of eating a school lunch.

"I don't know," said Mari Chris, 15, who is from the Philippines and likes to eat Chinese food and bagels off-campus during lunch hour.

When a friend told her that the cafeteria sometimes serves Asian-style foods, she smiled and said she would think about trying it.

It's news that would send Schobitz to the staff searching for recipes from the Philippines.

INDEX

Sweden, immigrants, 118, 151, 214, 262, 325
Syria, immigrants, 117, 148, 150–2

Terkel, Studs, *How Blacks and Whites
Think and Feel about the American
Obsession*, 137
Texas, 23–5, 137, 156, 161–2, 275–7
transnationalism, 8, 9, 13, 25–7, 30, 57–80,
81, 184, 204
transportation, 8, 26, 32–5, 37, 41, 58,
204, 216
air, 26–7, 58, 60, 68, 78–9
Erie Canal, 88
railroads, 32–7, 209–13, 227
ships, sailing, 2
ships, steam, 2, 26, 33, 59, 205, 209–10,
212, 279, 290
travel, 27, 45, 48, 55, 58, 60, 79–80, 105,
146, 209, 212, 290, 300, 329
Turner, Frederick Jackson, "The
Significance of the Frontier in
American History," 160

Ukraine, immigrants, 91–2, 112–13, 117,
210, 227
unemployment, 7, 22, 58, 141, 153,
165, 184, 187, 232, 254,
266–7, 305
United States Commission on Human
Rights, 254
United States Commission on Immigration
Reform, 135–6

United States Public Health Service,
278, 282

Vietnam, immigrants, 18, 22, 36, 55–6,
131, 132
Von Steuben Day, 301
voting, 5, 133, 160, 166–7, 180, 228, 260–2

West India, immigrants, 183–5, 187–94,
197–201, 234, 238–42, 251–8; *see also
individual countries*
Wilson, Pete, 133–4, 140, 145, 159
Wilson, Woodrow, 133–4
working class, 144, 164, 170, 175, 244–50,
255, 258, 261
World War I, 2, 4, 28, 134, 264, 327
World War II, 4, 5, 6, 15, 35, 83, 93, 96, 112,
115, 117, 127, 138, 142, 292, 322, 325,
326, 328, 331, 332, 335
women, 28–9, 33, 45–6, 82–3, 100–3, 119,
147–50, 152, 203, 212–13, 215–30,
231–3, 234–77, 292, 307–8, 313;
see also India, immigrants; Ireland,
immigrants; Italy, immigrants; Jamaica,
immigrants; Mexico, immigrants

Yezierska, Anzia, *Bread Givers*, 107
Yiddish language, 106–7, 148, 237, 283,
303, 315–16, 322–3, 332
YMCA/YWCA, 111–12

Zangwill, Israel, *The Melting Pot*, 320